On the Road to the Wolf's Lair

On the Road to the Wolf's Lair

GERMAN RESISTANCE TO HITLER

—

THEODORE S. HAMEROW

THE BELKNAP PRESS OF
HARVARD UNIVERSITY PRESS
Cambridge, Massachusetts
London, England
1997

To the memory of the Rubinlichts

Frontispiece: Claus von Stauffenberg (far left) and Adolf
Hitler at the "Wolf's Lair," the Führer's headquarters in East
Prussia, on July 15, 1944. In the background is the conference hut where five days later Stauffenberg's bomb almost
killed Hitler. (Bilderdienst Süddeutscher Verlag)

Library of Congress Cataloging-in-Publication Data

Hamerow, Theodore S.
On the road to the wolf's lair : German resistance to Hitler /
Theodore S. Hamerow.
  p. cm.
Includes bibliographical references and index.
ISBN 0-674-63680-5 (cloth : alk. paper)
1. Anti-Nazi movement—Germany. 2. Hitler, Adolf,
1889–1945—Assassination attempt, 1944 (July 20).
3. Bureaucracy—Germany—History. 4. Germany. Heer—
Political activity. 5. Germany—Politics and government—
1933–1945. 6. Church and state—Germany—History—
20th century. I. Title.
DD256.3.H335 1997
943.086—dc21   96-44364

Designed by Gwen Frankfeldt

Contents

Part IV The Beginnings of Resistance

Part V Between the Threat of Victory and the Danger of Defeat

Part VI Death and Transfiguration

Illustrations

Preface

My purpose in writing this book was not to present a comprehensive account of the anti-Nazi movement in Germany during the Third Reich. Such an undertaking would have had to be not only encyclopedic in scope but tedious in detail. To try to deal with all the various organizations, groups, circles, and factions that have by now come to be included in the resistance against the Hitler dictatorship would have led, in my opinion, to little more than a lengthy scholarly catalogue. I decided therefore to concentrate instead on the central components of the resistance, on the elements that, because of their military or administrative or cultural importance, were in a position to form a systematic, organized opposition to the Nazi regime. These elements included high-ranking army officers, upper-level civil servants, and prominent religious leaders. Many of them became directly involved in the most dramatic manifestation of the resolve of these men to overthrow the Third Reich, namely, the attempt on July 20, 1944, to assassinate Hitler in the "Wolf's Lair," his headquarters near Rastenburg in East Prussia. They have admittedly not been neglected by scholars studying the National Socialist era. In fact, they have been observed, investigated, scrutinized, and analyzed at great length. But I felt that a reexamination of what they did and especially of why they did it was in order, now even more than before.

In other words, I have chosen to focus not on the plans, strategies, tactics, and deeds of these resisters, but on their ideas, ideals, motives, and aims. It is clear that most of them did not oppose National Socialism from the outset. Indeed, at first they generally regarded the Third Reich as a significant improvement over the ineffectual Weimar Republic. Very few were actually out-and-out Nazis, but they were prepared by and large to work with the Nazi regime for the attainment of common goals and purposes. Yet a decade later they sacrificed their lives in a desperate effort to overthrow a government whose establishment they had initially greeted with hope and satisfaction. Why? What led them to change their minds? What caused them to turn against the Hitler dictatorship, which they had at one time willingly served? Those were the questions that first drew my attention to the German resistance, and those are the questions I have tried to answer in writing this book.

In the course of my research I received the support of many individuals who helped me gain access to essential historical sources. To name them all would require a very long list, too long for most readers. But there are a few obligations I feel I must acknowledge publicly. First of all, I want to thank Ulrich Goerdeler for generously giving me permission to examine his father's papers without questioning me about my personal background or political outlook. If in this book I have occasionally been more critical of Carl Goerdeler than members of his family would like, I want to assure them that I have always regarded him as a kind, decent, and honorable man. On that point at least there can be no dispute.

I also want to express my appreciation to Sabine Herrmann of the Bundesarchiv in Koblenz. During my several visits to that important archival depository, she was invariably helpful in locating materials essential for my research. More than that, she arranged on a few occasions to have copies of documents I needed sent to me by mail, thereby saving me the time and expense of a special trip. I will always remember her kindness. Paul Rood assisted me by providing materials from the National Archives and from the Library of Congress in Washington, D.C. He always treated my frequent requests for help courteously, expeditiously, and effectively. I am in his debt. Finally, I would like to say thank you to Judith L. Tuohy of the interlibrary loan department of the University of Wisconsin Memorial Library. Not only did she obtain for me materials from other libraries in this country as well as abroad, but she tried, not always with success, to calm a nervous and importunate author. I am very grateful to her.

There are many other obligations incurred in the writing of this book, obligations I can best acknowledge by voicing my appreciation to the various archives whose personnel made their resources available to me. I am indebted to the Bundesarchiv in Koblenz, invaluable for all students of German history, but especially useful to those interested in the period of the Third Reich. I also had an opportunity to examine some of the materials in the Bundesarchiv-Militärarchiv in Freiburg, another major archival institution, for data regarding the soldiers who took part in the resistance. The Institut für Zeitgeschichte in Munich has an important collection of eyewitness accounts, memoirs, and depositions pertaining to the Nazi era. The Evangelisches Zentralarchiv in Berlin gave me access to confidential information regarding Otto Dibelius, even when that information was not always flattering or edifying. I was able, moreover, to examine Max Habermann's account of the German National Union of Commercial Employees written early in 1934, which is among the holdings of the Deutscher Handels- und Industrie-Angestellten-Verband in Hamburg. As for archival collections outside Germany, the National Archives in Washington, D.C., contains materials reflecting the general attitude in the United States toward the attempt to assassinate Hitler in the summer of 1944, while the Leo Baeck Institute in New York has interesting information concerning Adam von Trott zu Solz. Finally, the Public Record Office in Kew, England, provided me with documents showing how the British Foreign Office viewed the German resistance. To all these archives, my sincere appreciation.

There are also important obligations of another sort I feel I should acknowledge. I do so with great pleasure. After completing the first draft of this book, I asked three of my friends, colleagues, and fellow historians to give me a candid evaluation of its contents. The assessments of Christopher R. Browning, Sterling Fishman, and Konrad H. Jarausch were very useful to me in making several essential revisions. In those cases where all three agreed on the need for some change or correction, I complied without hesitation. I also accepted in almost all instances alterations recommended by two of the three. But where it was one on one, my opinion against that of a single reviewer, I'm afraid I became more obdurate. Sometimes I would act on his suggestion, but at other times I would stick to my original view, assessment, or formulation. Was that wise? Or was I simply reflecting an author's stubbornness and vanity? I shall never be quite sure. In any event, I want to thank my three reader friends for their efforts, which unfortunately were not always successful, to improve the quality of this book. The least I can do is absolve them from any responsibility for its shortcomings.

My research into the German anti-Nazi movement has led to the publication of two articles presenting in a preliminary and abbreviated version some of my present findings. The first of these, "The Conservative Resistance to Hitler and the Fall of the Weimar Republic, 1932–34," was published in *Between Reform, Reaction, and Resistance: Studies in the History of German Conservatism from 1789 to 1945*, ed. Larry Eugene Jones and James N. Retallack (Providence and Oxford, 1993), pp. 433–463. The second article, entitled "Cardinal Faulhaber and the Third Reich," appeared in *From the Berlin Museum to the Berlin Wall: Essays on the Cultural and Political History of Modern Germany*, ed. David Wetzel (Westport, Conn., 1996), pp. 145–168. The views and arguments advanced in these two items appear in an expanded and elaborated form on the following pages. The great bulk of the book, however, has not been previously published in any other version. I should also note that in the text that follows all translations are my own unless otherwise noted.

In conclusion, I want to say that the completion of my study of the German resistance leaves me with mixed feelings. Until recently I looked forward to finishing this book with great anticipation. It seemed to be a heavy burden that I had to bear day after day, never entirely free from its importunity, always preoccupied with researching, analyzing, formulating, revising, and writing, rewriting, and rewriting again. There were times when I thought it would never end. But little by little I became accustomed to the unceasing task, so onerous and yet so challenging, so wearisome and yet so satisfying. Without fully realizing it, I grew used to it, attached to it, almost addicted to it. I began to look forward to grappling with the next page, the next paragraph, the next sentence, the next word. Slowly, imperceptibly, almost insidiously, I became hooked. And now it is over. There will be no more poring over the notes, determining where to begin, deciding how to express a thought, wondering what to say next, pondering where to stop, and always revising, polishing, improving, and agonizing. Strangely, I think I shall miss all that.

It is a gross misrepresentation to pretend today that the supporters of the Nazi system at that time had all been devils, while its opponents had been nothing but angels. The reality looked different; the picture was often the reverse.

ALEXANDER VON STAUFFENBERG (1955)

Introduction: From Collaboration to Resistance

Early on July 21, 1944, a few hours after the failure of the attempt on his life, Adolf Hitler declared in a radio address to the German people that those involved in the plot constituted "a very small clique of ambitious, unscrupulous, and at the same time criminally stupid officers." They were, he repeated, "a very small group," which, as "happened in 1918," had sought "to stab [the nation] in the back." To make the point still more emphatic, he stated once again that "the circle which these usurpers represent is extremely small." It was important to the leader of the Third Reich to convince his listeners that the nation was still behind him, that those who had sought to overthrow him were only a handful of traitors, defeatists, opportunists, and cowards. The war would go on, regardless of cost or sacrifice. And once final victory had been won, the plotters would be remembered only as renegades whose lack of patriotism had led them to dishonor and infamy.[1]

The attitude of the Allies toward the failed coup was not much more favorable. They were committed to wage war until the enemy agreed to unconditional surrender. There were to be no negotiations, no compromises. Hence the plot to assassinate Hitler seemed to the statesmen of the anti-Axis coalition nothing more than an attempt to escape the consequences of defeat. The uprising of 1944, they reasoned, like the uprising of 1918, was designed simply to protect Germany against just retribution for its aggression. But this time the scheme would not work. On August 2, addressing the House of Commons, Winston Churchill described the events at Hitler's headquarters two weeks earlier as "potent . . . manifestations of internal disease" in the opposing camp. He conceded that they might prove "decisive . . . one of these days." Yet "it is not in them that we should put our trust, but in our own strong arms and the justice of our cause." The failed coup had changed nothing. "The highest personalities in the German Reich are murdering one another, or trying to, while the avenging armies of the Allies close upon the doomed and ever-narrowing circle of their power." Military operations would have to go on until the other side had been crushed.[2]

This critical view of the German resistance against Hitler remained essentially unchanged during the early period of the Allied occupation of Germany. To the vanquished, experiencing the humiliations and hardships of the postwar years, the failed coup seemed an act of treachery that helped hasten the collapse of their nation. Those who participated in it had violated their oath of loyalty; they had weakened the will of their country-men to fight to the bitter end. The victors, by contrast, saw in the resisters primarily political opportunists who had supported Hitler as long as he produced easy successes, and then turned against him when his intuition and statecraft began to sour. They first opposed the Weimar Republic for being too democratic; then they opposed the Third Reich for being too authoritarian. How could anyone trust them? Expediency and self-interest seemed their only guiding principles. The occupation authorities, commit-ted to a doctrine of collective guilt, found little difference between those who turned against Hitler when the war began to go badly and those who remained loyal to him in the face of approaching defeat. Both were only trying to evade the penalty for the crimes committed by the Third Reich.

That attitude began to change, however, after the coming of the cold war. As the differences between the Soviet Union on the one hand and the United States and Great Britain on the other intensified, each side was forced to reassess its view of the recently defeated enemy. The vanquished came to be regarded less and less as inveterate aggressors or blind ultrana-tionalists. They were now viewed as potential auxiliaries, mercenaries, or even allies. Leaders on both sides of the iron curtain abandoned plans for the long-lasting punishment and subordination of the Germans in favor of a policy of conciliation. The process of German rehabilitation thus began much sooner than had been anticipated at the time of the collapse of the Third Reich.

Politically that meant the establishment in 1949 of two sovereign and independent German states, each with its own constitution, government, and army. And ideologically it meant the abandonment of the doctrine of collective guilt. For both the Federal Republic of Germany and the Ger-man Democratic Republic it became important to affirm that not everyone had supported Hitler. There had always been a clandestine but vigorous resistance to the Third Reich. Therefore a distinction had to be made between "good" and "bad" Germans, between resisters and collaborators, between heroes and villains. This altered view of the opposition to National Socialism was not only critical to the new political order in Central Europe as a means of legitimizing the claim to authority of each of the two Germanys. It was also accepted by the victors in the war. For how else could either the Americans or the Russians justify the abandonment of their contention that since the Germans were not to be trusted, they would have to undergo a long process of occupation and reeducation? In the atmosphere of the cold war, the existence of a courageous and extensive German resistance against the Third Reich became an ideological necessity.

Significant differences of opinion regarding the nature of that resistance nevertheless persisted. East of the iron curtain the true heroes of the struggle against Hitler's tyranny were the workers, peasants, and intellectuals, especially those inclined to Communism, who had risked their lives for a better social system. As for the conservative army officers and bureaucrats responsible for the unsuccessful coup of July 20, 1944, they were usually dismissed as willing supporters of National Socialism who had turned against it only when the regime began to threaten their privileged position in the class hierarchy. In the West, meanwhile, those who had opposed the Third Reich out of sympathy with the Soviet Union were viewed mostly as agents of a foreign power. Here the heart of the resistance was believed to be that small group of men who had risked and lost their lives trying to assassinate Hitler. It was they who had demonstrated to the world that not all Germans succumbed to the spell of Hitler's success, that some Germans resisted National Socialism to the end in the name of freedom and justice. They were the true spiritual founders of the new Germany.

With the renewed political and economic importance of Central Europe came also a rapid growth in the perceived size of the resistance. In both Germanys researchers began to discover more and more sources of opposition to Hitler. They included clandestine cells of left-wing antifascists who continued to denounce the Nazi regime even in the days of its greatest success. They comprised middle-of-the-road organizations like the White Rose, a group of university students and young academics who secretly distributed leaflets attacking the government, or the Kreisau Circle of aristocratic, religious, and socialistic intellectuals who met intermittently to discuss plans for a just political order after the fall of the Third Reich. And they embraced countless ordinary men and women, their names unknown in many cases, who had found the courage to scrawl an anti-Nazi slogan on a wall, to engage in political debate with a colleague or neighbor, to condemn the regime's religious policy, or to denounce the treatment of the Jews. The resistance expanded to include not only officers and bureaucrats, but businessmen, professionals, teachers, students, white-collar workers, industrial workers, farmers, unskilled laborers, and even housewives, adolescents, and pensioners. If the numbers seemed inflated at times, this was surely understandable in a nation eager to demonstrate that Germans as well as non-Germans had opposed the tyranny of National Socialism.

But it also made the task of examining and analyzing the resistance much more difficult. Could any valid generalization, any broad conclusion be reached about a movement that appeared so diverse in its social origins, economic interests, political convictions, and ideological commitments? The problem seemed insoluble. That was why the historian Martin Broszat, writing more than thirty years after the war, drew a useful distinction between "resistance" and "opposition" to the Third Reich. According to him, the "historically structured concept of 'resistance'" has to be clearly separated from the "moral and political concept of legitimacy" subsumed under the term "opposition." The distinction is necessary to make clear the "effective limitation of the hegemony of National Socialism." Broszat meant that certain organizations—the churches, for example—retained a measure of "immunity" in relation to the regime. There was, moreover, "a social milieu and tradition," especially in the armed forces and the civil service, which displayed a "resistant tenacity" with regard to the Third Reich. To put it more simply, certain military, bureaucratic, and religious institutions in the public life of Germany preserved a degree of autonomy under the Hitler dictatorship that enabled them to form an organized and systematic resistance to its policies. Their central position within the state apparatus provided them with a measure of protection against the demands and pressures of the regime.[3]

The opposition may have been just as brave and idealistic as the resistance, just as dedicated and selfless. It may in fact have been more courageous because it was more vulnerable. But the subordinate position of its members limited their effectiveness. They could not go beyond futile acts of protest or defiance. Their isolation and marginality condemned them to ineffectualness. Their circumstances restricted them to acts of individual disobedience that posed no real threat to the Third Reich. Their chief historic function has been to remind posterity that National Socialism never succeeded in completely suppressing the yearning for freedom and justice in Germany.

The resistance, however, was in a position to form a coherent, effective challenge to the regime. Its members were generally wellborn, affluent, educated, and influential. Some of them, occupying high places in the military and the bureaucracy, managed to make plans for the overthrow of the Third Reich while appearing to serve its purposes. They were the ones who nearly succeeded in assassinating Hitler in the summer of 1944. Others held important offices in religious life. Though not directly involved in plots against the Nazi government, they could openly criticize many of its policies as violations of Christian doctrine. Their influence and popularity provided them with a degree of security against reprisals by the authorities.

This resistance against Hitler comprised three distinct groups united by a common rejection of National Socialism. Two of the groups, dissident army officers and disaffected civil servants, worked in secret to bring about the downfall of National Socialism. The third, composed of prominent churchmen, expressed in public its reservations about the government's program. All three shared a growing hostility toward the Nazi system.

But what led them to oppose that system in the first place? For about a generation after World War II the answer seemed clear. The members of the resistance represented that other Germany, that better Germany, the Germany that had never yielded to the tyranny of totalitarianism. They were motivated by principles of decency and humaneness, which the Third Reich could never completely suppress.

In 1948 Hans Rothfels, who a decade earlier had been forced into exile by Nazi bigotry, wrote the first scholarly, analytical account of the resistance. It was published—and this reflects the mood of the immediate postwar years—not in Germany but in the United States, and by a publishing house often critical of official American policy (Henry Regnery). Rothfels maintained that the resistance "has left behind ideals which are not bound up with locality or nationality," thereby displaying "a unique character." Its members had to face a cruel but inescapable reality: "to fight for liberation was to fight for defeat." But they did not shrink from that reality. They recognized that "the only way of solving this dilemma was to substitute a positive for a negative ideal, an ideal which transcended the struggle against the Nazis or against external oppression and which was not fulfilled with the overthrow of a regime or the removal of tyranny from just one nation." The motive inspiring them was "basically human and at the same time of universal validity." They must be seen in retrospect as "standard bearers in the midst of chaos."[4]

This interpretation of the resistance may have seemed overgenerous to some readers in 1948. Within a few years, however, it became widely accepted, remaining the orthodox view for more than a generation. The reasons were obvious. A rehabilitated and democratized Germany needed heroes; it needed to show the world that the barbarity of National Socialism was to some extent counterbalanced by the idealism of its opponents. Those who died in the resistance became the martyred forerunners of the Federal Republic. Their self-sacrifice was perceived as an act of conscious atonement for the crimes committed by the Third Reich. They provided moral legitimation for the postwar political order in Central Europe.

The statements of many members of the resistance as they prepared for their doomed coup furnish considerable support for this idealized interpretation. Early in the summer of 1944, for example, General Ludwig Beck, the leading military figure in the plot to overthrow Hitler, argued that the attempt must be made despite the insistence of the Allies on unconditional surrender. "The decisive thing is not what happens to this or that individual personally," he maintained. "The decisive thing is not even the consequence for our nation. It is rather the unbearable reality that for a long time crime after crime and murder after murder have multiplied in the name of the German people, and that it is a moral duty to put a halt with all available means to these crimes committed in the usurped name of our people." The words bespeak unmistakable decency and courage.[5]

Equally moving is the statement of another member of the military resistance, Henning von Tresckow, made shortly after the Allied landing in France. "The attempt against Hitler must take place at any cost," he insisted. "For what matters is no longer the practical goal, but that the German resistance movement dared, before the world and before history, to risk its life in a final gamble. Everything else is by comparison a matter of indifference."

On the morning of July 21, 1944, moreover, after the failure of the coup, Tresckow declared calmly, just before taking his life, that the effort to overthrow the Third Reich had to be made, whatever the outcome. "Now the whole world will assail and revile us," he said in his farewell to a close friend. "But I am now as before of the unshakable conviction that we acted correctly. I consider Hitler to be not only the archenemy of Germany but also the archenemy of the world. When I appear in a few hours before God's seat of judgment to give an account of my actions and my omissions, I think I will be able to defend in good conscience what I have done in the struggle against Hitler." And then he invoked a familiar Old Testament account of human atonement and divine forgiveness. "If God once promised Abraham that he would not destroy Sodom if there were only ten just men there, then I hope that for our sake God will also not annihilate Germany." No participant in the plot could complain of his fate, he continued. "Whoever entered our circle thereby put on the shirt of Nessus." And finally, "the moral worth of a human being begins only at the point where he is ready to lay down his life for his conviction." Who can remain untouched by this expression of willing self-sacrifice?[6]

The bureaucratic members of the resistance could be equally eloquent. They too condemned the crimes committed by the Third Reich; they too spoke of the need for atonement and redemption. In a memorandum composed late in the war, Carl Goerdeler, the former mayor of Leipzig, dwelt on the brutal treatment of the civilian inhabitants of the occupied areas of the Soviet Union. Not only had the Nazis exterminated Russian Jews "in the same bestial way" they had earlier murdered German Jews. They had also behaved toward the Russian population in general "with the most brutal ruthlessness, with plundering, with terror, with the forced conscription of people for labor in Germany." Men and women of the white race had been driven to slave markets "like Negroes in Africa a hundred years ago!" As for the other "tragedies" inflicted on Eastern Europe by the Hitler regime, "there is no need to elaborate on that."[7]

The civilians in the resistance, moreover, displayed the same steadfastness as the soldiers in facing the executioner after the failure of the coup. Fritz-Dietlof von der Schulenburg, one of the younger participants, a jurist by training, told a colleague on the night of July 20, 1944, after it became clear that Hitler had survived the attempted assassination, that he had no regrets about his involvement in the plot. "We must continue in spite of that," he said calmly. "We must drain this cup to the dregs. We must sacrifice ourselves. Later people will understand us." During the interrogation that preceded his execution three weeks later, he expressed no remorse and asked for no clemency. Like Tresckow, he remained convinced to the end that he had acted rightly.[8]

If the churchmen seem less heroic, that is only because the dangers they faced were less deadly. They did not as a rule become involved in conspiratorial activity. Their criticism of the Third Reich, while public, was generally indirect. They may have made themselves vulnerable to charges of disloyalty or disobedience, but not of treason. And yet they too displayed remarkable courage by openly condemning many of the policies of the Third Reich.

Theophil Wurm, the Lutheran state bishop of Württemberg, was even bold enough to send a letter to Hitler himself in the summer of 1943 protesting against the "final solution" of the "Jewish question." He urged the Führer, "in the name of God and for the sake of the German people," to put an end to "the persecution and annihilation to which many men and women within the German sphere of authority are being condemned without a judicial verdict." Though expressing special concern for the "so-called privileged non-Aryans," those married to "Aryans" and the children born of such marriages, he also maintained that "measures adopted for the extermination of the other non-Aryans are in clearest violation of God's commandment and undermine the foundation of all Western thought and life, namely, the God-given right to human existence and to human dignity in general."[9]

Some prominent Catholic clergymen were equally daring. On July 13, 1941, for example, Bishop Clemens August von Galen of Münster denounced from the pulpit the oppression, lawlessness, and brutality of the Nazi regime. "Justice is the only firm foundation of any political system," he preached. "The right to life, to security, and to freedom is an indispensable part of any moral organization of the community." A government that tolerates disregard for the law, that permits persecution of the innocent, "undermines its own authority and the respect for its power in the conscience of the citizens of the state. . . . *Iustitia est fundamentum regnorum!*" To make such statements in the midst of a brutal war, in defiance of a totalitarian dictatorship, took courage.[10]

In short, there is a considerable body of scholarly evidence to support the contention advanced by Rothfels that the men of the resistance acted on principles transcending national interest or national welfare, out of motives that were of universal validity. The eulogistic school of historiography on the attempt to overthrow Hitler appears to be based on solid, incontrovertible data. Yet almost from the beginning a few dissenting voices challenged the orthodox interpretation. No one can doubt the courage or dedication of those who paid with their lives for repudiating National Socialism, they conceded. But what was the basis of that repudiation? Were they inspired primarily by a selfless humanitarianism above national interest or political advantage? Was their goal solely the establishment of a new German polity based on freedom and justice? Had they always opposed bigotry and authoritarianism? And if not, when did they begin to turn against the Third Reich? And why? In other words, the question of the motivation of the resistance would not go away. Suggestions, speculations, even bald assertions could be heard that its members had acted out of expediency rather than idealism, out of parochial rather than universal concerns. The eulogists had to contend from the outset with a small group of skeptics and critics.

Not surprisingly, the dissenters were to a considerable extent foreigners. It was after all psychologically easier for outsiders to find fault with the martyred heroes of the new Germany. Within five years after the appearance of Rothfels's idealized account, a distinguished British scholar, John W. Wheeler-Bennett, published the first major critical treatment of the resistance. It dealt mostly with the soldiers who had participated in the attempted coup of July 20, 1944, but it touched by implication on the civilians as well. The author conceded that "the abortive *Putsch . . . ,* and all that it stood for, was more than a mere military revolt or a gesture of frustrated ambition." It was "a considerably wider and more complex affair" than either the German or the Allied wartime leaders had acknowledged. Those who participated in it were inspired by "a higher loyalty than fealty to a régime or even to a Leader." The plot to assassinate Hitler should not therefore be dismissed as "a hot-bed of militarist reaction." And yet, "neither was it made up entirely—as some have since sought to show—of *preux chevaliers, sans peur et sans reproche.*" Though admittedly containing "elements of democracy," it was "certainly not an essentially democratic movement." The resistance was inspired not only by a yearning for freedom or a demand for justice. It also had a practical goal.

The nature of that goal, Wheeler-Bennett argued, is apparent. "The one motive which was common to all within the conspiracy was a deep desire to save their country from a catastrophe of cataclysmic proportions." In other words, they were first and foremost German patriots. What drove them to their desperate attempt was "the closing in of the avenging armies upon the doomed Reich." Some of their leaders, to be sure, had recognized quite early the "moral and physical" danger of National Socialism. Nevertheless, "it was not until full disaster stared the [military] commanders in the face that they could be brought to share this point of view and to agree to take action—and that only if and when Hitler had been eliminated." His assassination thus became a patriotic duty. Those who tried to carry it out were "by no means all democrats," nor were they "all free from responsibility for the Nazi régime." There was nothing base about what they did, however, nothing dishonorable. They were inspired by love for their country. They assumed that "a new government of the Reich, backed by an army which . . . could still mitigate the gravity of defeat by inspiring respect among its adversaries, might achieve some other and more favorable terms for Germany than Unconditional Surrender." The members of the resistance sought above all to protect their nation against the consequences of defeat.[11]

Those who advanced this point of view were at first dismissed in the Federal Republic as faultfinders and naysayers. The foreigners among them were often accused of being anti-German; the Germans were widely viewed as disloyal or even traitorous. They were giving support to the hatemongers abroad, to the preachers of war guilt and collective responsibility. And yet a small group of revisionist scholars continued to argue and dispute, to probe and question, especially since a growing body of historical evidence seemed to support many of its contentions. Indeed, by the 1980s the critical school had gained enough acceptance to challenge the eulogists and idealizers on almost even terms. Germany, restored and rehabilitated, was finally secure enough to begin dispensing with mythical heroes and martyred saints. The time had come to undertake a dispassionate, balanced, rigorous, and unflinching reexamination of the resistance.

Such a reexamination seemed to reveal with increasing clarity that the men who had sought to overthrow the Nazi regime acted out of a combination of motives, some idealistic, some practical, sometimes selfless, sometimes expedient. Many of those who later denounced Hitler had in fact originally welcomed his coming to power. They had regarded the Weimar Republic with the same hostility that they subsequently displayed toward the Third Reich. The doctrines of democracy filled them with as much aversion as the policies of totalitarianism. They often found it difficult to decide which was worse, Germany's victory or Germany's defeat in the war. Like Faust, they seemed to sigh and agonize: "Zwei Seelen wohnen, ach! in meiner Brust."

General Beck provides a good example. Shortly before the failed coup he insisted that the crimes being committed by National Socialism in the name of the German people had to be stopped, whatever the cost. But a decade earlier his attitude had been quite different. In the early 1930s he argued that Hitler should be appointed chancellor, because he represented the only chance Germany had of regaining military power. According to an old friend, Beck at that time "expressed himself to me unreservedly in favor of National Socialism and would not acknowledge my serious doubts." Soon after the establishment of the Third Reich, he rejoiced at the "political revolution" taking place. "I hoped for it for years, and I am delighted that my hope did not deceive me. This is the first real ray of light since 1918."[12]

Henning von Tresckow is another case in point. In the summer of 1944, just before committing suicide, he described Hitler as the archenemy not only of Germany but of the world. During the 1920s, however, he denounced "the Anglo-American (also known as Jewish) democratic-capitalistic idea" whose triumph would mean the "enslavement of the world by commercialism." He announced in the officers' club in Potsdam his support of the Nazi demand for "breaking the chains of usury," and he tried to influence members of his regiment "in favor of National Socialism." Indeed, Hans Bernd Gisevius, one of the few members of the resistance to survive the war, described Tresckow's early attitude toward the Third Reich as highly favorable. "He was for many years able to see only the side of National Socialism attractive to a soldier: the assertion of discipline, the reestablishment of military primacy, and the revision of the Versailles Treaty." Many of the soldiers who later turned against Hitler shared this view.[13]

The civilian resisters were originally of the same opinion. Many of them cheered the fall of the Weimar Republic, which appeared to them to embody all the weaknesses of mass rule, party politics, military ineffectualness, and crass materialism. The Third Reich, by contrast, seemed to hold out the promise of a civic and spiritual revival. Clearly, the duty of every patriotic citizen was to support its efforts.

Carl Goerdeler, who sacrificed his life in the attempt to end the Hitler dictatorship, had been full of hope at the time of its establishment. As early as 1929 he was complaining that "all parties suffer from fear of the voters," which had made them incapable of coping with the approaching economic crisis. In memorandums submitted to President Hindenburg in 1931 and 1932, he argued that the parliamentary system was now finished because it had placed "the interest of the parties above the welfare of the state." That was the "curse of parliamentarianism." The "mobilization of all popular energies" was the only way of avoiding a national catastrophe, and that meant "a dictatorship lasting for years." As for the Reichstag, "if it creates difficulties for the task of saving the fatherland," it would have to be dissolved.

The year after Hitler came to power, moreover, Goerdeler wrote to him to express approval of "the elimination of rule by the parties in Germany and its fortunate replacement by the amalgamation of party and state." This vital reform would not have been possible without the concentration of "the authority of the party and the authority of the state in the hands of one person." Only the Nazi regime, he felt, had made possible the recovery of Germany.[14]

Schulenburg was even more enthusiastic. In 1944 he faced the executioner with calm courage, but in 1933 he greeted the executioner's arrival with rejoicing. Long before the Nazi victory, the "red count" was inveighing that under republican rule the state, "formerly a living organism bound to the entire community," had become a "cover organization for special interests and for functionaries." The system of administration had been turned into "a battlefield and a source of booty" for the parties, while "anemic" government officials, increasingly submissive to the "party bosses," were becoming "alienated from the people." In 1932 he joined the National Socialist Party, and when a year later Hitler became chancellor, Schulenburg was jubilant. The establishment of the Third Reich represented a major defeat for the "powers of Jewry, capital, and the Catholic Church." The republic had destroyed "the old Prussian civil service, which possessed outstanding qualities of intelligence, character, and accomplishment." But then "the unknown soldier of the world war, Adolf Hitler," created a new core of resistance, so that the Nazi movement became "the incarnation of the faith and will of the German people." The country was finally emerging from the demoralization and defeatism of Weimar.[15]

Similarly, the church leaders who toward the end of the Third Reich came out openly against many of its policies were in the beginning highly supportive. Bishop Wurm had welcomed the establishment of authoritarian government in Germany. He hoped that the end of the secular and "materialistic" republic would lead to a national spiritual revival. In November 1932, just before the triumph of the Nazi movement, he spoke approvingly about the concept of a "Christian state" recently invoked by the ministry of Franz von Papen. He favored a regime "which makes it possible to be a Christian"; he supported a system of "politics based on faith." He rejoiced at the quest for "values that have been lost," a quest that could not be dismissed with glib phrases about "reaction or restoration." As for National Socialism, the Protestant Church should show "a measure of understanding" for "a powerful popular movement, even though it contains dubious elements and its leadership is by no means unobjectionable."

A few months later, after Hitler had come to power, Wurm's reservations about dubious elements and objectionable leadership in the Nazi Party had largely disappeared. In March 1933 he praised the new government for overcoming "the danger of a Bolshevization of the German people, a danger that was becoming ever more threatening as a result of our impoverishment." The youth of Germany in particular had learned that an improvement in material conditions could be achieved not by "the imitation of Russian methods of coercion," but only through "a reorganization of state and economy reflecting the character of its own nation."

By April Wurm sounded even more positive. After mourning the fate of the "organized Protestant Church in Russia," which had reportedly "ceased to exist," he spoke "with joy" about the efforts of National Socialism to initiate an "urgently needed purge of public life." German

Protestantism would regard such a purge "with approval" and would "gladly assist it with advice." In his view, what the Third Reich sought was not only the material but the spiritual revival of the nation.[16]

Bishop Galen underwent a similar change of heart. During the war he too criticized the Nazi regime for disregarding the norms of law and justice. But when that regime was first established, his attitude had been quite different. After a brief period of vacillation, shared with most other members of the Catholic hierarchy, he became an avowed supporter of the new order following the conclusion of a concordat between Germany and the Vatican on July 20, 1933. In a pastoral letter a few months later he thanked God that "the top leaders of our fatherland . . . have recognized and are trying with a firm hand to eliminate the terrible danger that threatened our beloved German people as a result of the open propaganda for godlessness and immorality." The agreement concluded with the Papacy would finally make it possible for the church to exercise freely its influence over "the education of our youth and over family and communal life."

By the following summer, Galen was even praising the enlightened social policy of the Third Reich. During "the period of liberalism and Marxism," he declared at a gathering of Catholic workers, the Weimar regime had encouraged "a new defection from the church." Its "idolatry of mammonism" had left no room for "the dignity, for the honor, and the right" of the working man. "Unconscionable seducers" of the lower classes had taught that "might is more important than right," that labor relations should be based on class antagonism and greed. But now "the developments of a new era promise to crush mammonism and Marxism," making possible the creation of a "new and better social order." Specifically, "the program of the [Hitler] government envisions the corporative reconstruction" of society. The duty of every Catholic, indeed, of every Christian, was to support this effort.[17]

Most members of the resistance followed a similar pattern. They were generally hostile to the republic, they were distrustful of parliamentary government, they were resentful of their country's military weakness, and they were opposed to the individualism and "materialism" that Weimar seemed to foster. Only a few of them were out-and-out Nazis. Generally they regarded Hitler's followers as a little crude and simple-minded, often intemperate, sometimes rough, but with their hearts in the right place. National Socialism appeared to them a useful partner in the struggle against the hated republican regime. Not only did it have popular appeal and a mass following, but many of its doctrines and beliefs were essentially sound. Frequently those who later formed the resistance were at first sympathizers, supporters, and allies of the Third Reich. They eventually turned against it owing to disagreement over policy or method rather than proclaimed principle.

Following the failure of the attempt to assassinate Hitler, for instance, one of those arrested for complicity, Count Nikolaus von Üxküll, declared that he had initially been favorable to the regime. "After the seizure of power [by the Nazis], I was an avowed adherent of the Führer, and I was also convinced that he would lead us to great achievements." Berthold von Stauffenberg, who joined the resistance even before his better-known brother Claus, described his original attitude toward the Third Reich in similar terms: "In the domestic area we had for the most part completely supported the basic ideas of National Socialism." Those ideas, according to his testimony, had seemed to him and his friends "healthy and forward-looking." A police report regarding the unsuccessful coup stated that the arrested participants in general claimed to have at first supported the Nazi regime. "For the most part they assert that in the beginning they had nothing against National Socialism. On the contrary, they regarded the assumption of power [by Hitler] with sympathy." There is no reason to question this assertion.[18]

What then made these members of the resistance change their minds? What made them turn against a government whose establishment they had originally greeted with approval? Was it the Third Reich's suppression of political dissent? Its disregard for civil rights? Its aggressive foreign policy? Its virulent racism? On this point there is little conclusive evidence. They themselves offered various explanations, none of them altogether satisfactory or persuasive. They almost never conceded that they had been mistaken in their initial assessment of National Socialism, that they had perhaps underestimated its inherent brutality or overlooked its essential malevolence. Rather, National Socialism had altered in the course of time; it had abandoned its original principles; it had become intoxicated with success; it had been corrupted by power. If only it had remained true to its original ideal of selfless service to the nation. Hitler was the one who had changed, not those who tried to assassinate him. In short, the participants in the coup of July 20, 1944, maintained that they were motivated primarily not by a fundamental opposition to the ideology of the Third Reich, but by a rejection of the means it adopted in the name of that ideology.

The police summaries of the interrogation of those involved in the assassination plot emphasize this point. "The same people often maintain," according to one report, "that they were basically in agreement with the main objectives of the National Socialist Party, but that their favorable attitude gradually began to weaken as a result of the practical application [of its principles]." Another report states that "the intoxication of the initial enthusiasm" with which the members of the resistance claimed to have greeted the Third Reich became "watered down considerably" in the following years, because "the behavior of National Socialism in practice has . . . often been in quite stark contrast to the proclaimed principles." In summary, "a large number of those interrogated state that they had declared themselves in agreement to a very large extent with the objectives of the National Socialist Party in 1933." Finally, "many other people who have been arrested in connection with [the attempted coup] have made similar declarations."[19]

But should such declarations be taken at face value? Should they not rather be ascribed to a desire by men fearing execution to mitigate the severity of the punishment awaiting them? That possibility must certainly not be dismissed. Yet long afterward, some of those who had been close to the resistance continued to maintain that National Socialism had originally not been without important redeeming features. A decade after the war, for example, Alexander von Stauffenberg, a historian by profession, both of whose brothers had perished in the plot against Hitler, was still wrestling with the question of whether the Third Reich represented the same malignant principles in the beginning as at the end. He wondered whether National Socialism "was absolutely evil from the outset, or whether we should advance here a hypothesis of development." Was it not possible that a state based on law, "though under authoritarian auspices," might have emerged out of the Nazi system, if its leadership had not degenerated with the passage of time, as the last restraints on its power were removed? "The latter is, on the basis of all historical analogies, the more likely [interpretation]," he concluded.[20]

Clearly then, understanding the motives and purposes, the ethos, of the resistance requires a close examination of the process by which its members were transformed from allies into opponents of the Third Reich. What first aroused their doubts regarding National Socialism? And when? At what point did their misgiving turn into suspicion, suspicion into resentment, resentment into hostility, hostility into rebellion? And what sort of political and social system did they seek to establish in place of the Nazi regime? Only a careful scrutiny of the words and deeds of those who risked their lives to overthrow Hitler can provide an accurate assessment of their hopes and plans for a new and better Germany.

I

The Rejection of Weimar

Behind the petty activities of the [political] parties stand dark forces . . . , alien to the history and character of the German people, forces which admittedly march in step with German destiny on unessential questions of German life, but which are always on the opposing side whenever essential issues, whenever the final struggle is being decided.

FRITZ-DIETLOF VON DER SCHULENBURG (1931)

1

Opposition to Democracy

Although Wheeler-Bennett's assessment of the resistance is generally regarded as highly critical, he could at times sound quite lenient, even sympathetic. His contention, for example, that "there were certainly elements of democracy about it," elements discernible not only in the handful of "Socialist and Trade Union representatives" but also in its "aristocratic members," is too generous. In fact, the great majority of those involved in the attempt to overthrow Hitler fundamentally opposed democratic principles. They openly said so. Indeed, they came to regard the Nazi regime as a product of popular forces and energies unleashed by democracy. The dominant values of the social groups from which most of them came—the officer corps, the civil service, and the church hierarchy—emphasized loyalty to legitimate authority embodied in the old monarchical order. For these strata the fall of the empire in 1918 and its replacement by a republic resulted from the violation of a sacred tradition. They were never able to accept it.[1]

The members of the resistance generally shared this view. The older men looked back with nostalgia to the imperial era in which they had grown up. To them it always remained the golden twilight of a vanished age of national glory. The younger ones were not as monarchical in their political sympathies; newer forms of authoritarian rule attracted them. But young and old alike remained united in a common hostility to Weimar. In view of their class origin, could any other attitude have been expected? The soldiers and bureaucrats among them came as a rule from aristocratic or upper-middle-class families, families of affluence, education, influence, and privilege. Their position within the social elite of Germany had been a reward for their loyalty to the crown, whereas the republican regime represented an implicit threat to their patrician status. Both conviction and self-interest fed their opposition to the new democratic political system.

The reasons for the antagonism of most churchmen to the republic are less obvious, but they are basically similar. Admission to the clergy, even to positions of ecclesiastical leadership, was not as restricted as in the officer corps or the civil service. Yet here too class background played a significant role. More important, the values of the established churches seemed clearly in conflict with the spirit of Weimar. To Protestantism in particular the alliance of crown and altar appeared essential for the defense of religious values. German Catholicism was more independent in its outlook, more wary of the imperial order against which it had waged a bitter conflict during the 1870s. Yet the hierarchy was even more suspicious of the new republican regime than of the old monarchical system. For Weimar represented that spirit of "secularism" and "materialism" which seemed a greater threat than the anti-Catholic bias of the empire had been. Worse than that, the republic tolerated the forces of Socialism, Communism, and atheism. At times it even appeared to sympathize with them. Both major churches thus regarded the democratic system with suspicion and fear. Both would have preferred a more traditional form of political authority.

Most members of the resistance made no secret of their opposition to republicanism. On the contrary, they expressed their rejection of Weimar openly and persistently. What they had to say constituted in fact a comprehensive critique or repudiation of the new political order. That critique was directed first of all against the historic act of insubordination against legitimate authority that had led to the overthrow of the monarchy. During his interrogation by the security police following the failed coup against Hitler, General Hans Oster emphasized that under the empire the officer corps had never doubted that the established system was impregnable. That it might some day "fall apart" seemed simply "not conceivable" to the professional soldier. "There were no politics for us. We wore the king's uniform, and that was enough for us." They were by background and training, by instinct almost, conservative and royalist. "To read the [liberal] *Berliner Tageblatt* or the *Frankfurter Zeitung* in the officers' club was taboo."

Hence the collapse of the empire as the result of a "revolt," Oster testified, "shocked and surprised" the officer corps "in the most painful way." The replacement of the monarchy with a "fragmented party state" affected most of its members like "a hammer blow to the head." They felt a profound aversion toward the new "November state." Still, what were they to do? After "the most difficult inner struggles," they decided "with a heavy heart" to serve the "socialist republic." Thereby they hoped "to help our nation survive this difficult period."[2]

Ludwig Beck, writing at the end of November 1918, corroborated Oster's later recollection. A major on the general staff, he could not believe what had been happening during the last few weeks. The fall of the old order was "so monstrous" that he often thought he was dreaming. He did not doubt, "even for a moment," that the revolution had been planned "long in advance." It had attacked the armed forces from the rear at a time when the high command was being forced to exert every effort to prevent a military catastrophe. "I know of no revolution in history that was carried out in such a cowardly fashion, a revolution that—and this is actually much worse—has aggravated beyond any doubt the difficult situation in which we have been for a long time now, leading perhaps to complete ruin."

The consequences were bound to be disastrous, Beck believed. How could anyone fail to see that? It was "madness" to initiate a revolution in a country that might still have achieved "an acceptable peace and a healthy peacetime economy," but only through "the most vigorous application of all its energies and the complete preservation of its intricate organism." What had happened could be compared to a patient suffering from a serious lung ailment who is forced to undergo an operation for appendicitis. "Not even the best organism can endure that." The revolutionary uprising had not only been an act of treachery, of political betrayal. It had also condemned Germany to defeat, weakness, humiliation, and oppression. Those responsible for it were guilty of an unpardonable crime against their people.[3]

This view was widespread among the members of the officer corps, including those who later joined the resistance against Hitler. Professional soldiers, however, had to be discreet about what they said in public concerning the republic's origins and doctrines. They were required to maintain at least the appearance of neutrality in political questions. Their attitude toward the new order must therefore be ascertained mostly from private conversations and personal letters, from hints and allusions, from diaries, reminiscences, memoirs, and autobiographies. In contrast, the civilians—the bureaucrats and the churchmen—could express their opinions more freely, protected by those same democratic principles that they scornfully rejected. Thus the most vocal and systematic criticism of the revolution came from their ranks.

The views of Cardinal Michael von Faulhaber of Munich are especially illuminating, because he was one of the few religious leaders who might have been expected to feel some sympathy for Weimar. Most of the other

members of the resistance, coming from conservative aristocratic or bourgeois families, had been brought up in the belief that obedience to monarchical authority was a solemn civic duty. But Faulhaber's background and
experience were different. Only fifty years earlier his church had been
engaged in a bitter struggle against the state. Even after the *Kulturkampf*
came to an end late in the 1870s relations between the two had remained
strained. Catholics were generally regarded by the imperial authorities with
suspicion and distrust; when seeking advancement in the civil service or the
armed forces, they faced pervasive discrimination. Hence the Center Party,
which represented their confessional interests, became a supporter of political reform, entering during World War I into an informal coalition with
the parties of the liberal middle and the moderate left in order to achieve
democratic reform and a compromise peace.

The establishment of the Weimar Republic meant liberation for the
Catholics of Germany almost as much as for the Socialists or the Jews. They
were now free to broaden their political influence and compete on even
terms for the highest offices in government. Indeed, because of its pivotal
position, the Center Party succeeded in gaining a parliamentary importance
far out of proportion to the size of its following. It held the chancellorship
in eight of the seventeen ministries between 1919 and 1932, and was
represented by cabinet members in each of the remaining nine. Thus a
prominent churchman like Faulhaber, a man of lower-class background,
the son of a baker, might have been expected to regard favorably a regime
committed to the equality of political opportunity. Yet he never became
reconciled to the new order; he found it too radical, too secular, too
individualistic. Worst of all, it had originated in an act of disobedience that
was unpardonable. Nothing it did could expiate the sin of subverting
legitimate authority.

This was the unmistakable implication of Faulhaber's famous speech of
August 27, 1922, before a large Catholic gathering in Munich. He conceded that, as a rule, compromise was essential for the reconciliation of
opposing views and interests. But principles must stand, "like the eternal
stars," above compromise; there is a limit beyond which flexibility and
accommodation should not go. For Faulhaber that limit had been reached
in the great national debate regarding the establishment of the republic
"The revolution was perjury and treason; it will remain in history tainted
with hereditary fault and branded with the mark of Cain." The new order
did achieve some successes, he admitted; it deserved credit, for example,
for making "the road to higher offices" more accessible to Catholics.
Nevertheless, a man of "moral character does not base his assessments on

successes; a crime cannot be sanctified because of its successes." Whatever Weimar's accomplishments, its origin in an act of political betrayal remained illegitimate.[4]

The loud public outcry provoked by Faulhaber's speech led him to modify what he had said or at least to try to explain its meaning. Three weeks after condemning the revolution as "perjury and treason," he assured the Bavarian envoy to the Vatican that he had never meant to cast aspersion on the Weimar constitution or on the republican form of government. "A constitution can be adopted legally without thereby legitimizing the preceding revolution. A child born out of wedlock can become a decent human being without thereby providing justification for motherhood out of wedlock as such." All he had sought to do was oppose efforts on the left "to bless the revolution of 1918," just as he opposed schemes on the right to organize a counterrevolution.

Writing at the same time to a member of the Papal State Secretariat, the cardinal reiterated that he had not intended to condemn "the present republican form of the state," nor had he advocated "the violent overthrow of the present constitution of Weimar." He declared once again that a constitution could be adopted legally, even though the revolution that had made it possible remained an act of illegality. Faulhaber proceeded to provide an additional justification of his position. Some leaders of the Center Party, he explained, were basing their political decisions on "election tactics and opportunistic viewpoints and momentary successes" rather than on "eternal principles." His purpose had been to warn them, "without talking about politics," against "opening for Bolshevism the gates to the German people by endless compromises and alliances with the Social Democrats." The great danger he perceived in the republican regime was a willingness to accept radicalism, whether in a Socialist or a Communist form, as a valid expression of the popular will.[5]

Still, what many members of the resistance found most objectionable in Weimar was not its illegitimate revolutionary origin or its alleged leftist inclination but its commitment to the principles of democracy. To them democracy was a form of government that, behind a facade of lofty phrases about the "rights of man" and "government by the people," promoted private gain at the expense of public welfare. Power under parliamentary rule was exercised not by the masses, the theoretical source of civic authority, but by politicians and demagogues, by sects and factions, by the "party system," which manipulated the voters to its own advantage. The republic had undermined the sense of common purpose in Germany. It had unleashed a war of class against class, interest against interest, ideology against ideology. How could the country cope with the consequences of military defeat and economic privation under such a regime? Only a return to a traditional form of authority and a renewed faith in hierarchical leadership could save the nation from permanent decline.

Even before the end of World War I, Ulrich von Hassell, just starting out on what was to become a distinguished diplomatic career, warned against the attempts of the imperial government to liberalize the political system as a means of bolstering public morale. Early in January 1918 he pointed in a newspaper article to the harmful effects of parliamentarianism, which determines policy by counting votes instead of considering national needs and interests. The great danger, he argued, lay in "that disguising of economic demands with political slogans and that adulteration of political lines of thought with economic egoism." Forms of government based on an unrestricted franchise were bound to become corrupted by private interests. Unfortunately, "defenders of the so-called rights of the people" failed to recognize "that they are being manipulated like puppets by the wire-pullers of international capitalism, and that the mechanistic realization of their doctrines is incompatible with true freedom." Since the introduction of parliamentary government would be contrary to the nation's historic traditions, it remained essential to preserve an aristocratic upper chamber in the legislative system as a counterweight, "though an inadequate one," to a democratic lower chamber.

A general suffrage seemed to Hassell acceptable only "in an organic form." That is, the method of representation should be based on "the various forms of self-government," on "occupational organization" and on "local self-government." As late as September 1918, after it became clear that Germany had lost the war and that only a democratization of the empire might still prevent military collapse and social upheaval, he continued to oppose an unrestricted franchise. Instead, he advocated a national parliament derived from the "occupational structure" of the country. More concretely, "first rebuild local administration organically, and then on this basis let the national representation develop, also organically." Until that became possible, however, the existing political system should be maintained unchanged. "The bulwark of an upper chamber [in the legislature], strong in composition and authority, is indispensable for us, as long as the dethronement of mechanistic parliamentarianism has not become an accomplished fact." Hassell remained to the end a bitter opponent of popular sovereignty.[6]

The establishment of the Weimar Republic only strengthened the members of the resistance in their distrust of democracy. What had hitherto been an abstract apprehension now became a terrible reality. They saw in the new order a regime that seemed to lurch from crisis to crisis, from failure to failure, without a sense of direction, unable to guide the country in its hour of need. But could anything better be expected from a government that, abandoning national tradition, had turned to alien doctrines of selfish individualism and ineffectual parliamentarianism? Sooner or later the republican system would have to go.

Hassell's rejection of democratic principles during the twilight of the empire was echoed by Schulenburg thirteen years later during the twilight of Weimar. In 1931 the young government official, still in his twenties, directed a bitter attack against the republic, an attack that reflected also the views of many older participants in the resistance. For him as for them, the basic cause of the ineffectualness of the new order lay not in its practical policies and objectives but in its theoretical beliefs and assumptions. The latter ultimately led to the rise of a party system, under which sound government had become impossible.

"The individual party cannot produce a pure political idea or follow a consistent political policy," Schulenburg argued. Within the party structure any original idea would of necessity be "smothered" by "narrow party interests." Parties by their nature did not unite but divide a nation through the confrontation of their "special interests." They could only paper over the differences separating them; they could not reconcile or transcend those differences. While the leftist Social Democratic Party, "champion of a fictitious international community of the working class," the liberal State Party, "agent of international finance capital," and the Catholic Center Party, "outpost of Rome in Germany," were for the moment joined in defense of the Weimar Republic, their sole purpose was to preserve a "fragmented, impotent state," which had abandoned any policy based on "political will." All that united them was their common pursuit of "purely extraneous goals."

A government based on such essentially incompatible elements, according to Schulenburg, must necessarily adopt a policy of "cunning stratagems" suited to shifting circumstances rather than a strategy of "planned action derived from a single purpose." It might try to disguise the lack of inner unity by overemphasizing the common platform on which the cabinet partners had agreed. But in the long run all those "hysterical cries about republic, constitution, and flag" could not conceal the lack of any "creative political idea" on the part of the regime. Indeed, the people were beginning to realize that the progovernment parties were not guided by political objectives but by "alien forces outside the state and opposed to the state."

Schulenburg did not identify those alien forces more closely, but there could be little doubt whom he meant. In any case, he concluded, there was a growing awareness that the parties supporting the republic were united by nothing more than "personal and egotistical goals," namely, "the protection of sinecures and offices." The regime was simply too feeble, too corrupt, to be saved by political devices, expedients, or palliatives. Its weaknesses were inherent and fundamental; they were the inevitable weaknesses of democracy. Only a more disciplined, more authoritarian form of government could save Germany.[7]

Long after the fall of the republic, after the "ineffectual" party system had been replaced by a ruthless totalitarianism, most members of the resistance remained convinced that the parliamentary regime had been destroyed by its own basic shortcomings, the inevitable shortcomings of mass democracy. Their opposition to Hitler did little to soften their criticism of Weimar. As late as 1941, while Germany's wealth and manpower were again being consumed in a ruinous world war, Goerdeler was still describing the failings of republicanism in terms similar to those employed by Hassell and Schulenburg. Like them, he remained convinced that the brief experiment in parliamentary rule had failed because of the innate defects of any political system based on popular sovereignty, namely, governmental ineffectualness, partisan selfishness, divided will, and irresolute purpose.

Hence, although the Third Reich had turned out to be brutal and tyrannical, the resisters did not want to bring about a restoration of the old discredited republican regime. "The Weimar constitution failed," Goerdeler explained, "precisely because of its addiction to being mathematical." What ruined it was not primarily the authority conferred on parliament but the system of proportional representation. That system, "while theoretically the fairest," reduced the constitution to a mere "machine." As a result, there was no longer any "organic suffrage." The voter did not vote for men who had gained his confidence, whom he had found "in his usual, everyday surroundings" to be honest and experienced. Instead, he voted for a list on which, under the best of circumstances, only a few names were familiar to him through "pretty speeches" delivered at "occasional election rallies." In other words, the voter cast his ballot for a "paper program" that each party tried to make more palatable with "demagogic bacon crumbs." There was thus no "organic connection" between those who elected and those who were elected, only "a temporary and more or less fragile community of interest." Could any good come from such a system of voting?

What made the situation worse, according to Goerdeler, was the economic crisis produced by Germany's military defeat in 1918. The "dictate of Versailles" had inflamed "national passions" still further. During those difficult postwar years, "material desires" became increasingly important, so that in the end a majority of the population voted for men who "made the greatest number of material and unrealizable promises to the greatest number of people" rather than for those in whose honesty it had confidence. Such a suffrage of the "logarithmic table" was bound to lead to a fragmentation of the nation and to the encouragement of reckless demagogy.

Goerdeler concluded that the system of government in Germany after 1933 resembled in important respects that which had been in force before 1933. Both represented "a mixture of fanatical idealism and unrestrained materialism," both suffered from too much doctrinal zeal combined with too much selfish appetite. But now idealism as well as materialism had passed its peak. Those two contradictory forces could not be completely suppressed, he acknowledged, because they were "natural and vital in man." They could be controlled, however, and even harmonized through "restraint." Yet that was attainable only on a foundation of "reason, justice, a sense of order, an awareness of responsibility, decency, and experience, as well as love of the people and of the fatherland." Neither the Weimar Republic nor the Third Reich had shown itself capable of providing such a foundation. It was apparent to Goerdeler that only some new political system, disciplined and forceful but just and humane, could be entrusted with the task of building a new Germany.[8]

In summary, the political rhetoric of the resistance, like that of the antirepublican conservative movement in general, resounded with certain stock phrases and concepts. These included first a condemnation of the teachings of popular democracy for being "mechanistic" or "materialistic," for exalting expediency and egoism above loyalty and self-sacrifice. Then came a denunciation of parliamentary government for opening the door to partisan politics, to the party system, which disguised a selfish quest for private gain with glib phrases about freedom and equality. Third, Weimar represented the triumph of special interests over the common good, pitting class against class and occupation against occupation, fragmenting and paralyzing the national will. And finally, behind the screen of civil liberties and parliamentary institutions lurked "sinister" and alien forces manipulating the political system for their own financial gain. The true allegiance of these schemers and intriguers, these cunning wire-pullers, unmistakably described though usually unnamed, belonged not to their country of birth but to their religion or "race."

Accordingly, to most of the men in the resistance the problems the republican regime faced were not contingent or fortuitous. They were not simply the result of poor judgment, mistaken policy, bureaucratic inefficiency, political inexperience, or bad luck. They were endemic and inherent. They were the outward manifestation of an inward flaw in the form of government. Weimar might survive a particular crisis, it might overcome this or that temporary difficulty. But it could not provide a consistent or effective system of authority. Only its replacement by a more courageous, more forceful regime could save the country from civic impotence.

On November 11, 1923, on the fifth anniversary of the signing of the Armistice, Ludwig Beck reflected on the disastrous situation in Germany. Inflation had reached catastrophic proportions, threatening the economy with total collapse. The French had occupied the Ruhr, the country's richest industrial region. A secessionist movement seemed to be gaining strength in the Rhineland. Communists had recently been admitted to the state governments in Saxony and Thuringia; now they were no doubt plotting to seize power in Berlin. Where would it all end? The only way out was a new national government—authoritarian, resolute, and disciplined.

"Conditions at home and abroad are forcing us to follow a different course," he wrote to General Konrad Ernst von Gossler, his wartime commander. "Social Democracy has mismanaged everything; the democratic blessings are no longer effective. We need iron leadership that can reestablish authority, force people to work, and provide bread for the industrious." Could someone be found in Berlin to provide such leadership? "If not," Beck feared, "we will soon have famine and civil war everywhere, and France will have her ultimate success." Clearly, the coming winter would be hard; there was every reason for concern. And yet, "we must not lose courage even now." The most important thing was "to prevent a disintegration of the troops," and for that the country would have to rely on methods "only a dictator" could employ. There was no alternative.[9]

The crisis that filled Beck with such anxiety started to recede, however, in the course of the next few months. In fact, the middle 1920s became Weimar's brief summer of hope, a time of renewed faith and optimism. The inflation came to an end, and the French withdrew from the Ruhr. Rhenish separatism collapsed, and the appeal of Communism to the working class gradually diminished. There was even a brief, unexpected prosperity, which held out the promise of Germany's complete political and economic rehabilitation. In those few years of renewed confidence, opposition to the republic began to sound less strident and insistent. The conservative members of the resistance, like most political conservatives, appeared more favorable to the new order or at least more resigned. They did not grumble quite as much, and they did not advocate a return to authoritarian rule with quite the same vehemence. Still, they continued to have serious doubts about the stability of parliamentary government, about its capacity to provide effective leadership over the long haul. At heart they remained distrustful of any political system based on popular sovereignty.

Consider Johannes Popitz. A highly respected economic expert, he served successively as German state secretary under Weimar, as Prussian finance minister in the Third Reich, and finally as a member of the cabinet that the resistance hoped to install after Hitler's assassination. This last distinction cost him his life. Even during the heyday of the republic, however, he expressed occasional doubts about the fairness or efficiency of representative democracy. In an essay published in 1926, for example, he wondered whether a legislative structure based on universal suffrage could provide adequate representation for those taxpayers who must bear the heaviest financial burden. "The general franchise structures the representative bodies that approve [taxes] in such a way that the people in the higher income categories who must feel the weight of additional payments directly are not the ones who have a strong influence in the representative bodies, but in general rather the people who represent the less affluent groups in the population are." This disparity between political and economic power under the republic made an equitable system of taxation virtually impossible.[10]

As the brief prosperity in Germany gave way to a new financial crisis, Popitz's criticism of Weimar became sharper and more explicit. Addressing a group of industrialists in the fall of 1930, he complained that "the distribution of the greater part of the German national income" was determined not by the "market mechanism" but by a "noneconomic will," namely, "the will of the state." And what was the nature of that will? How was it shaped and determined? By the "parliamentary democratic method," Popitz argued, which helped create not a "monocratic" but a "polycratic" form of political authority. That meant first of all that the dominant influence molding the state's will originated in "the interests of the parties," in "compromises made by [parliamentary] coalitions," as the country had unfortunately discovered through the "daily conduct of national policy." But worse still, under the polycratic system public finances were not treated as a single entity. "There is no one director of the will [of the state]." Rather, the republican regime had several directors, "who are

admittedly connected with one another," but not closely enough to provide "united leadership." Built on disunion and compromise, Weimar
seemed to Popitz incapable of supplying the firm guidance that the German economy needed so urgently.[11]

The evolution of Goerdeler's attitude toward the republic followed
roughly the same pattern: first a grudging acceptance of Weimar, then
growing criticism of the regime, and finally an open demand for a more
authoritarian constitutional structure. Even before the coming of the
depression, the gifted conservative civil servant had begun to turn from
municipal government to national politics. By the end of the 1920s he was
complaining that since "all parties suffer from fear of the voters," they were
incapable of dealing with the approaching economic crisis. He saw little
chance that parliamentary methods could bring about the political and
financial reforms needed to save the country. One possible solution was an
"enabling act" giving the president the right to issue emergency decrees
without the approval of the legislature. If the chancellor objected to such
a policy, he could be dismissed and replaced by someone more pliable. The
protests of the Reichstag were to be simply disregarded. A resolute statesman, Goerdeler maintained, would be able "to pursue for years a systematic policy capable of leading [the nation] through a difficult period, even
if there is a lack of capital." The goal of such a policy must be to save
Germany from chaos by a "mobilization of all popular energies." Here in
rough outline was the strategy the president and the chancellor were in fact
to adopt four years later.[12]

The great depression, which started just as Goerdeler was composing
his prescription for dictatorial rule, revived and intensified the criticism of
Weimar. The political resentments that had been allayed by the brief
prosperity of the middle 1920s reemerged more virulent than ever. All the
familiar charges about the disastrous effects of the party system, about the
outrageous injustices of the dictate of Versailles, about the greed and
selfishness of the special interests, and about the sinister schemes and
manipulations of alien forces rose to the surface once again. Among the
conservative critics of the regime, who were rapidly gaining strength,
could also be found many of the participants in the resistance. They too
believed that the economic crisis was a result of the weaknesses of popular
democracy. They too declared that the parliamentary system was incapable
of solving the problems facing the nation. They too favored the establishment of an authoritarian form of government. They too looked forward to the end of the republic. They too contributed to the downfall of
Weimar.

In that feverish atmosphere of a dying political system, the officer corps increasingly abandoned its ostensible neutrality on questions of public policy. It still insisted that its members were strictly nonpartisan and apolitical, that they stood above party and ideology, that they served only the nation. Long afterward Hans Oster testified that General Hans von Seeckt, chief of the army command in the early years of the republic, had taught the armed forces that involvement in politics would be incompatible with their status and mission. "We were trained in the decisive years of our military development to become apolitical soldiers." A policy of scrupulous aloofness from public affairs had been accepted as the only way to rebuild a disciplined and effective military force that could form the basis for an expanded army. "The words 'party' and 'politics' had an unpleasant sound, as far as we were concerned."[13]

But this portrayal of a strictly apolitical officer corps serving only the interests of the nation was in fact too idealized. The armed forces during the republic were never entirely above party and ideology; they were always tacitly predisposed and partisan. It would have been unrealistic to expect otherwise. The leaders of the army did avoid taking sides in public on questions of government policy. Still, even during Weimar's brief prosperity, their private conversations and letters leave little doubt regarding their political sympathies. And once the great depression came, the partisan inclinations of the officer corps became increasingly apparent. The attitudes of its members hardened; their words became less discreet and ambiguous. There could no longer be any question about their feelings toward the disintegrating republican regime.

Tresckow, for example, always critical of the Weimar experiment in democracy, became more and more vociferous as the economic crisis worsened. "If you are smart, you will vote for [the conservative leader Alfred] Hugenberg," he told a relative who had republican sympathies. "If you are ardent, you will vote for Hitler." During a train ride near the army training camp at Döberitz outside Berlin, he teased playfully, "Whoever votes for [Chancellor Heinrich] Brüning better get out. Here they shoot with live bullets." Behind his little jest was an awareness that the armed forces were eager for an end to the parliamentary system.[14]

The same view appeared in a more serious form in a letter written in the summer of 1932 by Lieutenant Hellmuth Stieff, who twelve years later manufactured the bomb that almost blew up Hitler. Here he described to his wife the political mood of the army leaders during the last days of Weimar, a mood he himself shared. "The parties are the misfortune of Germany." Their irresponsibility had made impossible any consistent or fruitful national policy, which the country needed so desperately "to lead us out of our misery." As a result, "the government must be freed from the chains of parliamentarianism so that it can work independently, supported by the confidence of the president and the power of the army." After all, the president and the army represented in a symbolic way "the idea of national unity." Since they stood "above the parties," they alone were qualified, "working solely for the welfare of the state," to bring about a reconciliation of the opposing political and social forces. They, and not the Reichstag, provided "the only basis for a government of the sort we need now." The republic was finished; the time had come for a dictatorship.[15]

The civil servants in the resistance were equally convinced that the republic was facing political bankruptcy, that the Weimar system could not go on much longer. Even Popitz, always the discreet, circumspect bureaucrat, argued in characteristically ponderous and convoluted language that the regime had arrived at a total impasse. "State and economy are in crisis," he declared in a newspaper article early in 1931. Those in charge—Popitz meant President Hindenburg and Chancellor Brüning—were trying to save the country by following "the will of the constituted leaders" of Germany. One part of the state apparatus, however, the part opposing rule by presidential decree, sought "to undo this work of salvation and render the will of the leaders ineffectual." How would this creeping paralysis of the nation's capacity to function end? Popitz cautiously and indirectly suggested the introduction of an authoritarian constitutional structure.[16]

Schulenburg, the youthful bureaucratic firebrand, was more explicit in his criticism of the republic. He considered the fatal weakness of Weimar to be that corrupting party system which dedicated conservatives never tired of denouncing. What made it so dangerous, he maintained, was its erosion and fragmentation of the country's political will. "The inability of the party [system] to lead the state was aggravated by the fact that not one party (which is after all still something unitary) but several parties took charge of the government." Those parties, in their essence "alien to the state," had originated in "entirely different views of the world"; they moved in "entirely different directions." And the inevitable result was that "political ideas" became less important than "the wishes of the party bosses." Such a system was inherently incapable of saving Germany from disaster. For Schulenburg there was only one thing to do. On February 1, 1932, he joined Hitler's crusade for national salvation, becoming member number 948,412 of the Nazi Party.[17]

By then even the churchmen of the resistance were becoming more outspoken in their opposition to the republic. Actually, they had never concealed their distaste for Weimar. To them it had always seemed to be tainted by the baneful influence of secularism and materialism. They had never ceased yearning for a return to the traditional values of the monarchical system. But their criticism of the new order had usually been indirect, restricted to the realm of morals and doctrines. As the republican regime began to collapse, however, they turned more openly to politics and economics, to constitutional issues and ideological conflicts. They became avowed adversaries of the republican regime.

Bishop Wurm, for example, saw in the decline of Weimar an opportunity to revive the ideals and allegiances of orthodox religious faith. He spoke with hope about "the ideas of the old Prussian conservatism," which were being embraced by the authoritarian, antiparliamentary cabinet of Franz von Papen. He admitted that slogans about establishing a "Christian state," however sincere, aroused a "vague uneasiness" in his mind. "We know that such slogans can be seriously misused, and that a Christian state in the sense that it compels people to be Christian will never again return." Still, a government that made being a Christian easier by acting on Christian principles and beliefs "should be welcome to us." For Wurm the end of the republic meant a chance to build a better, more virtuous political system.[18]

The rejection of democracy by most clergymen, including those who later turned against the Nazi regime, is even more apparent in the case of Otto Dibelius, general church superintendent of the eastern region of Prussia. He made no attempt to hide his aversion to Weimar behind pious generalities. He was openly, defiantly political. "The parliamentary system," which "we as Protestant Christians never held in very high regard, . . . has passed its peak," he declared with satisfaction at the beginning of 1931. The country should prepare to accept a "new authority" in government. How that new authority was to be established could be left to those "who bear responsibility for our political life," but it must display a sense of "Christian morality." What mattered to Dibelius was that the corrupt, ineffectual republic would finally come to an end.[19]

The only prominent member of the resistance to defend the democratic system in its hour of crisis was the young Protestant theologian Dietrich Bonhoeffer. In the summer of 1932, only a few days before the great Nazi victory in the parliamentary elections of July 31, he condemned the principles and objectives of the new radicalism on the right. "Hitler's nationalistic party abuses democratic opportunities and seeks the establishment of a dictatorship," he stated at a youth peace conference in Czechoslovakia. And then came an uncanny prophecy. "The victory of the Hitler party would have unforeseeable consequences not only for the development of the German people but also for the development of the whole world." All Christians must therefore unite in a struggle against the forces "that mislead countries into a false nationalism, that promote militarism, and that threaten the world with an unrest out of which a war could arise." Bonhoeffer had somehow sensed what the consequences of Weimar's collapse would be.[20]

But who could hear him amid the turmoil and chaos of a disintegrating political system? To most of the men of the future resistance the republic appeared hopelessly weak, confused, divided, and corrupt. Any other regime, they felt, however authoritarian, however intolerant, would be an improvement. The nation needed firm, determined, even ruthless leadership to regain its rightful place among the nations of the world. Only a decade later did they gradually come to realize that a disciplined and efficient dictatorship might prove an even greater danger to Germany than a fumbling, stumbling, fragmented, and bewildered democracy.

2

Breaking the Shackles of Versailles

The conservative critics of Weimar saw two fatal weaknesses in the republican regime: first, a party system that served special interests and selfish goals; and, second, an indifference to military strength and diplomatic assertiveness, to the need for boldness in international affairs. Indeed, one led to the other. A democratic form of government, they believed, was by its nature bound to suffer from a neglect of national defense, from an aversion to armed force and political militancy. Hence the new order in Germany was doomed to ineffectualness in that perpetual test of strength which determined relations among the states of the world. Parliamentary authority was synonymous with diplomatic incompetence.

This view played an important part in the great debate over Germany's defeat in World War I. There was no difference of opinion regarding the tragic consequences of that defeat. But who was responsible for it? Who should bear the blame? To those who supported the republic the answer seemed clear. The collapse of the empire was the consequence of a reckless foreign policy that had jeopardized national security in order to realize ambitious plans for expansion. It was a case of hubris and nemesis. The government, ignoring the wishes of the people as expressed through the Reichstag, had embarked on a risky, dangerous course likely to lead to war. And now the country would have to pay the price for the monarchy's folly. There was only one consolation in all of this. A new political system, more responsible, more responsive to the popular will, would hereafter avoid the mistakes of the imperial regime.

The conservative opponents of the republic saw the situation quite differently. To them the defeat of Germany resulted not from the aggressive or irresponsible policies of the monarchical system but from the intrigues of its domestic adversaries. At a time when all national energies should have been directed toward winning the war, they undermined public morale with their criticisms and accusations. Instead of waiting until victory had been achieved, they took advantage of the military struggle to press their demands for extensive reform. They brought about the erosion of the national will to fight, the spread of doubt and defeatism. And so, what the enemies abroad could not achieve by force of arms, the enemies at home accomplished by treachery and sedition. Was it any wonder that Germany lost the war?

The conservatives conceded that those responsible for the defeat of 1918 had not been in agreement on ultimate objectives. Some wanted to imitate the example of England and France by establishing a parliamentary form of government in which parties representing special needs and interests would determine national policy. But others had even more sinister designs. They sought the complete transformation of long-established social and economic relationships, abolishing private property by means of a dictatorship of the proletariat. Their ideal was the Bolshevik regime in Russia. Both groups of opponents of the monarchical order, however, the democrats no less than the radicals, had helped undermine a basically sound system of authority in Germany. They were the ones responsible for the military catastrophe.

In this debate concerning the nation's defeat, the members of the resistance were generally on the side of the adversaries of the republic. They maintained that the diplomacy pursued by Germany's statesmen before the war had been basically reasonable and defensible. They believed that the armed conflict had resulted from irrational fear and envy on the part of the Entente powers. They argued that the political parties which demanded civic and social reform while hostilities were still in progress had undermined the national will to fight. And they insisted that the disastrous outcome of the military struggle had been a result not of losses on the battlefield but of plots and intrigues on the home front. In short, they shared the views of the conservative opposition to Weimar.

On November 24, 1918, Ulrich von Hassell published an assessment of the causes and likely consequences of Germany's surrender two weeks earlier. Analyzing the political views of many supporters of the old order, he admitted that "our hearts beat faster" at the sight of Germany's prewar naval expansion, "though not because we had become 'imperialists' in the sense of having plans for world domination." Still, there are always a few "visionaries" whenever exciting new movements emerge in a nation. The voices of such ideologues, Hassell conceded, were "perhaps also the loudest." More important, however, "our [foreign] enemies as well as the Philistines at home did (and are doing) their best to place the blame for every folly, for every exaggeration resulting from the excessive enthusiasm of some individuals, on the whole [nation], claiming that they are typical." This was completely unjustified.

What had actually motivated the supporters of the government's policy was "the unmistakable feeling that Germany had to achieve influence in the world, if it did not want to decline spiritually and materially among the great powers of the world." They had believed that "the attempt had to be made to establish and assert our economy and culture as an independent force in the world alongside Anglo-Saxondom, which grasps at everything like an octopus." Was that so wrong?

Looking back, Hassell refused to admit that he and those who shared his views had been mistaken. Germany should pay no attention to that "wretched type of negatively disposed Philistine" who opposes every bold move, who in the struggle for lofty objectives knows no greater triumph than to say, "I told you so." Anyone looking objectively at the prewar situation, especially at developments overseas, would have to agree that the "impetuous upward movement" of Germany's commerce and industry had emerged out of "the full vital force of our nation." And precisely that vitality had aroused the hostility of England, whose goal became *Germaniam esse delendam*.

Hassell conceded that the imperial government had not been without fault. He claimed that even before 1914 he had been one of those who recognized and deplored "the aimlessness and disunity of our policy," the "noisy fanfares," the "mistaken ways of seeking understanding," and especially the "misperception of the English character." But those were errors of judgment or weaknesses in leadership, not fundamental flaws in the political system. Particularly for those who had discerned the tactical mistakes of the imperial regime without distorting or exaggerating them, the outcome of the war represented "a terrible collapse of our hopes." They had assumed that the old order could be improved and strengthened. "We had believed in our nation and in its power, but we had underestimated its lack of political talent." Now they would have to pay for that misjudgment.

Yet Hassell refused to give up hope. He admitted that the return of peace was no occasion for celebration in Germany. For the time being, "all roads leading upward again" seemed closed. "German influence in the world [has proved to be] a dream, destroyed once and for all. [Before us stretches the prospect of] wage slavery at home and a decline to Holland's level of power abroad." Still, the nation must not yield to despair; it must not accept the bleak situation resulting from military defeat as "an unalterable fate." Above all, it must not lose courage.

That would not be easy, Hassell warned. To remain hopeful required "an enormous store of confidence and faith in the mission of our people." But there was no choice. The Germans would have to find strength in that spirit of resolve which had animated them before the war. "A difficult task lies before us, a long struggle upward against foreign resistance and domestic folly." Loyal, patriotic citizens, however, would not shrink from the task facing them. "Let all of us who believe in a German future on . . . a [conservative] foundation unite! Let us get to work!" The nation had in the course of its long history overcome defeat and humiliation before. It would surely face up to its responsibilities now.[1]

To Beck the situation seemed much bleaker than to Hassell. The latter believed in the possibility of recovery through dedication, sacrifice, boldness, and hard work. The former saw nothing but suffering and chaos. Hassell, moreover, admitted that Germany's catastrophe stemmed partly from the weaknesses and miscalculations of the imperial government. Beck was convinced that the nation had simply been stabbed in the back. The dark, evil forces of subversion had long planned to overthrow the government, choosing a time for their revolution when every ounce of energy should have gone toward the defense of the fatherland. It had all been so treacherous, so contemptible. "I had until then considered such an abyss of vileness, cowardice, and unscrupulousness impossible," he wrote to his sister-in-law on November 28, 1918. "In a few hours five hundred years of history have been destroyed." It was "monstrous."

And what would happen to poor Germany now? "I am pessimistic," Beck admitted. The Entente powers would not prove charitable in dealing with their defeated foe. "Certainly the French know only one thing: revenge, revenge, and once more revenge. And anyone who expects anything else from them is a fool." The future would be dark indeed, "unless we succeed soon through negotiation in establishing a [permanent] government." Therefore a national assembly should be convoked at once. Otherwise, "the Entente will, in my opinion, continue to advance and perhaps occupy all the large German cities." But even that would not be the worst thing. If the country had to choose between rule by the left-wing Spartacists and a foreign occupation, the latter would be "more acceptable." Nevertheless, there should be no illusion that "France wants selflessly to establish law and order here among us." Far from it, "France wants to destroy Germany. That is my firm conviction on the basis of my long knowledge of the French national character."

Under such circumstances, who could tell what the future would bring? Beck saw for the time being no way out of "this chaos." Meanwhile, the men leading the provisional government of Germany were wasting "millions upon millions for their purposes." By their "amateurish and partly even criminal interference," they were undermining the loyalty of the army at the front and of the country as a whole. "Our industry is being paralyzed and our commerce remains paralyzed; in short, our burden of indebtedness is growing at a frightening rate. Where will all of this lead?" Beck did not pretend to have the answer, but he felt sure of one thing. "There is law and order in the Entente states, and they will not allow themselves to be trifled with very long." Germany's situation could only get worse.[2]

Beck was in fact closer to the truth than Hassell. He was certainly closer than those who hoped that the establishment of a democratic regime would protect Germany against the worst consequences of military defeat. Many supporters of the republic assumed that by embracing the political ideology of France and England they would gain the sympathy of the victors, paving the way for a peace of reconciliation. They were badly mistaken. The war had aroused deadly passions and hatreds that could not be appeased by changes in the form of government. Seven months after Beck's bleak prophecy, the National Assembly meeting in Weimar was forced to accept the "dictate" of Versailles. Consequently, the republican regime had to face new charges and accusations from the defenders of the old order. The bitter debate regarding the war became exacerbated by an even more bitter debate regarding the peace.

That debate raged despite unanimity of opinion in Germany regarding the Treaty of Versailles. All parties, all ideologies, from the Communists on the far left to the nationalists and ultranationalists on the far right, agreed that the victors had imposed a Carthaginian peace on the vanquished. Even Bonhoeffer, certainly no jingoist or revanchist, declared shortly before the collapse of Weimar: "A feeling of having been treated unjustly prevails in Germany because of the one-sided declaration of the Treaty of Versailles regarding the guilt of the German people for the world war. The League of Nations does not enjoy full confidence here either." This "sense of injustice" as well as the "national consciousness" in general were being exploited by "extreme elements," so that "the work of peace encounters an entire series of domestic and foreign problems." Without saying it in so many words, Bonhoeffer shared the view of virtually all his countrymen regarding the basic unfairness of the peace settlement.[3]

What did arouse controversy in Germany was the question of what to do about it. On this issue there were sharp differences of opinion. Those who supported the republic generally advocated a policy of "fulfillment." They argued that the old imperial order had by its shortsighted, reckless foreign policy contributed to the outbreak of the war, and now the country would have to pay for those mistakes. The Treaty of Versailles was manifestly unjust, but to defy its provisions would simply make a bad situation worse. The only reasonable course was to accept the peace—accept the territorial losses, financial reparations, and military restrictions—in the hope that thereby the nation could little by little regain political and economic stability. By living up to the terms of the settlement, Germany might even in time reacquire a measure of influence in international affairs. There was no alternative.

On the other side were the advocates of "repudiation," most of them conservative opponents of Weimar. To them the provisions of Versailles seemed so outrageous, so humiliating, that Germany must never accept them, come what may. In the months prior to the signing of the treaty on June 28, 1919, they urged its outright rejection, even if that meant an Allied occupation of the entire country. Afterward they preached open defiance of its provisions, attacking the republic for its acquiescence in a monstrous international injustice. The weakness of the government in opposing the designs of the nation's enemies, they maintained, reflected its lack of resolve. The democratic system was turning out to be as ineffectual in foreign as in domestic policy. Only a more authoritarian regime could protect the country against the rapacity of its neighbors.

And then there was a third group, probably the largest of all, a group that recruited many of its members from the right but that also attracted considerable support among followers of the republic. It advocated a policy of ostensible "fulfillment," but only as a means of achieving tacit "repudiation." That is, its strategy was to appear to observe the terms of Versailles in order to alleviate, revise, or circumvent them. It recognized that a direct confrontation with the victor states would be futile and would only result in still greater hardship for Germany. A seeming reconciliation with them, however, might effect what open defiance could not yet accomplish.

Allaying the fears of France in particular might open the way to a revision of the territorial settlement in Eastern Europe. The renunciation of all future German claims to Alsace-Lorraine, for instance, would surely not be an excessive price to pay for the elimination or diminution of the Polish Corridor. Similarly, the prompt remittance of reparations would encourage foreign loans and investments, helping to reinvigorate the nation's economic structure and military capability. The important thing was to comply with the treaty now in order to abrogate it later. Under existing circumstances, a strategy of deception seemed justifiable. Was not the Versailles settlement from beginning to end based on injustice, oppression, hypocrisy, and coercion? Any means of circumventing it would be morally defensible.

Most of the members of the future resistance against Hitler belonged to the second or the third of these groups. More precisely, they generally started out as overt "repudiationists" and ended up as feigned "fulfillers." At first they maintained that the peace conditions on which the Allies insisted were so outrageous that they must be rejected, no matter what. Martin Niemöller, for example, the nationalist naval officer who later became a Protestant clergyman and eventually an outspoken critic of Nazi policy, refused early in 1919 to turn over two German submarines to the British in accordance with the terms agreed to by the new government in Berlin. "I have neither wanted nor concluded this armistice," he declared defiantly. "As far as I am concerned, the people who promised our submarines to England can take them there. I will not do it." His commander was not unsympathetic; he did not charge Niemöller with insubordination. Instead, he ordered another officer to perform the hateful duty. Under the circumstances, it was probably a reasonable solution. Niemöller's honor remained unsullied, while the British got their submarines.[4]

Some of the men in the resistance were even prepared to go beyond noncompliance. In the period before the acceptance of the treaty, they advocated the use of armed force to prevent the "mutilation" of their country. To Goerdeler the overthrow of the old order represented not only treachery, defeat, and humiliation. It also meant a terrible personal loss. He recognized that the collapse of the empire signified that his native region, Posen and West Prussia, would probably become part of the new Polish state. The thought was unbearable. An integral part of Germany would fall under alien rule; its language would be suppressed, its culture eradicated, its people Polonized. Something had to be done, however perilous or desperate, to prevent such a national calamity.

In June 1919, on the eve of the signing of the peace in Versailles, Goerdeler argued that "the only possibility of saving the German nationality in the east and [preserving] the eastern frontier region for the Reich is the military overthrow of Poland." But he had little hope that the National Assembly in Weimar would follow this advice. In view of its defeatist attitude, "the peace will be signed." It was therefore necessary for the eastern region "to act independently." Such action, he maintained, "if prompt and militarily successful," would win the support of the local population, "even though the party leaders are at present hesitant." Under existing conditions, any means were justified—sabotage, conspiracy, putsch, or armed uprising—to prevent the partition of Germany.[5]

Nothing came of his plan to forestall the execution of the Treaty of Versailles. Posen and West Prussia became part of Poland, providing a constant source of friction between Berlin and Warsaw. But the members of the resistance could not bring themselves to accept the consequences of Germany's defeat as final. They generally continued to consider the peace no more than a temporary suspension of hostilities, which would be resumed at a more opportune moment in the future. Though it was best to appear for the time being to accept the treaty, they waited impatiently for the chance to abrogate it, by peaceful negotiation if possible, by military force if necessary. Most of them acquiesced in Weimar's policy of fulfillment only because they saw in it a means of repudiation. They never became reconciled to Versailles; they always regarded it as a national humiliation. They felt that to the extent the republican regime accepted the treaty in good faith, it was betraying the country's honor. Under the circumstances, governmental deception became a patriotic duty, while compliance with solemn diplomatic agreements was almost an act of treason. The usual norms of conduct in international affairs were in effect turned upside down.

Above all, the demilitarization of Germany could never be accepted as permanent, whatever the cost. To the conservative opponents of Weimar, and that included most of the future resisters against Hitler, a national revival required military strength first of all. The armed forces as restricted by Versailles—an army of only 100,000 professional soldiers, a minuscule navy of six battleships, and no air force—could not challenge the French. Rather, their chief mission should be to form the basis for a future large military establishment capable of reasserting the country's rightful position among the states of Europe. In other words, the acceptance of demilitarization today was to lead to its rejection tomorrow.

Late in World War II General Oster described what had been his view and that of the other members of the officer corps regarding their principal task during the Weimar period. "We were all convinced that, given the political conditions of the time, [service under the republican regime] was the only way that could lead to our goal, that is, an army that would again be disciplined and effective, and that would provide the foundation and precondition for a future further expansion of [what became] our *Wehrmacht* of today." Hence the fall of the republic meant for the armed forces "a deliverance from the conflicts of conscience that had confronted them during the period of the [Weimar] system!" Now they could finally begin that process of rearmament for which they had been waiting so impatiently since the fall of the empire.[6]

The other participants in the resistance generally agreed that of all the restrictions imposed by Versailles, none was in the long run as harmful as demilitarization. For how could Germany safeguard its vital political and diplomatic interests without a strong army? Rearmament was of the utmost importance. To Ludwig Beck the greatest danger facing the country in 1923, the most critical year during the early period of the republic, was not the raging inflation or the occupation of the Ruhr or Rhenish separatism or even the Communist threat. It was the "disintegration of the troops." The other problems could be solved one way or another, by negotiation or tenacity, by boldness or deception. They represented a temporary setback; at worst they would lead to a strategic retreat. But permanent military weakness meant permanent political impotence. The key to the revival of Germany, the one indispensable condition, was the creation of an army "that would again be disciplined and effective."[7]

A policy of ostensible fulfillment would gain more than just an opportunity for remilitarization. It would also provide the chance to undermine Versailles by diplomatic means. After his arrest in 1944, Goerdeler boasted of how he and other prominent conservatives had prepared the way for Germany's recovery by evading the peace treaty while seeming to accept it. "We worked, worked, worked; we neglected our families; we drudged in order to . . . abrogate the dictate of Versailles." It was unfair to ignore their achievements or to dismiss the successes won by Foreign Minister Gustav Stresemann, who had sought goals similar to theirs. "Nothing could be achieved by force without an army, so that left only shrewdness. The single heroic deed [of the 1920s], the struggle in the Ruhr, cost us what was left of our currency." Hence those who had followed a course of dissimulation displayed both "determination and sagacity." Goerdeler pointed to the example of Hans Lohmeyer, the former mayor of Königsberg, whose propaganda campaign against the Polish Corridor was so "clever" that after 1930 even the French recognized the "absurdity" of the territorial settlement in the east. Given the international situation during the Weimar years, the only effective way to oppose Versailles was to pretend to submit to it.[8]

The chief advantage of such a policy, however, to Goerdeler no less than to most other members of the resistance, was the opportunity it provided for German rearmament. They were convinced that cajoling and reassuring the French could lead only to limited successes. Revisions and modifications in the peace treaty were perhaps attainable through diplomacy, but outright abrogation was out of the question. Without a strong army, the nation would never regain its rightful boundaries, and it would never liberate its sons and daughters groaning under foreign domination. Even Dibelius, man of God, preacher of the Gospel, was convinced that only armed might could put an end to the wrongs of Versailles. "Where there is no power," he declared in 1931, "there is also no justice in this world." That clearly meant remilitarization. "As long as Germany is powerless, she will be unable to achieve effective protection for the [German] minorities [abroad]. As long as Germany is powerless, she will never have reasonable and acceptable frontiers. As long as Germany is powerless, there will be no peace on earth." The only way to achieve harmony and equity was to beat plowshares into swords and pruning hooks into spears.[9]

The conviction of so many men of the resistance that a political revival of Germany depended on a military revival reflected their general view of international relations. They remained profoundly skeptical of the contention that the end of the world conflict in 1918 had initiated a new era in diplomacy. To them all talk about outlawing armed force, about renouncing "recourse to war for the solution of international controversies" or not seeking a solution to disputes among states "except by pacific means," was pious humbug. They regarded organizations like the League of Nations and treaties like the Paris Peace Pact as only the means by which the winners in the war hoped to maintain their domination over the losers. Behind the smoke screen of lofty phrases about international amity and justice, the haves were abusing and exploiting the have-nots. Diplomacy would continue to be based, as in the past, on the use of military power. It could not be otherwise; indeed, it should not. For armed conflict between states helped separate the strong from the weak, the bold from the timid. It fostered heroic qualities in men and in nations. It performed a positive function.

The importance of military power was self-evident to Henning von Tresckow. After leaving the army following the monarchy's collapse, he had found employment in the Potsdam banking house of the Jewish financier Wilhelm Kann. But that experience did little to shake his conviction, expressed even before he rejoined the armed forces in 1926, that the various races and peoples were so different that an enduring peace between them was highly unlikely. A lasting harmony in international relations or a league of nations of "actual, enduring significance" could be achieved only on the basis of an idea alien to the German spirit, an idea "Anglo-American" or "Jewish" or "democratic-capitalistic" in nature. Its victory would lead to the enslavement of the world by "commercialism." And yet the forces of the radical left were now allied with those of the capitalistic middle in a futile quest for eternal friendship among states. "The Communist or Marxist idea, even if it is motivated by the best intentions, performs in this connection the role of a servitor [of the capitalists]." A regime like the Weimar Republic, espousing half-baked theories of diplomatic reconciliation and international understanding, was by its nature incapable of bringing about the revival of Germany.[10]

Dibelius was equally convinced that the "new diplomacy" of the postwar period was only a sham. The victorious statesmen in control of the League of Nations were simply playing the "old game," so that the task facing German diplomats in Geneva was certainly "not enviable." The country would have to adopt a more assertive foreign policy. It might sound very Christian, he conceded, to preach that a nation should not strive for power, that it should seek harmony rather than confrontation. "In the world of today," however, such a view would serve simply "as a reinforcement of injustice and hatred on this earth." The peace of justice advocated by Christianity could be achieved only among states enjoying equal rights. "To win back this equality of rights will be the task of the German people in the coming decades. The task has been assigned to us by God." Since the meek had not yet inherited the earth, only force could put an end to the injustices of Versailles.[11]

In short, the men of the resistance generally saw in the Weimar regime's foreign policy the same basic flaw they saw in its domestic policy: indecisiveness. Could anything better be expected from a political system dependent on parties and coalitions, on compromises and concessions, on an endless bartering for the spoils of office? The diplomacy pursued by the republic was admittedly not altogether ineffectual. Here and there it did achieve some modest success; it did manage from time to time to effect a minor revision in the terms of Versailles. But it would never be able to gain full equality for Germany among the great powers. For that, the government was simply too weak, too timid, too irresolute.

The rise of Hitler therefore, seemed to many of the future resisters not only understandable but encouraging. They did not all became ardent supporters of National Socialism; in fact, only a few of them ever joined the party. But they saw in it a sign of growing popular condemnation of the republic's faintheartedness. The nation was finally waking up; it was demanding more forceful leadership. Hitler admittedly had his shortcomings: he was a little too extreme, too rigid perhaps, too naive or fanatical. Given his background and education, he could hardly be expected to be an accomplished statesman, another Bismarck. Yet, to the extent that he was helping to hasten the fall of Weimar, he was performing a valuable function. He and his followers were preparing the way for a great national awakening in Germany. Once the republic had come to an end, the Nazis would have to accept the guidance of men with superior training and greater experience. The historic role of Hitler would then be finished. But for the time being, he was enlisting masses of patriotic, dedicated, loyal citizens in the cause of political revival. To conservatives seeking a more assertive foreign policy, he appeared a useful ally.

Early in 1932 Hassell, then the German envoy to Yugoslavia, explained in a newspaper interview in Belgrade the reasons for the growth of National Socialism. To describe it as a danger to international stability was nonsense, he insisted. After all, when Hindenburg had become a candidate for the presidency of Germany seven years earlier, that too had been portrayed abroad as a "threat of war" or an "election for catastrophe." Now it was clear that all those alarmist predictions had been baseless. "Sometime in the future, perhaps, people will also recognize that the name of Hitler does not mean revenge and things of that sort for the world and for the millions of Germans who follow him, but rather that it is simply the expression of a passionate demand for, and at the same time the absolute necessity of, giving Germany finally full equality of rights."

Hassell insisted that his country sought nothing more than to break the shackles of Versailles. The winners in the war could not expect to base their security permanently on the subjugation of the losers. The only way to preserve peace in Europe was by a policy of revisionism. "I don't know a single German, and I don't believe that there is a single reasonable German, who thinks of revenge or things of that sort. But I also don't know a single German who considers the present situation of Germany in the world any longer tolerable." Hitler was not a threat to stability in international relations. He was a symptom, a warning that harmony could not be built on oppression and that tranquillity could not be achieved through inequity. Justice was the key to peace.

And justice, according to Hassell, demanded the end of reparations and of unilateral disarmament. "These are the two subjects that occupy above everything else the thoughts of all Germans today." The victor states would have to recognize that the vindictive policy of Versailles could no longer be enforced. "The fate of the world, that is, the question whether Germany, Europe, and the entire world will grow calm and thereby achieve a sound and prosperous state, depends on whether the incubus of reparations and military inequality is lifted from Germany." If so, the rise of Hitler would pose no danger to the peace of the world. Otherwise, there was no telling what might happen.[12]

Whether Hassell actually believed that reparations and demilitarization were chiefly responsible for the spread of National Socialism is open to question. He was too experienced, too shrewd, not to recognize the effect of economic hardship and social unrest on the decline of Weimar. But his duty as a German diplomat stationed in a country allied with France required him to minimize the implications of Hitler's political success by portraying it as primarily an expression of popular resentment against Versailles. The members of the officer corps, by contrast, felt less need to disguise their true feelings. They had been waiting for a more authoritarian regime ever since the fall of the empire. And now their hopes were about to be realized. Shortly before his execution for participating in the plot against Hitler, General Oster recalled that the professional soldiers welcomed the coming of the Third Reich. "The return to a strong national policy, rearmament, and the introduction of conscription," he testified, "signified for the officer [corps] a return to earlier traditions." Under Weimar the soldier had served out of a sense of loyalty to the nation, not to the government. But under the Third Reich he had pursued "with his heart" the objectives of "the National Socialist work of reconstruction." For here at last was a political system that fostered once more the proud military spirit of Germany.[13]

The attitude of the officer corps toward the disintegrating republic was not determined entirely by ideology, however. There were also important practical considerations. Under Versailles, the chances of the professional soldiers for promotion were severely limited by the small size of the army. They were prohibited, moreover, from acquiring training in the most advanced techniques and technologies of warfare. While the armed forces of neighboring states were gaining new knowledge and expertise, those of Germany were largely condemned to the dull routine of garrison duty. Both idealism and self-interest thus helped turn them against the republic. Under a National Socialist regime, a regime committed to the repudiation of the peace settlement, conditions were bound to improve. Before the officer corps dangled the prospect of expanded opportunities for advancement, training, innovation, and proficiency. Its members would finally be able to compete on even terms with the officers of the leading foreign armies.

Is it any wonder that so many of them welcomed the rise of Hitler? After the establishment of the Third Reich, an officer in the war ministry who was known to have reservations about the new order told the French military attaché in Berlin that by 1933 "perhaps 60 percent of the army was Nazi." The estimate does not appear farfetched, and it seems to apply as much to those who later decided to resist Hitler as to those who remained loyal to him to the end.[14]

Opposition to Versailles even helped turn most clergymen, especially Protestant clergymen, against the republic. They also felt that Weimar was too timid, too indecisive, in defending the national interest. Of course, they usually expressed their criticism of the government in religious rather than political or military terms. They argued that the new democratic regime was indifferent to Christian values, that it was secular in outlook, that it favored the eventual separation of church and state. Under republican rule the country was becoming alienated from traditional loyalties and pieties; it was turning to liberalism, materialism, even atheism. That shift in turn made a reassertion of Germany's claim to a position of leadership in Europe all the more difficult. Only a conservative form of government was capable of bringing about a national revival. According to one estimate, some 80 percent of Protestant ministers favored the parties of the right. And here again, there is no discernible difference between those who eventually became critics of the Third Reich and those who remained its supporters.[15]

Dibelius is a case in point. As early as June 1933 he was forced into retirement because of his differences with National Socialism regarding churchly governance. But only three months before, on March 21, he had participated in the solemn religious service in the Nikolai Church in Potsdam celebrating the opening of the new Reichstag dominated by the Nazis. He delivered from the pulpit a sermon that must have met with the approval of the most ardent of Hitler's followers. A new and happier day was dawning for the nation, he declared. And yet, at that exalting moment his thoughts continued to dwell on the Germans forced to live under alien rule. "The burdens of the past still weigh down upon us. Hundreds of thousands of our brothers and sisters, whom God has summoned to be members of a free people, are still groaning in foreign bondage." Now there was hope; there was confidence. The new order would put an end to the injustices that the old order had been too weak to oppose. "With God to a new future!" Dibelius preached to his countrymen. "In millions of hearts burns the hope that this future will become a future of renewed German freedom." Under National Socialism the nation would achieve its liberation at last.[16]

What Dibelius and most other members of the resistance saw in the Third Reich in 1933 was what so many of their compatriots saw. To them it did not represent oppression, brutality, bigotry, or injustice. It meant a revival of German pride and German patriotism. It meant a rejection of the slights and humiliations that the nation had been forced to endure under Weimar. Hitler was an instrument not of despotism but of liberation. He was somewhat crude and unpolished perhaps, somewhat flamboyant and melodramatic. He might sound at times like a tub-thumper or rabble-rouser. But he was a patriot, a nationalist; there could be no doubt about that. He would break the shackles of Versailles, he would end the subordination of the fatherland, he would assert its claim to diplomatic and military equality; above all, he would inspire in his countrymen a renewed faith in their destiny. Under his leadership, as Dibelius prophesied, Germany would march "with God to a new future!"

3

The Struggle against Materialism

The conservative opponents of the Weimar Republic believed that its weakness in domestic politics and international affairs reflected a more fundamental defect: the lack of spirituality. In their view, the measures and policies that governments adopt are based ultimately not on practical considerations but on faith, on conviction. The day-to-day activities of any system of authority rest on a foundation of ideas. beliefs, loyalties, and allegiances. The old imperial order, for example, had accepted the primacy of public over private welfare, of collective need over individual profit. It had taught the virtues of patriotism, steadfastness, and self-denial. And thereby a country that had for centuries been weak and divided succeeded in achieving unity and power. What had made the creation of the German Empire possible was more than military proficiency or economic enterprise. It was idealism and spirit. But that spirit was different from the spirit of the French or the English. It was less rationalistic and mechanistic; it was more spontaneous and instinctive, more ardent and pure. It was the real source of the nation's strength.

The new republican regime, however, had undermined that spirit. It had not only abandoned time-honored political institutions and surrendered territories historically German. It had also eroded the faith of the people in their own destiny. It had rejected, in the name of reform and progress, the ideals forming the foundation of national greatness. That was Weimar's most serious offense. For how could the country overcome the corruptions of the party system and the injustices of the Versailles dictate without the faith that had inspired its achievements in the past?

Most of the men of the resistance shared this view of the republic. During the Third Reich, Niemöller recalled the "great misery" that had "oppressed our people like a heavy burden after the end of the war." There had been a lack of "leadership," a lack of any "great goal." Worse still, there had been a lack of "the inward and moral foundations for a true popular will and activity." After leaving the navy, he had begun to doubt whether "the national enthusiasm, which was [still] alive among the young people and the veterans who had served at the front, was strong and pure enough to create something new in the future." There was no lack of courage, he acknowledged. But there was a lack "of any strong, unifying force and of any norms that ultimately impose a sense of duty." The republic's abandonment of traditional values and allegiances had created that lack.[1]

Some of the resisters conceded that Weimar had its ideals too, but they were ideals alien to the German spirit. They were importations from abroad; they were too rational, too calculating. They were based on the assumption that the principles governing national life could be reduced to axioms and formulas. They manifested a fundamental error. The men of the resistance generally agreed with Pascal that "the heart has its reasons which reason knows nothing of." Hence a national revival could not be achieved by a regime that embraced the rationalism and materialism of Western Europe. Only by rejecting cold, bloodless calculation could the German people regain a sense of purpose. The republican regime, however, constantly striving for compromise and expediency, failed to see that. It was too busy with political buying and selling, with parliamentary horse trading, to be able to pursue idealistic goals. Its besetting sin was sober rationality.

The call for a struggle against materialism grew louder during the last years of Weimar. Most of the resisters shared the general conviction of the conservative movement that the underlying causes of the national crisis were spiritual rather than secular in nature. In the fall of 1930 Hellmuth Stieff, then still a junior army officer, wrote to his wife that the time for a rebirth of idealism had arrived. "Every rationalism, every cold calculation, comes to an end at some point and becomes lifeless." That was the unmistakable lesson of history. "The decisive thing always remains pulsating life, the heart." The demands of the vital, instinctive forces in man could not be ignored. "Rationality and reason are good, as long as life retains its rights in the process. But if they become an end in itself, they produce a life-destroying effect." The political and military leadership of the nation should therefore never disregard "the soldier's elixir of life, his selfless love of the fatherland." Once that was impugned, "he will rebel, if he still has enough spirit." And if not, then "he is simply a mercenary serving for pay." The armed forces were now facing such a test of their spiritual steadfastness.[2]

To the soldiers in the resistance the decline of Weimar thus meant an opportunity to revive the national sense of patriotism. To the churchmen it represented a chance to lead the country back to traditional religious values, to faith, piety, spirituality, and idealism. Dibelius, who had never disguised his hostility to the republican regime, welcomed Hitler's rise to power for precisely that reason. Germany would finally experience a rebirth of morality. "We want to be free again from the spirit that knows only material things," he preached from the pulpit a few weeks after the establishment of the Third Reich. He meant the spirit of the failed experiment in democracy, the spirit "that believes that economy is destiny, that subordinates man to machine, and that, from the skyscrapers of New York to the powerhouses of south Russia, is willing to recognize only this one type of mechanized man." The real enemy was the soulless, materialistic, rationalized, and brutalized mentality of big-city life, which conservative thinkers tirelessly anathemized. But Dibelius was confident that a new era of spirituality was beginning for his people. "We want to be once again that for which God has created us," he declaimed. "We want to be Germans again. But we will be Germans only when faith in God, the Father of our Lord Jesus Christ, becomes the pulse beat of our life." With the help of National Socialism, Christian beliefs and Christian values would defeat the forces of secular rationalism.[3]

Even Popitz, the respected financial expert, a man who had spent his life amid charts, graphs, and statistics, was now inveighing against the crass materialism of Weimar. On April 26, 1933, speaking before the exclusive Mittwochs-Gesellschaft, he too criticized the rationalistic spirit of the fallen republic. The forces that had led to its collapse included the "mental outlook" of a large part of the German people. That outlook had unfortunately been "almost exclusively materialistic"; it had ignored, "consciously or because of its skeptical attitude," the "religious or ethical aspects" of life. Worst of all, it had repudiated "national loyalty," if not by denying its value outright, then by failing to embrace it "inwardly" or by suppressing its "outward manifestations." Weimar had been a "powerless" political system, a state "alienated from the nation." Popitz described its constitution as "formalistic," "disunited," and, in that favorite locution of his, "polycratic." The civil service had lost all sense of a "community of conviction." The "constantly changing ministries" lacked any "broad idea," while parliament and its parties only served as a screen for those familiar sinister "forces alien to the state." A form of government so fundamentally flawed was bound to end in a national crisis.

But now there was hope, Popitz went on. The failure of the republican regime had led to the emergence of "a growing national opposition." That opposition had at first been divided, partly shaped by the yearning for "tradition," partly committed to "armed resistance," and partly focused on "one person, the person of Adolf Hitler." At last the long period of struggle was over. Weimar had been overthrown; a revolution had taken place in Germany. It had been a legal, bloodless revolution, however, without a "march on Rome," carried out in accordance with the "pliant" constitution of the dying republic. For Popitz the crisis had finally come to an end; a new day was dawning for the nation.[4]

Many members of the resistance agreed that the rejection of rationalism would lead to a great moral revival. The Third Reich would help foster principles and ideals that Weimar had ignored or disparaged. Clergymen in particular, especially Protestant clergymen, saw in National Socialism an ally in the struggle to revive religious faith. Although the republican regime had not interfered with the practice of Christianity, and had in fact carefully observed the legal autonomy of the two major denominations in accordance with laws governing relations between church and state, its attitude toward organized religion was one of neutrality, perhaps even indifference. It tolerated rather than encouraged Christian beliefs and doctrines. It was basically secular in outlook. And that outlook in turn helped encourage nonconformity in culture and morals. To the devout, the spread of what they considered indecency and licentiousness, especially in the big cities, was a direct result of the materialism embraced by Weimar. Hitler, they anticipated, would encourage a return to piety, morality, virtue, and idealism. He would put an end to vice and licentiousness, to agnosticism and godlessness. Under his government Germany would experience a rebirth of spirituality.

For Bishop Wurm the choice between a corrupt democracy and a righteous dictatorship was easy. Shortly before Weimar's collapse, he had spoken favorably about the ideals of Prussian conservatism, ideals that were being "brought back to life" by Chancellor Papen. People should not be coerced into being Christian, he agreed. But a government that fostered the Christian faith by "displaying it in the basic outline of its goal" should be welcome to all members of the Protestant Church. They should greet the revival of "politics based on belief"; they should welcome the search for "values that have been lost." The disintegration of the republic meant new hope for a religious revival.

A few weeks after Hitler's appointment to the chancellorship, Wurm made it clear that National Socialism was living up to his high expectations.

The new regime deserved praise, he announced, for crushing "at great sacrifice" the "terror" of the far left, for bringing together strata of the population that had become estranged, and for waging a struggle against "the disruptive influences in our cultural life." A few weeks after that, on March 25, 1933, he declared in a letter to the Lutheran clergymen of Württemberg that Germany had finally found "united, purposeful leadership" after a highly dangerous period of "confusion and division." The Protestant Church should not remain indifferent to the work of national regeneration, he wrote. On the contrary, it should be grateful that "the complete collapse of our nation and state and the victory of the destructive powers were at the last moment averted." The Third Reich had become for Wurm Germany's moral savior.[5]

The Catholic churchmen in the resistance were somewhat less enthusiastic. Far from feeling much affection or loyalty toward Weimar, they too believed that the republican system represented the forces of modernism and materialism, that it was hostile to religious traditions and moral values. But they also regarded National Socialism with suspicion. What would be the fate of the church under a regime which taught that all public institutions, religious as well as secular, must subordinate their particular interests to the general welfare of the state?

Once the Third Reich was established, however, they began cautiously to seek an accommodation with the new order. The government in turn tried to reassure the leaders of the church by loudly proclaiming its support for religious ideals and values. As a consequence, whether out of conviction or expediency, German Catholicism began to display greater sympathy toward the Third Reich than it had ever shown toward Weimar.

Bishop Galen illustrates the point. In the early 1940s he was to become "the lion of Münster" by defying the authority of National Socialism. But in the early 1930s he welcomed its establishment and supported its program. At first, he remained silent regarding the political transformation that had taken place. He was still troubled and suspicious, unsure about what direction the new regime would follow. But Hitler's conciliatory policy persuaded him little by little that Catholicism had nothing to fear from the Third Reich. On the contrary, collaboration between them might prove of great benefit to the church. By the fall of 1933 he was praising the government for having shown a "firm hand" in dealing with the terrible dangers that had threatened the country. National Socialism had become Germany's protector against the forces of "godlessness and immorality." The church would be free to pursue its work in the religious education of the young and the moral guidance of family and communal life. All Catholics should show their gratitude for "these gifts of divine Providence" by the "most loyal fulfillment of their duty in the service of God, of the church, and of the fatherland." The downfall of Weimar had made possible a new flowering of religious faith among the German people.

Gradually the bishop's support for the Third Reich began to erode. In the course of World War II he became in fact a fearless and persistent critic of its policies. But that in no way diminished his antipathy toward the republic. Indeed, the tyranny of National Socialism seemed to him ultimately a providential retribution for the sins committed by Weimar. Even as late as the summer of 1945, preaching amid the ruins of Münster, he preferred not to dwell on the Nazi regime, which had led Germany to catastrophe. Instead, he expatiated once again on the moral and spiritual failings of the republican system. "Broad circles of the German population unfortunately abandoned more and more their faith in God, their faith in Christ and the church." Even those who remained loyal Catholics did not always have the courage to oppose a "dechristianizing public opinion." They were not always brave enough to resist the "wanton and immoral practices of the fashionable world" or to organize "business life, social life, and family life" in accordance with the teachings of Christianity. In the "fashionable world of public affairs" people were reluctant to admit that they were Christians. At "great political gatherings" they hardly dared "utter God's name with proper respect" or invoke the name of God, "the ultimate source of justice, freedom, and truth." Was not such a regime bound to end in disaster?

Galen was not talking about "the last 12 years, in which we no longer had any real popular representation." He was referring rather to the "previous period," when the nation was governed by a constitution which began with the "untrue assertion" that "the authority of the state originates in the people." Yet did not Saint Paul teach that "there is no power but of God"?

Admittedly, there had been many supporters of Weimar who interpreted the constitution to mean simply that those exercising authority in the state were to be chosen by the people. But "the real authors and defenders" of that constitution had deliberately worded it to mean a rejection of government "by the grace of God," thereby renouncing their "responsibility to God." After all, Friedrich Ebert himself, the first president of the republic, had made the "awful and fatal" declaration at the opening of the Reichstag that the German people had now been liberated from all "dependence ordained by God." That meant they had been liberated from "respect for

God, obedience to God, and hope in God." Could such impiety go unpunished? The Third Reich was merely the instrument of divine retribution; the basic cause, the fundamental reason, was Weimar.[6]

Cardinal Faulhaber was less oracular. Indeed, he sounded by contrast almost matter-of-fact. Yet he too condemned the "corruption" bred by big-city life. He too denounced the "hedonism," the indifference to "decency," and the tolerance of "smut" that had followed Germany's defeat in the war. He too deplored the indifference of the new government to "lax standards" and "loose morals." All this seemed to him to prove that a secular, democratic state must inevitably breed materialism and immorality. How could spiritual values thrive under a political system indifferent to the teachings of religion?

Always hostile to Weimar, the cardinal observed its decline without regret. But the Third Reich made him uneasy as well. Like Galen, he wondered what would happen to the church under a regime which insisted that confessional and denominational interests bow to national and racial needs. The doctrines of Catholicism seemed on the surface incompatible with the principles of National Socialism. Still, he too was gradually reassured by the new regime's initial policy of moderation. Maybe Hitler's bark was worse than his bite; maybe all those denunciations of "insidious" and "unhealthy" clerical influence in public life were only rhetoric. Now that the Nazis were in power, they might become more restrained, more reasonable. Certainly the possibility of a fruitful cooperation between secular and spiritual authority should be encouraged.

What impressed Faulhaber particularly was the new government's widely publicized campaign for the "purification" of public morals. Bars and cabarets featuring nudity were warned to provide more sedate forms of entertainment; commercialized vice became less prevalent or at least less conspicuous; plays and movies began to turn from social criticism or bedroom comedy to preaching and moralizing; nightclubs and cafés frequented by homosexuals were closed by order of the police. Soon after coming to power, the Nazi authorities could boast of having created a more "wholesome" social and cultural environment.

Faulhaber welcomed all these changes. Here finally was a regime working to bring about a return to traditional values. Its efforts deserved support. Late in 1933, in the course of one of his Advent sermons, the cardinal spoke with approval of the government's resolve to promote public decency. There was still no cause for complacency, he admonished. It would be "Jewish pharisaism" to claim that the Germans had now become "much better than other races" or that "our big cities were gardens of virtue compared to Sodom and Gomorrah." But at least a start had been made; there was some hope for the future. "In recent months, thank God, a great deal of immorality has been swept away with an iron broom out of the public life of our people." This achievement deserved public acknowledgment. Unlike Weimar, the Third Reich was committed to a restoration of national morality.[7]

To most of those who later formed the resistance, spiritual decline and moral corruption were not the only dangerous consequences of the materialism the republican system had embraced. They found the spread of social antagonism equally ominous. Weimar seemed to them to reject the view that the various classes in society were essentially harmonious and complementary, that they were organically interrelated and interdependent. Instead, it apparently assumed that organized economic interests in the community were by nature irreconcilable, that one could prosper only at the expense of another. The regime thereby helped promote domestic strife, pitting rich against poor, propertied against propertyless, capital against labor. In short, Weimar embraced the Marxian concept of class conflict.

The resisters always saw in Marxism the sworn enemy of national unity and purpose. Of course, not all supporters of the republic were in their opinion radicals. Some were simply misguided, impractical middle-of-the-road liberals. Nevertheless, the strongest supporter of Weimar was the Social Democratic Party, committed in theory to a Marxian ideology. And competing with it for the support of the lower classes was the Communist Party, which openly promoted revolutionary struggle. Hence the republic appeared to many of the resisters to be a stalking-horse for subversive forces on the far left. The greatest danger to the nation, they believed, was not a bumbling bourgeois democracy but a ruthless Communist dictatorship.

Their apprehension intensified after the coming of the great depression. The rise in unemployment and the spread of privation were clearly bound to encourage radicalism among the masses. Where would it all end? In the spring of 1931 Dibelius spoke with grave concern about the campaign against religion being waged by the leftists. "The new attack against Christianity originates in Moscow," he warned. The "Communist freethinkers" had no real ideology for which they were prepared "to live and die"; the conflict they had initiated was not actually a struggle between "belief and unbelief, between Christianity and paganism." It was rather a "political struggle," a struggle waged for the purpose of "political propaganda." The Marxists were convinced that their goal could be achieved only "when the Christian religion has been destroyed." And what was that goal? Nothing less than the "dictatorship of the proletariat."

Dibelius then launched into an elaborate explanation of why the dictatorship of the proletariat really meant the subordination of the proletariat. In Russia, he expounded, it was not the lower classes that ruled but "a small group of those in power." The worker in the factory had to obey orders as unquestioningly as anyone else. Whoever challenged those orders endangered his own life. The chief purpose of this system of coercion was "to secure for the people a greater share . . . of earthly possessions." But for Dibelius that was precisely the point. Under a Marxian system "possessions other than earthly are of no use." Spiritual values ceased to have any importance in human existence. "Eating, drinking, clothing, housing—those are the aims of life." Radicalism's emphasis on the pursuit of material goals deprived the working man of the moral dignity of his calling.[8]

This was a fundamental issue for the resisters, especially for the churchmen among them. They believed that economic antagonisms and class conflicts could be reconciled through a recognition of the spiritual mission of all social strata in the community. Each had a function to perform, each had a task to fulfill. Their differences were not a sign of incompatibility but of harmonious diversity. All classes contributed, each in its own way, to the welfare of society. But a comprehension of the organic nature of the nation's economy depended on an acceptance of its moral foundations. And here Marxism exerted a pernicious influence. By emphasizing that material interests were the sole basis of social relationships, by teaching that class solidarity was more important than national loyalty, Marxism encouraged anarchy, unleashing a war of all against all. The government had a duty to protect society against such a danger.

That was also the gist of Galen's criticism of Weimar in June 1934. Under the republican regime, the regime of "liberalism and Marxism," he declared, labor had been treated with "contempt." In vain did the Catholic Church urge society "to honor work" and "to respect the human dignity of the worker." Society had remained deaf. Amid the "idolatry of mammonism" there was no room for "the dignity, for the honor, and the right" of the working man. As a result, "unconscionable seducers" could preach that might makes right; they could say to the workers: "You have the might, now seize the right." The church had recognized and characterized Marxism as "false doctrine," but that warning had been largely ignored.

Fortunately, there had been some groups in Germany that refused to be misled. Even in that materialistic age, the bishop recalled with satisfaction, Christianity did not die out; it persisted, for example, in the "big cities of industry" or among the "Catholic working-class population." The church, "the bride of Christ, of the workingman of Nazareth," continued to preach the dignity, value, and honor of labor. In consequence Catholic workers did not yield to the enticements of those who insisted that might makes right. Instead, they joined in Christian labor organizations to strengthen one another in the struggle against the "seductions of Marxism." Thereby they had earned the thanks of "the entire German nation, of its government, and of [its] bishops." And now that "the developments of a new era" promised to uproot "mammonism and Marxism, those two enemies of a true labor movement," Catholic workers could claim the right to participate in the building of "a new and better social order." Galen saw in the Third Reich the means of finally restoring the moral foundations of the economic system.[9]

What made social antagonism during the Weimar era seem especially dangerous was its alleged incitement from abroad. Many members of the resistance, like millions of other Germans, believed that subversion was being spread among the masses by a radical agitation directed from the Soviet Union. Not only their own country but Europe as a whole was threatened by a vast conspiracy organized by the various national Communist parties under the direction of planners and organizers in the Kremlin. The implacable enemy of Western civilization was "Bolshevism." Yet the republican government in Germany could not or would not see the danger. Some of its supporters were so doctrinaire in their devotion to constitutional rights that they would rather face disaster than suspend or restrict them. Others were too weak or indecisive to halt the growing red menace. And still others were in secret sympathy with the subversive designs of the far left. Only the overthrow of Weimar could save the country from the threat of social chaos, civil war, and Communist dictatorship.

After the establishment of the Third Reich, Hassell described the danger from which the new regime had saved Germany. "Bolshevism," he maintained in a lecture early in 1937, was not to be regarded simply as a political and social system "that we consider false and dangerous." It was much worse than that; it was "an expression of an un-European form of thought" threatening to "poison and corrupt our innermost being." By now all Germans had learned how great had been "the contagious force of this [false] doctrine," how deep "the deadly germs had penetrated into the lifeblood of our nation."

What had protected the Continent against the "un-European Bolshevik spirit," Hassell argued, was National Socialism and Fascism. They were not only defending one particular political and social doctrine against another. They were leading their nations out of the "contagion zone of the eastern, un-European way of thinking" toward attitudes and beliefs firmly rooted in the "European character." Germany and Italy were being summoned to fulfill their "European mission," the mission of "Dante and Goethe," in the name of a "lofty ideal." The realization of that ideal, however, would require the application of "all spiritual forces" and the strict observance of "moral conduct," in keeping with that familiar phrase of Benito Mussolini's about "the German-Italian Axis." Grateful for being free at last from the Communist menace, Hassell overflowed with praise for the regime to which he was to fall victim a few years later.[10]

Wurm was equally convinced that National Socialism had saved Germany from Bolshevism. Even before the fall of the republic, while most Protestant clergymen still could not decide between the conservatism of the old school represented by Hindenburg and the new right-wing radicalism of Hitler, he displayed considerable sympathy for the Nazi movement. In the spring of 1933 the bishop boasted that "I have for a long time also taken Hitler quite seriously," while so many others had looked down on him and his party with "superciliousness." Indeed, "at a time when everybody was still groveling before [Chancellor Heinrich] Brüning [between 1930 and 1932], I told anyone who would listen that we had a choice only between a dictatorship by Hitler and a dictatorship by Moscow." Wurm preferred the former, even if it should not prove very "convenient." That was the reason he gave for refusing to sign a statement supporting Hindenburg in the presidential election of the previous year, although other prominent churchmen had endorsed it without seeking his advice. In the face of the danger of international Communism, the Nazi movement seemed to him the only source of protection.[11]

The Catholic leaders in the resistance were more distrustful of National Socialism than the Protestants, but the threat of Bolshevism aroused their apprehension as well. The republican regime appeared indifferent to the Communist danger; at times it even seemed to flirt with Marxist doctrine. How then could it defend the nation against the Kremlin's machinations? As early as September 19, 1922, Faulhaber had written to Giuseppe Pizzardo of the Papal State Secretariat that his speech a few weeks before characterizing the overthrow of the monarchy as "perjury and treason" had been intended to warn the members of the Center Party against an alliance with the Social Democrats. For by making concessions to "moderate" or "reasonable" Marxists, they would be "opening for Bolshevism the gates to the German people." As far as he was concerned, the conciliatory rhetoric of "democratic" socialists was, whether deliberately or unintentionally, a screen for the plots of the Comintern.

Indeed, the fear of international Communism continued to haunt the cardinal's political thinking throughout the Weimar period and beyond. In November 1933 he joined the other Bavarian bishops in signing a declaration urging support in the forthcoming plebiscite for Hitler's decision to withdraw from the League of Nations. Thereby Catholics would prove once again their devotion to "people and fatherland." But, equally important, they would demonstrate their agreement with "the farsighted and energetic efforts of the Führer to save the German nation from the horrors of war and the atrocities of Bolshevism." National Socialism might not always be free of political extremism or antireligious bias, but there could be no doubt about its determination to oppose Communist expansion.[12]

Even after the outbreak of World War II, after it became clear that Hitler's foreign policy was not only demanding increasingly heavy sacrifices but might end in military defeat, most Catholic churchmen continued to support the regime as a bulwark against Marxism. The attack on the Soviet Union in particular was seen as a sacred crusade to crush the forces of godlessness. And what good Christian could oppose that?

In September 1941, after he had already begun to voice public criticism of the government's brutality, Galen bestowed his blessing on the struggle against atheistic Communism initiated three months earlier. The purpose of that struggle, he declared in a pastoral letter, was "to thwart the military, coercive effort of Moscow to impose the Bolshevik heresy and despotism on Germany and Western Europe." The armies of the Third Reich, guarding the Atlantic coast and the shores of the Mediterranean, had also begun battling "the Bolshevik opponent in the east." The bishop prayed for divine assistance in "the defense of our people and nation against the Bolshevik threat." Yet he was thinking not only of his own countrymen. He also hoped for "the liberation of the Russian people, who have for nearly 25 years been infected and almost destroyed by the plague of Bolshevism." Galen was not blind to Nazi ruthlessness, but in the regime's campaign against international Marxism he perceived an instrument of the divine will.[13]

The struggle against "materialism," against the secular and democratic values of Weimar, helped lead many of the resisters toward an acceptance of the Third Reich. To them National Socialism did not initially mean brutality and oppression, conquest and genocide. They saw in it rather a means of liberation, a rejection of corruption in domestic politics and weakness in international relations. It meant a repudiation of the modernism and individualism that the republic seemed to incarnate. Above all, it represented a return to traditional beliefs and loyalties, to discipline, authority, morality, patriotism, and idealism. They were too shortsighted, too zealous, and too dogmatic to recognize the dark totalitarian forces they were helping to unleash. In the end they became victims of a brutal regime that they themselves had supported in its rise to power.

At the time of Weimar's collapse, however, they had few doubts regarding the new order in Germany. Some of them even became avowed Nazis, persuaded that the rise of the Third Reich signified a great political and spiritual revival. Schulenburg, for example, declared in the spring of 1934 that while republican politicians had been the slaves of "alien international forces," Hitler created in the National Socialist Party a "new core of resistance." All those who still had "faith and will," who still had "courage to make sacrifices and willingness to perform deeds," rallied to his movement. Thereby the nation found the means to shape its life "in accordance with its own laws and its own character." The party, "hardened by struggle and terrorism," became "the incarnation of the faith and will of the German people." Under Hitler's leadership, the country would march toward a glorious future.[14]

Schulenburg was an exception, however. Most of the men in the resistance were allies and auxiliaries of National Socialism rather than true believers. They were fellow travelers. Although they welcomed the establishment of the Third Reich, they preferred to dwell on the positive accomplishments of the new order without endorsing all of its principles and doctrines. In a sermon delivered in October 1933, Niemöller emphasized the new sense of faith and value that had recently emerged in Germany. "Occupation and status, race and nation, are once again accepted by us today as realities. They make demands on us from which we cannot escape." This new awareness of collective responsibility represented "a liberation, in reality, indeed, . . . a deliverance." Society had been going in circles in a narrow "prison courtyard" of selfishness and greed. "Now the gates have been forced open, and we see numerous tasks to which we are summoned." The Hitler regime was reawakening a sense of moral mission and purpose in the country.[15]

Dibelius did not even wait until the fall of Weimar to proclaim his sympathy for National Socialism. As early as the spring of 1931 he rejected the contention of liberals in the "so-called [political] middle" that there was little to choose between the extremism of the right and of the left. "From the Protestant point of view, such an equivalence is impossible." The Communists had declared war against the Christian religion in all its forms. They had shown in the Soviet Union "in what inhumane ways the war of annihilation against Christianity is being waged." They were even trying to spread atheism in Germany. The Nazis, by contrast, had shown themselves "quite friendly" toward the Christian churches. They had abjured violence, moreover; they had repeatedly announced that "they want to reach their goal in a legal way." Could there be any doubt who was preferable?

Two years later, after Hitler had come to power, Dibelius expressed satisfaction that under the new regime the work of moral and spiritual reconstruction would finally begin. "There can be no serious dispute among Protestant Christians regarding the goal being sought." The important thing was that "Christian standards" were again in force in Germany, and that the "Christian atmosphere," which had fallen victim to "modern secularization," was being restored. He conceded that the concept of a "Christian state" should not lead to economic regimentation or religious coercion. But as a political system opposed to "the utilitarian state [preaching] so-called religious neutrality," and as a collective protest against a form of government that is "nothing more than a gigantic instrument for the secularization of all of life," the "Christian state" had "a good Lutheran meaning." The Third Reich was now making possible the creation of such a state.[16]

The clergymen in the resistance were not the only ones to see in Hitler at first a defender of morality. The bureaucrats and the soldiers also believed by and large that under his regime the nation would experience a rebirth of idealism. Long afterward the official investigation into the plot to assassinate Hitler reported that a large number of the participants testified that "they had declared themselves for the most part in agreement with the objectives of the National Socialist Party in 1933." Berthold von Stauffenberg, for instance, stated that he had supported many of the "basic ideas" of the regime, including "the community of the people, the principle of 'collective welfare before individual welfare,' . . . the emphasis on rural life and the struggle against the spirit of the big cities, . . . and the determination to [create] a new system of law that was German in character." He had found those ideas "healthy and forward-looking." Even now, as he faced the executioner, they did not seem to him altogether bad.[17]

The struggle against materialism thus led most members of the resistance into collaboration with National Socialism. For them the fundamental flaw in Weimar, the basic cause of all its other failings, had been the lack of any inspiring ideal, any transcendent faith. This flaw is what accounted for everything else, for the corrupting party system, the bartering and huckstering of public office, the timidity in international affairs, the weakness in the military system, and the decline in national morality. This is what turned them against the republic. They assumed that spirituality could be built on repression, that idealism could be revived through dictatorship. But they were mistaken. Their quest for virtue led to tyranny, their defense of tradition fostered brutality, their call for harmony invited destruction. They ended up paying a terrible price for their mistake.

4

That Perennial "Jewish Question"

Among those "basic ideas" of National Socialism that, according to Berthold von Stauffenberg's testimony following his arrest in 1944, he and the
other resisters had found "healthy and forward-looking" was the "concept
of race." Essentially, that concept meant anti-Semitism. For behind all the
theorizing by the Third Reich about racial differences, and behind all the
pseudoscientific lecturing on the distinctions between brachycephalic and
dolichocephalic types, between Nordic and Mediterranean peoples, between Teutonic and Slavic characteristics, between Occidental and Oriental mentalities, and between the white and the colored races, there was only
one fundamental principle that remained beyond debate or compromise:
hostility toward Jews. Everything else could be negotiated, modified, or
even ignored. When it suited their interests, the leaders of the Nazi regime
became the oppressors of Norway and Holland but the partners of Italy
and Spain. They despised Poles and Russians but embraced Slovaks and
Croats. They sought the support of the Japanese in the struggle against the
Anglo-Saxons. They even tried to incite dark-skinned nationalists in India
to rebel against the rule of Caucasian Great Britain. They were almost
always pragmatic in their attitude toward racial doctrine, almost always
ready to subordinate theory to practice, principle to expediency. On only
one issue did they refuse to make concessions: the "Jewish question."[1]

In the view of National Socialism, Jews differed fundamentally from
non-Jews. There could be no reconciliation, no understanding between
them. The two coexisted in a state of covert, undeclared warfare, so that
anti-Semitism was really a weapon of self-preservation, a means of racial
survival. The Jewish community would always remain unassimilated and
unassimilable. Germany had in the past been able to absorb many other

alien elements. It had succeeded in incorporating and nationalizing Polish and Bohemian aristocrats, Lithuanian and Slovene peasants, French Protestants, Flemish Catholics, Dutchmen, Danes, Italians, and Swedes. But the Jews were different. They might pretend to feel and behave like the Germans, but that was only a screen for their schemes to exploit the Germans. What they really wanted was to dominate the political, economic, and cultural life of the nation. Nothing could change that. The only solution was a rigid separation of the two inherently incompatible "races."

Many members of the resistance shared at least some of these views. Admittedly, there were important differences between them and the rabid, fanatical anti-Semites of the Nazi Party. They typically displayed the fashionable bigotry of the exclusive drawing room or the elite gentlemen's club. They looked down with condescension on the Jewish parvenu who might have acquired a great deal of money but could never attain the social status that only family and tradition bestowed. Yet they also agreed by and large that the Jews were an alien element incapable of being fully assimilated into German society. The traits separating the Nordic from the Judaic character were too profound to be bridged by tolerance or liberality. Something had to be done, legally and equitably, of course, to reduce the influence of Jewry, to diminish its importance in commerce and finance, to control its growth in learning and the arts, and to counter its promotion of radicalism and subversion. On this point almost all the resisters agreed.

None of them foresaw how the Third Reich would ultimately try to solve the Jewish question. If they had, they would have been horrified. They would never have considered organized, systematic extermination an acceptable means of dealing with racial problems. But that racial problems existed and that something had to be done to resolve them appeared self-evident to most members of the resistance. They had no clear idea of how to deal with them; they advanced no concrete proposals for their solution. And yet they spoke with growing concern about the "Judaization" of German culture, about the "excessive" or "unhealthy" influence of Jews in politics, and about the "parasitical" or "exploitative" role of Jewish moneylenders in the economy. The anti-Semitic rhetoric of National Socialism did not seem to them entirely baseless.

The attitude of the soldiers among the resisters is hard to determine with precision, because they spoke about the Jewish question so infrequently. For one thing, the armed forces had been taught to avoid discussion of controversial questions of public policy. They were expected to be above party or ideology; they were supposed to be loyal only to the nation. For another, there were virtually no Jews in the officer corps and very few among the bureaucrats and politicians with whom the high command had to deal. Hence to the members of the military the Jewish question was something remote and abstract, something that did not affect them closely. They could afford to regard it with a certain detachment.

Still, the few comments soldiers in the resistance did make suggest that they generally shared the casual bigotry prevalent in conservative circles of German society. They too identified Jews with the "destructive" forces of liberalism, radicalism, pacifism, capitalism, and modernism. When during the 1920s Henning von Tresckow criticized the idea of permanent peace among the nations of the world, he characterized it as "Jewish" in origin, designed to ensure the triumph of the spirit of commercialism. In the 1930s Wilhelm Canaris, the enigmatic naval officer who was soon to direct the German counterintelligence while at the same time obstructing the German war effort, sought to ingratiate himself with the Third Reich by affirming the gravity of the Jewish question. Whether out of conviction or opportunism, and probably a little of each, he spoke of the need, "in view of contemporary events," to awaken a "consciousness of the eternal values of faith, race, nationality, and the social community." Though not a virulent anti-Semite, Canaris shared the widespread dislike for Jews that National Socialism exploited and encouraged. This attitude was common to most members of the military.[2]

The bureaucrats were much more outspoken on the Jewish question. Not only did they face fewer restrictions on the expression of views regarding public issues, but they had greater personal contacts and sharper professional rivalries with Jews prominent in politics and economics. The abandonment by the republican regime of the monarchy's semiofficial policy of discrimination against the Jewish community had the effect of intensifying the competition for influence within the bureaucracy and hence the hostility toward ethnic outsiders.

Popitz provides a good example. During his long career as a government financial expert, he had come to know well many of his Jewish colleagues. In the late 1920s, moreover, he had loyally served Finance Minister Rudolf Hilferding, whose family had only recently emerged from the ghettos of Galicia. Nowhere in his writings is there any evidence of anti-Semitic prejudice. Yet after his arrest for complicity in the plot on Hitler's life, he testified that he had long felt that the influence of Jewry in national affairs was excessive. "As a quite knowledgeable expert on conditions in the period of the [party] system, I was entirely of the opinion regarding the Jewish question that the Jews must disappear from political and economic life." The only reservation he had pertained to the means, not the ends, of

Nazi racial policy. "I did repeatedly recommend a somewhat more gradual approach in the method employed, especially for reasons of foreign policy." Was he only trying to placate the authorities, to win their leniency, to lighten his punishment? Perhaps, although he must have sensed that nothing could save him now from the executioner. In all probability, his assertion that during Weimar he had believed Jewish influence to be excessive was quite sincere.[3]

Similarly, Goerdeler, though an avowed conservative critic of Weimar from the outset, displayed no anti-Semitic bias in his speeches and writings. On the contrary, when the Nazis came to power, he personally helped protect Jewish shopkeepers in Leipzig against plundering storm troopers. Yet he too believed that it was important to curb the influence of Jews in politics and economics. His only major concern in this regard was that the elimination of alien forces from national life be carried out fairly and equitably. Otherwise, he was prepared to support the program of National Socialism, including its racial policy.

Thus in the memorandum Goerdeler submitted to Hitler in the summer of 1934, he urged that the government's anti-Semitic measures be enforced with strict adherence to legal norms. "What the law has provided will hardly be questioned by reasonable people abroad as a means of self-protection, as long as everything is now carried out with iron discipline and the avoidance of excesses and petty persecutions." If this advice were disregarded, however, "we [would] only be forced to make ever greater concessions." There was no reason, for example, why the playing of Felix Mendelssohn's music should not be discouraged or even prohibited, provided it was not done officially on "grounds of racial policy." What appeared to concern Goerdeler most was the execution rather than the content of Nazi racial legislation.[4]

Hassell's flirtation with anti-Semitism began much earlier, almost immediately after the establishment of the republic. He was one of those participants in the resistance who had not been content merely to grumble about the "undue importance" Jews had acquired in public life. He tried to do something about it. Having become a member of the executive committee of the conservative German National Party following the fall of the monarchy, he proposed a compromise on its stand regarding the Jewish question that sought to avoid both too much bigotry and too much toleration. "The development and training of [the nation's] energies in all areas of public life," he suggested, "is the best protection against an excessive growth of harmful alien influence, especially against the domination of Jewry."

Yet this was not enough for most members of the German National Party. The platform they approved in 1920 declared that only a strong sense of nationality, "which consciously protects the nature and character [of our people] and remains free of alien influence," could provide the foundation for a strong German state. "We therefore oppose every manifestation of a disintegrative, un-German spirit, whether emanating from Jewish or other circles." It was especially important to put a stop to the "ever more dangerous emergence of the domination of government and public life by Jewry." For that reason "the influx of people of alien origin across our frontiers should be halted." Hassell might have preferred a more discreet or restrained tone in the declaration, but the one they actually adopted did not seem to shake his faith in the conservative movement.[5]

Schulenburg was some twenty years younger than Hassell, and the generational difference in their experiences and convictions was reflected in their attitude toward the Jewish question. Hassell's anti-Semitism derived from a genteel, aristocratic assumption of superiority characteristic of the patriciate of the old imperial order. Schulenburg expressed the sense of alienation of an interwar generation of young, conservative nationalists outraged by the Versailles peace settlement, scornful of the weakness of Weimar, and convinced that their nation was being victimized by the conspiratorial schemes of international Jewry. Hassell did join the Nazi Party in the fall of 1933, but out of expediency rather than principle. Schulenburg, however, felt with all his heart that only National Socialism could save Germany from political decline and moral decay. One became a fellow traveler of the Third Reich, the other a true believer.

Hence for Hassell a systematic application of the national energies to the protection of public life could provide a sufficient safeguard against "harmful alien influence," including "the domination of Jewry." But for Schulenburg the problem was much more complicated. During the last years of Weimar he saw all about him "dark forces" controlling the political parties, forces "alien to the history and character" of Germany, forces that pretended to be German in allegiance but that were always "on the opposing side" whenever "essential issues" were being decided. It was quite clear whom he meant. After the Nazi victory Schulenburg identified by name those "dark forces" that had dominated the republican regime: "the powers of Jewry, capital, and the Catholic Church." Now that Hitler had come to power, he rejoiced, they would be defeated and crushed.[6]

The most vocal anti-Semites in the resistance, however, came from the Protestant clergy. Indeed, German Protestantism as a whole was generally critical of Weimar and of the "unhealthy" and "unchristian" influences in public life that parliamentary democracy nourished. Most of the church leaders yearned for a return to the traditions and pieties championed by the old monarchical order. Like other conservatives, they firmly believed that the republic had been established by a treacherous rebellion against legitimate authority, that it placed the interest of the parties above the welfare of the community, and that it acquiesced in the military weakness and diplomatic humiliation of their country. But they saw the most serious fault of the new government in its indifference to Christian values, its attempt to restrict the role of religion in national affairs, its advocacy of secularism and "materialism," its tolerance of the "immorality" of big-city life, and its flirtation with radicalism and "Bolshevism."

For many of them anti-Semitism became a justifiable means of self-defense against the dangers threatening the state. Since the attitudes and values of Jewry were, in their view, fundamentally incompatible with the spirit of Germany, valid reasons existed for adopting protective measures against a small but dangerous racial minority. Such measures would not really victimize Jews; they would simply safeguard Germans.

Niemöller, for instance, the most equivocal and contradictory figure in the resistance, was convinced at first that a Hitler dictatorship would be far preferable to the secular, democratic, and materialistic republic. He eventually turned against the Third Reich, denouncing the government's religious policy and paying for his audacity with seven years in a concentration camp. But during Weimar he believed that an authoritarian right-wing regime was the only salvation for Germany. Always unpredictable, often inconsistent, he combined faith in the golden rule with conservative, ultranationalistic zealotry; he opposed autocratic rule in the church but supported it in the state; he embraced simultaneously Christian universalism and German jingoism. How should a man of such disparate and incompatible views be characterized? Niemöller can never be accused of lacking courage, but his displays of insufficient discernment, tolerance, compassion, or even good common sense are puzzling and distressing. Long after his death, he remains an enigma.

What is clear is that to him the political and economic role of the Jewish minority was a threat to the German majority. Not even the most strenuous efforts at assimilation by one side or at tolerance by the other could bridge the differences separating the two "races." At his trial early in 1938, Niemöller testified that Jews seemed to him "unpleasant and alien." That would hardly be surprising, he explained, in someone who came from "an old Westphalian family of peasants and theologians," and who was "a former imperial naval officer." Still, whether one liked it or not, Jews who converted had to be accepted as equal members of the Christian community. The Bible did not permit the church "to replace baptism with the family tree." Nor should God be conceived "in our image, the Aryan image." He would have to be accepted as he actually was, made manifest "in the Jew Jesus of Nazareth." This "truly distressing and great vexation" had to be endured "for the sake of the Gospel." There was no avoiding it; it was part of the divine scheme of things, inscrutable but inescapable.[7]

Niemöller's view of conversion helps explain his defense in 1933 of "non-Aryan" Protestant clergymen—twenty-three of them in the entire country, not counting those who had "non-Aryan" wives—clergymen whom the Nazi authorities were trying to remove from their positions in the church. To support them, he admitted, required a high degree of "self-denial" on the part of the Germans, who "as a nation have had to endure a great deal under the influence of the Jewish people." It was understandably hard for them to accept pastors of alien racial origin. But only by doing so could they demonstrate their faith in the Christian Church as a "community that extends beyond national affinities." No dispensation from this difficult obligation was possible.

Still, while Protestant ministers of Jewish descent should not be disowned, neither was there any need to flaunt them. They could be expected in fact, according to Niemöller, to display "appropriate discretion" so as not to cause "offense" to the ethnic sensibilities of their fellow Christians. It would be better if they did not belong to the governing body of the church or participate prominently in its missionary work. Was that too much to ask, considering the "frailty" of most Germans regarding questions of nationality and race? Surely not. Some concession to popular passions and prejudices was justifiable and would have to be made. As for the more than half a million "non-Aryans" who had still not converted to Christianity, their fate seemed to Niemöller to be properly the concern of world Jewry, not of the Protestant community in Germany.[8]

For pure, undisguised animosity toward Jews, however, no member of the resistance could surpass Dibelius. There are interesting parallels between him and Niemöller. Both were Protestant ministers who eventually turned against National Socialism because of its increasing interference in churchly governance. Both were hostile toward parliamentary democracy, both were outraged by the Versailles peace settlement, both condemned the secularism and "materialism" of the Weimar regime, and both attributed Germany's misfortunes at least to some extent to the machinations of a greedy, cunning, and unscrupulous Jewish minority.

Nevertheless, in his virulent anti-Semitism Dibelius far outstripped Niemöller. As early as 1928, during Weimar's heyday, he described his position regarding the Jewish question bluntly and unequivocally in a circular letter labeled "confidential," which was distributed among the clergymen under his jurisdiction. "I have always considered myself an anti-Semite, despite the bad sound the word has acquired in many circles." Who could deny that in "all the disintegrative manifestations of modern civilization" Jewry had played "a leading role"? The cultivation of the nationality "to which God has assigned us," the reinforcement of the love of country, a new sense of rootedness in the soil, and a conscious rejection of "modern asphalt culture," those were the goals to which "every Protestant church will categorically commit itself." In this context anti-Semitism was an essential safeguard of the nation's moral heritage.[9]

The great depression only intensified Dibelius's hostility toward Jews. For him they were the ones responsible in large part for the economic crisis, which had been precipitated by Jewish capitalism and which was being exploited by Jewish radicalism. When Hitler came to power, Dibelius was jubilant. Here was a regime that would finally put an end to destructive alien influences over national affairs. And when the foreign press presumed to criticize the boycott of Jewish businesses organized by the Third Reich in the spring of 1933, he became outraged, launching into an anti-Semitic tirade that must have pleased even the most ardent Nazi Jew-baiters.

Public opinion abroad, Dibelius charged, was not shaped by government officials or parliamentary leaders. It was determined by "entirely different forces," namely, "economic capital and the press, which is dependent on it." Those forces had established connections between various countries, connections that, "as everyone knows," were to a considerable extent "in Jewish hands." This influence accounted for the foreign hostility toward National Socialism.

That the Jews should feel threatened by "a national movement with anti-Semitic tendencies" was quite understandable, Dibelius expounded. After all, had they not been closely implicated in the revolution of 1918 and in the "Socialist domination" of Germany? Every child was familiar with the large number of Jewish names, names like Rosa Luxemburg and Rudolf Hilferding, which had become prominent in politics after the establishment of the republic. Even more familiar were Jewish profiteers and swindlers like Julius Barmat, Max Sklarek, and "all the others, whatever their names." These facts could not be ignored. "Even though we as Protestant Christians are ever so sensible of the obligation not to do an injustice to anyone, there can be no doubt that the Jewish element has played a leading role in the sinister events of the last fifteen years." More than that, while Jews constituted only 1 percent of the German population, their share of important offices in government and administration far exceeded this proportion. Under Weimar "the number of Jewish judges, Jewish politicians, and Jewish officials in influential positions has grown measurably." Currently, with their predominance in jeopardy, the Jews were trying to stir up public opinion abroad against the Third Reich.

England and America could not understand the problems Germany faced in dealing with the Jewish question, Dibelius went on. "The Anglo-Saxon race is far too robust and tough to let itself be weakened by Jewish immigration." But the Germans were geographically close to the "great recruitment centers of Jewry in Galicia and the interior of Poland," so the danger facing them was far more acute. All the Third Reich was trying to do was protect them against this danger. To achieve that, it would first of all have to close the eastern frontier of Germany to Jewish immigration. But more important, it would have to foster "the firmness of our own [national] character," so "it will not succumb to an alien race." And that would prove an impossible task, "unless our Christian conscience makes the [sense of] responsibility toward the nationality that God has given us a force in the life of every individual." For Dibelius anti-Semitism had almost become a solemn religious duty.[10]

Hostility toward Jews was much less pronounced among the Catholic churchmen in the resistance. Although not above an occasional platitude about Jewish sophistry or cupidity or radicalism, they rarely engaged in systematic anti-Semitism. The lack of Niemöllers or Dibeliuses among them reflected the obvious similarity in the position of Jews and Catholics in Germany. Both were religious minorities exposed to bigotry on the part of the majority. Both were charged with insufficient patriotism or even disloyalty to the nation. Both were suspected of greater sympathy for their coreligionists abroad than for their compatriots at home. And both were denounced by the Nazis for being "international" or "cosmopolitan" in their allegiance, for serving the interests of sinister alien forces. The common experience of discrimination thus encouraged a measure of mutual understanding between them. Occasionally it even led to open expressions of sorrow by Catholics, by laymen as well as clergymen, at the sufferings the Jewish community had to endure. In anti-Semitism they perceived the specter of anti-Catholicism; in the persecution of Jews they foresaw the persecution of Catholics.

Thus in 1934 a priest, who understandably preferred not to reveal his name, declared in a religious periodical that it was "a sacred task of the church" to oppose "sinful racial pride and blind hatred of the Jews." It should instead seek "atonement for all the sins committed by Christians against Jews," and pray for "the return of Israel to God and Christ." Every Good Friday the church offered a prayer for all people, "including the Jews," that they might see Christ and gain faith in him. But why only on Good Friday? And why in Latin, a language incomprehensible to the people? "Would it not be appropriate to translate this prayer for the people and to make clear and impress very urgently on the consciousness of every ordinary Christian the fact that hatred toward the Jews is a sin and injustice, and that the Christian has an obligation, toward them as well, to pray, to bless, and to love?" Asking questions of this kind during the Third Reich required courage.[11]

The leaders of the Catholic Church, however, including the resisters among them, were much more cautious or even afraid, though not for their personal safety. They could have faced arrest and imprisonment, if convinced that religious duty required them to defy the Third Reich. But what troubled them was the thought that by openly condemning anti-Semitism they might be endangering the position of the Catholic community. They knew of influential groups within the National Socialist Party that regarded Catholicism as a sworn enemy, groups that would be only too glad to find a pretext for restricting its freedom of action. A determination to defend Catholic interests at all costs, to avoid anything that might have interfered with the performance of the church's sacerdotal and pastoral functions, helps explain the silence of its leaders regarding anti-Semitism. They feared that by speaking out for the Jews they would jeopardize the position of the Catholics.

The dilemma of a churchman torn between the conflicting demands of Christian universalism and denominational self-interest, between transcendent faith and religious expediency, appears clearly in the case of Faulhaber. The cardinal had gained an early reputation as an opponent of National Socialism by emphasizing in his Advent sermons of 1933 the central position of the Old Testament in Catholic theology. He boldly attacked those who argued that the Old Testament, being Jewish in origin and hence incompatible with the spirit of Germany, should no longer be considered part of the Holy Scriptures. Perceiving this argument as a direct challenge to the authority of the church, he felt that he must not remain silent. It had become his duty to respond.

What Faulhaber had to say was not only unambiguous but defiant. Before the death of Christ "the people of Israel were the bearers of the revelation," and their prophets, "whom the spirit of God awakened and enlightened," had aroused the popular conscience with the living word. The New Testament, to be sure, was superior to the Old; it must always occupy "the place of honor." But the Old Testament was also an integral part of the Christian Scriptures. Its books were "sacred," its words were "inspired by the Spirit of God," and its contents were "building stones for God's kingdom." On this point there could be no compromise.[12]

The cardinal's private correspondence during the early months of the Third Reich reveals, moreover, that his sympathies were not confined to the Judaism of antiquity. In a letter to Alois Wurm, editor of a Catholic periodical, he condemned the new government's anti-Semitic campaign. "This action against the Jews is so unchristian that every Christian, not only every priest, would have to stand up against it." To Eugenio Pacelli, the papal secretary of state, later Pius XII, he described the persecution of the Jews as "unjust and painful." What troubled him especially was that "also those [Jews] who have been baptized for ten or twenty years and are good Catholics, even those whose parents were already Catholic, are still legally considered to be Jews, and are to lose their positions as physicians or lawyers." Judaism, in his eyes, was not a racial but a religious concept. Writing to Professor Theodor Steinbüchel in Giessen, he made clear that he felt some concern even for those Jews who had remained Jews. "We certainly want no [Jewish] predominance that is disproportionate to the actual number of Jews, but we cannot deny them every right in the German fatherland without destroying the foundation in natural law of our own love of the fatherland." Clearly, Faulhaber cannot be accused of being an anti-Semite.[13]

Nevertheless, in his public declarations he said nothing in defense of "non-Aryans," whether Catholics or Jews. Even in his Advent sermons he emphasized that he was fighting for the Old Testament, not for the people of the Old Testament. He was treating questions of theology rather than of politics or even of morality. He stated at the outset that "my Advent sermons will deal only with this Israel of biblical antiquity," repeating a few sentences later that "as for our Advent sermons, they will discuss only pre-Christian Judaism." As if to underscore his resolve to avoid challenging the regime's racial policy, he explained that the church did not oppose efforts "to keep the special character of a people as pure as possible" or "to deepen the sense of a people's community through reference to its community of blood." More than that, "from the point of view of the church, there is no objection to honest research on race and cultivation of race," provided they did not turn into "hatred of other peoples." Religion and racism were not really incompatible.[14]

In confidential statements the cardinal revealed why he was so reluctant to condemn anti-Semitism openly. He feared that thereby he might endanger the position of the church. "We confront new situations from day to day," he cautioned the Bavarian episcopate in March 1933, "and the present Jew-baiting can turn just as quickly into Jesuit-baiting." Early in April he informed Pacelli that it was impossible for now to oppose the government on the racial question, because "the struggle against the Jews would at the same time become a struggle against the Catholics." And writing concurrently to Alois Wurm, he sounded annoyed and impatient with those demanding a stronger stand. "For the higher authorities of the church there are far more important questions at present [than anti-Semitism], since schools, the continued existence of Catholic societies, and sterilization are even more important for Christianity in our country."

Faulhaber remained convinced that it was best, for Jews as well as Catholics, to endure in silence the racial injustices of National Socialism. To criticize, to condemn, to resist would only make matters worse. The wisest course was to submit and wait.

That was the gist of his letter of March 30, 1933, to Cardinal George William Mundelein of Chicago. He spoke first about "the untrue reports of bloody atrocities in Germany" that had appeared in the American press, and about the attacks against the new government "because of its struggle against Communism." As a result, the Nazi authorities had organized a boycott of all Jewish business establishments. And now "tens and tens of thousands of large and small and very small businesses are being hit hard, and many families are being financially ruined or at least placed in the greatest difficulty." The journalists for the foreign press had failed to realize what a dangerous situation they were creating for the Jews of Germany. "I [therefore] ask Your Eminence to use all your influence to persuade the newspapers abroad that have until now reported atrocities to issue a declaration that they have become convinced of the baselessness of their earlier assertions." That would be the prudent thing to do. Faulhaber's main concern was the defense of his faith and the welfare of his flock. He never pretended to be more than a protector of Catholic interests.[15]

For the men in the resistance, then, anti-Semitism was generally no obstacle to an acceptance of the Third Reich. On the contrary, most of them agreed with National Socialism that the Jews had gained an unhealthy influence over the national life of Germany. They rejected the ruthlessness and brutality of the methods by which Hitler's followers proposed to curb that influence. But that there was indeed a Jewish question and that it had to be solved one way or another seemed to them quite evident.

Even among the handful of supporters of Weimar who later joined the resistance, anti-Semitism was not entirely unknown. Julius Leber illustrates the point. Born out of wedlock to a family of village laborers, married to the daughter of a "non-Aryan" school principal, the editor of a republican newspaper in Lübeck, a devoted lifelong Socialist, he might have seemed to be the last person to engage in condescending bigotry. Yet the sense of ethnic superiority was at times too much even for him.

Analyzing the reasons for the fall of Weimar, for instance, Leber did not dwell on the policies or tactics of National Socialism. He emphasized rather the weaknesses of the democratic regime he had supported, weaknesses aggravated by ambitious but incompetent Jews. His essay on the collapse of the Social Democratic Party, composed in the summer of 1933, stressed the unfortunate role played by Paul Hertz, the Jewish secretary of the Socialist caucus in the Reichstag. He and his followers had become "very influential and often decisive." Yet he was only a "typical representative of that Jewish intermediate [social] stratum which has indeed already climbed the first steps to success, but has not yet reached a high level of cultural and personal self-confidence." Properly supervised, he might have proved useful to an effective party leader; he did have "persistent diligence" and "expertise in many areas." But acting independently and authoritatively, "Hertz was bound to have a harmful effect." Because of him "all parliamentary achievement and organization dissolved into isolated struggles over financial and social lawmaking."

In his comments regarding the Third Reich Leber was much more lenient. Writing to his wife that same summer while under arrest by the Nazi authorities, he argued that "given the state of German life and of the German economy today, given the conflict between the generations, given the general misery and the extensive destruction of property," anyone in power would be apt to fail within six months, "if he leaves the decision regarding himself and his achievements to the people." Desperate times required desperate measures, even dictatorial measures. "How little the world outside understands events [in Germany] is shown by its reaction to the so-called atrocity propaganda. As if the essential thing were whether a few Jews or Social Democrats or clergymen were being mistreated. . . . That is not very important." It could have been Hassell or Goerdeler or Popitz speaking.[16]

Bonhoeffer was the only one among the resisters to come out clearly and unequivocally against anti-Semitism. But what made him more tolerant and understanding than the others is not entirely clear. Was it that he had grown up not in some small-town parsonage or on an aristocratic landed estate or in the household of a monarchist civil servant, like so many members of the resistance, but in the family of a well-known Berlin psychiatrist and neurologist? Did his frequent travels abroad, to Spain, America, and England, help widen his outlook and deepen his sympathy? Or did the marriage of his sister to a "non-Aryan" lawyer, whose chances for professional advancement were threatened by a pervasive ethnic bigotry, make him more sensitive to the injustices of anti-Semitic prejudice? Whatever the reason, there can be no doubt about his courageous rejection of the racial doctrines of the Third Reich.

Bonhoeffer was not entirely free of common religious biases and stereotypes, however. He too believed that there was something called the Jewish question with which society had to contend. After the Nazis came to power, he even declared that "the state is without doubt justified in adopting new approaches" to that question. As for the Christian Church, it must view the history of the Jews "with a shudder" as "God's own, free, terrible way of dealing with his people." An end to their suffering could come only with "the conversion of Israel." So far Bonhoeffer was only repeating the cultural and theological commonplaces of traditional Christianity.

And yet there gradually emerged out of those familiar phrases about the historic transgression and punishment of the Jews an indirect but unmistakable condemnation of anti-Semitism. "From the point of view of Christ's church," Bonhoeffer insisted, "Judaism is never a racial but a religious concept." One can become a Jew through the acceptance of "God's law," but there is no such thing as a "racial Jew." And since someone who received baptism thereby became a full-fledged "member of our church," its leaders could not allow the treatment of that member to be dictated by the state. The member had to be accepted as a Christian without differentiation or discrimination.

Not only that, Bonhoeffer argued that officially sanctioned oppression even of unbaptized Jews was morally and theologically wrong. "No state in the world" could deal conclusively with "this enigmatic people," because "God has not yet dealt with it." The task of "humanitarian organizations" and of "individual Christian men who feel the calling" was therefore to point out to the state "the moral aspect of its measures at any given time." Indeed, if necessary, they should not hesitate "to accuse the state of violating morality." As for the Christian Church, it should avoid glib "moralizing" about the "curse" pronounced against the Jews because of their refusal to accept the Gospel. Instead, it must feel humbled by the experience of "that rejected people," so important in the history of salvation. The words expressed, clearly though implicitly, a repudiation of National Socialism's racial policy.[17]

The other resisters were as a rule less broad-minded. Only a few of them can be described as out-and-out anti-Semites. The great majority viewed with skepticism the contention of rabid Nazis that international Jewish bankers were trying to gain control over the world through the power of money. Nor did they generally believe that international Communism had emerged out of a conspiracy by world Jewry to rule the Aryan race. But most of them did regard Jews with distrust and dislike, sometimes even with hostility. They felt that there were too many Jewish businessmen in Germany, too many Jewish politicians, too many Jewish radicals, and too many Jewish academics, intellectuals, and artists. Something had to be done to deal with this problem. Not quite sure what that something should be, they by and large supported, in principle at least, the initial measures adopted by the Third Reich to restrict the influence of Jews in the political, economic, and cultural life of their nation. They failed to see the ultimate cost, in human life and human conscience, of solving the Jewish question.

II

Establishing the New Order

Hitler's revanchist military program accorded with the views dominant in the army. Its realization was therefore greeted and supported by us. All our reservations and hesitations were pushed aside by the successes of the Hitler government in the diplomatic and military area.

BERNHARD WATZDORF (1963)

5

The Collapse of the Republican Regime

The fall of Weimar resulted directly from the depression; that conclusion seems clear and incontrovertible. Admittedly, important groups in German society had opposed the republic from the start, for a variety of political, diplomatic, moral, or ideological reasons. But after the early, chaotic postwar years, they began little by little to lose their support. The achievement of governmental stability, the revival of the national economy, and the increasing importance and influence of Germany in European affairs, all helped to reinforce the republic. Even some of those who had at first regarded it with distrust for being too unstable or too ineffectual or too timid came to feel that the parliamentary system offered perhaps the best chance for a national revival. Ten years after its establishment, a growing majority of Germans was prepared, with varying degrees of enthusiasm, to support the new order. The prospects for Weimar appeared bright.

The increasing acceptance of the regime was clearly reflected in the results of the Reichstag elections. The political parties supporting the parliamentary system gained strength steadily. The Social Democrats, the strongest partner in the republican coalition, increased their share of the total vote from 20.5 percent in the election of May 4, 1924, to 26.0 percent in the election of December 7, 1924, and 29.8 percent in the election of May 20, 1928. The Catholic Center Party, which played a pivotal role in Weimar politics, raised its percentage in the two elections of 1924 from 16.6 to 17.4, but then fell to 15.2 in 1928. The percentages for the middle-class Democratic Party, the weakest member of the government bloc, followed roughly the same pattern: 5.7, 6.3, and 4.9. All in all, the major parties supporting the regime enlarged their portion of the Reichstag vote from 42.8 percent in the spring of 1924 to 49.7 in the fall of that year and 49.9 in 1928. With the help of the People's Party, which had grudgingly also come to accept the republic, the supporters of the regime appeared to be firmly in control.

Conversely, its opponents on the left as well as the right were gradually losing strength. In the two elections of 1924 the percentage won by the Communist Party fell from 12.6 to 9.0, before rising again to 10.6 in 1928. The German Nationalists, the largest of the conservative parties, increased slowly from 19.5 to 20.5, but then fell sharply to 14.2 percent. And as for the National Socialists, at that time only a fringe group of political extremists, their share dropped from 6.5 to 3.0 and then 2.6 percent. The combined total for the three most important antirepublican parties thus declined uninterruptedly from 38.6 to 32.5 and then 27.4 percent. By the late 1920s those who favored the republic, even if not always with great conviction, outnumbered those who were firmly opposed by at least 2 to 1.[1]

The economic crisis that began at the end of the decade changed the outlook for Weimar dramatically. Just as the relative prosperity of the previous five years had strengthened the republican regime, so the calamitous depression of the next four undermined it. Those who had once supported the government out of hope gradually turned against it out of disappointment. And while the defenders of the parliamentary system were losing their confidence and courage, its opponents were finding new assurance and strength.

The close connection between economic conditions and political preferences was again revealed graphically in the results of the Reichstag elections. The gains the republican forces had made in the late 1920s suddenly turned into losses in the early 1930s. In the election of September 14, 1930, the percentage of the vote won by the Social Democratic Party, the linchpin of the Weimar bloc, fell from 29.8 two years earlier to 24.5. In the election of July 31, 1932, it fell again to 21.6 percent, and then again to 20.4 in the election of November 6, 1932. The Center Party did considerably better. It did drop from 15.2 percent in 1928 to 14.8 in 1930, but then climbed again to 15.7 and 15.0 in the two elections of 1932. While working-class voters remained by and large loyal to the Socialist ideal and many Catholic voters continued to support the Catholic party, middle-class voters were deserting middle-class democracy in droves. The Democratic Party, now renamed the German State Party, was decimated by the depression, its share of the vote dropping precipitously from 4.9 percent in 1928 to 3.8 in 1930 and to 1.0 in each of the two elections of 1932.

All in all, the total of those voting for the republican coalition fell without interruption from 49.9 percent in 1928 to 43.1 in 1930, 38.3 in the summer of 1932, and 36.4 in the fall. About a fourth of Weimar's supporters defected as a result of the economic crisis.

The losses suffered by the prorepublican forces became gains for the antirepublican forces. The opposition to the regime, which had for five years been in steady retreat, suddenly found itself making rapid advances. Its gloomy forebodings of defeat gave way to exhilarating prospects of victory. The Communist percentage of the vote for the Reichstag climbed from 10.6 in 1928 to 13.1 in 1930 and to 14.5 and 16.9 in 1932. Most of this increase came from disillusioned and embittered Social Democrats. But the German National People's Party, the old-school conservative opponent of Weimar, failed to capitalize on the spreading disgruntlement of the electorate. Its share of the ballots actually declined from 14.2 percent in 1928 to 7.0 in 1930 and 5.9 in July 1932, before rising modestly to 8.5 in November 1932. The portion of the growing antirepublican vote that the Nationalists failed to get went mostly to the big winners in the politics of the depression, the National Socialists. Their percentage of the electorate rose with unexpected rapidity, from 2.6 in 1928 to 18.3 in 1930 and finally to 37.4 and 33.1 in 1932. No other party had won such a high proportion of the vote since the balloting for the Weimar National Assembly in 1919.

By the time Hitler became chancellor, it was clear that Weimar had suffered irreparable losses. The successes of the antirepublican bloc had been of such magnitude that the parliamentary system was no longer capable of reversing them. The combined share of the Reichstag vote received by the opposition had grown from 27.4 percent in 1928 to 38.4 in 1930, 57.8 in July 1932, and 58.5 in November 1932. As a result of the depression, the distribution of political power between the opposing camps had become inverted. Now it was the antirepublican bloc that grew with each election at the expense of the prorepublican bloc. The final collapse of Weimar appeared to be only a question of time.[2]

The sense that they had lost control of the situation, that they now faced unavoidable defeat, seemed to demoralize and paralyze the defenders of the republic. Reluctant to alienate the electorate by harsh measures for coping with the depression, but afraid that without harsh measures the far right or far left might seize power, they suffered in an agony of indecision. They would not say yes and they would not say no. Long before Hitler became chancellor, the parliamentary system had thus ceased to function. What the Third Reich overthrew was not an operative democratic regime but a paper constitutional construct without life or substance.

As early as 1930 the Reichstag acquiesced in the resolve of Chancellor Heinrich Brüning to govern by means of the presidential emergency powers. Though a member of the Center Party, he had become convinced that the economic crisis required decisive action with or without legislative approval. When the Reichstag refused to support his attempt to balance the budget by an increase in taxes and a reduction in expenditures, including those for social welfare, Brüning induced President Hindenburg to promulgate the necessary measures by the special constitutional authority vested in his office. And when the Reichstag voted against this strategy, the chancellor called new elections. The result was a dramatic gain for the Nazis and an impressive one for the Communists. Frightened by the signs of a growing radicalization of the electorate, the Reichstag decided to "tolerate" Brüning. It would not approve his measures because they imposed new hardships on a suffering nation, but it would not reject them either because that might mean the chancellor's replacement by an avowed opponent of Weimar. The republican leaders continued to cling to Brüning in the forlorn hope that his antiparliamentary policy could somehow, in the long run, save the parliamentary system.

Hence the locus of power, fixed by the constitution in the legislature, suddenly shifted to the office of the president. A tired, bewildered, erratic octogenarian became the decisive force in the political system of the foundering republic. By granting or withholding the use of his emergency powers, he could in effect appoint and dismiss chancellors and cabinets. Schemers, intriguers, plotters, and wire-pullers began to vie for influence over the confused and unpredictable old man. Government in the last years of Weimar degenerated into a labyrinth of Byzantine politics.

In May 1932 Hindenburg withdrew his support from Brüning, replacing him with the conservative Franz von Papen. An antiparliamentary ministry now headed a parliamentary government. But Papen's attempts to obtain a popular mandate in two Reichstag elections served only to strengthen the far right and far left. In December he was replaced by another conservative of the old school, Kurt von Schleicher. And when he too failed to come even close to winning mass support, the president was forced to turn to the one prominent political figure who was not only authoritarian, conservative, and nationalistic but also popular. Hitler's appointment as chancellor on January 30, 1933, had by then become almost inevitable. The last chance for the survival of the republic disappeared more than two years earlier with the introduction of a presidential semidictatorship. Thereafter the only choice was between a traditionalist regime dominated by the old political and social elite of Germany and a new radical authoritarianism, populist, egalitarian, and militant in outlook. The establishment of the Third Reich represented the victory of the latter.

The members of the resistance generally viewed the final agony of Weimar with satisfaction. They may have felt some uncertainty or uneasiness about what would take its place, but that any new regime, whether traditionally or radically authoritarian, would be an improvement seemed indisputable to most of them. As a rule, they would have preferred Hindenburg or Papen or Schleicher to Hitler. But even Hitler was bound to be better than the indecisive, timid, and corrupt politicians of the republic. His rhetoric might sometimes sound intemperate; his program was in part perhaps visionary and impractical. But the responsibilities of office would no doubt make him more moderate and more realistic. Without training or experience in statecraft, he would have to rely on the guidance of professional bureaucrats. And that would establish an informal but effective alliance between the old ruling elite and the new. National Socialism would maintain law and order, winning popular support for the regime, while conservative civil servants, who had played a decisive administrative role under the monarchy as well as the republic, would continue to shape and execute government policy. It seemed an ideal arrangement.

Even those few resisters who had started out in the labor movement often expressed mixed feelings about the disintegration of the republic. They too had their doubts about the ability of the parliamentary system to cope with the effects of the depression. Some of them in fact suggested, directly or implicitly, that a retreat from democracy might be the only way to overcome the dangers that confronted the state.

In the case of Max Habermann, a leader of the German National Union of Commercial Employees, such views were not surprising. He had long been a harsh critic of the republic. The members of his union were white-collar workers—clerks, tellers, cashiers, bookkeepers, and salespeople—most of them conservative and nationalistic, antirepublican and anti-Semitic, clinging desperately to a threadbare lower-middle-class respectability, terrified of sinking into the gray, faceless mass of the urban proletariat. Habermann faithfully reflected their prejudices and predilections.

Even after the Third Reich suppressed the National Union along with all other independent labor groups, he continued to proclaim his loyalty to the new order. He boasted that as early as 1930 he had urged Brüning, publicly as well as privately, "to strive for an understanding with Hitler regarding domestic politics." His organization had even arranged a meeting between representatives of the Nazi Party and the Center Party to discuss the possibility of mutual support. During the brief Papen chancel-lorship, moreover, the National Union had tried to persuade the president that only Hitler could end "the confusion in domestic politics," because "he alone would be able to direct into a useful channel the enormously swollen revolutionary wave sweeping over the German people." Now that the new order had been established, Habermann was eager to convince its leaders of his long-standing loyalty to National Socialism.

The harsh dictatorship introduced by the Nazis did not dampen his enthusiasm. The Third Reich still seemed to him far superior to the Weimar Republic. "Although the [National Union] as a social force with a spiritual and political character of its own has foundered in the storms of Adolf Hitler's national revolution," he wrote in February 1934, its mem-bers could feel confident that the "precious metal" of what they had once advocated would now become part of "the new forms of national commu-nal life" being created by National Socialism. Their labor organization had fought honorably in "the eternal struggle of the German people for the Reich," helping to create a more disciplined and effective form of political authority. Was that not something to be proud of? After all, "hundreds of thousands" had been schooled by the National Union to become recruits "whom Adolf Hitler could enlist in his fighting units as people educated in the national spirit." Habermann exuded admiration for a regime that a decade later would drive him to suicide.[3]

The Catholic trade unionist Jakob Kaiser, in contrast, had long been a resolute defender of the republic. His faith in the principles of constitu-tional freedom and representative government appeared unshaken by the tragic social consequences of the depression. As late as September 1932 he was urging at a meeting of Catholic labor leaders the maintenance of "a parliament based on direct popular elections as an expression of the politi-cal will of the people." Only through democratic institutions "are one-sided special-interest groups kept in check," he claimed; only through political liberty "can the spiritual and economic energies of the entire people be balanced and made fruitful." There seemed to be no doubt about his opposition to dictatorial rule.

Yet even Kaiser was by then groping for some magic formula, some spell, some nostrum for ending the political and economic crisis. He declared that he was no blind supporter of "formal democracy" as represented by "pure parliamentarianism." What the country needed was the estab-lishment of "economic corporations" to express the popular will "in addi-tion to parliament." By the end of the year he was even arguing that "the National Socialists must somehow be included within the state," that "their positive force must somehow be made available to the state," provided this could be achieved "without the danger of a party dictatorship." For that matter, a Hitler chancellorship was nothing to fear, as long as "adequate guarantees and agreements can be reached against sliding into a dictatorship." To Kaiser, as to so many other Germans on the eve of the Third Reich, almost any means of avoiding a national collapse appeared acceptable.[4]

The political and economic crisis had an even more profound effect on Julius Leber. Here was a man whose faith in Weimar looked unshakable. He had for more than a decade denounced rightists and superpatriots in the pages of the *Lübecker Volksbote*. He had joined the Reichsbanner Schwarz-Rot-Gold, the quasi-military organization of republican supporters. He had served for nine years as a Socialist member of the Reichstag. His credentials as a defender of the parliamentary system were impeccable. Yet after the victory of the Third Reich, he displayed an unexpected understanding for the government that had revoked the democratic constitution, dissolved the political parties, including his own, and put him in prison. The dictatorial regime, he came to feel, was only trying to accomplish what the republican regime had failed to achieve. It was seeking the same ends by different means. Its efforts should not be blindly condemned, even by former defenders of Weimar.

What was happening in Germany, he concluded by the summer of 1933, had its origins in the world war. Ever since, Europe had been going through a fundamental change whose ultimate outcome remained unforeseeable. But the goal was already clear, namely, "the end of the capitalistic epoch with its egoistic economic liberalism, and the proclamation of human labor as the foundation of social value." In its own way the Third Reich had been trying to achieve that goal. If it failed, then the "birth pangs of social transformation" would go on, the "idea of a socialism based on class would revive," and no power on earth would then be able to keep that idea from gaining "new effectiveness." National Socialism apparently assumed that it would take a long time to bring about the end of economic liberalism. But that was in all probability a mistake. "The capitalistic system and the mental outlook . . . dependent on it are writhing in convulsions that cannot be long endured." The crisis would have to end soon, one way or another.

In the meantime, Leber argued, National Socialists and Marxian Socialists could agree that both were seeking a similar goal, that both were trying "to build for the working man a better future on the firm foundation of justice and freedom." That similarity had been obscured by "the political struggles and passions" of recent years. It would soon become apparent, however, that "those fighting honorably in the hostile camps are closer to one another in spirit than they are able or willing to admit today." The consequences of the depression had almost persuaded Leber that the new order was, potentially at least, better than the old. Why then should not the two opposing sides regard each other with greater understanding, respect, and perhaps even sympathy?[5]

While the handful of republican resisters was trying to adjust, psychologically as well as ideologically, to the establishment of the Third Reich, most of the others greeted its arrival with open arms. The fall of Weimar represented for them the beginning of a new era full of challenging opportunities. A more effective form of government would now be established, the humiliating restrictions imposed by Versailles would be abrogated, the pursuit of private gain would be replaced by a commitment to collective welfare, and harmful alien influences in politics, economics, and culture would be suppressed once and for all. Out of the ruins of the republic would emerge a renewed sense of national pride and national purpose. It was all so exciting.

True, not many members of the resistance believed that National Socialism was the best means of bringing about the revival of Germany. Most of them, especially in the armed forces, would have preferred a Hindenburg dictatorship to a Hitler dictatorship. Hitler seemed to them too much of an upstart and adventurer. Bernhard Watzdorf, who in 1932–33 attended an army school training officers for general-staff duty in violation of Versailles, recalled thirty years later that "aristocratic officers in particular . . . stated that they felt no sympathy for Hitler, especially because of his lowly social origin, and that they as officers would only reluctantly accept the authority of a former corporal." Yet as far as "the important diplomatic and military questions" were concerned, the establishment of the Nazi dictatorship did not confront the officer corps with a "fundamental political decision." After all, Hitler's "revanchist military program" reflected views that predominated in the armed forces. "Its realization was therefore greeted and supported by us." In short, the military revival of Germany seemed more important to the professional soldiers than the political ideology or social background of the statesman responsible for it.[6]

The officers who later joined the resistance welcomed the establishment of the Third Reich as much as those who did not. Some of them were in fact enthusiastic. General Beck, for example, the son of a successful Rhenish metallurgical engineer, seemed largely free of the social prejudices displayed by many aristocratic members of the officer corps. He had been sympathetic to Hitler since at least the beginning of the depression. According to the later testimony of General Alexander von Falkenhausen, Beck during the last years of Weimar "unreservedly" supported the Nazi movement. Another witness, General Eugen Ott, corroborated this recollection. He remembered that in 1930 Beck had, "in a discussion lasting for hours," criticized the government's cautious attitude toward National Socialism, expressing "great hope in Hitler and [his] movement." In the fall of that year, moreover, he had celebrated the results of the Reichstag election in which the Nazis had made important gains. Beck himself provided additional evidence. In a letter written in March 1933, he greeted with enthusiasm the "political revolution" for which he had hoped for so many years and which had now finally taken place. It was the "first ray of hope" since the end of the war. There can be little doubt about his feelings regarding the victory of the Third Reich.[7]

Canaris's attitude was similar to Beck's. He too came from a middle-class family; his father had been a prosperous Ruhr industrialist. He too was free of that feeling of social superiority with which aristocratic officers often regarded the Nazi movement. He too believed that Hitler expressed the fundamental political hopes and aspirations of the German people. One of his former colleagues, Admiral Conrad Patzig, described him as an "enthusiastic National Socialist." His friend Otto Wagner wrote, moreover, that "like most Germans," Canaris "felt at first only the dynamic, vital forces that the Nazi movement imparted to the nation as a whole," adding dryly that "after all, at first almost all of us went along." And Werner Best, a high-ranking official in the SS who knew Canaris well, confirmed his early admiration for the Third Reich. "As a nationalist [he] was at first convinced that the [Nazi] regime was better than anything which had preceded it, and that for the time being there was simply no other way." He tended therefore to judge individual developments, personalities, and activities in the light of this political conviction. But "above all he wanted to see the idea of a German national state realized cleanly." For him the Hitler dictatorship meant primarily a rebirth of national pride and patriotism.[8]

The younger men in the military resistance generally shared this favorable view of the new order. A few of them did have early misgivings about some of the harsher doctrines of National Socialism. Watzdorf remembered that at the time of the establishment of the Third Reich, "Captain [Hellmuth] Stieff, who already at that time displayed a pronounced interest in political questions and who later participated in the conspiracy of July 20, 1944, against Hitler, rejected the [Nazi] measures against the church and the persecutions of Jews." Yet Stieff's attitude toward the dying republic had been even more critical. He felt that since parliamentary democracy had proved incapable of coping with the problems confronting the nation, it would have to be replaced by some authoritarian form of rule. "The parties are the misfortune of Germany," he had written to his wife in August 1932. "The government must be freed from the chains of parliamentarianism." He was expressing the commonplaces of conservative political rhetoric on the eve of Weimar's collapse.

Not surprisingly, within half a year after the establishment of the Third Reich, Stieff had made his peace with the new order. Listening on the radio to the congress of the National Socialist Party in Nuremberg in September 1933, he found the speeches of Hitler and Joseph Goebbels "very good." The former in particular made an excellent impression; what he had to say was "simply fabulous." It had by now become clear to Stieff that National Socialism differed from Italian Fascism in that it dealt with problems "much more thoroughly and fundamentally, at their root." Mussolini might still be better as a practitioner of *Realpolitik*. "But Hitler has far overshadowed him as the founder of a new and doubtlessly epochal view of the world." Stieff's misgivings had vanished; he had now become a believer.[9]

Even Claus von Stauffenberg, the most important and dramatic figure among the younger members of the military resistance, the man who planted the bomb that almost killed Hitler in the summer of 1944, was at first a supporter of the new order. Admittedly, the form and extent of his support have been the subject of considerable debate. Soon after the war the story surfaced that on the day when Hitler was appointed chancellor, Stauffenberg, dressed in full uniform, had led a jubilant procession through the streets of Bamberg to celebrate the occasion. When his superiors reprimanded him for taking part in a political demonstration, he had expressed the view to some of the other officers in the regiment that "the great soldiers at the time of the Wars of Liberation [against Napoleon] would surely have shown more feeling for such a genuinely popular manifestation." The incident suggested that Stauffenberg must have been, at least initially, a devoted follower of National Socialism.

Yet little by little the story was shown to be largely apocryphal. The subsequent testimony of contemporaries proved inconsistent and sometimes contradictory. No newspaper account of the event ever appeared, moreover. The report was possibly based on a misunderstanding of remarks made by Stauffenberg, remarks that were overheard and misinterpreted. They may have pertained to the case of another officer, Hasso von Manteuffel, who had publicly saluted the Nazi swastika in the erroneous belief that it had now become the national flag. He had thereupon received a reprimand from the regimental commander, and it was perhaps in this connection that Stauffenberg made a comment about the attitude of the soldiers who had fought in the Wars of Liberation. In any event, to conclude from such an incident that he was an ardent supporter of National Socialism would clearly be unjustified.

Still, that he was at least sympathetic seems beyond dispute. Like almost all other members of the officer corps, he found the new order vastly superior to the old. Heinz Greiner, who knew him in the early 1930s, reported after the fall of the Third Reich that Stauffenberg had been delighted because "the people rose up against the chains of the Versailles Treaty, . . . the misery of unemployment was eliminated through the creation of work, and other measures providing social relief for the working population were initiated." His approval of Hitler's welfare program had apparently rested on a "religious (Catholic) basis."

Another of Stauffenberg's acquaintances during those years, Rudolf Fahrner, emphasized even more strongly his early favorable view of the Third Reich. "Any merely disapproving remark about Hitler," he later reported, "[was]—with great concern for an 'impartial' evaluation of him—received by Claus Stauffenberg very reservedly and skeptically." He felt that Hitler, despite "all the low qualities in his nature," had expressed "fundamental and genuine longings for a revival," so that even people with "idealistic thoughts and lofty objectives" were attracted to him. Stauffenberg had argued, moreover, that the victory of the Third Reich was in part ascribable to the enemies of Germany, "who believed that they could build peace on the Versailles Treaty." They had unwittingly provided Hitler with his strongest arguments, enabling him to appear as a "defender of the justifiable interests of any nation." But, even more important, Hitler's success rested on his social measures. "He had thereby established from within an effective position against Communism." Views such as these could be heard in every officers' club in Germany in 1933.[10]

They were widespread in the bureaucratic resistance as well. Though many of its members had been opposed to the republican regime from the outset, they had at first been careful not to express their objections publicly. It was important, they felt, to maintain the appearance of aloofness from partisan politics. But the coming of the depression emboldened them. Their criticism gradually became more open and defiant. Goerdeler, for example, began to warn that it was "out of the question" for any "parliamentary combination" to "agree on and carry out the reform required by the economic and political situation of today." Hence "[those with a] capacity for political judgment must achieve greater influence," putting an end to "the absolutism of the parties and of parliament." The nation yearned to be free from "the pushing and pulling of partisan political groups that, with an eye to the fickle mood of the crowd, forget too easily the welfare of the whole and the future of the community." The only solution was an authoritarian form of government.

What Goerdeler had in mind was a Hindenburg dictatorship, but in 1933 he quickly became reconciled to a Hitler dictatorship. It was at least better than Weimar. National Socialism might have some weaknesses, but the experience of power would no doubt teach its leaders to be more moderate and responsible. In any case, many of the Nazi Party's basic ideas were sound; they deserved the support of loyal and patriotic citizens. As late as 1944, after his arrest for participation in the conspiracy against Hitler, Goerdeler wrote that the Third Reich had given the nation "two good things," namely, "the recognition that life is a struggle [which] demands work and accomplishment," although, he hastened to add, "it must become a struggle ennobled by the observance of God's command-ments," and "the doctrine that we must help one another and make the system of compensation such that capital does not earn excessive profits." To the end of his life he continued to believe that the Nazi regime, with all its cruelties and brutalities, had been an improvement, at least initially, over the corrupt, ineffectual republic.[11]

Popitz regarded the fall of Weimar with the same sense of relief. The only choice before the nation, he felt, had been "reform or revolution." The former had been tried, first by Brüning and then by Papen and Schleicher, in the form of a "presidential reform." But it had failed because of the absence of a "leading personality" and the lack of any "connection to the popular movement." That had left only the "revolution" repre-sented by Hitler. His was a unique revolution, however, "without blood-shed or at least without struggle, and in legal form." There could be no doubt that failure to rebuild the state on a "national and authoritarian basis" would result in political and economic chaos. The only question was whether National Socialism would leave room for "personal values and private initiative," that is, whether it would follow the rigid Italian Fascist model or encourage the emergence of a "caste of leaders based on a sense of responsibility and knowledge, united with the people and serving the people." To Popitz the latter seemed more likely.[12]

Schulenburg was much more positive. One of the few members of the bureaucratic resistance who was not only antirepublican but pro-Nazi, he had throughout the early 1930s raged against party politics and parliamentary government. The leaders of Weimar seemed to him to be motivated by nothing more than "personal and egotistical goals"; their chief concern was simply "the protection of sinecures and offices." They served as a facade for the "alien forces" of international capitalism, Catholicism, and Judaism. But "the unknown soldier of the world war, Adolf Hitler," had succeeded in organizing an effective opposition against the corrupting, demoralizing republican regime. His movement had become "the incarnation of the faith and will of the German people." Its victory would lead to a rebirth of national pride and greatness.[13]

The most vocal critics of Weimar among the resisters, however, were the Protestant clergymen. The soldiers and bureaucrats were after all expected to maintain a semblance of neutrality on questions of public policy. Although they expressed themselves with increasing boldness after the start of the depression, there were limits to what they could say against a government they were supposed to serve. But no such inhibitions restrained the churchmen. They were free to voice their political preferences and predilections, especially in the guise of moral or theological homilies. They could loudly criticize the republic for its secularism and materialism, for its indifference to spiritual values, and for its permissiveness toward "vice" and "immorality." They did not have to try to disguise their hostility to Weimar.

Bishop Wurm exemplified their attitude. Even before the collapse of the republic, he had welcomed the rightward drift of the government toward a presidential semidictatorship. He had urged the Protestant Church, moreover, to display greater understanding for the motives and objectives of National Socialism. Once the Third Reich was established, he rushed to express his support. The new order would mean a religious and moral revival for Germany. As for the repressive measures adopted by the Hitler government, that was a price well worth paying for the great benefits it would bring. Having always thought "realistically" about "human possibilities and realities," having never accepted "the liberal cult of ideas," Wurm described himself as less repelled than some by the "disagreeable side effects" of the "great purification." The German people had become accustomed to the "luxury of an unrestrained freedom of opinion even in the most dangerous times." But now they would have to learn to exercise that freedom, "which must return someday," with the restraint normally displayed by "the Latin and the Anglo-Saxon." Until then, the Protestant Church should not obstruct the "process of unification" with "criticism about details." He proclaimed, "with complete conviction," his support for the Third Reich.[14]

Niemöller's acceptance of National Socialism had begun much earlier. He himself declared that he had consistently voted for the Nazi Party since 1924, although he had not joined it because of his conviction that clergymen should not become directly involved in partisan politics. He was on friendly terms with many of Hitler's followers, occasionally even using the Nazi salute. In the events of 1933 he saw the opening of a new era of religious faith and spiritual devotion in Germany. "Among many sections of our people," he preached to his congregation in Berlin, "the hope has sprung up that there will now be a new meeting between our nation and the Christian Church, between our nation and God." He hoped that as a result of the revived confidence which the Third Reich was inspiring in German Protestantism, "obstacles will be swept away and the way made clear" for a happier future. Even fifty years later, toward the end of his life, Niemöller recalled that after the ordeal of Weimar, "it was a kind of liberation when Hitler came." What had happened afterward could not entirely expunge the memory of that exciting new beginning.[15]

As for Dibelius, no member of the resistance, with the possible exception of Schulenburg, welcomed the victory of National Socialism with such joy. After long years of denouncing parliamentary government, the Treaty of Versailles, the spirit of materialism, and the machinations of international Jewry, he celebrated the coming of the Third Reich as the start of a process of national regeneration.

On March 21, 1933, having been chosen to deliver the sermon at a religious service preceding the opening of the new Reichstag, Dibelius justified the repressive measures recently introduced by the Nazi government. "The state is power," he preached. "When questions of life or death for the nation are at stake, then state power must be applied vigorously and thoroughly, whether in foreign or in domestic affairs." After all, did not Luther himself denounce the rebellious peasants who had risen against legitimate authority four hundred years earlier? "When the state uses its office against those who undermine the foundations of the political order, especially against those who destroy marriage with corrupting and coarse language, make religion [seem] contemptible, and slander the [sacrifice of life] for the fatherland, then it uses its office in the name of God." National Socialism had gained in Dibelius an eloquent defender of its high moral mission.[16]

While the Protestants in the resistance rejoiced, the Catholics brooded and worried. In the past the Nazi movement had often attacked their church for its allegiance to an alien pope, for its defense of confessional separatism in education, and for its insistence on the autonomy of religion in relation to the state. Now that Hitler was in power, would he try to diminish the influence of Catholicism in state and society? Would there be a new struggle between secular and spiritual authority, a new *Kulturkampf*? Such were some of the questions that troubled the leaders of the church in the weeks following the establishment of the Nazi regime.

The first hint of a possible reconciliation came from Hitler himself. In a speech to the Reichstag on March 23, 1933, outlining the program of the new regime, he declared that "both Christian denominations" were "the most important factors in the preservation of our nationality." He would therefore respect the agreements they had concluded with the state governments of Germany. "Their rights are not to be infringed."

Catholic Church leaders responded with an almost audible sigh of relief. A conflict between Catholicism and National Socialism might be avoided after all. They might still be able to reach some compromise or understanding, some reasonable accommodation. It was important not to allow this opportunity to slip away.

The first member of the hierarchy to respond to the government's overture was Faulhaber. There was a certain logic in that. Fundamentally opposed to the republic, condemning its illegitimate origin in an act of rebellion, denouncing its commitment to liberalism and secularism, the cardinal shared some of the basic convictions of the Nazi movement. On March 24, only a day after Hitler's declaration before the Reichstag, he replied, indirectly but unmistakably, to the hint at a rapprochement. He urged the Bavarian episcopate "to exercise more tolerance toward the new government in spite of everything." Not only was the Third Reich in power, he explained, but it had acquired that power legitimately, "as no revolutionary party has yet done." Besides, the pope himself had described Hitler as "the first statesman, after the Holy Father, who had raised his voice against Bolshevism." The Catholic Church and National Socialism were about to start down the road to reconciliation.[17]

The evidence on the prevalent political attitudes of the resistance in 1933 thus points to the conclusion that its members were generally as opposed to the Weimar Republic and as favorable to the Third Reich as most of their countrymen. Indeed, they were more so. In the last free or rather half-free election to the Reichstag on March 5, after Hitler had already been appointed chancellor, after the opposition had been restricted and intimidated, after many of the leading anti-Nazis had been arrested and imprisoned, the two parties supporting the new regime barely got a parliamentary majority. The National Socialists received 43.9 percent of the votes and their coalition partners, the German Nationalists, 8.0 percent.

The three parties committed to the republic won the backing of about a third of the electorate. The Social Democrats got 18.3 percent, the Centrists 13.9, and the hapless Democrats 0.9, for a combined total of 33.1 percent. If to this is added the 12.3 percent obtained by the Communist Party, which opposed Weimar but also National Socialism, the proportion of voters rejecting the Third Reich comes to 45.4 percent. Clearly, the Hitler dictatorship was at first favored by only a small majority of the German people.[18]

Among the members of the resistance, the proportion of those supporting the new order appears to have been much higher. Admittedly, most of them sympathized with the German Nationalists rather than the National Socialists. They assumed that old-school conservatives would formulate and execute state policy, while the Nazis organized parades, held speeches, and enthralled the masses. Only a few sensed the danger in a Hitler dictatorship. Here and there some eccentric right-winger would warn them against an alliance with the Nazis. Ewald von Kleist-Schmenzin, for example, left the German National People's Party because of its participation in the Hitler cabinet. He maintained that it had thereby abandoned the ideal of a strong conservative government independent of political factions and legislative majorities. "I did not fight against the parliamentary system and for an authoritarian state leadership," according to his self-vindication, "in order to disguise the replacement of a party government of the left with an opposing party government. As a conservative, [I fought] rather [to establish] a truly independent government resolutely committed, of course, to the fatherland." He rejected the new order because it seemed to him too much like the old.[19]

On the opposite fringe of the resistance were a few steadfast defenders of the republic, most of them active in Weimar politics, men like Wilhelm Leuschner, Carlo Mierendorff, Adolf Reichwein, and Theodor Haubach. Should Julius Leber and Jakob Kaiser be included in this group? Perhaps. And then there was always Bonhoeffer, politically unaffiliated but courageous and unflinching in his opposition to National Socialism. Six months before the establishment of the Third Reich, he stated publicly that Hitler's movement "abuses democratic opportunities and seeks the establishment of a dictatorship." Its victory would have "unforeseeable consequences" not only for Germany but for "the development of the whole world." He denounced the forces that "mislead countries into a false nationalism," that "promote militarism," and that "threaten the world with an unrest out of which a war could rise." Bonhoeffer had recognized where a Nazi regime was likely to lead.[20]

Most members of the resistance were not as perceptive, however. They entered into an alliance with National Socialism, convinced that the results would benefit them as well as their nation. They thought they could use Hitler to regain political stability and military primacy for Germany. How could they have foreseen that it would be the other way around, that Hitler would first use them, then discard them, and finally destroy them?

6

The Military and the Third Reich

Popular support for the new order in Germany gained strength steadily throughout the first two or three years following its establishment, the years of reconstruction and consolidation. What had started out as a cautious acceptance of the political experiment in dictatorial rule turned into a widespread conviction that the Nazi regime was bringing about a great political and military revival. The weaknesses of the Weimar Republic began to seem all the more glaring in light of the achievements of the Third Reich. There appeared to be a new sense of purpose and direction in the nation, a new feeling of hopefulness and confidence. Even many of those who had at first warned that the victory of National Socialism would mean civil strife and international conflict were now wondering whether they might not have been mistaken. Perhaps Hitler was more than a wild-eyed demagogue. Perhaps the regime knew what it was doing after all. The new dictatorship looked so much more effective than the old fumbling democracy had been.

There were, to begin with, the impressive gains by the Third Reich in foreign affairs. The government succeeded by 1936 in removing all of the restrictions imposed on Germany by the peace settlement. Hitler had sensed that the economic depression made the continued maintenance of the Versailles system impossible. The victor states, especially France, which had for more than a decade insisted on strict enforcement of the terms of the treaty, found themselves forced to acquiesce in its piecemeal dismantlement. The spread of social discontent at home made them reluctant to risk armed conflict abroad. Faced by mounting unemployment and growing discontent, they hesitated to make a bad situation worse by trying to collect German reparations or to enforce German disarmament through military might. They felt compelled instead to make concessions to the Third Reich that they had stubbornly refused to grant to the Weimar Republic.

As a result, the Versailles system rapidly disintegrated. Even before Hitler came to power, the reparations question, which had been a source of so much friction between France and Germany during the 1920s, was settled once and for all at the Lausanne Conference of June–July 1932 with the cancellation of all future payments. In October 1933 the Nazi government announced its withdrawal from the League of Nations, thereby formally expressing its rejection of Weimar's policy of fulfillment. In January 1935 the Saar region voted in a plebiscite for reunion with Germany, in accordance with the terms of the peace treaty but in defiance of its intent and spirit. Two months later the Third Reich officially denounced the disarmament provisions of Versailles, reintroducing conscription and increasing the army to thirty-six divisions. And a year after that, with the remilitarization of the Rhineland in March 1936, came the final step in the reassertion of Germany's military sovereignty. The entire structure of international relations established after the war was in shambles.

The Third Reich introduced equally profound changes in domestic policy. The Hitler dictatorship swiftly dismantled the democratic political system established under the republican regime. There was in fact a certain parallelism between the objectives pursued by the new order at home and abroad. In both spheres the Nazi government sought to remove the limitations imposed on the authority of the state. In both it employed the threat or the use of force to obtain compliance. And in both it exploited the fear of economic instability and social unrest to attain its political ends. Thereby it succeeded with remarkable rapidity in completely transforming popular attitudes and expectations regarding domestic as well as foreign affairs.

The establishment of the Third Reich, in other words, initiated a drastic reconstruction of the system of civic authority in Germany. Within six months all the parties except the National Socialists were dissolved, some by persuasion, others by coercion, and still others by a combination of the two. The independent labor unions, whether Socialist, liberal, or Catholic, were replaced by the Labor Front controlled by the government. The civil service was purged of members believed to be opposed to the new order. The judiciary lost most of its independence, while the police received vastly expanded power. Arbitrary arrest and imprisonment became the accepted method for dealing with political dissidents. Finally, the Hitler regime vigorously promoted anti-Semitism, first informally, through economic boycotts, social ostracism, and a miscellany of petty persecutions, and then formally, through the Nuremberg Laws of September 15, 1935, which deprived all Jews of the rights of citizenship. The Third Reich accomplished nothing less than a revolution in the form of government and the structure of power.

Most Germans accepted the new order willingly, many of them even enthusiastically. Some had always entertained doubts about the efficacy of popular democracy. How could the new government bring about a revival of the nation, they reasoned, without rejecting the values and beliefs of Weimar? Others, who may at first have been troubled by the repressive methods employed by National Socialism, gradually overcame their scruples. Maybe there was no other way. Maybe pitiless measures were required for survival in a pitiless world. Public opinion, in short, became progressively more favorable to the new regime during the period of its establishment and consolidation.

What accounted for the growing acceptance of the Third Reich even more than the repudiation of Versailles was the alleviation of the economic crisis. For the victory of National Socialism coincided with the rapid emergence of Germany from the great depression. The reasons for this recovery are still in dispute, however. The economy may have been headed for an upturn in 1933 regardless of the form of government. Or the program of public works introduced by the Hitler government may have provided the necessary stimulus for an industrial revival. Perhaps secret rearmament during the early years of the Nazi regime helped encourage investment and employment. The combination of all these factors could in fact have been the decisive element. In any case, the Third Reich was able to claim credit for leading the nation out of economic misery and social chaos. This claim in turn helped convince millions of Germans that the new order, though perhaps high-handed and dictatorial, had saved them from privation, despair, and ruinous class war.

The attitude of the officer corps toward the Third Reich paralleled that of the population at large. If anything, it was more favorable. For the armed forces had never become reconciled to the postwar republican regime. They had always felt repelled by its antimilitaristic rhetoric, its espousal of social egalitarianism, and its rejection of the traditions and loyalties of the old monarchical order. Above all, they were opposed to the policy of fulfillment, to the government's passive acceptance of the military restrictions imposed by Versailles. What they wanted was a program of rearmament, whether overt or covert, which would regain for the nation full military equality with the other great powers. That was essentially why they remained inwardly hostile to Weimar; that was why they welcomed the victory of National Socialism. They saw in the new order an opportunity to end the humiliating restrictions imposed on the German army by the victors in the world war.

Hitler did not disappoint them. His remilitarization program was exactly what the armed forces had been looking for. Not only would the shameful subordination of Germany come to an end, but they would have new opportunities for professional advancement, for technical improvement, and for social recognition. Is it any wonder that the professional soldiers supported the Third Reich with such conviction? In an affidavit submitted to the International Military Tribunal in the fall of 1945, Field Marshal Werner von Blomberg, who had served as minister of war in the Hitler cabinet, summarized the attitude of the army leaders toward the Nazi regime during its period of consolidation. "Before 1938–1939 the German generals did not oppose Hitler. No reason existed for opposing Hitler, since he produced the successes they wanted." It was as simple as that.[1]

In his memoirs published more than a decade later, Erich von Manstein, one of the chief wartime commanders of the German troops on the Russian front, confirmed this characterization of the attitude of the senior military officers. "We must consider above all the fact of the extraordinary successes that Hitler's policy gained for the Reich before and during the year 1938," he wrote in defense of the armed forces. "Who could have been more impressed by them than the German army, the exponent of the national (not National Socialist) consciousness, the clamp that had held the Reich together in the time of its impotence, and the shield of the nation, although it became strong enough to protect the Reich only under Hitler." Its misjudgment, Manstein seemed to suggest, was not only understandable but excusable.[2]

The generals were not the only members of the armed forces to support the Third Reich. The junior officers showed at least equal enthusiasm. For them the new order meant an end to living on a lieutenant's meager pay for five, six, seven, or ten years. It meant an end to the dull routine of garrison duty and ceremonial parade. They could now see before them exciting new challenges and opportunities.

According to Bernhard Watzdorf, at that time one of the promising young members of the officer corps, Hitler's early diplomatic and military triumphs quickly put an end to "all our reservations and hesitations." He and the others became loyal followers of the new regime. "The introduction of general conscription on March 16, 1935, by which the prospects of a successful career assumed for us the appearance of reality, played a special role. With the introduction of conscription, the most important military restrictions of the Versailles Treaty were removed without any intervention by the powers responsible for the Versailles Treaty against this obvious violation of the treaty." What the old republican government had vainly tried to accomplish by years of pleading and negotiating, the new dictatorial regime achieved with one bold stroke. This diplomatic revolution in Europe effected by National Socialism inevitably made a deep impression on the armed forces of Germany.[3]

They were less enthusiastic about some of the domestic policies of the Third Reich. Occasionally members of the officer corps would even express private doubts and reservations. Still, those policies did not touch them directly. Why then, they asked themselves, should they be concerned about the violation of civil rights, the suppression of representative government, the growth of arbitrary authority, or the persecution of the Jews? After all, that was really none of their business.

"The soldier still lived until 1938 on an island, so to speak, little affected [by domestic affairs]," explained Manstein after World War II. "As for the fundamental questions of the loss of the political freedoms and of the freedom of expression of opinion, they had minor significance for the army." The armed forces, he emphasized, had always been prohibited from engaging in political activity. "In the years of the Weimar Republic . . . it was precisely the democratic parties [which] watched closely to ensure that no soldier, especially no officer, allowed himself to express political criticism in public. Hence the loss of political freedom could hardly be felt in the world of the army." Besides, "all soldiers were completely absorbed in the tasks imposed by the rapid expansion of the army and were burdened with its problems." How could anyone then have expected them to pay much attention to nonmilitary affairs?[4]

The only aspect of the domestic program of the Third Reich that did arouse serious concern in the armed forces was the one with a direct bearing on military policy. On the left wing of National Socialism stood a large group of ideological militants committed to a drastic social and economic reconstruction of Germany. Populist and egalitarian in outlook, they hoped to tear down the traditional hierarchical structure of society. The army in particular seemed to these Nazi radicals to embody the old order, exclusive and elitist in composition, monarchical and aristocratic in sympathy, lukewarm or even condescending toward the ideals of the new regime. Not until the armed forces had been completely reorganized could the national revolution initiated by the Third Reich be successfully completed.

In fact, the instrument of that reorganization already existed. The SA, the paramilitary defense organization of the National Socialist Party, seemed to the left wing to be everything the regular army was not. Indifferent to class origin or social background, rejecting distinctions of rank and status, committed to the principles of the Third Reich, it constituted a true people's army, plebeian in structure and radical in sympathy. The amalgamation of the SA with the regular armed forces, in which the former was bound to predominate by the sheer weight of numbers, would ensure the loyalty of the military establishment to the Nazi movement.

This proposal alarmed the members of the officer corps. They feared the loss of the autonomy of the army, of its immunity to party politics, of its protection against partisan pressures. But they also hoped that the government would shield them from the dogmatists within National Socialism. They perceived two Hitlers contending for the leadership of Germany, a good Hitler and a bad Hitler, one moderate, pragmatic, and realistic, the other doctrinaire, zealous, and fanatical. One was being advised by reasonable, traditional conservatives like Franz von Papen and Hjalmar Schacht. The other was being incited by wild radicals like Ernst Röhm of the SA and Heinrich Himmler of the SS. The crucial question was which of the two Hitlers would prevail.

Ludwig Beck exemplified the view of many army officers concerning the leadership of the Third Reich. Soon after the victory of National Socialism he expressed to a friend of his, General Wilhelm Adam, the hope that "the propagandist and demagogue Hitler," who had shown so much skill in rising to power, would gradually become a "real statesman." He saw in the new chancellor's entourage a number of "dangerous men," but he felt that the cabinet was essentially sound, especially Minister of War Blomberg and Foreign Minister Konstantin von Neurath, an experienced professional diplomat. In addition, President Hindenburg remained the embodiment of sober, sensible conservatism. Statesmen such as these would no doubt be able to resist the radicals in the Nazi Party and keep the government on the right course.[5]

The good Hitler did not disappoint the officer corps; he prevailed over the bad one. He decided to maintain his alliance with the middle-of-the-road conservatives by sacrificing the Nazi radicals. The "blood purge" of June 30, 1934, crushed the left wing of National Socialism in a wave of summary executions that included not only many party dissidents like Röhm and Gregor Strasser but also two prominent army generals, Kurt von Schleicher and Kurt von Bredow, who were suspected of intriguing against the government.

This move eliminated the last obstacle to a wholehearted collaboration between the armed forces and the Third Reich. The remaining doubts of the officer corps regarding the new order vanished. As long as the regime was willing to respect the autonomy of the army, the army was willing to support the program of the regime. It was a mutually advantageous arrangement. Three weeks after the blood purge the French military attaché reported to Paris that an unnamed source in the German war ministry, someone who was himself not in sympathy with National Socialism, had told him and several of his colleagues that a year before about 60 percent of the army had been favorable to the Nazi regime. By the spring of 1934 the proportion had fallen to only 25 percent as a result of uncertainty regarding the government's plans for the SA. "Today it is 95 percent." The civilian and the military leadership of Germany had entered into a close partnership.[6]

That partnership was officially established early in August when, after the death of Hindenburg, the functions of the presidency and of the chancellorship were combined in the office of the Führer. A day later Hitler personally received the oath of allegiance from the leaders of the armed forces, while throughout the country the enlisted men took a similar oath before their barracks in the presence of their officers. On August 19 this consolidation of power was approved in a general plebiscite by a majority of 88 percent. The political structure of the Third Reich was finally complete.

Throughout this period the members of the officer corps who were later to join the resistance against Hitler seemed as favorable to the new order as the ones who did not. There is no evidence that they were more critical of the goals pursued by the Nazi regime or of the methods employed to reach those goals. Like the others, they were impressed by the government's success in ending the restrictions imposed by Versailles. At last Germany would be able to regain military parity with the victor powers. And as for the harsh repression directed by National Socialism against its domestic opponents, that appeared to them to be an unpleasant but inescapable necessity. How else could the nation emerge from the weakness and confusion created by Weimar? In short, no distinction can be detected between the political attitudes of the future military resisters and those of the professional soldiers in general.

Again, Beck's views were typical. Sympathetic toward National Socialism throughout the last years of the republic, he was rewarded by the new order in October 1933 with the position of chief of the general staff. Though a little uneasy at first about the policies adopted by the Nazi regime, he became its faithful supporter following the blood purge. There could be no doubt now that Hitler had matured into a practical, responsible statesman. His objectives were clearly those long sought by all loyal and patriotic Germans. He deserved full support.

Speaking on the radio a year later in celebration of the seventieth birthday of General Erich Ludendorff, the brilliant if erratic strategist of World War I, Beck used the occasion to sing the praises of the Führer. "The German nation . . . under Adolf Hitler's strong leadership has found its way back to the heroic spirit and to respect for its own history." To the head of the Third Reich this expression of loyalty from the military establishment must have sounded pleasing.

In private comments Beck was less effusive, but he generally supported the government's policy, especially in foreign and military affairs. His brief, handwritten notes on the back of an army report of April 11, 1935, dealing with Germany's international position provide a valuable insight into his thinking. They show him to have favored the diplomatic goals pursued by the Third Reich, although he hoped to reach them without antagonizing France and England. "Rejection of an international court of justice" and "not to go too far with concessions" appear among his comments, but he also mentioned "reasonable proposals" and a "reasonable proposal for disarmament." He jotted down somewhat cryptically that the "cause of the general refusal [is] only the brutality of the policy," citing under this heading Germany's withdrawal from the League of Nations, the predominance of domestic over foreign affairs, the unsuccessful coup of the Austrian Nazis on July 25, 1934, which resulted in the death of Chancellor Engelbert Dollfuss, and the reintroduction of conscription on March 16, 1935. Among his concerns, moreover, were the territorial losses suffered under Versailles, specifically, "the case of the Saar," "Poland," and "Memel." Finally, he referred without comment to the "policy of violence and breach of faith."

While Beck had reservations about the tactics employed to achieve the regime's diplomatic objectives, he did not consider them irremediable. They could be corrected with only a little more discretion, a little more restraint. He warned in his notes that "if we [do not] make clear to them that nothing [bad] will happen, there will be no tranquillity." For that reason it was important that "for 2–3 years no extra ventures [should be undertaken], no revolutionary foreign policy." Toward the end, he summarized his view of Hitler's statecraft. "What is so bad is not what we are doing but how we are doing it." This concluding comment provides the key to his attitude toward the policies of the Third Reich. While the means it employed appeared to him sometimes crude and reckless, the ends it seemed to seek were essentially legitimate and justifiable. Beck's doubts about the methods of the Nazi regime in no way weakened his faith in its ultimate objectives. He remained at heart a loyal supporter of the new order.[7]

Canaris was entirely free from the misgivings that sometimes troubled Beck. He considered the Third Reich right in everything it did, in its foreign and in its domestic policies, in its methods and in its objectives, in its ideals and in its actions. Nothing could shake his faith, not the imprisonment of republican leaders nor the execution of Nazi dissidents nor the persecution of Jews. There were good reasons for whatever the government did. His superior officer, Rear Admiral Max Bastian, commented in November 1934 on Canaris's unswerving loyalty. "I must emphasize the tireless efforts of Captain Canaris . . . to familiarize his crew, through lectures delivered in person, with the wealth of ideas of the national movement and with the principles of the political structure of the new Reich. . . . [He] has served as a model in this regard."

The Hitler regime knew how to reward such devotion. On January 1, 1935, Canaris became head of the counterintelligence department of the armed forces. Here he long remained a faithful servant of the Nazi state, politically and ideologically as well as militarily. One of his colleagues in those years, Lieutenant Colonel Erich Pruck, later referred discreetly to his early unquestioning loyalty to the Third Reich. "In the case of Canaris the development from an obedient servant of the state to a supporter of the opposition occurred only gradually."

Werner Best, who had also known Canaris before the war, put it more bluntly. "Canaris never championed a political idea directed against the authoritarian state," he wrote in 1949. "He would at any time have assumed extensive functions of power in such a state—and [before the war] even under Hitler—in order to exercise them as he thought right." It would be a mistake, Best insisted, to view Canaris as someone who "knew everything ahead of time," who had been "always opposed" to National Socialism or had stood at the center of "the spider's web of the great conspiracy" against the Third Reich. This view was nothing more than a fiction of "foreign sensationalistic literature." The truth was less complicated. "A gifted officer conscious of his duty, an old nationalist, was called to an important position [and] did the best he could in fulfilling his task." All he had wanted was to serve his country.[8]

But that could be said about the other military resisters as well. All of them believed that in serving Hitler they were serving Germany, that in defending the Third Reich they were defending their nation and their people. They could not see, because they did not really want to see, the dark underside of National Socialism, its cruelty and oppressiveness, its rapacity and heartlessness, its dehumanizing worship of brute force. They knew only that the Nazi regime was making possible the political and military revival of their country, and for them that was enough.

Tresckow, for example, had become a sympathizer of National Socialism long before the victory of the Third Reich. Weimar had come to symbolize for him all the disastrous consequences of the military defeat of Germany: corruption and weakness, humiliation and demoralization, materialism and selfishness. Hitler represented an opportunity for the country's revival; his "national uprising," Tresckow felt confident, would follow the path of "justice and honor." The brutalities accompanying the establishment of the Nazi regime, the beatings, arrests, and sometimes murders of the opponents of the new order, failed to shake his faith. To him those were the unfortunate but unavoidable excesses that at first characterize every revolutionary reconstruction of society. They were the price of a political and military revival. Hans Bernd Gisevius, one of the few members of the resistance to survive the war, remembered Tresckow as "a Pomeranian landowner, a Prussian through and through, and an outstanding general staff officer," who perceived in the Third Reich the source of Germany's regeneration, reestablishing soldierly discipline, regaining military independence, and repudiating the unjust peace settlement. Did not achievements of such magnitude outweigh the occasional brutalities of the Nazi movement?[9]

Hans Oster had an essentially similar view of the Nazi regime. Testifying shortly after his arrest for involvement in the plot against Hitler, he spoke of the terrible shock suffered by the officer corps as a result of the defeat of 1918, of the long years of weakness, stagnation, discouragement, and hopelessness under the republic, and of the silent longing of the professional soldier for a more forceful form of government. And then came the Third Reich, boldly proclaiming the beginning of a great national renewal. To the armed forces it was a "deliverance." He and the others welcomed the reestablishment of "a strong national policy, rearmament, and the introduction of conscription." Here was that "return to earlier traditions" for which they had vainly hoped during Weimar. No wonder they supported the program of the Hitler dictatorship "with all [our] heart."[10]

The younger officers in particular were sympathetic to the new regime, not only for ideological reasons but out of practical considerations. They would emerge at last from that genteel impoverishment to which they had long been condemned; they would finally find free scope for their talents and ambitions. Stieff, who had been a second lieutenant for five years and a first lieutenant for seven, made it to captain a year after Hitler became chancellor. The reintroduction of conscription on March 16, 1935, moreover, meant that still greater opportunities would open to the members of the officer corps. It was a striking contrast to Weimar.

"Captain Stieff was on duty at the entrance to the State Opera [in Berlin]," Watzdorf recalled afterward, "at the same time when the introduction of conscription was proclaimed at an official ceremony. After the conclusion of the celebration he dispelled our misgivings about a [possible] intervention by the victor powers in the First World War, and told us joyfully that Blomberg had welcomed Hitler in front of the Opera with the news that it was now clear that France did not propose to take any military measures against Germany. Stieff considered this matter a victorious battle for us as well." The magnitude of the diplomatic success of National Socialism seemed to the young army officer to outweigh by far its occasional lapses and excesses.[11]

The remilitarization program convinced even Erwin Rommel, the most popular German troop commander in World War II, the best-known soldier recruited by the resistance, that the new order was unquestionably superior to the timid, ineffectual Weimar regime. Though at first cool toward the Third Reich, he gradually began to overcome his doubts and scruples. But what finally made a believer out of him was the reintroduction of general conscription in the spring of 1935. That proved to him conclusively the efficacy of National Socialism.

According to Hans Speidel, an old comrade-in-arms of Rommel's who had served as his chief of staff on the western front, he started speaking of Hitler as the "unifier of the nation" responsible for ending the divisiveness of the party system, and as Germany's "liberator from the shameful provisions of the Versailles Treaty." More than that, he praised the Führer's social program, describing him with admiration as "the man who eliminated unemployment." He even expressed confidence in the "peaceful goals and ideals" of the Nazi regime, convinced of Hitler's intention to follow a middle-of-the-road policy. He regarded the rearmament program of the Third Reich as clear, tangible evidence of the successful reassertion of Germany's sovereignty. There was no reason, however, why France and England should feel threatened by it. On the contrary, it seemed to Rommel that they would probably welcome German remilitarization as "a bulwark against Bolshevism." He became persuaded that National Socialism, far from being a danger to the stability of Europe, would prove to be its protector and defender.[12]

Nevertheless, the soldiers in the resistance did not support unquestioningly everything the Third Reich sought and did. Some of them had doubts about one or another of its policies, about measures adopted against political dissidents, for instance, or laws regulating religious institutions, directives concerning the armed forces, or disabilities imposed on members of the Jewish community. Sometimes they would grumble and complain, privately as a rule, but even openly on occasion. Yet their dissatisfaction was never directed against the Nazi system as such; they criticized only this or that action, this or that decision. They did see dangerous elements within National Socialism—ideologues, zealots, extremists, and fanatics—elements that had to be opposed. But National Socialism as a faith and as an ideology seemed to them fundamentally sound. They hoped that it could eventually be purged of its superficial imperfections, but in the meantime its essential truths were not to be ignored or repudiated. In other words, while the military resisters criticized the Third Reich now and then, they always did so within the framework of its own basic beliefs and purposes. They refused to acknowledge that the shortcomings they found in the regime were not incidental but inherent.

The blood purge of June 30, 1934, provides a good illustration of their attitude. Oster was one of the few army officers who condemned, at least in private, the lawless, arbitrary execution of those suspected of disagreeing with Hitler's policies. What shocked him most, however, was not the illegal or extralegal nature of the operation, and certainly not the suppression of the SA, but rather the army's failure to protest against the murder of two of its general officers. He felt that such passive acquiescence would weaken the political influence of the armed forces to the advantage of the National Socialist Party and the SS. As a matter of fact, no sooner was the blood purge over than the SS began to form an armed force of its own designed to conduct military operations in competition with the regular army. What was the point of eliminating the brownshirts, Oster wondered, only to have them replaced by the black uniforms of the Nazi elite corps?[13]

Rommel displayed a similar attitude. He too was shocked by the events of June 30, 1934. What motivated him was not sympathy for the SA, although there were rumors that he himself had once been a storm trooper. The story was certainly untrue; it may have originated in his service as liaison officer with a government program to provide young boys with premilitary training. But there can be no doubt that he was outraged by the blood purge, especially by the murder of Schleicher and Bredow. Two members of the armed forces had been killed in cold blood, and yet the perpetrators had never been tried and punished. They had not even been arrested. That was simply scandalous. "Now would be the time," Rommel exploded to a friend, "to get rid of Hitler and his entire gang."[14]

Still, criticism of the Nazi regime by the future army resisters rarely went beyond muttering and grumbling. They all managed sooner or later to suppress their misgivings in view of its vigorous defense of the national interest and its rapid expansion of the armed forces. It was hard to fight success. Shortly after the blood purge Oster took the oath of allegiance to Hitler and accepted an appointment to military counterintelligence, where he worked diligently and conscientiously under the direction of a loyal servant of the Third Reich, Admiral Canaris. Similarly, Rommel's hostility turned into admiration as a result of the reintroduction of conscription. Less than a year after denouncing "Hitler and his entire gang," he was singing the praises of the "unifier of the nation." As for most army officers, resisters and nonresisters alike, they felt nothing but relief at the elimination of the SA. Claus von Stauffenberg, for example, his wife recalled after the war, compared it to the bursting of a festering boil as a result of which healthy conditions could finally be restored. He saw in the blood purge only the removal of a powerful and dangerous rival.[15]

That same subordination of moral scruples to national and professional interests is discernible in the attitude of the soldiers in the resistance toward the government's racial program. Very few of them were out-and-out anti-Semites. They generally regarded Jews with disdain rather than hatred. Some of them even felt at heart that the treatment of "non-Aryans" by the Third Reich was not altogether fair or honorable. Yet they were unwilling to say so openly. Why risk the career of a lifetime for the sake of a small, alien minority? Why oppose a regime that was doing so much good for the fatherland to uphold some remote and abstract principle of toleration? It was easier to turn away, to suggest that charges of racial persecution were greatly exaggerated, or to argue that the welfare of the many was more important than the security of the few.

Carl-Heinrich von Stülpnagel, the German military governor in France during the war who became a leading participant in the plot to overthrow Hitler, expressed dissatisfaction a decade earlier with at least some aspects of official racism. He complained to his family, for instance, according to his son's recollection, about the renaming of the street on which they lived in Berlin from Lindenplatz to Theodor-Fritsch-Platz in honor of an anti-Semitic publicist who had been an early convert to National Socialism. "Father regarded with the greatest disapproval the monument to Theodor Fritsch, which had been recently erected there." What angered him most was that a winged dragon with unmistakably Jewish features had been engraved on the base of the monument. That seemed to him in poor taste. Yet Stülpnagel's opposition remained confined to complaints about the changing of a street name and the displaying of a tasteless piece of sculpture. He could not bring himself to break with a regime whose broad political objectives he supported, a regime, moreover, that recognized and rewarded his professional talents with a promotion from colonel to brigadier general in 1935 and to major general in 1937. It would take more than discrimination against "non-Aryans" to make a resister out of him.[16]

Stieff's situation was similar. He too had some misgivings at first about the anti-Semitic doctrines of National Socialism. Watzdorf remembered that at the time Hitler became chancellor, Stieff opposed his "measures against the church" and his "persecutions of Jews." Yet ten years later, after his arrest for participating in the attempt to overthrow the Third Reich, he testified that, though apolitical throughout the Weimar years, he had "embraced National Socialism unreservedly at the time of [its] seizure of power." The sense of participating in a great national revival had transformed him into a supporter of the new order.

This testimony should not be dismissed as the desperate effort of a doomed prisoner to escape the hangman. In a letter to his wife written much earlier, immediately after Hindenburg's death, Stieff overflowed with enthusiasm for the Third Reich:

> But *le roi est mort, vive le roi!* We soldiers must not remain standing still. And as we become bound by a new oath to our new commander in chief, we can best express our thanks to our great model [Hindenburg] by fulfilling our duty toward our new leader, as we fulfilled it toward Hindenburg, firmly trusting in God and believing in the future of our fatherland. And the more closely we are committed to the Führer, the more he will depend on us for the success of further developments. I am firmly convinced of this in view of the Führer's pure character, and that gives me strength again to look to the future with new hope in spite of all the blows of fate.

That Stieff would a decade later try to assassinate the Führer would have seemed in the summer of 1934 incredible.[17]

A few of the military resisters even embraced the government's anti-Semitic policy, whether out of expediency or conviction or a little of each. Canaris, convinced of the existence of a serious "Jewish problem," proposed in 1935–36 a solution that bore some resemblance to the one actually adopted by the Nazi regime during the war. Since it was out of the question for "Aryans" and "non-Aryans" to coexist harmoniously, a carefully planned, equitable separation of the two "races" was really the best way out. Believing that England and France would someday return to

Germany the colonies they had "stolen" at Versailles, he suggested that one of these be set aside for the resettlement of the German Jews. They might even establish there a state of their own. Those who chose to remain in Germany temporarily should be identified as the citizens of such an independent Jewish state by wearing a Star of David. This sign would not only alert Germans to the presence of Jews but might even protect the Jews themselves against anti-Semitic fanatics. Was that not reasonable?[18]

Canaris's insensitivity toward the victims of Nazi racism was common among the members of the officer corps. In this regard there was again little difference between those who became members of the resistance and those who did not. Indeed, throughout the early years of the Third Reich, the armed forces supported not only the ends but the means of the new order. They did not view themselves as the auxiliaries or subordinates of National Socialism. They were its allies, its partners. The government and the army were fighting for the same great cause: to break the shackles of Versailles, to bring about the military revival of the fatherland, to restore a sense of patriotic duty, and to reawaken a feeling of national pride. Such were the goals the civilian and the military authorities were jointly trying to attain.

At times the struggle admittedly demanded suffering and sacrifice. On occasion it might even lead to excess and injustice. But that was inescapable in a period of fundamental political and ideological reconstruction. Individual hardship was the cost of collective welfare. The military resisters recognized the regime's brutal treatment of its adversaries, of republicans, Marxists, Jews, and dissenting Nazis. But they preferred to look the other way; they told themselves that this was the price to be paid for a great national rebirth in which they were destined to play a glorious part. As Canaris's friend Otto Wagner put it following the collapse of the Third Reich, "after all, at first almost all of us went along."[19]

This photograph of Dietrich Bonhoeffer was taken in London in July 1939, during his return trip from the United States to Germany. (Bilderdienst Süddeutscher Verlag)

Martin Niemöller as he appeared early in 1938 at the time of his trial for opposing the religious policies of National Socialism. (UPI/Corbis-Bettmann)

7

The Bureaucracy and the Third Reich

The members of the officer corps did not regard their collaboration with the Hitler government as an endorsement of all the regime's methods, policies, and principles. They believed rather that they could support the military and diplomatic objectives of National Socialism without necessarily supporting its political and social doctrines. After all, they had been able to perform their professional duties under Weimar without compromising their ostensible neutrality on questions of public policy. Why then should they not be able to maintain that same neutrality under the Third Reich? Throughout the early years of the new order the armed forces remained firmly convinced that they could retain their autonomy, that their approval of the Nazi system did not have to extend beyond its remilitarization program, and that the government and the army would always remain partners in the defense of the national interest.

The members of the civil service, by contrast, found it difficult to maintain the appearance of neutrality. They were visibly and directly involved in the day-to-day execution of the policies of the Third Reich, in the enforcement of political authoritarianism, in the introduction of economic regulation, in the furtherance of social reformism, and in the promotion of racial purification. There was no aspect of public life in which they did not play a central role.

They had admittedly managed to play the same role under the Weimar system without disguising their reservations about many of its principles and objectives. But that had been different. For one thing, National Socialism was far less tolerant of dissent, even private dissent, than the old republican regime had been. Moreover, National Socialism appeared so much more efficient, purposeful, energetic, and dedicated than popular democracy. Finally, to many German bureaucrats in the early 1930s Hitler seemed to be the only defense left against the danger of social chaos arising out of the depression. He had his shortcomings, no doubt. He could sound dogmatic and intemperate; he could rant and rave, swagger and bully. Still, he was head and shoulders above those timid, drab political hacks who had been in power during the preceding fifteen years—Friedrich Ebert, Philipp Scheidemann, Josef Wirth, Hermann Müller, or Heinrich Brüning. Like it or not, he was the nation's last hope.

Even more important, the Third Reich appeared to most civil servants to embody many positive qualities that had been conspicuously lacking in the republican regime. National Socialism preached patriotism and the subordination of private interest to collective welfare. It sought to end the Versailles system and reawaken a sense of pride and confidence in the German people. It rejected materialism and hedonism, personal selfishness and class egoism. It spoke of the need of society for ideals and convictions, for principles and beliefs. Did not such views deserve support by all Germans who loved their country? And who could support them with greater devotion than the bureaucracy, committed heart and soul to service to the nation? The readiness of so many civil servants to accept the Third Reich, in other words, was based on principle as well as expediency.

In fact, the bureaucracy and the military showed strikingly similar attitudes toward the new order. Both regarded themselves not as auxiliaries or subordinates of National Socialism but as its partners, its allies in the struggle for Germany's revival. Both clung to the view that a distinction could continue to be made between state and party, administration and government. By serving the one they were not necessarily endorsing the other. Hence their efforts in support of the nation should not be construed as an expression of unqualified support for the regime.

The civil service, like the armed forces, thus failed to recognize the revolutionary implications of the new totalitarian system in Germany. Its members went on believing, basically because they wanted to believe, that the Third Reich, like the Weimar Republic or the German Empire, was only a transient form of government adopted by an enduring national community. In obeying the first, they were promoting the last. If the Nazi regime ever ceased to express the fundamental needs and interests of the nation, it could be and undoubtedly would be replaced by some other system of authority better suited to changing times and circumstances. The bureaucracy would then serve that new authority with the same diligence and loyalty with which it had served the old.

This distinction between government and nation, this failure or rather unwillingness to recognize that the Third Reich was undermining the autonomy of the civil service, encouraged its members to work for the new order despite their occasional doubts or misgivings. The rewards that National Socialism bestowed on those who served it faithfully—the promotions, raises, encomiums, and distinctions—helped promote their compliance. As in the case of the professional soldiers, there was little difference between those bureaucrats who later turned against the regime and those who did not. At first they all seemed equally enthusiastic regarding the establishment of dictatorial rule in Germany.

Admittedly, Goerdeler declined Hitler's invitation in the fall of 1933 to join the National Socialist Party, but he hastened to assure Rudolf Hess that his refusal did not imply any objection in principle to the Nazi ideology. A few months later, moreover, he accepted an appointment as price commissioner of the Third Reich, and soon thereafter he was assisting in the drafting of new legislation on local government. Although Popitz, like Goerdeler, chose not to join the Nazi Party, he became in the spring of 1933 Prussian minister of finance under Hermann Göring. Hassell, who had been promoted shortly before Hitler came to power from the German legation in Belgrade to the embassy in Rome, sought to make his position more secure by entering the party in 1933. This move helped him to hold on to his ambassadorship for six years, during which he worked hard to reduce friction between Germany and Italy over the Austrian question and to prepare the way for the Rome-Berlin Axis. As for Schulenburg, a party member long before the victory of the Third Reich, he was rewarded with an appointment to the staff of Gauleiter Erich Koch, the "uncrowned king" of East Prussia, and later with the less prestigious but more independent position of county commissioner of Fischhausen near Königsberg.

None of them seemed to fear that by supporting the new order he might be jeopardizing the autonomy of the civil service. None appeared to believe that he was abandoning the principle of nonpartisanship, the doctrine of neutrality on political questions that the bureaucracy had in theory always tried to uphold. Each was convinced that by serving the Nazi regime he was only serving the German nation. What blinded them to the totalitarian nature of the Third Reich was the feeling that their country faced an unprecedented crisis only Hitler and the Third Reich could remedy.

After the failure of the plot to assassinate Hitler, Ralph C. Busser, who before the war had served for ten years in the American consulate in Leipzig, described Goerdeler in a letter of August 5, 1944, addressed to

Secretary of State Cordell Hull as a committed defender of democracy who had opposed the Third Reich from the start:

> Dr. Goerdeler, being a man of remarkable political vision, foresaw that the overthrow of the Republic and the rise of Hitler and his fellow gangsters to supreme power would have tragic consequences for the German people. He often expressed to me and others the fear that Hitler's revival of German militarism, the suppression of political and civil liberties, the chauvinistic propaganda, and the aggressive foreign policy of the Nazi regime, would eventually bring Germany into mortal conflict with the democratic countries.

The tragic outcome of the attempt by the resistance to overthrow the Third Reich helped persuade not only Busser but many other foreign observers that Goerdeler was one of those "good" Germans who had consistently and courageously opposed National Socialism.[1]

Yet an examination of what Goerdeler had to say a decade earlier, during the period of consolidation of the Nazi regime, shows that he too believed that the new order had saved Germany from disunion and weakness. In a memorandum submitted to Hitler in August 1934, he expressed approval of the government's political program. "The elimination of rule by the parties in Germany and its fortunate replacement by the amalgamation of party and state have as their inner logical precondition the concentration of the authority of the party and the authority of the state in the hands of one person." Goerdeler no doubt meant to sound encouraging and supportive to the Führer. He then went on to speak of the "great achievement" of National Socialism in effecting "the end of the party system." He concluded by praising the regime for removing the boundaries between the various German states and regions, thereby creating "a precondition, which has almost never existed in German history, for the forging of a unitary Reich." None of this suggests that Goerdeler had at once foreseen that the overthrow of the Weimar Republic would have "tragic consequences for the German people."

It may be, of course, that Goerdeler was merely trying to flatter Hitler, that he was hoping to gain the regime's confidence and favor. By praising the new order he may have been seeking to influence its direction. Yet his condemnation of the party system, his advocacy of a concentration of political authority, and his support for the centralization of the administrative system, all appeared in the advice he had given Hindenburg two or three years earlier. There is nothing in his statements, whether public or private, to suggest that he inwardly opposed the announced goals or principles of the Nazi movement.

His only concern seemed to be that the regime might prove too doctrinaire in choosing those entrusted with the execution of its program, too insistent on ideological purity in filling top positions in the bureaucracy. He strongly urged the new government not to spurn the energies and talents of its conservative allies. "It would be truly a pity," his memorandum to Hitler pleaded, "if the soberest judgments, the richest experiences, and the finest characters to be found among the German people were not enlisted now in making use, to the greatest national advantage, of the conditions that have thus been created." In speaking of "the soberest judgments, the richest experiences, and the finest character," Goerdeler was probably thinking of himself and of others like him, traditionalists of the old school who were willing to work with the Third Reich in creating a new and greater Germany.[2]

Popitz was not quite as favorable toward National Socialism, but he too came to believe that it offered the only alternative to political paralysis, economic crisis, and social chaos. At first he spoke somewhat disparagingly about Hitler's supporters, describing them in February 1932 as "great landowners whose property is in difficulty, peasants and handicraftsmen, young people not overly capable of thinking, and worthy widows of government officials." The growing strength of the Nazi Party derived not only from "the economic despair of large groups" of the population but also from "the failure of the other parties . . . regarding the question of the national [interest]." Popitz initially considered Hitler's militant, unquestioning nationalism to be his main source of strength.[3]

A year later, however, in April 1933, three months after the establishment of the Nazi regime, he acknowledged that there was more to it than that. The Third Reich now appeared to him to represent the victory of idealism over materialism, faith over selfishness. He spoke of "the mental attitude of the greatest part of the [German] people," which under Weimar had been "almost exclusively materialistic, rejecting, consciously or through a skeptical outlook, religious or ethical considerations, and while not ignoring the national interest, not embracing it inwardly either or displaying concern for it only outwardly." The state had come to be dominated by "pluralistic" forces "favoring private interests, and lacking any total idea." But all that was changing; a sweeping revolution was taking place.

That revolution had been provoked, according to Popitz, by the attempt of the republican regime to exclude from public affairs the masses of Germans joining "the national movement that was represented more and more by Hitler." Now that he had triumphed, however, his government would no doubt seek "an increase in the power it had seized at the expense of the previously existing rights of freedom of the individual." In other words, the establishment of the Third Reich meant a "fundamental reconstruction of the organization of the state." The only question was "whether the national enthusiasm will lead permanently to a new spiritual attitude among the people, or whether a materialistic outlook will again prevail, misusing the [national] movement for the assertion of special interests and for the provision of security in state positions." On this last point Popitz sounded cautiously optimistic.[4]

All in all, his view of the new regime was sympathetic. Though not wildly enthusiastic, he regarded it as a vast improvement over Weimar. It deserved the support of all Germans. Long afterward, following his arrest for involvement in the plot against Hitler, he understandably exaggerated his approval of the Third Reich. He claimed he had embraced it unquestioningly. "I support the National Socialist state in every respect," he told his interrogators, "and I see in it the historic necessity, in view of the internationalism and Judaization during the period of the [party] system and in view of the unendurable crises of the parliamentary parties, of uniting the German people within their total national boundaries and of governing them in the only way in which they can be governed, given their geographic position." What had impressed him almost as much, he added, was Hitler's vigorous and effective economic policy. "For me as an old Prussian administrative official, the right of the state to direct entrepreneurship was self-evident." Imprisoned, isolated, and frightened, facing imminent execution, Popitz was obviously eager to emphasize his approval, at least in principle, of the doctrines and ideals of National Socialism. Yet there can be little doubt that he had in fact accepted the Hitler regime initially as the only safeguard of the nation against political paralysis and social conflict.[5]

To the older participants in the bureaucratic resistance, to men like Goerdeler and Popitz whose formative experiences had been shaped by the prewar monarchical order, the Third Reich represented essentially an acceptable alternative to Weimar. They would have preferred, however, a national leader less radical, less doctrinaire than Hitler, if not a member of the old imperial dynasty, then at least a loyal supporter of traditional values and loyalties like Hindenburg. But to the younger participants National Socialism was more than a weapon against the hated republic. Deeply affected by the postwar confusion and demoralization of Germany, they often saw in the Third Reich the basis for a great national awakening, for a rebirth of the sense of pride and the willingness to endure struggle and sacrifice. Their acceptance of the new order reflected a profound conviction, a heartfelt yearning. Many of them became ardent, dedicated believers in the Nazi system.

Schulenburg is a good example. For him Weimar represented the betrayal of all those traditions on which the nation's greatness had been founded. Its leaders, the "formal possessors of state authority," had "failed" miserably. They had allowed themselves to be enslaved by "alien international forces," by capitalists, papists, and Jews. The only source of opposition to the spreading political decadence had been the Nazi Party, which came to form "a new core of resistance" against the republican regime. It succeeded in attracting all those who had not yet lost their "faith and will," their "courage to make sacrifices" or their "willingness to perform deeds." It embodied the resolve of the nation "to shape its life in accordance with its own laws and its own character." It became nothing less than "the incarnation of the faith and will of the German people."

Once victorious, however, National Socialism faced new dangers, dangers inherent in success and power. The same temptations that had undermined Weimar would in the future threaten the Third Reich. To Schulenburg it was of crucial importance that the new regime maintain the purity of its motives and principles. He rhapsodized about the lofty moral mission of Hitler's movement, which should never yield to selfishness or greed. "The party must always concentrate on its essential character and its unique task. It is by its nature an eternal movement. It must struggle day after day to keep its idea pure and its faith alive and to infuse its will with new strength." His belief in National Socialism was lyrical and mystical in nature, transcending mere logic or reason, rooted in a transcendent idealism and spirituality.[6]

The older members of the bureaucratic resistance, less susceptible to the high-flown rhetoric of the Third Reich, remained somewhat skeptical of its strutting, posturing, and sloganeering. Yet they too were impressed by the new spirit of resolve and dedication that the Nazi regime seemed to be fostering in Germany. Although approving of Hitler primarily as the only alternative to the inept and corrupt republican system, they were not motivated solely by sober judgment, by the careful weighing of possibilities and choices. They were also responding, sometimes almost in spite of themselves, to the call of the new order for determination and sacrifice, duty and patriotism. Their collaboration with National Socialism derived not only from calculation but also from conviction.

In his memorandum to Hitler in the summer of 1934, for example, Goerdeler, after describing the practical measures needed to attain the government's goals, dwelt on the ideals and principles on which those measures should be based. The "freedom and welfare" of the German people could be achieved only "through power and its application." The means to be employed, however, constituted "an organic whole." It would no longer be enough, he warned, to apply "judgment and skill" piecemeal to the various parts of the program of the Third Reich. What was needed was "an absolutely organic and compatible domestic and foreign policy, which should provide our people with an existence under the best possible conditions, which must be based on experience, [and] which enlists the best available skill and knowledge." Above all, such a policy should combine "the idealism of the National Socialist movement with the hard lessons of a difficult but successful and glorious past." Goerdeler's view of the Third Reich did not fundamentally differ from Schulenburg's.[7]

Even Popitz, the hardheaded economist and sober, experienced government bureaucrat, was surprisingly susceptible to the Nazi mystique of idealism and spirituality. Analyzing in the spring of 1933 the reasons for the Weimar Republic's collapse, he focused first on its structural and organizational weaknesses. It had represented pluralistic forces and special interests. Its constitution had been "formalistic," "disunited," and of course "polycratic." The bureaucracy had ceased to constitute a "community of conviction"; the successive cabinets, constantly bickering, constantly changing, had lacked any "broad idea"; the parliament and the parties had become nothing more than a tool of "forces alien to the state." How could such a shoddily constructed form of government provide the nation with effective leadership?

But then Popitz turned from the constitutional and administrative inadequacies of the republican system to its moral and spiritual shortcomings. He described the unhealthy mental attitude it had fostered, an attitude "almost entirely materialistic," indifferent to religious and ethical teachings. He condemned especially its lack of a sense of national pride and dignity, Weimar's most serious failure and the main cause of its downfall. But now that a more idealistic regime had come to power, Popitz hoped for "a new spiritual attitude among the people." A change in the collective outlook of the nation would surely lead to a different form of leadership "based on a sense of responsibility and knowledge." Otherwise, Germany would relapse into "chaos in state and economy." Popitz saw in National Socialism's fervent idealism its most heartening aspect.[8]

The bureaucratic resisters, unlike their military counterparts, were attracted to the Third Reich chiefly by its domestic program. They perceived Hitler as the country's savior from the disastrous party system and from the terrible danger of Bolshevization. He alone could revive a feeling of collective purpose among the people; he alone could oppose the disruptive forces of liberalism and materialism. But they were by no means indifferent to his call for a diplomatic and military revival. They too felt that the injustices of Versailles must be rectified, that Germany should not remain disarmed in a world bristling with armaments, and that their countrymen ought not to be required to pay reparations for a war for which the other great powers were at least equally responsible. They too hoped that the territorial boundaries established by the peace settlement would someday be revised, freeing the more than a million Germans groaning under foreign oppression. And they too believed that a vigorous foreign policy was essential for domestic stability and progress. In this regard as well there was little apparent difference between them and the leaders of the Third Reich.

Hassell, for example, insisted in 1932, while still stationed in Belgrade, that the rise of National Socialism in Germany did not mean "revenge and things of that sort." It reflected rather the yearning of the German people for "full equality of rights." Was that yearning unjustified or unreasonable? Did it really pose a threat to the stability of Europe? The same hysterical fears had been expressed by the opponents of Germany when Hindenburg was elected president seven years before. Those fears had proved false then and they would prove false now. Hitler was no more a warmonger than Hindenburg.

All his countrymen wanted, Hassell explained, was justice. They did not seek vengeance or hegemony or conquest. Their goal was simply to remove the "incubus of reparations and military inequality," which had been forced on their nation at Versailles. They did not regard "the present situation of Germany in the world [as] any longer tolerable." And who could blame them? The losers were being forced to indemnify the winners for a military conflict for which they had all been equally at fault. The losers remained disarmed, while the winners were continuing to expand their armies and enlarge their arsenals. Was that fair? To Hassell it was clear that only with the end of reparations and demilitarization would the world "grow calm and thereby achieve a sound and prosperous state." Otherwise, distrust and fear would continue to fester in international relations. Hitler was not a cause of diplomatic tension; he was its symptom, its result. Once the economic and military inequities of Versailles had been rectified, Germany would be free to concentrate on domestic reform and reconstruction.[9]

Goerdeler's objections to the peace settlement were more extensive. Born in the eastern border region that had been lost in 1919, he was not content with arguments for an end to reparations and demilitarization. He also sought a major revision in the boundary between Germany and Poland drawn at Versailles. He had no other urgent demands for territorial expansion, no grand schemes for aggrandizement and conquest. His efforts as price commissioner to deal with the consequences of the economic depression had helped convince him of the need for international cooperation. And that in turn curbed his resentment against many of the inequities of the peace treaty. But he never wavered in his commitment to the reacquisition of the lost provinces in the east. That commitment always seemed to him a sacred patriotic duty.

The Polish Corridor in particular, separating East Prussia from the rest of the nation, represented "a thorn in the flesh of German honor." Once it had been removed, Germany might become reconciled to the other frontiers established in 1919. But until that happened, there could be no peace in Europe. If need be, Goerdeler was even prepared to contemplate a "short war" against a diplomatically isolated Poland. Such views were bound to meet with Hitler's satisfaction and approval. Indeed, both men were revisionists; both opposed the Versailles system; both regarded the elimination of the Polish Corridor as a major objective of German diplomacy. And their agreement on the direction of foreign policy helped strengthen their agreement on the direction of domestic policy.[10]

All of the bureaucratic resisters, moreover, moderates and militants alike, deeply resented criticism of the Third Reich by foreigners. They resented it even when they agreed with it. They found it intolerable that outsiders should presume to lecture them on the wickedness of chauvinism or the immorality of dictatorship. How could they know what it was like to be a German, to suffer national oppression and humiliation, to face defeat, revolution, occupation, and extortion? Where had the French or British or American liberals been when Germany was being bullied and exploited? What did they understand about the ruinous policies pursued by Weimar? The Germans might justifiably perhaps argue among themselves about the strengths and weaknesses of the Third Reich. But for foreigners to assume a tone of moral superiority was arrogant and infuriating. The national pride of the members of the bureaucratic resistance rebelled against what they viewed as alien presumptuousness.

Even Adam von Trott zu Solz, the young lawyer and former Rhodes scholar who paid with his life for opposing Hitler, shared at first the feeling that outsiders could not really grasp what was happening in Germany and should not therefore pass judgment. A man of tolerant outlook and cosmopolitan taste, broad-minded, generous, affable, and kindhearted, he

had from the outset had his doubts and misgivings about National Socialism. Yet he too bristled at the expression of those same doubts and
misgivings by foreigners. His patriotism was offended by criticism from
abroad of his country and of his government, however justified, however
valid.

Early in 1934, for example, he wrote in labored, ponderous English to
a friend in Great Britain that if the new regime offered him a political
appointment, he would accept. Anticipating that this decision might arouse
surprise and disappointment among his acquaintances abroad, he rejected
their right to condemn his willingness to serve the Third Reich:

> You cannot as an Englishwoman understand this, especially not the issue on
> the moral side, for it is based on something (so it seems to me) essentially
> different from the kind of indignation that is so lavishly displayed in England
> over anything that happens in this country—and I fundamentally disclaim the
> categories on which that English capacity of moral judgement is based. It is
> based on the untold and never fully articulated cruelty of social relationships,
> on the very inhumanity of a system that is at least being contested though as
> yet not articulately over here.

England criticizing Germany was simply the pot calling the kettle black. It
would be better, Trott suggested, for the British to solve their own
problems before presuming to tell others how to deal with theirs.[11]

In sum, the bureaucrats in the resistance, like the soldiers, generally
supported the Third Reich. They too believed that it was far superior to
Weimar. More than that, they felt that its policies and objectives were in
essence sound. They saw their nation emerging from confusion and demoralization, regaining confidence and faith, rejecting materialism, return-
ing to traditional values and ideals. At home there was a new resolve to
deal with the problems of unemployment and privation. Abroad the government was displaying fresh courage and strength in demanding an end
to the Versailles system. Could any patriotic German remain indifferent to
this exciting national revival?

The willingness of the bureaucratic resisters to serve National Socialism
did not appear to them calculating or demeaning. They regarded themselves not as the mercenaries of the regime but as its allies, perhaps even its
guides and tutors. The leaders of the Third Reich, they believed, were no
doubt motivated by love of country. Their ideals were pure, their objectives
valid. But they lacked polish and experience, subtlety and skill. Here the
members of the civil service could play a valuable role. They could correct
the deficiencies of the new order; they could provide it with professional

expertise and technical knowledge. They could warn it against dangerous policies or reckless experiments. Such a collaboration between government and administration, between party and bureaucracy, would prove mutually beneficial. The regime would receive expert advice and guidance, while the bureaucracy obtained greater recognition of its talents and accomplishments. It seemed an ideal arrangement.

The belief in such a tacit alliance helps explain the general readiness of the bureaucratic resisters to approve the political, administrative, economic, and ideological changes introduced by the Third Reich. The end of parliamentary government and of the party system appeared to them not only acceptable but desirable. They had always regarded the republican experiment in democracy as risky or futile. The curtailment of individual rights and the expansion of police powers were, in their opinion, essential for the restoration of stability in public life. Increased government regulation of wages, prices, profits, and the relations between capital and labor accorded with their belief that freedom of enterprise must be subordinated to collective economic welfare. And the regime's racial policy reflected a view that in varying degrees most of them shared, namely, that under Weimar the Jews had gained excessive influence in politics and finance. Something had to be done to deal with that problem.

Hence, the participants in the bureaucratic resistance accepted the anti-Semitic teachings of the Third Reich without much hesitation. Schulenburg epitomized their attitude. An ardent supporter of National Socialism, he too believed there was a Jewish question that had to be resolved before the national revival of Germany could be successfully completed, although he did not quite know how to resolve it. Still, its solution was not an obsession with him. He did not become a Nazi because he was an anti-Semite; he became an anti-Semite because he was a Nazi. More simply, racism was not central to his political thinking. His acceptance of it reflected an uncritical faith in the doctrines and dogmas of the Third Reich. He believed unquestioningly what the party told him, that international Jewry was one of those sinister, conspiratorial forces that had gained control over Germany after the defeat of 1918. Now that the corrupt republic had been overthrown, the new order would put an end to the unhealthy alien influences exploiting the nation's weakness. In what way that was to be accomplished, by what means, through what measures, and with what weapons, remained vague. Schulenburg was simply not sure.[12]

Popitz had a more complex attitude toward anti-Semitism. Schulenburg had reached manhood during the poisonous and malevolent postwar years.

Like many young people of his generation, he felt surrounded by dark conspiracies, plots, intrigues, and machinations. In that venomous atmosphere bigotry inevitably flourished. But Popitz was a child of the prosperous, optimistic, relatively tolerant imperial era. At no time, either before or after the war, did he display overt hostility toward Jews. Some of them had in fact been his colleagues and associates in the civil service. During those years he had never criticized their prominent role in public affairs or in economic life or in education and culture. Even after the establishment of the Third Reich, when it was not only safe but expedient to express anti-Semitic opinions, he had remained silent. Following his imprisonment in 1944 for plotting against Hitler, however, he strongly condemned the "Judaization" of the political system under Weimar. On the basis of his long experience as a government official, he had come to the harsh but inescapable conclusion, according to his testimony, that "the Jews must disappear from political and economic life."

His only reservation regarding the racial program of National Socialism, Popitz explained, pertained to its means, not its ends. He had favored a "somewhat more gradual approach," especially "for reasons of foreign policy." In the course of his interrogation he repeated that a "solution to the Jewish question" was "unavoidable," and this meant "elimination [of the Jews] from political and economic life." What he had objected to was the "violent procedure" followed by the regime, "the destruction of property, the arbitrary imprisonment, and the annihilation of life." That was wrong, partly because "it could not be reconciled with law and morality," partly because it was "dangerous on account of the views that would inevitably spread among the people regarding the value of property and human life," and partly because of "the great danger of strengthening international opposition to Germany and its form of government." A less drastic method of solving the Jewish question would have been preferable.[13]

Goerdeler held similar views. They too were shaped by the values of the old, prewar monarchical order. Though an avowed critic of Weimar, he like Popitz avoided anti-Semitic rhetoric or racial sloganeering. Indeed, Busser assured Secretary of State Hull in the summer of 1944, that "Dr. Goerdeler never faltered . . . in his opposition to the Hitler regime, which he loathed on account of its racial and political persecutions, its propaganda against the Christian Churches, its educational perversion of the German youth, its aggressive militarism, [and] its tyranny and reign of terror. He particularly denounced the Nazi persecution of the Jews and of others on account of their race, religion, or political beliefs."[14]

That Goerdeler was indeed opposed to the violent persecution of Jews is clear. He was too much a Prussian civil servant of the old school, too much a devout Christian and decent man, to countenance rabid bigotry. In fact, as mayor of Leipzig he had tried early in 1933, following Hitler's appointment as chancellor, to defend Jewish businesses against Nazi thugs and marauders. Yet he too, like most members of the resistance, believed the Jewish question simply could not be ignored. The Germanic and the Semitic racial characters were too dissimilar, too incompatible, to coexist in harmony. There had to be a separation between them—peaceful, just, deliberate, and orderly—but a separation nevertheless. Goerdeler objected to the anti-Semitic program of the Third Reich because of its method, not its avowed goal.[15]

This view emerges clearly from his comments in the memorandum he submitted to Hitler in August 1934. He pointed out that "men who have gained experience abroad and whose judgment can be trusted" had repeatedly emphasized the need "to consolidate German racial policy." Excessive measures against the Jews would only draw unwanted attention from foreign observers. As for Mendelssohn's music, an official admission that it was being excluded from the German orchestral repertoire because of the composer's Jewish background might prove quite embarrassing. "After all, it is conceivable that no living German composer would be able to produce a better composition." To Hitler such views must have seemed timid but certainly not disloyal.[16]

Finally, there were those bureaucratic resisters who reacted to Nazi anti-Semitism by minimizing its severity or even denying its existence. Trott belongs in this category. Personally generous and fair-minded, he had many Jewish friends, in Germany as well as England, with whom he remained in touch even after the establishment of the Third Reich, knowing that his loyalty to them would be viewed by the Nazi authorities with disapproval. Yet his patriotism, his deep sense of national pride and dignity, led him to reject foreign criticism of the Hitler dictatorship, even when he must have known that it was at least partly valid.

Early in 1934, for example, having read in the *Manchester Guardian* an unfavorable account of the treatment of Jews in Germany, he felt compelled to write a letter to the editor protesting against this attack on his country's reputation. It was not true, he insisted, that the "partiality of German courts forms an instrument of anti-Semitic persecution." Having served for several months as a legal aide in Hanau, he was familiar with economic and social conditions in the Prussian province of Hessen-Nassau. Although some of the Jewish tradesmen there were indeed facing difficulties "owing [in part] to political reasons," many others "were doing the same business as before." He had never heard of "any case of active persecution." The charge simply could not be true.

Nor was there anti-Semitic discrimination within the court system itself, Trott maintained. "I have been present at a great many cases brought up by or against Jews, and I can therefore assert this fact from personal observation." All efforts to influence the outcome of legal proceedings by the disclosure that one of the litigants was Jewish were rejected "with unhesitating firmness." Indeed, Trott found that at the district court to which he had been assigned, his supervising judge was himself a Jew and several of the lawyers were "of Jewish extraction." A government regulation, moreover, protecting debtors against creditors in cases resulting from an overall decline in the national economy was applied impartially to "such Jewish businesses as had suffered general deterioration." He himself had seen this regulation invoked "with extreme liberality" to save "the very shaky business of a Jewish shopkeeper." How then could anyone speak of bias or discrimination in the legal system?

Trott admitted that the economic position of the Jews in Hanau had worsened. But whose fault was that? "[It] cannot possibly be attributed to local or national but only to foreign boycotting." The Jews in other countries, trying to help their coreligionists in Germany, had organized a campaign of economic reprisal against the Third Reich. But thereby they had only hurt those they hoped to assist. The chief result of "this assumed 'aid' of German Jewry from abroad" had been the terrible losses suffered by Jewish businessmen in consequence of "the compulsory sale of stocks on a closed market to meet their obligations." For their sake, the boycott of Germany should be dropped.

As for anti-Semitic excesses, Trott had often talked to SA men, men committed to the racial doctrine of National Socialism, who had assured him that they "would never consider themselves justified to execute it with methods of violence." Indeed, they had turned "with indignation" from any "suggestion of atrocities being committed in their presence." The orders they had received from their superiors clearly prohibited acts of brutality. The acknowledged fact that there were National Socialists among prisoners in the concentration camps "proves that those who do [not] obey these orders are finding punishments." Trott had succeeded in persuading himself, at least for the moment, that charges of the persecution of Jews in Germany were mostly a fabrication.[17]

Similarly, other members of the bureaucratic resistance, whether they approved of the regime's racial policy or merely acquiesced in it or simply dismissed it, did not generally regard official anti-Semitism as a serious obstacle to their collaboration with National Socialism. It was no more an obstacle than the overthrow of representative government or the violation of civil liberty or the growth of coercive authority or the repression of ideological dissent. They may not have always agreed with what the new order was doing, but their objections seemed to them minor in light of Hitler's great goals and accomplishments. What really mattered to them was that Germany faced an exciting and inspiring future. Should they remain aloof from this triumphant national revival? That was unthinkable. Like millions of other Germans, they marched forth to embrace a glorious destiny.

8

The Catholics: Church, Clergy, and National Socialism

The clerical resistance differed significantly from both the military and the bureaucratic resistance in the occupational status and function of its members. This difference in turn determined the form and content of its criticism of the Third Reich. To put it more explicitly, the military officers and civil servants who eventually came to reject the Hitler dictatorship were men close to the center of political power. Their profession made it possible for them to plan in a coherent and organized way for the overthrow of the regime. But it also forced them to rely on the techniques of plot and stratagem. They could not overtly express their objections to the doctrines or policies of National Socialism. They had to pretend to support them in order to subvert them. They had to appear to defend the system while actually working against it. In other words, they were compelled by their circumstances to form a conspiracy.

The churchmen in the resistance, however, could voice their views more or less openly. Not being part of the state apparatus, they were freer to criticize it. Religious institutions retained some degree of autonomy even under the Third Reich, and while that autonomy was in theory restricted to confessional questions, it was not always easy to determine the boundary between the spiritual and the secular. The role played by the churches during Weimar had clearly demonstrated that. Hence the clerical resisters could, indirectly at least, articulate political dissent in the guise of pastoral stricture.

They enjoyed yet another advantage. The soldiers and bureaucrats who harbored doubts about Hitler's policies had to be careful about expressing them. Any suspicion of disloyalty could lead to their dismissal or even imprisonment. They had no protection against the arbitrariness of the regime, no recourse against its dictatorial authority. But the members of the clergy could count on the sympathy and loyalty of their communicants. The higher the position of a churchman, moreover, the greater the degree of popular support on which he could rely. The arrest of a minister or a priest for incitement to civic disobedience might distress the members of his congregation, but the incarceration of a bishop or an abbot could lead to nationwide protests and demonstrations. Even a totalitarian government had to be careful about alienating public opinion.

It is not surprising, therefore, that the first major component of the resistance to voice open disagreement with the Third Reich was the clergy. From the very beginning some churchmen expressed, quite directly at times, their reservations about the new order. In fact, those reservations gradually came to form a coherent, systematic critique of many of the teachings of National Socialism. Yet the problem confronting the clerical resisters was the scope or range of their opposition to the regime. How far should they go in their criticism? Should they confine themselves to religious and moral issues or should they deal with political and racial issues as well?

At first glance the answer seemed simple enough. Church and state were separate and independent powers, one exercising spiritual, the other secular, authority. Neither had the right to trespass on the lawful jurisdiction of the other. But the problem grew more complicated. Do not almost all public issues have a moral dimension? And does not then the obligation of the Christian to observe the ethical teachings of his or her faith apply to those issues as well? If so, should not the leaders of the church point out to their communicants the spiritual danger in the political and racial policies of the Third Reich? That was the dilemma with which members of the clergy had to wrestle. Even when they generally agreed that they had the right and the duty to criticize the moral transgressions of the state, they had trouble determining how far that criticism should go. Should it be restricted to the denominational interests and concerns of the church or should it include moral imperatives transcending confessional boundaries, embracing all of humanity? In deciding what their attitude toward the Nazi dictatorship ought to be, the churchmen had to confront questions of this sort.

The conclusion at which they almost invariably arrived was that their first duty was to protect their church and its members. That meant they did not hesitate to challenge the state when they felt that it was encroaching on denominational autonomy or authority. But their challenge rarely went beyond the narrow boundaries of churchly jurisdiction. It rarely touched

on the fundamental problem of the relationship between moral commandment and political power. It remained within the limits of formal legality.
Hence the clerical resistance during the early years of the Third Reich was
directed not against the established system as such but only against specific
policies that it had mistakenly adopted and that it should therefore properly
correct. The church leaders who criticized those policies insisted that they
were not opposed to the new order in principle. On the contrary, they
supported its purposes and objectives. They were merely trying to prevent
occasional errors, to point out possible pitfalls. They were acting not out
of hostility but out of loyalty. In essence, their strategy for dealing with the
regime represented the triumph of confessional expediency over religious
universalism.

Of the two major Christian denominations, the Catholics were more
successful than the Protestants in reaching an understanding with the
Third Reich. That development was somewhat surprising. Before Hitler's
victory the Protestant Church had not been unfavorably disposed toward
him and his movement. Indeed, some of its leaders, while maintaining an
ostensible political neutrality, had expressed support for many of the
demands of National Socialism, for a national revival, for instance, or for
the end of the Versailles system or the rebirth of patriotism and idealism in
Germany. The Catholic Church, meanwhile, had generally viewed the Nazi
Party with fear and suspicion. It had felt threatened by a radical ultranationalist ideology that regarded the papacy as a sinister, alien institution,
that opposed denominational separatism in education and culture, and that
at times appeared to promote a return to Nordic paganism. The establishment of the Third Reich seemed to many Catholics to portend the
coming of a bitter conflict between church and state.

They were mistaken, however. Both the regime and the hierarchy, each
for its own reasons, wanted to avoid a test of strength. To Hitler it was
important to show the world that, far from being a fanatic or ideologue,
he was a pragmatist and a moderate. The policies he proposed to adopt
would prove reasonable and responsible. The Catholic Church, for its part,
was anxious to avert an open confrontation with the new order, to reach
some sort of understanding or agreement, to live and let live. Each side
privately hoped for an accommodation.

The first step was taken by the new chancellor in March 1933 when,
seeking to justify his assumption of dictatorial power, he described "both
Christian denominations" as "most important" for the defense of the
German nationality. His government would respect their rights. The
Catholic leadership rushed to accept this implicit offer of the olive branch.

On the day after Hitler had spoken, Cardinal Faulhaber urged the church to display greater tolerance toward the Nazi regime. After all, that regime had come to power by legal means, unlike the revolutionaries who prepared the way for Weimar. Even more important, he pointed out, the pope had referred to Hitler as the first head of government in Europe to oppose Bolshevism openly. Why then should not Catholicism and National Socialism try to work together to bring about the political and spiritual revival of Germany?[1]

The cautious rapprochement between church and state that started in the spring of 1933 turned into mutual admiration by the summer, following the government's conclusion of a concordat with the papacy on July 20. Each side began to proclaim its respect and support for the other. Admittedly, those professions were not always entirely sincere. Secret fears and suspicions continued to linger; bitter memories of past recriminations and conflicts remained alive. But outwardly all was harmony. The regime and the hierarchy regularly exchanged expressions of regard and approval. All major differences between them seemed to have been resolved at last.

Clerics in particular eagerly demonstrated their good will. In October 1933 Bishop Galen thanked providence for the resolve of the Third Reich to suppress "the open propaganda for godlessness and immorality." The concordat concluded with the Vatican was helping the regime to protect "our beloved German nation" against "the terrible danger" of secularism. It had therefore become the solemn obligation of all Catholics to fulfill faithfully their duty to their god, their church, and their fatherland. In June 1934 Galen once again condemned the godless spirit of the Weimar period, the period of "liberalism and Marxism," when the "idolatry of mammonism" had threatened to undermine the dignity and honor of the German worker. Now a "new era" was promising to create a "new and better social order," he claimed. A year later, in December 1935, he maintained that all Catholics "stand united behind the Führer" in "the struggle for Germany's freedom, honor, and equality of rights, for the end of the economic crisis and of unemployment, for social reconciliation, and for the reconstruction of the national community destroyed by the effects of so-called liberalism." And in March 1936, following the remilitarization of the Rhineland, he proclaimed jubilantly that "the Führer, to whom divine providence has entrusted the direction of our policy and the responsibility for the fate of our German homeland, has by his courageous resolve broken the chains in which, after the unfortunate outcome of the war, hostile powers kept our nation permanently imprisoned, as it were." Galen did not intend "to discuss and to judge political questions." Still, "as a German and as a bishop," he wanted to thank the Führer "for everything he has done for the right, the freedom, and the honor of the German people." There could seemingly be no question about his loyalty to the new order.[2]

Faulhaber, who gained an early though exaggerated reputation as a critic of the Third Reich, was equally effusive. He too wanted to ingratiate himself with the new order; he too wanted to demonstrate his support for the Führer and the Führer's program. In July 1933, a few days after the signing of the concordat, the cardinal sent Hitler a handwritten letter overflowing with praise. "What the old parliaments and parties did not achieve in 60 years, your statesmanlike farsightedness has made a reality of world history within 6 months." This "handclasp" with the papacy, "the greatest moral power in world history," represented "a great deed of immeasurable benefit" to Germany's reputation throughout the world. It would bring to the spiritual life of the nation "an increase in faith and thereby an increase in the moral strength of the people." All the world would now see that "Adolf Hitler can not only deliver great speeches . . . , but . . . he can also perform deeds of historical greatness." Faulhaber concluded with an outpouring of gratitude. "God preserve our chancellor for our nation." What other German statesman had shown so much understanding for the church?[3]

Four months later, in November, the cardinal joined the other bishops of Bavaria in appealing to all Catholics to endorse in the forthcoming plebiscite the government's decision to leave the League of Nations. By doing so they would support "peace among nations and the honor and equality of rights of the German people." More important, they would show not only "their loyalty to people and fatherland" but also their agreement with "the farsighted and energetic efforts of the Führer to save the German nation from the horrors of war and the atrocities of Bolshevism," to "maintain public order," and to "provide work for the unemployed." It almost sounded as if for German Catholics allegiance to the Third Reich had become a religious obligation.[4]

By the end of the year Faulhaber was also praising the determination of the regime to improve public morality. He welcomed this change from the attitude of Weimar, which had seemed to regard indecency and vice with indifference. The cardinal did hasten to admonish that a great deal still remained to be done. The big cities had not yet become "gardens of virtue"; they might indeed be compared in some respects to Sodom and Gomorrah. Nor had the German people as a whole any right to claim moral superiority over "other races." But there could be no doubt that conditions were getting better under the Third Reich. "In recent months, thank God, a great deal of immorality has been swept away with an iron broom out of the public life of our people." National Socialism deserved the gratitude of all Germans for the improvement of moral conduct as much as for the reassertion of diplomatic independence or recovery from the economic depression.[5]

A year afterward, shortly before Christmas 1934, Faulhaber even suggested that Hitler's statecraft reflected the teachings of Christianity. Meditating on the significance of a religious holiday celebrating "the entry of the Prince of Peace," he turned his thoughts to the recent achievements of the Third Reich. "The Führer has committed himself to peace in bold and strong words, in fateful hours when demonic forces were at work cranking up the engines of war." His efforts to find a peaceful solution to international disputes and conflicts had clearly earned him the support of his countrymen. "The history of our people will be thankful to him for having now saved our people twice, perhaps even three times, from the horrors of war." The struggle to regain for Germany a prominent position among the great powers was, in the cardinal's view, inseparable from the struggle to maintain the stability of Europe. By seeking diplomatic equality, the Nazi regime was promoting world peace. As he contemplated the Savior described in the New Testament, Faulhaber was reminded of the one revealed in *Mein Kampf*.[6]

Relations between the Catholic Church and the Third Reich were not always harmonious, to be sure. There were in fact frequent differences and arguments, even quarrels and clashes. They focused largely on the role under the new order of confessional schools, youth organizations, workingmen's clubs, and cultural societies. Their ultimate source, however, was the incompatibility of a totalitarian regime claiming jurisdiction over all collective civic or social activity with a religious community insisting on a measure of autonomy for its faith and its organization. Still, both sides were anxious to avoid an open clash. The church hierarchy in particular went to great lengths to emphasize that what it objected to was not the ideology of National Socialism but the way that ideology was being interpreted by subordinate officials. Its members maintained that while they continued to serve the system loyally, a doctrinaire, overzealous bureaucracy was distorting and weakening that system. They themselves were merely trying to influence from within some of the regime's policies and measures, not to challenge its ideals or goals. They sought to strengthen the Third Reich by pointing out the tactical mistakes that a few of its dogmatic, shortsighted officials were committing.

Faulhaber had sensed from the outset that, despite their constant expressions of mutual regard, church and state might before long become embroiled in controversy. This emerges clearly, for example, from the comments in his letter to Hitler of July 24, 1933, congratulating him on the conclusion of the concordat. After praising the Führer for this accomplishment, the cardinal expressed his hope that the agreement with the papacy would not remain "confined to paper" but would be acknowledged as a "mutual solemn agreement" possessing "life and reality" in those provisions that "contain duties" as well as in those that "contain rights and concessions." There could be no doubt about Hitler's own commitment to both the letter and the spirit of the treaty, Faulhaber hastened to add, but what about his followers and subordinates? Would they prove equally fair-minded and farseeing? "God grant that the lower grades of the first, second, and third level [of the administrative system] will not lag too far behind the statesmanlike greatness of the Führer with regard to the execution of the concordat." He must have suspected that a written agreement between Berlin and the Vatican would not of itself be a guarantee of harmony between church and state in Germany.[7]

The cardinal's apprehension proved fully justified. Throughout the early years of the Third Reich friction grew between the regime and the hierarchy regarding their respective spheres of authority. On the surface all seemed tranquil, but beneath there were constant challenges and confrontations. By the end of 1935 Galen was proposing that the Catholic bishops issue a pastoral letter protesting against the underground war being waged against the church. His draft spoke of "the struggle unleashed against Christianity" in which Catholics were "duty-bound" to defend their faith. Yet they were preparing for battle reluctantly, "with a heavy heart," knowing that it would make more difficult "the revival of the German nation, which Adolf Hitler wants and leads," and "for which we wholeheartedly desire success and pray to God every day." The loyalty of the church to the Third Reich remained unshaken, he maintained, no matter what.

Galen could not emphasize this point enough. Catholicism and National Socialism were not opponents but allies. "We and the faithful whom we lead stand united behind the Führer," ready, "as Germans and as Christians," to support him with every ounce of strength. But Catholics felt hurt and rejected in view of "the mistrust kindled and inflamed by influential circles" that "consider the renunciation of Christianity, of its dogmas and of its moral doctrine, a test of national trustworthiness." It was absolutely untrue that Catholics sought "separate political goals" or that their organizations were dominated by "discontented outsiders" who hoped for the failure of "the renewal movement and the policy directed by Hitler." In fact, Catholics would prove "the most trustworthy collaborators" and "the most loyal followers" of the regime, once the barriers erected against them because of their "inherited Christian faith" were removed.[8]

In sum, the leaders of the church adopted a strategy of defending their religious interests not by opposing but by supporting or at least appearing to support the Third Reich. They had concluded that overt resistance would be futile. It would only precipitate a conflict in which the odds clearly favored the other side. By remaining ostensibly loyal to the regime, they might be able to exert some influence on the shaping of its policy. They might gain the support of the moderates in the government against the extremists. They might form an alliance with the realists and pragmatists in the Nazi Party against the dogmatists and ideologues. They might even appeal successfully to the practical statesman in Hitler, to his sense of reasonableness and restraint. Collaboration seemed the best way to defend German Catholicism.

By adopting this strategy of acquiescence, however, the leaders of the church subordinated the transcendent moral imperatives of their faith to its practical denominational needs. They were prepared to oppose some of the measures of the Third Reich, but for reasons of confessional expediency or utility rather than ethical principle. They insisted that their criticism of the government's religious policy derived from sympathy and support for the ideals of National Socialism, not from antagonism. They sought to perform the role, essentially, of a loyal pressure group within the established system competing with other loyal pressure groups for influence and authority. Their chief concern was the protection of the traditional function of the clergy in providing spiritual guidance of the faithful through pastoral care and religious ministration. As for the moral or ethical implications of the ideology of the Third Reich, that was not something for which they were willing to jeopardize the institutional interests of the church.

The resolve of the hierarchy to protect Catholic ecclesiastical rights at all costs determined its attitude toward official anti-Semitism. Its members were not bigots as a rule. They often shared some of the popular ethnic prejudices and stereotypes of their society, but thoroughgoing racists were a rarity among them. They felt, nevertheless, that to protest against the government's policy concerning the Jews would be a violation of the boundary separating spiritual from secular authority. It would only invite retaliation by the regime and encroachment on the authority of the church. The chief responsibility of the Catholic leadership was to safeguard the Catholic community. The fate of the Jews was properly the concern of world Jewry.

Some of the members of the lower clergy did display considerable courage and compassion in defending the victims of the Third Reich's anti-Semitic program. A priest in the Rhineland, for instance, had to pay a fine of five hundred marks for "abusing the pulpit" in a sermon that characterized the vilification of the Jews as unjust. Another priest, this one in Bavaria, described the stories circulating in Germany about the pernicious influence of Jewry as a pack of lies. And then there was the anonymous "German Roman Catholic priest" who in a Munich theological journal urged his coreligionists to oppose "sinful racial pride and blind hatred of the Jews," and to seek "atonement for all the sins committed by Christians against Jews." The leaders of the church, however, were not as bold, chiefly because they felt that they could not afford to be. Their main task, they remained convinced, was to defend the position of Catholicism in Germany by conciliating, appeasing, cajoling, and flattering the Nazi regime.[9]

Only when official anti-Semitism trespassed on their jurisdiction did members of the hierarchy protest, and then not on the basis of any fundamental moral or religious principle, but because of some encroachment on legally established ecclesiastical rights and prerogatives. For example, when the school superintendent of Münster, Wilhelm Glowsky, issued a directive in the fall of 1933 that religious instruction regarding All Souls' Day should be combined with classroom discussion of the "demoralizing power" of the "people of Israel," Bishop Galen objected vigorously. The superintendent had clearly violated the boundary between the authority of the state and that of the church. Hence Galen had not only the right but the duty to protest.

The connection between the directive and the significance of All Souls' Day seemed "very loose, not to say artificial," he wrote to Glowsky. Besides, some of the children might become confused about "Catholic teachings regarding the historical mission of the people of Israel in salvation during the pre-Christian period and regarding the obligation to act with charity toward all men." As "an appointed guardian of the values of the faith," Galen felt obliged to oppose any infringement on its jurisdiction. He reminded the school superintendent that under earlier agreements between the government and the episcopate and under article 21 of the concordat of July 20, 1933, any change in the content of religious instruction could be introduced only "with the consent of the higher church authorities." Since no such consent had been obtained, the current curriculum would remain in effect. There was nothing fainthearted about this gesture of defiance toward the Nazi authorities, but it was the only time prior to the war that the bishop spoke out openly on the subject of official anti-Semitism.[10]

Faulhaber's attitude can be ascertained more precisely because it appears with greater clarity in both his private letters and his public statements. His personal correspondence shows that he disapproved of the regime's racial policy, particularly regarding "non-Aryan" Catholics, those who had converted or whose parents had converted from Judaism. Though faithful members of the church, they continued to be regarded by the authorities as racial Jews subject to legal discrimination. Yet the cardinal also expressed privately some sympathy even for those who remained loyal to their ancestral religion and tradition. They too, it seemed to him, should be treated with fairness and compassion.[11]

In his public declarations, however, he remained just as cautious as Galen and just as eager to avoid a confrontation with the regime. On only one occasion did Faulhaber express in public views that might be construed as indirect criticism of a basic tenet of the Third Reich. In his Advent sermons of 1933 he denounced the Nazi extremists who were arguing that the Christian Scriptures should be purged of the "Jewish" Old Testament. This issue did not simply involve some vague moral imperative, some abstract religious principle. The anti-Semitic zealots had clearly crossed the line between secular and spiritual authority. They were in fact trying to undermine the basis of Catholicism. Neither accommodation nor acquiescence was possible any longer; the cardinal had to face the enemy head on.

The opponents of the church, he began, had recently formed a loud chorus demanding insistently, "Away with the Old Testament!" Given "the present state of mind," this outcry might well succeed in shaking "the foundations of faith in the soul of the nation." Not even Christ was safe from the subverters of true religion. "Some wanted to save him with a forged birth certificate," claiming that "he was not really a Jew but an Aryan, because Aryans had lived in Galilee." Others, recognizing that Christ could not be Aryanized on the basis of any historical evidence, were saying: "If he was a Jew, then we must certainly reject him." Here was a grave threat to all of Christianity. "Confronting such voices and movements, the bishop cannot remain silent."

Faulhaber then proceeded to reemphasize the central position of the Old Testament in Catholic theology. Before the coming of Jesus, he preached, Judaism had been a bearer of the revelation, and its prophets had been enlightened by God. Obviously, the Old Testament, being subordinate to the New, could not claim primacy in the Christian Scriptures. Yet its writings were also sacred; they were also inspired by the spirit of God; they were also "building stones for God's kingdom." It would be a mistake to exclude its stories from the religious instruction provided in public schools, because they clearly had a "high pedagogical value." The cardinal concluded by appealing to Protestants to join with Catholics in preserving for the German people this "precious instructional material" for a Christian education.[12]

The Advent sermons earned for Faulhaber a widespread but unfounded reputation as a critic of the Third Reich. All those opposed to the regime, at home as well as abroad, who had been waiting impatiently almost a year for some prominent public figure to speak out against National Socialism, thought that they had finally found their champion. Had he not defended the Old Testament, thereby defying, implicitly at least, the dogmas of anti-Semitism? By emphasizing the sacred mission of the Jews in antiquity, was he not indirectly voicing sympathy for the Jews of today? In short, did he not really express in religious terms his opposition to the new political system in Germany? Faulhaber became overnight a hero to the adversaries of the Hitler government.

But they misjudged their man. The cardinal simply wanted to uphold the teachings of Catholicism, protect the integrity of the Holy Scriptures, and maintain the jurisdiction of the church in questions of religion. He was fighting for the Old Testament, not for the people of the Old Testament. He was arguing for the divine mission of the Jews in biblical times, not for their civic equality in the 1930s. What concerned him above all was the welfare of his flock and the defense of his faith.

In all fairness, Faulhaber never pretended to be more than a protector of Catholic interests. Those who saw in him a principled opponent of National Socialism had simply succumbed to wishful thinking. Indeed, he went out of his way to underscore that his Advent sermons did not address political or even moral issues and concerned only religion and theology. They would focus, he declared right at the outset, solely on "this Israel of biblical antiquity," promptly reiterating for added emphasis that "they will discuss only pre-Christian Judaism."

There was a fundamental difference, he went on, between the Jewish community of antiquity and that of modern times. Therefore "aversion to the Jews of today should not be transferred to the books of pre-Christian Jewry." As if to reassure those whose anti-Semitism went beyond a dislike for contemporary Judaism, the cardinal pointed out that the Old Testament was not really Jewish at all. The Jews had merely been the vehicle through which God had made his word manifest to mankind. "Christianity did not become a Jewish religion because of its acceptance of these books," according to the first of his Advent sermons. "These books were not written by Jews. They were inspired by the spirit of God, and are therefore God's word and God's books." In any case, the role of Judaism in the Bible had no actual bearing on its role in Germany.

Faulhaber hastened to make clear, moreover, that he did not reject in principle the government's racial program. There was no fundamental conflict between the teachings of Catholicism and of National Socialism regarding hereditary ethnic differences. As far as the church was concerned, "honest research on race and cultivation of race" were quite permissible. Nor was there anything wrong with a resolve to keep "the special character" of a nation "as pure as possible" or to encourage "the sense of a people's community" by emphasizing "its community of blood." The cardinal's only admonition was that racial pride must not lead to "hatred of other peoples," to rejection of "the means of grace" provided by religion, or to "opposition to Christianity." In short, "race and Christianity are in themselves not incompatible; they are rather separate categories [of reality]." Official racism was no reason why church and state could not work together, each in its own way, for the general welfare of the German people.[13]

Faulhaber's determination to observe outwardly a scrupulous neutrality regarding the regime's anti-Semitism became even more apparent late in the summer of 1934, when a Swiss newspaper published the erroneous report that he had recently preached a sermon against racial hatred. On the basis of this misinformation, the Jewish World Conference meeting in Geneva had expressed its approval of what it believed to be his condemnation of religious bigotry. The endorsement embarrassed the cardinal profoundly. The last thing in the world he wanted was public praise or support from an international organization of Jews. He had been trying so hard to demonstrate that his church in no way opposed the basic objectives of the Third Reich, that it was in fact pursuing a course of strict noninterference in the Jewish question. But the conference had by its unwelcome approbation played into the hands of the anti-Catholic forces in National Socialism. It became imperative to control the damage.

On August 31 Faulhaber's secretary sent off an indignant letter to Geneva. The sermon that had been reported in the Basel *National-Zeitung* two weeks earlier never actually took place; indeed, it was "a fabrication from its first sentence to its last." Even in his Advent sermons "Cardinal Faulhaber . . . defended the old biblical writings of Israel, but took no position on the Jewish question of today." Above all, "Cardinal Faulhaber objects to the fact that his name was mentioned at a conference which is demanding a commercial boycott of Germany, in other words, economic warfare." His secretary simultaneously sent copies of the letter to the Ministry of the Interior in Berlin and to the Bavarian Political Police in Munich. The cardinal was eager to demonstrate to the authorities that he had nothing to do with the efforts of world Jewry to resist the Third Reich's anti-Semitism.[14]

He even seemed to feel that the foreign press should not dwell too much on the persecution of Jews in the Third Reich. Stories on this subject published abroad, in his view, were often exaggerated and sometimes reflected an underlying hostility toward Germany. In a letter to Cardinal George Mundelein of Chicago, Faulhaber spoke of inaccurate reports regarding anti-Semitic atrocities in Germany published in foreign newspapers. Some of those responsible for such reports harbored leftist sympathies, no doubt, directing their attacks against "the new government in Germany" because of its opposition to Communism. Besides, what good did stories about Nazi anti-Semitism do? They had only induced the Hitler government to organize a boycott of Jewish stores. As a result, many businesses had suffered serious losses, and some had been ruined. That was what the correspondents for the foreign press had accomplished with their stories, most of them fabricated, about racial persecution in the Third Reich. Faulhaber concluded by asking Mundelein to try to persuade the newspapers that had printed accounts of alleged anti-Semitic atrocities in Germany to publish a retraction acknowledging the "baselessness" of those accounts. "Urgent speed is needed," he insisted.[15]

All in all, while the cardinal believed that "non-Aryans" who converted to Catholicism became thereby entrusted to his pastoral care, the great majority of Jews, those who continued to practice Judaism or who abandoned religion altogether, were not really his responsibility. He disapproved of the persecution directed against them by National Socialism, but he remained convinced that the hardships they faced were properly the concern of their coreligionists in other countries. "We may assume," he wrote early in April 1933, "and we have already seen this in part, that the Jews can help themselves." Two days later he used that same phrase in another letter: "The Jews can help themselves." When pressed to take a more forceful stand against racial injustice, he sometimes became irritated and petulant. "I receive inquiries from various sources," he informed the editor of a religious journal, "asking why the church is not doing anything against the persecution of Jews. I am puzzled by this, because despite the agitation against the Catholics or against the bishop, no one is asking what could be done against that agitation." The church authorities had to deal with "far more important questions at present" than the fate of German Jewry, questions like denominational schools, Catholic organizations, and sterilization of the physically or mentally disabled.[16]

Behind Faulhaber's annoyance with those who were urging him to come out openly against the regime's racial program, behind his peevish insistence that the church had more important things to do than worry about the Jews, was a profound fear concerning the future of his own religious community. He was afraid that by publicly condemning racism he would be endangering Catholicism. He knew of influential groups within the National Socialist Party that regarded the church as a sworn enemy, groups that would be only too glad to find a pretext for restricting its freedom of action. Should he then jeopardize the safety of his own flock for the sake of some small, alien ethnic minority? That was the dilemma with which the cardinal had to grapple.

During the months following Hitler's appointment as chancellor, Faulhaber repeatedly expressed his fear that to speak out for the Jews, even for the converted Jews, would jeopardize the situation of the Catholics. At the end of March 1933 he advised against calling a conference of the Catholic bishops to assess the new order in Germany. The situation facing the country seemed to be changing "from day to day," he warned, and "the present Jew-baiting can turn just as easily into Jesuit-baiting." Early in April he used similar language in counseling avoidance of a confrontation with the Nazi regime over anti-Semitism. "Thus we have no cause to give the government a reason for turning the Jew-baiting into a Jesuit-baiting." A few days later he reiterated his deep concern about the future. "We bishops are being asked at present why the Catholic Church does not intercede for the Jews, as has happened so often in the history of the church." But that was impossible for the time being, he explained, because "the struggle against the Jews would simultaneously become a struggle against the Catholics." As late as December, long after the conclusion of the concordat, the cardinal voiced alarm at the dangers facing the church. He feared that "the Nordic-Germanic creed" was now intended to become the "3rd religion in Germany." With the tacit approval of the government, "the struggle against the Jews and the Catholics has become quite openly a struggle against Christianity in general." Faulhaber saw before him the threat of a bitter struggle between secular and spiritual authority, a struggle in which the church might have to endure persecution, oppression, suffering, or even martyrdom.[17]

The cardinal was therefore determined to defend Catholic interests at any price, to avoid anything that might interfere with the performance of the church's sacerdotal and pastoral functions. And that resolve necessitated acceptance or at least acquiescence in the fundamental tenets of the Third Reich. He felt that his responsibility to his religious community required him to avoid antagonizing those in power, whatever his private convictions. This does not mean that he was really at heart a principled opponent of the Nazi regime. He approved in fact of many of its avowed objectives: the improvement of public conduct and morality, for example, and the fostering of faith and idealism, the alleviation of economic hardship and social distress, and the revival of political and military assertiveness. His chief aim, however, was always to protect the interests of the church. To achieve that end he was prepared to swallow any doubts, any scruples, regarding the new order. Solicitude for confessional welfare and parochial advantage remained his primary motive.

The other members of the Catholic hierarchy generally shared Faulhaber's views. They too were eager to avoid a confrontation with the regime. Behind their professions of loyalty and support for National Socialism lay a profound concern for the future of the church. Sometimes that concern found expression in open protests against a particular policy of the government, against this or that decision, this or that measure. But the ecclesiastical leaders submitting those protests went to great lengths to emphasize that they were doing so as faithful adherents of the Nazi system, not as principled opponents or even as neutral bystanders. They always insisted that they sought to strengthen the Third Reich and make it more effective, more popular. Hence they carefully avoided raising issues other than those of ecclesiastical authority or jurisdiction. Like Faulhaber, they were willing to temporize and equivocate, to accommodate and compromise, and to subordinate universal moral principles to pragmatic denominational needs.

9

The Protestants: Church, Clergy, and National Socialism

The Third Reich's relations with the Protestant Church appeared to follow a course directly opposite to the one taken in dealing with the Catholic Church. At first National Socialism and Catholicism had regarded each other not only as rivals but as adversaries. One side saw in the other a religious institution subservient to a foreign pontiff and indifferent to the interests of its own nation. The other in turn viewed the first as hostile to traditional Christianity, as promoting an idolatrous worship of the state. There had seemed to be no room for compromise between them. Hence the appointment of Hitler as chancellor was widely believed to portend the coming of a protracted struggle between spiritual and temporal authority in Germany. Yet the two managed to settle or at least to submerge their differences. Before long they were ritually exchanging public expressions of mutual regard, assuring each other of loyalty and support. Behind those assurances a good deal of distrust remained; old suspicions continued to linger and rankle. But outwardly all was harmony. The leaders of both Catholicism and National Socialism felt it best to pretend that the serious disagreements between them had been finally resolved.

In the case of the Protestant Church, the situation was reversed. Initially Protestantism and National Socialism had seemed to have a great deal in common. At times they even appeared to be partners or confederates. Both favored a revival of traditional values, both denounced the spirit of liberalism, both opposed popular democracy, and both demanded a rejection of Versailles. In short, a common hostility to the Weimar Republic made them look like natural allies. Many Protestant clergymen expressed some sympathy for the ideas of the Nazi Party, and quite a few became outright supporters. Thus most leaders of the church greeted the establishment of the Third Reich with hope and confidence. Yet within a few months differences between the new order and the ecclesiastical establishment began to emerge, differences that soon became acute enough to divide German Protestantism. While the Catholic hierarchy moved from distrust to collaboration, the Protestant leadership moved from support to opposition. The response of each to the Hitler dictatorship seemed entirely at variance with what had been expected.

Yet in fact each denomination faced the same problems in dealing with the government; each confronted the same demands, pressures, and threats. The differences in the way they dealt with them merely reflected the differences in their respective institutional structures and organizations. The German Catholic Church was recognized as being by its nature semi-independent of national authority. Part of a worldwide ecclesiastical community subject to a non-German pope, it could not be controlled by the National Socialist system directly. Its claim to autonomy had to be respected, at least on paper; its freedom of action had to be acknowledged, in theory if not always in practice. That was why the conclusion of the concordat in the summer of 1933 seemed simply to confirm long-established confessional rights and freedoms. Actually, no written agreement, however solemn, however explicit, could protect Catholicism against the insistence of a totalitarian regime on control over all aspects of national life. Yet that insistence had to be expressed indirectly; it had to appear to observe the autonomous status of the church. Hence the struggle between religious and political authority, though fierce, remained largely submerged. Each party, for reasons of its own, helped maintain the fiction that their relations were cordial and harmonious.

In dealing with the Protestant Church, by contrast, the Third Reich could afford to be direct. Protestantism was free of any supranational connection; it was independent of any foreign authority. Indeed, it often boasted that whereas the Catholics were subject to alien influence, its own communicants rejected all outside control or supervision. Their church was a truly German church. But this absence of external ties only made them more vulnerable to internal pressures. Their undivided allegiance to the nation undermined their ability to oppose governmental domination. The Third Reich could seek to gain hegemony over Protestantism by open means, by encouraging among its members loyalty to the new regime and by removing from denominational leadership clergymen considered insufficiently dedicated or enthusiastic.

Nevertheless, the struggle remained essentially a contest over churchly governance. The opposing sides had no basic disagreement regarding the regime's political, economic, social, or even racial policies. Both agreed that the Third Reich was far superior to the Weimar Republic and that its program deserved the support of all right-minded, patriotic Germans. The only issue dividing them was whether the Protestant Church could simply be the faithful ally of the Third Reich, or whether it should become an ecclesiastical branch of National Socialism by abandoning its claim to ideological autonomy.

In dealing with the Protestants the government did not adopt the same strategy as with the Catholics—the strategy of pressure, threat, and intimidation behind a facade of cordiality. It could act more openly in seeking to Nazify German Protestantism. The church itself, the clergy as well as the laity, included many adherents to National Socialism. By encouraging them informally or by giving them overt support or especially by exercising one-sidedly its right to supervise ecclesiastical administration, the state could strengthen its hardcore supporters. Nevertheless, the struggle was not simply between church and state but also between opposing groups or factions within the church. This was to a large extent a civil war.

Hence it remained possible for those who opposed ecclesiastical Nazification to insist that they were not in fact hostile to the regime. They objected to the new system of churchly governance, not the new system of political authority. They questioned not the ideology of National Socialism but the way that ideology was being interpreted and applied by overzealous bureaucrats. The regime in turn made it easier for them to defend this claim by deliberately leaving the formulation of religious policy in the hands of subordinate officials. Hitler himself appeared to stand above the fray, so that his ostensible noninvolvement in the church struggle left him free to advance or retreat, intimidate or conciliate. The antagonism of the ecclesiastical resistance was thereby directed at those members of the bureaucracy who were immediately responsible for regulating relations between temporal and spiritual authority: Minister of Church Affairs Hanns Kerrl, Administrator of the Protestant Church August Jäger, and Reich Bishop Ludwig Müller, the regime's chosen instruments of ecclesiastical Nazification.

Thus on closer inspection the differences in the relationship of the Catholic Church and of the Protestant Church to the new order appear to be superficial differences of style or method rather than substance. The tactics and strategies may have been dissimilar, but the goal of the Third Reich was in both cases the same: the subordination of spiritual to temporal authority.

The response of each denomination to the assault on its autonomy was also the same. Each sought to defend itself by emphasizing its loyalty to the Nazi system and by insisting that its opposition to the government's religious policy was motivated precisely by that loyalty. In other words, German Protestantism, like German Catholicism, restricted the scope of its struggle to the issue of confessional rights and interests. It too subordinated the broad moral principles of religious faith to the limited pragmatic needs of ecclesiastical governance. It too loudly proclaimed to the world its support for the doctrines and purposes of the Third Reich. Basically, it sought only a measure of internal autonomy regarding ecclesiastical administration. Its resistance rarely went beyond the bounds of denominational concerns.

A pastoral report in the summer of 1934 from the town of Schwabach in northern Bavaria described the main source of dissatisfaction among the Protestant laity. At the time of the establishment of the Third Reich, local members of the church had "rejoiced wholeheartedly" because they assumed, "on the basis of the personal declarations of our Führer Hitler as well as the program of the National Socialist Party," that the new order would seek to attract the "Christian population." But this "initial joy" soon turned into disappointment. "Complaints from all our congregations are steadily becoming louder that as a result of the Sunday activities of the Hitler Youth, the SA, the SS, and other [Nazi] Party organizations, attendance at divine services is being affected more and more adversely." The younger generation in particular seemed to be growing indifferent to religious worship. "The continuing disruptions extend even to the teaching of the Christian religion, although that is part of the regular school curriculum." Protests to the authorities had here and there produced some result, but no lasting success was achieved "despite all the decrees issued from above."

Orders restricting meetings of Nazi youth organizations late in the evening were being ignored as well. Even teachers of nonreligious subjects often complained about that, but to no avail. The consequence was a noticeable "absentmindedness or fatigue" among the pupils receiving secular as well as religious instruction. It was especially disturbing that during the church's harvest thanksgiving observance the older boys in the district had been ordered by the SA to take part in athletic contests. Was this how National Socialism proposed to fulfill its promise to honor the German peasant? A few months later, moreover, on a day designated by the church as a time for repentance and prayer, military exercises had been conducted. What the Protestants of Schwabach were objecting to was not the regime's political oppressiveness or racial bigotry but its disrespect for religious worship.[1]

The main source of the disaffection of the ecclesiastical leadership, though somewhat different, was equally limited. While the laity complained about the government's interference with churchly instruction and observance, the clergy deplored its interference with churchly administration and governance. Many ministers regarded the attempt to Nazify German Protestantism with indignation or apprehension. Yet they too hastened to make clear that they were not rejecting the ideology of the Third Reich as such. On the contrary, they maintained in general that they were loyal supporters of the new order. Only on the religious question did they differ with it, and then largely for its own good. Since harmony between church and state was essential for the success of Hitler's program, those who tried to restore that harmony were not really his adversaries but his allies.

In the spring of 1934, in the midst of the struggle to defend the autonomy of the Protestant Church, Bishop Wurm continued to declare his faith in the Nazi regime. "No, there is no hostility toward the Third Reich," he announced from the pulpit, "no hostility toward the state, which, with the heartfelt support of the church, rejects and exorcises caste spirit and class hatred, no hostility concealed behind our concern for church and faith." Rather, the reverse was true. Behind the "noisy glorification of the state" by the extremists within National Socialism lurked an "aversion to the full evangelical truth" and a "lack of understanding for the true mission of the church." Zealots and ideologues had sought, "by promoting misunderstandings," to "confuse" the proper relationship between secular and spiritual authority. All he was therefore trying to do was clarify that relationship, so that the new order could turn without distraction to its historic task of national reconstruction.[2]

Thus for the Protestant as for the Catholic resistance, the chief concern, almost the only concern, was the defense of its confessional interests. The Catholics hoped to reach that goal by compromise and conciliation, by hiding their doubts behinds a facade of approbation. The Protestants expressed their disagreements with the religious policies of the Third Reich more openly. But even they did not oppose the Hitler dictatorship in principle. There was no reason why they should have, since they approved in essence of most of its avowed principles and objectives.

For the Nazi stalwarts, however, that was not enough. They wanted no compromise or accommodation; with them it was all or nothing. Whoever was not totally for the regime was totally against it. Early in 1934 the police commissioner of Bielefeld reported to Gestapo headquarters in Berlin that the Pastors' Emergency League, which played a central role in the Protestant resistance against ecclesiastical Nazification, was made up of irreconcilable enemies of the Third Reich. A "small minority" of its members, he claimed, consisted of "former Marxists," while a "larger number" had once belonged to "the German National People's Party and the [conservative] Christian Socialist People's Service." The "old political differences" between them had now been "completely subordinated to their common resolve to fight against the [new] system of ecclesiastical governance."

Those who had joined the Pastors' Emergency League, moreover, "with a few insignificant exceptions," felt no real "inward sympathy" for "the present state." Indeed, "until the most recent past" they had "more or less openly" waged war against the National Socialist movement or had tried to make it appear "contemptible." How then could there be any reconciliation with people of that sort? The police commissioner's report reflected the views of the Nazi true believer—dogmatic, unbending, and convinced that behind every doubt or reservation regarding the new order lurked subversion.[3]

A more accurate assessment of the churchly resistance came from the other end of the ideological spectrum. Despite its partisan rhetoric and bias, a report issued in November 1934 by the German Social Democratic Party in exile in Prague recognized the limited scope of the religious struggle against the Third Reich. It insisted, with too much vehemence perhaps, that Bishop Hans Meiser, spiritual leader of the Protestants in Bavaria, "can still be regarded today as a convinced personal supporter of Hitler from as early as the putsch period [of 1923]." Bishop Wurm was not much better. He had formerly been "a politician decidedly of the right, specifically, a German National member of the state legislature" in Württemberg, who had "earned his spurs, as far as followers of the Nazi Party are concerned, by his passionate hatred of Marxists." Behind this noisy vituperation was more than a grain of truth.

As for the Socialist analysis of the nature of the religious conflict in Germany, that sounded even more persuasive. "This was no struggle against the system, but a struggle within the system for a share in the dominance, power, and booty in the new authoritarian State." The shopworn phrases about "dominance, power, and booty" can perhaps be dismissed as doctrinaire declamation, but the argument that the ecclesiastical resistance was not a struggle "against the system" but "within the system" sounds convincing.[4]

Thus the leaders of the Protestant Church, with only a few exceptions, endorsed in general the establishment of a dictatorial regime in Germany. Some of them may have differed with the Third Reich on religious questions, but on political issues they were in agreement. Dibelius, as always, stood in the vanguard of the ecclesiastical apologists for the new order. No member of the Nazi Party could have defended its program with greater zeal or conviction. Even Hitler's suppression of civic liberty seemed to him to be in accordance with the teachings of the founder of German Protestantism. "We have learned from Dr. Martin Luther," he sermonized, "that the church must not obstruct the legitimate power of the state when it does what it is supposed to do, even when it acts harshly and ruthlessly. We know the terrible words with which Luther summoned the authorities during the Peasants' War to proceed mercilessly so that stability could be reestablished in Germany." The 1930s resembled the 1520s, a period of confusion and chaos, and Hitler was today's Luther preaching the need for law and order. "A new beginning in the history of a state always takes place in some measure under a constellation of power. For the state is might." The Third Reich was indeed about to demonstrate that.[5]

To Dibelius it was apparent, moreover, that Protestantism shared the ideals and aspirations of National Socialism to a far greater extent than Catholicism did. After all, "the Catholic bishops expect that during religious services political organizations will avoid anything that might appear to be a political or partisan demonstration." They even demanded that "the work of Catholic societies not be restricted." But Protestants voiced no such reservations. "The Protestant ecclesiastical leadership has never issued warnings against the National Socialist movement. It has never barred its clergymen from belonging to it." When the "Socialist" bureaucrats of the republican regime had demanded that the church take action against pastors who were Nazis, its bishops had invariably refused to comply.

Nor was there any need for Protestantism to prove its loyalty to "the great national goals that have now again been placed before the German people." The Protestant Church had always endorsed those goals "in clear and unmistakable words," during good times and bad, "in the prewar period as well as the dark days of the revolution and under the rule of the Weimar parties." And now they were about to be realized. Dibelius remained faithful to the ideals of the Third Reich long after his forced retirement from ecclesiastical office. He may have differed with the regime about religious governance, but he continued to be its ardent supporter regarding secular authority.[6]

Niemöller was somewhat less enthusiastic, but not by much. He too felt that the Hitler regime represented a repudiation of the spirit of Weimar, that it marked the beginning of a return to faith and morality. He too accepted its political goals and methods. Always a patriot and nationalist, always opposed to secularism and democracy, he had never disguised his hostility to the republic. Half a century later, well in his eighties, Niemöller still remembered that the establishment of the Hitler dictatorship had appeared to him to be an act of "liberation." It had meant a revival of traditional values, a restoration of religious beliefs, a reestablishment of political stability, and a rebirth of national pride. How could he have resisted the intoxication of that exciting, inspiring moment?[7]

His endorsement of the Third Reich was as a rule indirect, especially at first, wrapped circumspectly in biblical exegesis and moral exhortation. "Both as Christians and as a Church, we clearly find ourselves today at an altogether unique turning point," he told his congregation in Berlin early in March 1933, barely a month after Hitler's appointment to the chancellorship. The situation in Germany was similar to that described in the Gospels. "We may therefore feel, like Jesus' disciples . . . , that the cause must now go forward and that a new beginning has been made which cannot really fail to achieve success." Once again "confident voices" were being heard in the nation; once again there were "ideas and plans" to advance "the cause of Christianity." The new watchword was "nationality and Christianity," and "with a little skill something can thereby surely be accomplished."

But first serious obstacles would have to be overcome. "In these days" any political leader who "stands up publicly for the protection and preservation of the Christian Churches . . . falls no doubt easily and quickly under the suspicion of wanting to use God to further his [own] aims and plans." All good Christians would recognize, however, that "a German statesman bears a responsibility to God not to let the nation entrusted to his care lose its soul and thereby its life." There could be no mistaking which German statesman Niemöller meant.[8]

By the end of May his support for the new order sounded much more assured. His prayers were at last being answered; his hopes were coming true. "We are at present in the midst of a vast reconstruction of our Protestant Church," he declared from the pulpit. The press was devoting a great deal of attention to that reconstruction, and "the forces that press forward are filled, we may surely assume, with honest purpose and with an enthusiasm that is contagious and irresistible." Many Germans expected that under the Third Reich there would be a reconciliation between church and state, "between our nation and God." Indeed, faithful Protestants hoped "with all our heart" for a new fruitful relationship between temporal and spiritual authority. After all, National Socialism and Protestantism were not incompatible but complementary forces in the spiritual life of Germany.[9]

A few months later Niemöller appeared even more grateful for what the regime was doing to promote a national moral revival. By then an organized opposition to the policy of religious Nazification had already emerged. In fact, he himself had played an important part in the formation of the Pastors' Emergency League. Yet his resistance against the attempts of the Third Reich to gain a controlling influence over churchly governance did not diminish his support for what he regarded as its legitimate objectives. He had waited too long for the establishment of an authoritarian form of rule to turn against it now because of a dispute over ecclesiastical autonomy. In any case, it was not Hitler who was responsible for that dispute but his doctrinaire followers among the clergy and in the bureaucracy. Before long the Führer would surely correct the mistakes that had been committed in his name. In the meantime, those mistakes should not be allowed to obscure the great achievements of the new order. Niemöller's opposition to the regime remained narrowly restricted to the question of denominational authority. On all other issues he was supportive and even laudatory.

He extolled, for example, the spiritual awakening that the Nazi dictatorship was making possible. "We have rediscovered a forgotten truth," he preached at a harvest thanksgiving service in October 1933, "and we have learned once again that we are not independent, isolated individuals." Rather, all Christians were bound and directed to one another "by various connections and dependencies." Under the Third Reich "we feel once again that we are created beings . . . who are not simply what we would like to be but what we must be by virtue of a bond that has been placed and imposed on us." That truth brought a new awareness of vital concepts and values like "occupation and status, race and nation." Those concepts and values had now revealed to the German people "numerous tasks to which we are summoned," tasks from which "we are not permitted to withdraw." Niemöller did not define these tasks, but they were clearly similar to those implied in the common National Socialist slogans about "occupation and status, race and nation."[10]

Bishop Wurm stood somewhere between Niemöller and Dibelius, more explicit than the one, less fervent than the other. For him Hitler's victory meant an end to social unrest and class conflict, to the futile bickering of political factions and parliamentary parties, to the danger of Communist revolution and godless atheism. In a letter addressed to the Protestant clergy of Württemberg in the spring of 1933, he expressed his sense of profound relief. Germany was like a "beleaguered city" in which, after a "very dangerous period of confusion and division," a "united and purposeful leadership" had emerged as a result of the "cooperation of responsible men." The church must not remain indifferent to the great work of national regeneration. On the contrary, it should be thankful that "at the last moment" the "total collapse of nation and state" and the "victory of destructive forces" had been prevented. A glance at Russia would show what might have become the fate of Germany. In view of "the enormously difficult task" facing the Third Reich, it was the duty of the church "to bless the work of the men who today are at the top." More than that, the laity as well as the clergy should help foster that "inner unity" without which "even the strongest political leadership cannot achieve the great goals before the fatherland."[11]

Something else helped attract many Protestant churchmen to National Socialism, namely, its call for a military revival of Germany. Almost all of them were ardent patriots and nationalists. They resented the acquiescence of the republican government in the peace settlement; they prayed for a rectification of the injustices of Versailles; they demanded for their country a position of equality with the victor states; they even agreed that the threat or the actual use of armed force was the only means of ending Germany's subordination. In the establishment of the Third Reich they saw at last an opportunity to wipe out an intolerable national humiliation.

They also deplored the fate of the unfortunate Germans living under foreign domination, especially in Poland, who were struggling to preserve their cultural identity against an alien government, an alien language, and an alien religion. While rejoicing at Hitler's victory in the spring of 1933, Dibelius reflected on the fate of his nation's lost tribes. "Hundreds of thousands of our brothers and sisters, whom God has summoned to be members of a free people, are still groaning in foreign bondage." Yet they had never wavered in their loyalty to their ethnic heritage. "It is our pride and joy that our Protestant fellow communicants in the east who speak the German language but have been separated from Germany by the dictate of Versailles have preserved their connection with the inner life of the mother church." Now at last the oppressed had reason to hope. In the past the German people had often been forced to fight for their freedom, and they had always won "whenever a new surge of faith pulsated throughout their being." National Socialism was about to provide that "new surge of faith," making possible the political rebirth of Germany.[12]

Niemöller shared all those hopes and expectations. How could it have been otherwise? A former naval officer, an ardent patriot, an avowed opponent of the Weimar regime, he perceived in Hitler's victory the opportunity to revive national pride and greatness. Even after the outbreak of the struggle over churchly governance, he continued to endorse the regime's new assertive diplomacy. His reluctance to become involved in controversial issues of public policy did not extend to the abrogation of Versailles. When the government announced Germany's withdrawal from the League of Nations in October 1933, he joined several other leaders of the Pastors' Emergency League in sending the Führer a message congratulating him on his bold statesmanship. Even four years later, at the trial that led to his imprisonment in a concentration camp, Niemöller boasted how, after learning of Hitler's decision to withdraw from Geneva, he immediately sent off a telegram to express his support, "probably the first the Führer received regarding this action." He was still proud of that.[13]

Breaking the chains of Versailles seemed equally important to Wurm. He, like Niemöller, supported the diplomatic policy of the Third Reich while opposing its religious policy. In April 1934, in the midst of the struggle to preserve the confessional autonomy of the Protestant Church in Württemberg, he proudly proclaimed in the Ulm Cathedral his unyielding patriotism and conservatism. He was seeking to assure not only his fellow Protestants but also the Nazi authorities that he had always been ultranationalist and antirepublican in his convictions. He recalled how, after the fall of the monarchy, he had opposed the abandonment of "the black, white, and red [imperial] flag crowned with glory," how disappointed he had been that the bourgeoisie put its trust in "the siren song of President Wilson," and how bitter he had felt because the working class "hoped for better days [once] militarism was destroyed." His "heart bled" because under the republic the nation had become indifferent to "German honor and German greatness." But then his "heart filled with hope" when a new leader, "a man of the people," succeeded in impressing on even the "simplest person" the truth that "no social group can be strong and happy unless the fatherland is strong and happy." If only that unfortunate conflict over churchly governance could be resolved, Wurm was saying, he would be ready to support Hitler unreservedly.[14]

Still, what attracted the Protestant churchmen to National Socialism most of all, more than its domestic program or its foreign policy, was its "spirituality," its "idealism." They saw in it first and foremost a rejection of the materialistic values of Weimar, a rejection of individualism, liberalism, and secularism, of Mammon and the golden calf. The Germans would now return to time-honored beliefs, values, and loyalties. "We want to be free again from the spirit that knows only material things," Dibelius declared when the Hitler dictatorship was formally established. The end of the republic seemed to him to open the way for a great religious revival.

"We owe it to our people . . . to help validate Christian standards in the German fatherland and recreate the Christian atmosphere that has fallen victim to modern secularization." His support for the Third Reich was not radical but traditionalist in nature, he insisted; it served a profoundly religious purpose. "We Protestant Christians are fighting in good conscience for a Christian state." National Socialism had become in his view the champion of a revived spiritual faith.[15]

Yet the idealism for which Dibelius and many other members of the Protestant clerical resistance yearned was narrow in focus. It had no sympathy for the peace movement, for example, for a renunciation of armed force or even a reduction in military armaments. It had little concern for civil liberties, the freedom of opinion, the right of dissent, protection against arbitrary authority, and security from governmental repression. It questioned the contention that those who rule should take into account the views of those who are ruled, that public authority should rest on public consent. And it rejected the argument that all members of the community, regardless of political conviction or ethnic origin, should help determine the goals of the community. The idealism of the ecclesiastical leadership meant primarily submission to legitimate authority, obedience to established tradition, avowal of national loyalty, and acknowledgment of religious faith.

Hence for the Protestant resistance official anti-Semitism presented less of an obstacle to the acceptance of the Third Reich than for the Catholic resistance. The Catholics were often ambivalent in their view of the Nazi persecution of the Jewish community. They perceived a disturbing similarity between their own position and that of the Jews. They too were accused by Nazi zealots of being disloyal to the nation, of feeling a greater devotion to their coreligionists abroad than to their compatriots at home, and of forming, in alliance with international capitalism and Judaism, a conspiracy to dominate the world. In the propaganda employed by the new order to justify anti-Semitism they could hear the unmistakable echoes of anti-Catholicism. They did not dare oppose that propaganda openly. They were afraid that if they did, the regime would introduce repressive measures against Catholics like those it was directing against Jews. Therefore they decided to remain silent, to bow and acquiesce. But sometimes they felt troubled by the thought that they were perhaps protecting their own security by abandoning another unpopular, persecuted minority. The Jews were after all also victims of officially sanctioned prejudice, underdogs, and scapegoats. Should not the church do more to defend them?

Such doubts rarely assailed the Protestant leaders. Many of them had been opposed to the indulgent, tolerant spirit of Weimar, convinced that the republican regime was dominated by the forces of big business, Roman Catholicism, and world Jewry. The establishment of the Third Reich represented for them not only the victory of traditional authority over destructive revolutionism, but also the triumph of national religious faith over alien spiritual influence. They generally welcomed that victory with joy.

About Dibelius's attitude there could be no question. Even under the Weimar regime he had made no attempt to hide his hostility to democracy, republicanism, radicalism, individualism, pacifism, and Judaism. The triumph of the Third Reich appeared to him to open the way for a moral as well as material rebirth. He exulted. As for Nazi anti-Semitism, he portrayed it simultaneously as a shameless fabrication and a necessary corrective. In a shortwave radio broadcast to the United States in the spring of 1933, Dibelius assured the American public that stories about Jewish persecution by the Hitler dictatorship were largely invented. "On the basis of . . . false reports [world] Jewry has now started an agitation against Germany in several countries. . . . In order to break this boycott, the German National Socialists in turn have now initiated a boycott movement against Jewry in Germany." But that measure was only defensive, a means of self-protection. Besides, the government's counterboycott had been brief and restrained; it had been carried out "in orderly fashion and peacefully." Dibelius hoped that before long "a newly established order in national life will leave room for charity and justice." But that would depend on whether "[foreign] agitation against Germany stops or not." He concluded by urging his listeners in the United States not to rush to judgment. They should use their influence rather to ensure that "no false reports about Germany are hereafter circulated and believed."

Even while denying the severity of the Third Reich's anti-Semitic measures, Dibelius justified their adoption. How else could the nation oppose the excessive influence that Jewry had acquired in Germany? He declared his support for the efforts of the new government "to remove Jews from state administration, particularly from judicial posts," since Jews constituted less than 1 percent of the population. All the Nazi authorities were trying to do was restore conditions to "what they were formerly," before Weimar. Once that had been achieved, anti-Semitic resentment would no doubt diminish, and the Protestant Church, which represented "chivalry and charity," would then be able to assist in maintaining racial justice. Until then, however, the state had no choice but to try to establish a more equitable balance between Aryans and non-Aryans.[16]

Even after Dibelius himself fell victim to the same intolerance that the Third Reich had displayed toward Jews, he continued to consider its anti-Semitic program, in part at least, defensible. There was no connection in his mind between opposition to the regime's ecclesiastical policy and opposition to its racial policy. One was justified, the other was not. Many years later, in the autobiography he wrote toward the end of his life, he still recalled with satisfaction how he had closely scrutinized all requests from Jews for admission to the Protestant Church to make sure they were not motivated by a desire to escape racial discrimination. "They all claimed that they were coming for the most spiritual reasons and that they wanted to do anything the clergyman asked. . . . But eventually it almost always turned out that there was some external reason. I therefore became increasingly precise and rigorous in my demands. This gradually became known, and so in the end I was spared such requests for baptism motivated by purely external needs." To violate the sanctity of conversion by considerations of expediency or security or even self-preservation seemed to him deplorable.[17]

Niemöller was more charitable. He too believed that the Jews were collectively guilty of an unpardonable crime, the crucifixion of Christ, but held that their punishment should be left to divine judgment, not human retribution. In the summer of 1935 he sermonized about the "dark secret surrounding the strange history of this people that can neither live nor die, because it is under a curse." The Jews were undoubtedly "highly gifted," producing "idea after idea to benefit the world." But whatever they touched became "poison"; all they reaped was "contempt and hatred." Still, the true Christian should not contribute to their ordained punishment. He should rather keep in mind that "there is no license empowering us to add to God's curse with our hatred." After all, "even Cain receives God's mark, so that no one is permitted to slay him; and Jesus' command, 'love your enemies,' allows for no exception." The Nazi persecution of the Jews appeared to Niemöller to be a divine retaliation for an unforgivable transgression. Hence those witnessing that retaliation could not and should not try to mitigate its severity. They should view in silent awe God's terrible judgment.[18]

The Jews who converted to Protestantism were in an entirely different situation, of course; they were now full and equal members of the church. For Niemöller Judaism was not a matter of race but of faith, so that whoever accepted baptism, whether Aryan or not, became a Christian in the full meaning of that term. Yet he was prepared, for reasons of expediency, to retreat a step or two from this professed principle. At one point, for instance, he contemplated the establishment of separate Jewish-Christian congregations, still within the church, but segregating Aryans from non-Aryans. Although membership would be entirely voluntary, such an arrangement might help the ecclesiastical leadership avoid needless confrontations with the Nazi regime. He conceded, moreover, that while non-Aryan holders of churchly office could not be removed without violating Protestant doctrine, "this acknowledgment demands of us, who as a nation have had to endure a great deal under the influence of the Jewish people, a high degree of self-denial." He hoped therefore that Christians of Jewish descent would of their own accord agree to forgo positions in denominational administration or missionary work. That would really be best for all concerned. Niemöller continued to proclaim that in theory all Protestants were equal, but he was prepared in practice to make some concessions to the anti-Semitic prejudices of the Third Reich.[19]

A few members of the ecclesiastical resistance did speak out more boldly. Church Superintendent Martin Albertz of Berlin, for instance, helped draft a memorandum in September 1935, on the eve of the Nuremberg Laws formalizing the exclusion of Jews from the civic and social life of Germany, which denounced Nazi racial policy. "Where is Abel thy brother? For us too . . . there will be no answer other than the answer of Cain." Even if the church could do nothing to help the victims of anti-Semitism, should it not at least acknowledge its moral responsibility? "Why does it not pray for those whom this undeserved suffering and persecution affect? Why are there no religious services seeking [divine] intercession?"

Worse still, there were some Christians who "dare believe that they are justified or even called on to preach to the Jewish community regarding God's judgment and grace, despite the historic happenings of today and the sufferings for which we are responsible." That was unconscionable. "Since when does the evildoer have the right to pretend that his evildoing is the will of God?" Christians should beware of hiding the "abomination of our sin" behind the "sanctity of God's will." Otherwise, it might well happen that "the punishment of the defilers of the Temple would be inflicted on us as well, [and] we too would have to bear the curse of him who fashioned the scourge and drove them out." The attitude of the church to the persecution of the Jews served as the real measure of its devotion to the teachings of Christianity.[20]

The poignancy of this declaration of compassion for the victims of racial persecution was all the greater because it was so rare. And yet its fate was only too common. Albertz's memorandum circulated among his friends and associates in the resistance movement, but it was never submitted for formal consideration to either the ecclesiastical or the secular authorities. A copy was sent to England, where it remained neglected and ignored until after the war. Engaged in a bitter struggle to defend the autonomy of their church, even those leaders of German Protestantism who sympathized with the Jews hesitated to intensify the hostility of the Nazi dictatorship by directly challenging its anti-Semitic doctrines.

The only well-known member of the ecclesiastical resistance who from the outset criticized the regime's racial program, openly, repeatedly, and consistently, was Bonhoeffer. The young Protestant clergyman, still in his twenties, refused to be intimidated or silenced. Admittedly, his views sounded at times, especially in the early days of the Third Reich, similar to Niemöller's. He too spoke of "the curse that rests on this people"; he too maintained that "only the conversion of Israel" could put an end to its "period of suffering." No temporal state could solve the Jewish question, because God had not yet finished solving it. Therefore the Christian could only view the history of Jewry "with a shudder" as "God's own, free, terrible way of dealing with his people." But the Christian should at least refrain from "any glib moralizing" about the fate of the Jews, while waiting "full of hope" for those who "returned home" with a newborn faith "in the one true God in Christ." Such converts were to be received joyously as "brothers."

On this last point, that "non-Aryan" Christians were full and equal members of the church, Bonhoeffer was uncompromising. He insisted that "the community of those who belong to the church is defined not by race but by the Holy Spirit and by baptism." To transform the Protestant Church into a religious community restricted to "Christians of the Aryan race" would "rob it of its promise." Since Judaism was "never a racial but a religious concept, . . . the baptized Jew is a member of our church." In short, "for the church the Jewish question is different from what it is for the state." There could be and must be no retreat from this position.

Bonhoeffer even criticized the Nazi regime, indirectly but unmistakably, for its treatment of those Jews who had not converted and were therefore outside the formal jurisdiction of the church. They too seemed to him to have a valid claim to the moral concern of the Christian community. He categorically rejected the idea that anti-Semitism represented a providentially decreed punishment for an unforgivable collective crime. "It can never be the mission of a people to impose vengeance on the Jews for the murder at Golgotha." That had to be left to God. At the funeral service for his grandmother he spoke of the "great sorrow" she had felt, and by implication he as well, at "the fate of the Jews in our nation," a fate that the deceased had "shared and pitied." And in a lecture entitled "The Church and the Jewish Question," he declared outright that "it remains the task of humanitarian organizations and of individual Christian men who feel the calling to point out to the state the moral aspect of its measures at any given time, that is, to accuse the state, if need be, of violating morality." It was obvious which state and what moral violation he had in mind.[21]

Unlike most members of the clerical resistance, Bonhoeffer did not compartmentalize his opposition to the Nazi regime. He remained convinced that the struggle against the Third Reich's religious policies could not be separated from the struggle against its political, military, or racial policies. But most other ecclesiastical resisters did not share that view. What they sought was a return to the pieties and allegiances of the imperial era, when the state provided the church with influence and esteem, while the church preached loyalty and devotion to the state. The reestablishment of that mutually beneficial relationship was the main objective of their resistance against the Hitler dictatorship. They were fighting by and large not for religious faith or moral principle but for denominational autonomy and confessional authority. Their struggle, as the exiled Socialists in Prague had charged, was in essence not against but within the system.

III

The Flowering of the Authoritarian Coalition

In many respects I feel that the internal development of Germany—if only the European peace can be kept—bears more promise in its potential social and economic working out and [has] more honest and substantial bearing on a cooperative international future than the "powers" that have let Spain and Abyssinia happen.

ADAM VON TROTT ZU SOLZ (1937)

10

The Armed Forces under the Hitler Dictatorship

After the collapse of the Third Reich many Germans looked back with a certain nostalgia to the period from roughly the end of 1935 to the beginning of 1938, the bright summertime of the Nazi regime, the season of regained hope, security, confidence, and pride. That period, between the tensions and hardships of the political consolidation of the new order and the pressures and dangers of its diplomatic aggrandizement, seemed in retrospect a golden interlude, the high point of the Third Reich. The incessant squabbling of political parties and factions had been suppressed, the economic depression had come to an end, the danger of social upheaval had been eliminated, and the military restrictions of Versailles had been repudiated. How could anyone not have been impressed by achievements of such magnitude?

Here and there, to be sure, the government had used force, occasionally even excessive force, to establish and consolidate the Nazi regime. Prominent radicals had been exiled or imprisoned; Jews had been abused and humiliated, more perhaps than was necessary to reduce their influence in public life; and a few liberal bureaucrats and clergymen had been removed from office. But for almost everyone else conditions seemed much better than under the old order. The good Hitler managed to keep the bad one in check; the moderates in the National Socialist Party still had enough strength to restrain the extremists. If only the regime had been a little more cautious and realistic, if only the Führer had not succumbed to ambition and hubris, Germany might have continued to grow, progress, prosper, and rejoice.

This view obviously presupposed that the catastrophic outcome of the Hitler dictatorship was not logical but fortuitous. It rested on the assumption that the disastrous policies which led to war and defeat resulted from inexperience and miscalculation rather than from destructive forces inherent in totalitarianism. Yet even in the heyday of the Hitler dictatorship there were those who recognized that the regime was bound to become increasingly dogmatic and intolerant, and that the coalition between the old-line conservatives and the new radical rightists was only a screen for an attempt to end the distinction between state and party, between National Socialism and Germany.

The Protestant clergyman Günter Jacob, for example, a member of the ecclesiastical resistance in Prussia, predicted in 1936 that the Third Reich would sooner or later turn against those who were mere sympathizers and well-wishers, and that anyone who was not totally committed to its doctrines would eventually come to be regarded as its opponent. "Today's state, being a dogmatically constrained state, cannot by its nature be content with the loyalty of its citizens. . . . Today's state can recognize only followers and adversaries, but not loyal citizens. And Christian reserve must [therefore] appear to it as political opposition and violation of its sacred foundations." Indeed, the ideologues of National Socialism regarded any doubts and hesitations, whether religious or secular in nature, as clear evidence of subversive tendencies.[1]

That did not trouble most Germans, however, at least not at first. What mattered to them was the dramatic contrast between the early and the middle 1930s. They saw an end to the bewildering succession of chancellors and cabinets: the fall of Hermann Müller and the appointment of Heinrich Brüning in March 1930, the fall of Brüning and the appointment of Franz von Papen in May and June 1932, the fall of Papen and the appointment of Kurt von Schleicher in December 1932, and the fall of Schleicher and the appointment of Hitler in January 1933. The system of government had degenerated into a game of musical chairs, and an endless sequence of electoral campaigns and elections ensued: the vote for the Reichstag in September 1930, the preliminary vote for president in March 1932, the runoff vote in April 1932, the vote for the Reichstag in July 1932, another vote for the Reichstag in November 1932, and still another vote for the Reichstag in March 1933—a total of five bitter and emotionally exhausting elections in the space of less than a year.

They therefore welcomed the end of the Byzantine politics of the dying Weimar Republic, the schemes and intrigues, plots and counterplots, the backstage maneuvering and conspiring: Papen against Brüning, Schleicher against Papen, Papen against Schleicher, Nationalists against Centrists, Centrists against Socialists, Socialists against National Socialists, and all of them against Communists. It was a relief to many Germans to get off this dizzying merry-go-round of parties, platforms, politics, and politicians.

Even more important was the end of the economic crisis. Long after the fall of the Hitler dictatorship, those who lived through it often recalled how hard life had been in the early 1930s. They remembered the pitiful dole on which families of the unemployed had to live, the cramped, drab housing, the young people still residing with their parents because they could not find work, and the elderly forced to depend on the grudging charity of relatives. They recalled the demoralizing social manifestations of the depression, the spread of begging, stealing, cheating, and prostitution. Those were humiliating experiences for a proud people. But then came the Third Reich, and everything seemed to change. Suddenly there were jobs, most of them admittedly not very well paying, but jobs. Housing improved; families had a little more room, more comfort, more privacy. The new order suppressed public begging and reduced petty crime, and while commercialized vice was not eliminated, at least it became less blatant or importunate. Most important, the Third Reich appeared to restore hope and confidence to a nation that had sunk into profound discouragement.

Even those who did not have to endure privation during the depression felt relieved by the victory of National Socialism. The well-to-do classes had been watching with mounting concern the growth of economic tension and social resentment in Germany. They had felt threatened by the endless demonstrations and counterdemonstrations, marches and countermarches, strikes and riots, by the increasing clashes between police and protesters, between rightists and leftists, between nationalists and antinationalists, and between Communists and Nazis. Where would it all end? Was this not how things had been in Russia just before the Bolshevik revolution? Germany seemed to face the same situation, the same political confusion, the same class antagonism, the same breakdown of law and order, and the same left-wing conspiracy to seize power and expropriate wealth. To many landowners, businessmen, professionals, and shopkeepers, the victory of National Socialism meant essentially an end to the danger of social conflict and upheaval.

For all these reasons the Third Reich enjoyed its most solid and consistent popular support in the mid-1930s. Earlier there had been fears and uncertainties regarding the effect of the changes being introduced by the new order in state and society. Afterward public opinion fluctuated between wild rejoicing at Hitler's remarkable diplomatic successes and deep apprehension of a war provoked by his reckless international gambles. But the period from late 1935 to early 1938 was the high noon of the Nazi regime, bright and hopeful, rich in the promise of sound, steady progress.

This atmosphere helps explain the decline of what might be called the proto-resistance or quasi-resistance, the resistance that was basically the last gasp of Weimar. During the early years of the Third Reich die-hard supporters of the parties active in republican politics, mostly Communists and Social Democrats, tried to maintain an underground opposition in Germany. From time to time chalked slogans denouncing the Hitler dictatorship would appear on a wall or sidewalk, anti-Nazi pamphlets would occasionally be smuggled in from abroad and circulated surreptitiously, and sometimes even small, clandestine meetings would be organized to discuss and criticize the government's policies. By the middle of the decade, however, these faint attempts at organized political disaffection had come to an end. That was due in part to the increased efficiency and ruthlessness of the Gestapo, but mostly it reflected the growing acceptance of the new order by the German masses. Even many of those who had at first been opposed to National Socialism began to have second thoughts. Could they have been mistaken in their assessment of the Third Reich? Did the government in fact possess greater wisdom, skill, or talent than it had been given credit for? The rising popular approval of the regime clearly resulted from its perceived effectiveness.

This effectiveness seemed as evident in foreign as in domestic affairs. Hitler had come to power promising to free Germany from the restrictions imposed by Versailles. The promise had been largely fulfilled by the spring of 1936 with the remilitarization of the Rhineland, following the introduction of military conscription and naval expansion in the spring of 1935, and the elimination of reparations in the summer of 1932, even before the establishment of the Third Reich. Yet the Nazi regime remained at first isolated, regarded with distrust and suspicion not only by the democratic powers, France and England, but by Fascist Italy as well. What had kept the two dictatorships apart, despite their obvious ideological similarities, was the question of Austria. Mussolini had become that country's patron and protector, especially after the establishment of an authoritarian government in Vienna early in 1933. But the victory in Germany of National Socialism with its doctrine of a common political destiny of all Teutonic peoples seemed to threaten the independence of Italy's client. The prospect of an assertive and expansionist Third Reich on the Brenner Pass made the Duce uneasy. He was therefore prepared to swallow his antidemocratic scruples and collaborate with Paris and London to maintain the status quo.

In return for his support of their policies in Central Europe, however, he expected their support for his policies in East Africa. When he discovered during the war against Ethiopia that they in fact opposed him—only halfheartedly, to be sure, and not out of conviction but in response to the pressure of public opinion—he decided to change sides, even if that meant the abandonment of Austria. After all, he and Hitler had so much in common. They were both dictatorial, aggressive, nationalistic, and militaristic. They were both have-nots in international affairs, opposed to the Versailles settlement and eager for a new diplomatic order in Europe. Cooperation between them seemed eminently logical.

In October 1936, following their joint intervention in the civil war in Spain, the two dictators reached an understanding that, without establishing a formal alliance, initiated close collaboration between them in foreign policy. The conclusion of this Rome-Berlin Axis, as it came to be popularly known, signaled that the Third Reich had finally emerged from the international isolation to which it had been relegated since its establishment. A month later Germany and Japan signed the Anti-Comintern Pact, ostensibly designed to counter the machinations of international Communism, but in fact clearly directed against the Soviet Union. The Versailles system was now in shambles. The dominant role of the victor states had been replaced by a new dualism in international relations, a new balance of power. Two hostile camps faced each other, one hoping to preserve the status quo, the other determined to revise it. The establishment of the Third Reich thus helped create an opportunity to repudiate the peace settlement of 1919 once and for all.

This altered constellation of power in European diplomacy promoted pride and assertiveness among the Germans, defiance of the unfair demands of their country's hostile neighbors, and a new sense of national dignity. But Hitler sought more than that. He was not content with the end of reparations or the rejection of the demilitarization clauses of Versailles or even the reacquisition by plebiscite of the Saar region. To him those were small potatoes. What he really wanted was far-reaching expansion including not only territories that the German state had lost after the war but also some that had not even been within its prewar boundaries. An ethnic or racial mystique more than any historic or legal claim shaped his ambition.

On November 5, 1937, he presented his views at a secret conference of the top German military and diplomatic leaders. Present were the war minister, Field Marshal Werner von Blomberg, the commanders in chief of the army, the navy, and the air force—General Werner von Fritsch, Admiral

Erich Raeder, and Hermann Göring—Foreign Minister Konstantin von Neurath, and the Führer's adjutant, Colonel Friedrich Hossbach, who took down the minutes of the meeting. Five days later he finished drafting a memorandum, based on his notes, that summarized the proceedings. This document provides important insights into Hitler's thinking about the future direction of the Third Reich's foreign policy.

"The solution to the German question can be achieved only by means of force," he insisted, "and that can never be without risk." He did not hesitate to face that risk, although a decision would still have to be made on "the questions of 'when' and 'how.'" Hitler argued that hostilities should begin no later than 1943–1945, because "after this date only a change for the worse, from our point of view, can be expected." For the improvement of Germany's military and political position, the first objective of an armed conflict should be "to crush Czechoslovakia and at the same time Austria" so as to eliminate "the threat to our flank in the event of an advance against the West." It seemed to him "highly probable" that the British and even the French "have already quietly written off the Czechs and become reconciled to the fact that this question would someday be settled by Germany." As for the other states that might object to an expansion of the Third Reich—Italy, Poland, and Russia—they were even less likely to intervene than England or France. Hitler thus calculated that for the next six or seven years he could initiate a war for territorial expansion under favorable conditions.

Such a war would lead to obvious gains. The incorporation of Czechoslovakia and Austria would mean the acquisition of foodstuffs for five to six million people, "on the assumption that a compulsory emigration of two million people from Czechoslovakia and one million from Austria could be successfully carried out." Additional advantages would include the shorter and more defensible boundaries of Germany, the redeployment "for other purposes" of troops now guarding the southeastern frontier, and the possibility of expanding the armed forces "by up to about 12 divisions." The Hossbach memorandum makes clear that as early as the period of the consolidation of the Third Reich, maybe even earlier, Hitler had concluded that only war could provide him with the means of attaining his diplomatic objectives.[2]

Most Germans of course had no knowledge of Hitler's plans. They saw only that the government was standing up at last to those overbearing French and English politicians, rejecting their demands, defying their threats. But the members of the officer corps, and certainly those in top positions, must have recognized that the regime regarded a military conflict as not only likely but desirable. For how else could the nation achieve that territorial enlargement that, in Hitler's view, was necessary for its political stability and economic progress? Still, none of the leaders of the armed forces disagreed in principle with the conclusion that only armed force would be able to win the position of power to which Germany was rightfully entitled. They simply wanted the test of military strength to take place under optimum conditions, avoiding premature initiatives or unnecessary risks. They never questioned its ultimate purpose.

Some twenty years later Field Marshal Manstein did maintain that "criticism was quite openly expressed in military circles regarding the encroachments and blunders of the [Nazi] Party, and [these encroachments], insofar as they affected the military sphere, were sharply rejected." But his observation applies only to the efforts by some overzealous National Socialists to interfere with the organization and administration of the armed forces. Regarding the goals of Germany's diplomatic and military policy, there was no significant disagreement.[3]

More revealing is the affidavit submitted by Field Marshal Blomberg at the Nuremberg trial of the Nazi leaders. Until the late 1930s, he testified, the armed forces did not oppose Hitler's conduct of foreign affairs. Thereafter "some of the generals began to detest his methods and distrusted his judgment." But by and large they failed to take any "discernible position" against him. Why should they have? After all, "he produced the successes they wanted."[4]

Blomberg was in a position to know. He had been present at the meeting described in the Hossbach memorandum, when Hitler revealed his plans for an expansionist war to begin within a few years. Blomberg did not question the underlying reasons given for waging such a war. He tried rather to determine how to remove the obstacles to success and to maximize the chances of victory. He and Fritsch emphasized that England and France must not be made to appear as Germany's enemies. Perhaps they would then turn instead against Italy. As for a campaign to conquer Austria and Czechoslovakia, Blomberg drew attention to the strength of the Czech fortifications, "whose construction has now assumed the dimensions of a Maginot Line making our attack difficult in the extreme." Fritsch added that he had already ordered a study to be made of how best to conduct military operations in the southeast, "with special consideration for overcoming the Czech fortification system." Both generals sounded somewhat uneasy, but because of technical difficulties rather than moral scruples. Their reservations pertained to the means, to the techniques and methods, not to the ends, of Hitler's diplomacy. War was after all their trade.[5]

Members of the officer corps did not confine their support of the Third Reich to foreign affairs. They were also impressed by its domestic accomplishments, especially its restoration of political and social stability. Without officially abandoning the doctrine of noninvolvement in government policy, they made no secret of their conviction that the Nazi regime was far preferable to the old discredited Weimar system. Hitler had put an end to unemployment and privation, to left-wing agitation and Bolshevik conspiracy, to demoralization, hopelessness, humiliation, and defeatism. Could those entrusted with the defense of the nation remain indifferent to achievements of such magnitude? On October 15, 1935, at a ceremony celebrating the reopening of the War Academy, which had remained closed for fifteen years under the terms of Versailles, Blomberg spoke of the professional soldier's recognition of what the new order had accomplished. Although members of the officer corps had nothing to do with politics, he declared, they must know "where the sources of the nation's strength lie," they must learn to embrace "political thinking," and they must feel a need for "the joyful avowal of the Nationalist Socialist view of the world." For the armed forces the line separating loyalty to the state from loyalty to the government had by now become very thin indeed.[6]

Approval of the Nazi regime was just as strong among those officers who later joined the resistance as among those who did not. The younger men in particular were attracted by the boldness and determination of the new order. Less is known about their attitudes in the middle 1930s than about their feelings in the preceding period of the Third Reich's establishment or in the succeeding period of the emerging opposition against Hitler. But there are glimpses here and there of future resisters sharing in the widespread popular enthusiasm for the achievements of National Socialism. In 1936 Paul von Hase, head of an infantry regiment in Küstrin and later the military commander of Berlin, held speeches in praise of the Führer. At about the same time Claus von Stauffenberg, caught up in the new spirit sweeping across Germany, attended a lecture by Walther Buch, chief judge of the Nazi Party's high court. Shortly before, Stauffenberg's close friend Albrecht Mertz von Quirnheim had joined the SA, convinced that it was destined to become a true people's army entrusted with the defense of the fatherland. All three were to be executed in the summer of 1944 for participating in the plot to kill Hitler. Yet only a few years earlier they had seemed to be loyal, obedient soldiers of the Third Reich.[7]

The most ardent supporters of the new order within the armed forces, however, were to be found not in the army but in the navy. The army was too patrician in outlook, too much under the influence of the monarchical

and conservative traditions of the imperial era, to embrace National Socialism unreservedly. The navy, by contrast, had been shaped primarily by the
experiences of the twentieth century. Largely bourgeois in origin, less elitist
in spirit, more favorable to political engagement, its officers perceived in
the Hitler regime ideals and principles close to their own. Many of them
became avowed and enthusiastic adherents of the Third Reich.

But none could surpass Admiral Canaris in zeal or loyalty. He appeared
to be a Nazi through and through, at least until the outbreak of the war.
It was in fact this devotion to the regime that helped him gain in 1935 the
position of chief of German counterintelligence. His appointment was
strongly supported by the SS as well as the Foreign Bureau of the National
Socialist Party, both of which believed that they had found in him someone
whose ideological commitment was beyond question. They felt sure he was
one of them.[8]

Canaris did not disappoint them. Throughout the 1930s he continued
to sing the praises of the new order, to preach its doctrines and extol its
leaders. There was nothing of the nonpolitical officer about him. "Only
someone who is a good soldier, a good comrade, a fine fellow, and a pure
spirit can also be a good National Socialist and citizen," he declaimed.
"With us lip service is nothing, service by deed is everything. True soldierly
conduct and National Socialism are one and the same thing." It was no
longer enough for the man in uniform to acquire technical mastery of his
craft. He also had to become familiar with what was happening around
him, with political questions, with current affairs. He had to become aware
of "the eternal values of faith, race, nationality, and the social community."
Before the world war the military officer had "logically" been a monarchist;
under Weimar he had "logically" tried to preserve "the legacy of the
battlefront experience"; and now that "the battlefront experience of all of
us has found its realization in the National Socialist state," he ought
"logically" to be a National Socialist.

For Canaris loyalty to the nation and loyalty to the party had become
indivisible and indistinguishable. The separation of military service from
political activism seemed to him not only unrealistic but undesirable. The
principles and values expounded by the Third Reich were precisely those
embraced by the armed forces. Why then maintain an artificial barrier
between them? "We should always remember," he exhorted, "that National Socialism arose in the trenches and in the shell holes of the world
war, and that its creator, our commander in chief, always was and is a
soldier. The more familiar we become with National Socialist ideas, the
more we will discover that they are truly soldierly ideas." The watchwords

of the Nazi Party, "obedience, comradeship, closeness to the people, readiness to serve, and loyalty," were also the watchwords of the armed forces. In short, "whoever is a really good soldier will also be a good National Socialist." The difference between state and government had vanished.[9]

As late as the spring of 1938, after the first stirrings of doubt had begun to trouble some of the leaders of the armed forces, Canaris continued to insist that the fate of Germany was inseparable from the fate of Hitler. The Führer's great virtues, he declared at the beginning of March, "a sense of honor and duty, courage, a readiness to take up arms, a readiness to serve and sacrifice, leadership, comradeship, [and] a sense of responsibility," were those fostered by the soldier. He urged the officers under his command to avoid "the slightest appearance of a so-called reactionary outlook, even though it may not actually exist." And in those few cases where it might exist, "for the most part only out of stupidity," it would have to be "destroyed." There was no room in the military for doubters and waverers.[10]

Seven weeks later, after the annexation of Austria, he sounded even more enthusiastic. In a lecture given in Vienna, now the visible symbol of Hitler's triumphant statecraft, he suggested that the history of Germany during the preceding three hundred years had been largely a prelude to the victory of the Nazi Party. In founding the Prussian army in the seventeenth century, for example, the Great Elector had taken a momentous step based on "a National Socialist decision." Similarly, the soldier who had fought at the front in the world war became the "first National Socialist of the deed." At present Hitler's military program represented "the logical culmination of the officer's calling, which National Socialism has achieved purely and without compromise." In short, the Nazi regime was essentially "a means of training the individual to become a good German."

The armed forces were especially indebted to the Führer, according to Canaris. He had restored them to a prominent position in national life; he had translated their guiding principles into political realities. They owed him unquestioning obedience. "The soldier and officer," Canaris preached, "is today once again bound to his commander in chief by a personal oath, with the invocation of almighty God as a witness. To doubt this loyalty or to question the National Socialist trustworthiness of the armed forces or of the officer is a grave insult to the armed forces and to their officer corps." As far as he was concerned, the Nazi slogan "one nation, one Reich, one Führer, and one army" was "a slogan of pride and satisfaction."[11]

This eagerness to demonstrate his devotion to the Hitler dictatorship also helps explain Canaris's involvement in an issue far beyond the scope of his duties as head of counterintelligence. The plan he advanced in the middle 1930s to resettle the Jews of Germany in one of the overseas colonies that, he felt confident, England and France would eventually return to the Third Reich was not motivated by any morbid fear or hatred of Jewry. He was never an obsessive anti-Semite. He sought rather to show that he was not simply an apolitical naval expert indifferent to the questions of race and culture that concerned his government so deeply. Canaris wanted to underscore that he shared those concerns, that he too wished to contribute to a solution of the Jewish question. His proposal was a way of displaying his gratitude to those who had chosen him for an important military position in the belief that he would prove unquestioningly loyal to the National Socialist ideology.

Many groups in the Nazi movement, including the leadership of the SS, favored the idea of forcibly expelling the German Jews. In November 1938, less than a year before the outbreak of the war, in a secret meeting convoked by Hitler and chaired by Göring, leading government officials still expressed the hope of solving the racial problem by mass deportation. Among the conference's recommendations, as summarized by Undersecretary Ernst Woermann of the Foreign Ministry, were the following: the "Aryanization of the economy" should be carried out more expeditiously; the "expropriation of Jewish landed property, art objects, jewelry, stocks, etc." should receive serious consideration; the "question of compulsory labor for the Jewish proletariat" should be carefully examined; and "Jewish emigration should be promoted in every way." In this context, what Canaris had been suggesting clearly accorded with views common in government circles regarding the racial purification of Germany. There was nothing original or unusual about them; he exhibited neither more nor less anti-Semitism than most followers of the Third Reich. He was simply a faithful Nazi in naval uniform still confident that Hitler was leading the nation to a glorious destiny.[12]

Most of the future military resisters appeared less enthusiastic in their view of National Socialism. They were as a rule not so vociferous in their praise, not so ostentatious in their support. But they too remained convinced that the government's policies were essentially sound. Occasionally some of them would voice cautious concern about its repressiveness and extremism, its intolerance and arbitrariness. They even expressed a few veiled criticisms of the virulence of its anti-Semitic policy. But the most common doubts pertained to its aggressive diplomacy. Was the Third

Reich moving too fast? Was it making too many enemies? If a war came, would the Wehrmacht be ready? Would it not be better if the Führer waited a little longer before risking a test of military strength? The members of the officer corps did not question the need for a diplomacy of revisionism in international affairs. But they worried that Hitler might provoke an armed conflict before they were fully prepared.

General Beck provides a revealing insight into the attitude of many senior officers toward the Third Reich. Although he had originally greeted its establishment with great satisfaction as a way out of the chaos of Weimar, he began by the middle 1930s to feel a vague uneasiness regarding its methods and objectives. The regime now seemed to him too unrestrained, too unpredictable. Still faithful to the beliefs and values of the old empire, he found the new order increasingly puzzling and even disturbing.

In the summer of 1944, after the failure of the attempt on Hitler's life, Popitz told his interrogators that Beck had held a "view of the world bound by tradition," so that he had "no sympathy and understanding whatever for National Socialism." He had believed that the "vitality of the National Socialist state" was driving it to deal with many questions "prematurely and rashly." In his opinion, for example, the rearmament of Germany should have been carried out "much more cautiously and intensively." Moreover, many of Hitler's domestic policies had "needlessly" aroused abroad "an insurmountable aversion to National Socialism," providing, "especially for America," a "pretext for entry into the war." Even in rejecting the "dictate of Versailles," the Third Reich had pressed "too hard and too quickly." In short, according to Popitz, "Beck had no understanding whatever for the ideological élan of National Socialism."[13]

After the war there was even a tendency to portray the martyred general as an opponent of the Nazi regime almost from the beginning. He was frequently depicted as a member of the resistance of the heart and spirit long before there had been a resistance of the deed. Major Robert Holtzmann, who had known him during his years as chief of staff, recalled afterward that "at first [Beck] sought to make Hitler acceptable to me, . . . but gradually that diminished more and more, until after March–April 1935 the hymns of praise . . . ceased altogether." He did at times try to draw a distinction between the Führer himself and his rash or shortsighted subordinates. But "whether Beck was ever serious with his 'except for Hitler'" seemed to Holtzmann doubtful. In the postwar mood of remorse and soul-searching, the high-principled soldier who had turned against the Third Reich became an embodiment of the "good German" willing to risk his life to end the brutalities of National Socialism.[14]

Yet the evidence suggests that Beck did not in fact become a convinced opponent of the regime until 1938. He made occasional critical remarks about it long before then, but he continued to differentiate between the "well-intentioned Führer" and the "radicals" in the Nazi Party. Hitler, he assured Holtzmann in the summer of 1935, was really "above any odiousness." Even Ludendorff, who had participated in Hitler's failed putsch in 1923, considered Beck's credulity "shocking." The latter was still convinced that Hitler would sooner or later turn against the extremists among his followers, a shift that would strengthen the position of the army. In a radio address in April 1935, he praised the achievements of the new order. "The German nation . . . under Adolf Hitler's strong leadership has found its way back to the heroic spirit and to respect for its own history." Nothing in either his public or his private utterances to this point suggests that he was less than completely loyal to the Third Reich.[15]

The only aspect of Hitler's policy about which Beck had serious reservations was his diplomacy. And here the Führer's proposed methods rather than his avowed goals troubled Beck. He was afraid, as Popitz later put it, that the Nazi regime was pressing "too hard and too quickly" for a revision of Versailles, that it might provoke a war before Germany was ready. But he did not oppose in principle the use of armed force to satisfy what he regarded as his country's just demands for territorial expansion. Nor, in his opinion, should these demands be restricted to the boundaries of 1914, specifically, to the areas ceded to Poland by the peace treaty. He was also prepared to contemplate other acquisitions in Central and Eastern Europe, particularly Austria. His views on foreign affairs, in other words, resembled Hitler's. He simply wanted to proceed more slowly, more cautiously. "I'm afraid," he confided at the time of his appointment as chief of staff, "that we could become involved in a war before we are in a position to defend ourselves with some prospect of success." This fear led to his gradual alienation from the Third Reich.[16]

Beck spelled out his position in a memorandum of May 20, 1937, ten months before the Anschluss, dealing with a possible German intervention in Austria. He prefaced his conclusions with a quotation from Karl von Clausewitz. "The task and the right of the art of war in relation to politics is chiefly to keep politics from demanding things that are counter to the nature of war and from making, out of ignorance of the operations of the instrument [of war], mistakes in its use." His purpose, he wanted to make clear, was not to dissuade Hitler from his plans for aggrandizement but to ensure that those plans were put into execution under optimum conditions.

He announced his view at the outset. The armed forces were simply not ready for a major conflict. "Germany is, with regard to its army, still not in a position to invite the risk of a Central European war," he warned. "On the whole, it cannot physically wage war, either for the time being or in the near future." Beck did not question Hitler's reasons for contemplating military action; that was not his business. It was his business, however, to provide the Führer with a realistic assessment of the chances of victory. "Therefore, on the basis of my evaluation of the military and political and all the other factors pertaining to a military intervention in Austria to prevent a restoration of the Habsburgs, I advocate the view that a further pursuit of this idea on the part of the army cannot be justified." There is no evidence that this advice reflected any doubt regarding the propriety or legitimacy of Hitler's annexationist policy. It was simply a dispassionate professional estimate of the likelihood of success.[17]

Beck reacted similarly to the views advanced by the Führer half a year later, at the meeting of November 5, 1937, described in the Hossbach memorandum. He had not been present, but he learned almost immediately about Hitler's new aggressive plans. About two days afterward, Foreign Minister Neurath testified before the Nuremberg tribunal, he, Fritsch, and Beck had gathered to discuss the opinions expressed at the meeting. All three agreed that something had to be done "to get Hitler to change his ideas." According to their plan, Fritsch, who was to report to the Führer in a few days, would explain to him the military considerations that made his policy "inadvisable," while Neurath would shortly thereafter explain its political risks. Perhaps he would listen to reason.

But soon afterward Hitler left for his Bavarian retreat at the Obersalzberg, and the foreign minister could not see him until the middle of January. "On that occasion I tried to show him that his policy would lead to a world war, and that I would have no part in it." Such was Neurath's testimony eight years later, as he faced imprisonment or perhaps execution. "I called his attention to the danger of war and to the serious warnings of the generals." But the Führer would not listen. He insisted that "he could not wait any longer." Thereupon, Neurath declared before the court, "I told him that he would have to find another foreign minister, and that I would not be an accessory to such a policy." That at least was his recollection.[18]

As for Beck, he remained the good soldier for the time being, obeying orders from above despite private doubts and misgivings. It would take about another six months to transform the dutiful officer into first a dissident and then a resister. Both the Führer and the chief of staff were motivated by an essentially similar sense of patriotism. The difference between them lay in their understanding of what that patriotism demanded of them.

The other members of what became the military resistance had as yet not even started to doubt. They were still under the spell of the great domestic achievements of the Hitler government: the reestablishment of political stability, the revival of economic confidence, the enforcement of law and order, and the reawakening of national pride and dignity. They were equally impressed by Hitler's successes in foreign policy. The repudiation of Versailles, the rearmament of Germany, the formation of the Axis, and the new balance of power in Europe, all seemed to them unmistakable evidence of the Führer's masterful statesmanship. Even the possibility that his diplomacy might end in war did not deter them. They saw themselves on the road to Armageddon, to a great decisive battle between right and wrong, a battle for Germany's future. Could any challenge facing a soldier be nobler than that? They were ready to march under the banner of the Third Reich, to march and fight and die in order to defend the security and greatness of their nation.

11

Nazi Dominance and Bureaucratic Accommodation

There was a close parallel between the attitude of the military and that of the bureaucracy toward the Third Reich during the middle 1930s. Both believed the new order represented values and ideals that they had faithfully served under the old empire. Both assumed the nation would now return to traditional civic virtues like devotion to duty, obedience to established authority, respect for law and order, and the subordination of private to public interest. Under the republic they had continued to carry out conscientiously the official tasks assigned to them, but their heart had not been in it. They felt a profound distrust of popular democracy with its egalitarian, insubordinate outlook and its skeptical view of custom and tradition. They considered the Nazi regime an improvement over Weimar precisely because it seemed to favor a restoration of the hierarchical principle in state and society and to seek a return to conservatism in politics and economics.

There was still another reason, usually unarticulated and sometimes subconscious, for the sympathy that many civil servants felt toward the Third Reich. They assumed that while Hitler might excite and mesmerize the masses, he knew little about the art of governing. How could he? With little formal education and no practical experience in administration, he would be unable to direct affairs of state on his own. That would have to be left to the bureaucracy, to men who had devoted their lives to the intricacies of diplomacy and statecraft. In other words, an informal partnership would of necessity be established between those who governed and those who administered, between those who exercised power in theory and those who exercised it in practice. The former would organize rallies and demonstrations; they would hold speeches and shout slogans; they would provide the bread and circuses. The latter, in the meantime, would do what they had been trained to do. They would draft legislation, supervise the economy, maintain social stability, and formulate diplomatic policy. Those who appeared to be senior partners would in fact be junior, while those who were nominally junior would actually be senior. It seemed an ideal arrangement.

The bureaucratic resistance emerged only after this calculation proved seriously mistaken. For National Socialism began almost from the outset to display a will of its own. Its leaders were not content simply to follow the advice of the experts. They were determined, rather, to initiate policies derived from their own underlying ideology, ignoring the recommendations and warnings of senior civil servants. Those who objected were peremptorily ordered to comply and, if they failed to do so, were dismissed. It was increasingly apparent that the bureaucracy had become not the partner but the servant of the regime. The disillusionment that realization produced among some of its members gradually turned into disaffection.

The disaffected, however, generally ascribed their feelings not to frustrated professional aspirations but to violated political principles and betrayed civic ideals. What turned them against the Third Reich, they insisted, was its growing corruption, its increasing surrender to the temptations of power. The Nazi loyalists, not the bureaucratic resisters, had changed. While the former had gradually succumbed to self-aggrandizement, the latter had proved faithful to the doctrines of struggle, sacrifice, and service preached by the party. Those accused of being traitors had in fact remained true to the teachings of National Socialism. The real traitors were the opportunists in positions of power who, while proclaiming their devotion to those teachings, had abandoned them for advantage and booty.

After the failure of the attempt on Hitler's life in the summer of 1944, the official inquiry reported that the arrested participants maintained they had initially supported the Third Reich. Far from being opponents of National Socialism, they had in fact approved of Hitler's assumption of power. What had changed their attitude was "the conduct of National Socialism in practice." The prisoners spoke of "specific personal happenings and experiences" that appeared to them "in very stark contrast to the proclaimed principles" of the party. In this connection, they accused the regime above all of "a lack of honesty." According to one of them, Baron Ferdinand von Lüninck, the former governor of Westphalia, "a great deal of water diluted the wine of our initial enthusiasm" in the years following the Third Reich's establishment. They insisted that they had become opponents of the regime only after witnessing its betrayal of the principles it claimed to espouse.[1]

Exactly when this happened varied from case to case, but the shift almost never occurred before 1938. Until then civil servants may have occasionally muttered and complained, but they expressed no consistent, systematic criticism. They still assumed that they would remain the partners of National Socialism or, better still, its guides and teachers. The bureaucrats would manage to restrain the extremists in the party; they would influence and moderate its policies. Their prime duty now was to try to reconcile the interests of the government and the state, of the regime and the nation. Only toward the end of the decade, as they saw the allies and sympathizers of the Third Reich being increasingly replaced by hard-liners and hundred-percenters, did some of them recognize that Hitler really wanted compliant subordinates, not experienced advisers. Until then they faithfully continued to support the new order.

The only significant exception was Carl Goerdeler. He became the first major figure in the bureaucracy to grasp the essential character of the National Socialist movement, the first to recognize its rejection of historic tradition, its insistence on blind obedience, its reliance on brute force, and its quest for absolute power. Yet initially he too had seemed to be just another conservative member of the civil service pleased to see the end of Weimar. Even before the collapse of the republic, he had complained about "the absolutism of the parties and of parliament." The only way to put an end to "the pushing and pulling of partisan political groups" was, in his opinion, to assign "greater influence" to those who had demonstrated a "capacity for political judgment."

Hitler, he felt, agreed with him on this point. In the summer of 1934 he wrote to the Führer congratulating him on "the elimination of rule by the parties in Germany and its fortunate replacement by the amalgamation of party and state." He approved of "the concentration . . . of the authority of the party and the authority of the state in the hands of one person." Not only would this enable the government to cope with the economic depression but, by making possible a more centralized system of administration, it would create the precondition, "which has almost never existed in German history," for a "unitary Reich." The Nazi regime appeared to be exactly what the nation needed.[2]

Goerdeler did not limit his support for the new order to expressions of approbation. While continuing his duties as mayor of Leipzig, he also served as price commissioner of Germany from November 5, 1934, to July 1, 1935, and participated prominently in the drafting of the law on local government of January 30, 1935. He repeatedly endorsed the policies and applauded the aims of the Third Reich. There was little to suggest during those early years of the Hitler dictatorship that he was anything but a faithful supporter of the government.

In fact he was gradually becoming disillusioned with National Socialism. By 1936 his initial enthusiasm had given way to mounting doubts and apprehensions. His most serious disagreement with the new order pertained to its economic program. Always the cautious, prudent government official, he favored a deflationary monetary policy, noninterference with market forces, and international cooperation in the promotion of commerce. But the regime seemed to be moving in the opposite direction. It decided to embark on rapid rearmament, it sought to achieve economic autarky, and it favored bilateralism over multilateralism in international trade. Worst of all, it displayed growing impatience with those advocating a more moderate course. Nazi functionaries began to infringe on the authority of the civil service, at first indirectly, but then more openly and boldly. It became increasingly clear to Goerdeler that his hopes for a permanent sharing of power between party and bureaucracy had been unrealistic. The only choice before him now was submission or retirement. He did not hesitate long; on April 1, 1937, he resigned as mayor of Leipzig.[3]

This decision has often been ascribed to his dispute with local National Socialists regarding the removal of a statue of Felix Mendelssohn that stood before the Gewandhaus, the city's orchestral hall. But there must have been more to it than that. Although Goerdeler was never an ardent anti-Semite, he was prepared to tolerate nonviolent expressions of hostility toward Jews. Only a few years earlier he had advised Hitler that "if . . . Mendelssohn's composition . . . does not please us, then we should not perform it." Why then should he have reacted so strongly against a proposal to get rid of a statue of Mendelssohn? After all, that action seemed no worse than many other ritualistic manifestations of official anti-Semitism which he had been prepared to accept.

Following the fall of the Third Reich evidence began to emerge that there had actually been other differences between Goerdeler and the party bigwigs. A dispute had arisen, for example, over the elimination of a proposed church, whose construction the mayor had favored, from the plans for a housing project in Leipzig. It must have been galling to him to see his authority defied by Nazi intriguers and wire-pullers. Yet not the quarrel over Mendelssohn's statue, nor the disagreement regarding the construction of a church, nor the other frictions and irritations he encountered in his dealings with National Socialist functionaries explain Goerdeler's decision to resign from office. Ultimately, what led him to that decision was the recognition that the Third Reich would not tolerate any disagreement with its policies, however cautious, however reasonable. It demanded total submission, which he was not prepared to offer. He sensed at last, though he never admitted it to others or even to himself, that his earlier assessment of National Socialism had been fundamentally wrong.[4]

In July 1937, a few months after his resignation, Goerdeler wrote for his friends in England an account of what had led him to leave office. He dwelt on the moral and philosophical reasons for his decision. He said nothing about his disputes regarding the statue of Mendelssohn or the building of a church in the Leipzig housing project. He did describe in detail his loyal service to the Third Reich in the years following its establishment. His emphasis, however, was on betrayed principles and broken promises. National Socialism "had the opportunity to make the lofty ideal of comradeship in life and work the foundation of the national life of our country. It had the opportunity to unite the states of Germany inwardly as well." It could have even, "by inscribing achievement and comradeship, decency and justice on its banner," assumed "moral leadership" in a world "undergoing social change." Equally important, it could have secured "Germany's vital rights in foreign affairs." Not surprisingly, therefore, many loyal Germans, men like Goerdeler himself, had at first been ready to support it in the work of national reconstruction.

The Nazi movement failed to live up to its ideals, however. It committed "the [common] mistake of dictators"; it "snatched at power and abused power." And now "our task is to keep this abuse from harming the German people." More than that, Goerdeler acknowledged the essentially corruptive nature of the Hitler regime. By its totalitarian claim to power, "it touches the natural roots and moral foundations of collective human existence." Hence it must come into "an irreconcilable conflict" with the fundamental ethical forces on which society rests. "Yet since nature always prevails, and since a moral law making possible collective human existence is likewise a requirement of nature, the party must collapse for these reasons." The downfall of the Third Reich had now become for him only a question of time.[5]

Goerdeler was taking the first hesitant steps on the road that would lead him from moral opposition to organized resistance to political conspiracy and finally to the gallows. Still, he continued to believe to the end that National Socialism was not inherently or irretrievably evil. On the contrary, it had strengths as well as weaknesses, virtues as well as shortcomings. The weaknesses and shortcomings, unfortunately, began in time to outweigh the strengths and virtues. But that had not been inevitable. The fatal flaw in the Nazi movement lay in its policies and judgments, not in its doctrines or ideals. Its leaders had gradually succumbed to ambition, arrogance, vanity, and self-interest. But if they had only listened to the advice of those who urged more restraint and moderation, greater caution and prudence, things might have turned out quite differently. Goerdeler did not regret his initial approval of the Hitler government. He only wished that he and others like him had been more successful in curbing its impetuosity and ruthlessness.

Thus he continued to speak ruefully about what National Socialism might have accomplished for Germany, about its sound ideas but lost opportunities. Even after he left public office, he would at times refer with approbation to some of the measures it had initiated. Its proclaimed diplomatic objectives in particular often received his warm endorsement. An ardent patriot all his life, he considered the foreign policy of the Third Reich, especially in its early years, far better than Weimar's. A German government was finally trying to revise the frontiers established at Versailles. Perhaps it would eventually succeed in regaining some of the lost territories in Posen and West Prussia.

In August 1934 Goerdeler wrote to Hitler to remind him that "Germany simply cannot exist under reasonable conditions separated from its eastern borderland." The Polish Corridor especially seemed to him "a thorn in the flesh [of the country's] economy and its honor." Hence the nonagression pact that Berlin and Warsaw had concluded a few months earlier was largely worthless. "We cannot trust Poland." The Pilsudski regime would only exploit the treaty to advance its own interests. "Knowing the Pole through many years of daily contact, and familiar with his policy and that of Prussia, I am convinced that Poland only appears to be becoming independent of France." Actually, "behind the scenes" the two countries remained closely allied. "By playing this game, Poland gains a free hand to proceed against the German nation." Goerdeler tried to impress on Hitler that "the German people must fight for the security of their existence." But his admonition was superfluous; the Führer was already convinced.[6]

The need to revise the eastern boundary of Germany, to eliminate the Polish Corridor and reacquire at least a substantial part of Posen, was a familiar theme of conservative political rhetoric during the interwar period. There was therefore nothing unusual in Goerdeler's opinions on the subject, and he made no secret of them even under Weimar. But after the establishment of the Third Reich, his view of the territorial gains that the nation might legitimately seek began to expand in keeping with the new aggressive diplomacy of the Hitler regime. He no longer felt that it was enough to regain the lost provinces in the east, although that remained his chief objective. Now he was prepared to contemplate additional acquisitions, overseas as well as in Central and Eastern Europe, even of territories that had not been part of the German Empire. His differences with the Nazi government pertained to its methods, not its purposes. He remained convinced that national expansion could be achieved through bargaining and negotiation, through skillful diplomacy.

Early in January 1938, for instance, after traveling in Belgium, England, Holland, France, Canada, and the United States, Goerdeler composed a detailed report describing, among other things, how the Wilhelmstrasse might achieve its main objectives painlessly and effortlessly, without bloodshed. An agreement between Germany and America, he maintained, could be reached only by a settlement of the political disputes in Europe, above all, by a "guaranteed peace." This settlement would create a great opportunity for Germany. If the Hitler government would accept a negotiated resolution of diplomatic differences on the Continent, thereby facilitating the struggle of the Anglo-Saxon powers in the Far East against Japan, it would be in a position to reap rich rewards. Goerdeler was confident that a satisfactory agreement could then be worked out regarding German colonial demands, probably in the form of "a compact territory in West Africa," regarding the Anschluss of Austria, and even regarding "the Sudeten region and the [Polish] Corridor." It was really quite simple.

A reconciliation with England and America, moreover, would offer important economic advantages. Germany would gain free access to the world market, while the danger to its currency could then be met by loans from Wall Street. To a nation that had just emerged from a terrible depression, commercial expansion and financial stability would be of the greatest benefit. And it could all be achieved so easily.

Besides, what was the alternative? Should it come to a military conflict, Goerdeler believed, "especially against Czechoslovakia," the United States would in all probability not send troops to Europe, as it had done twenty years earlier. Aware of American isolationist sentiment, he considered direct intervention unlikely. But the United States would support England in every other way in a struggle against Germany. And that support might well prove decisive. A war should therefore be avoided at all costs, especially since its main objectives could be achieved through negotiation. The way to an understanding was still open, but only "up to a certain point." Germany should not miss this great opportunity.[7]

Goerdeler had by now broken with the Third Reich, and yet his opposition seemed at times inconsistent and vacillating. He continued to wrestle with doubts, with conflicting opinions and contradictory feelings. Indeed, he never succeeded in completely overcoming his ambivalence regarding the Hitler regime. Sometimes he would describe it as immoral, as undermining the ethical foundations of civilized society. But at other times he would concede that some of its doctrines had been worthy of support: loyalty to the national community, for example, the subordination of private to public welfare, and the fostering of ethnic pride. Sometimes he would condemn the heavy-handed diplomacy of the Nazi government, its strutting and posturing, its reliance on threat and intimidation. But at other times he would concede, directly or indirectly, the need for territorial expansion, for the inclusion of most ethnic Germans within a single German state, and for the reacquisition of overseas colonies. He never appeared to regret his early support for the Third Reich. He only regretted its failure to live up to the ideals and principles it had professed.

Most of the other members of what became the bureaucratic resistance seemed as yet untroubled by serious doubts about the new order. At the end of 1937 they were still where Goerdeler had been at the beginning of 1933. They continued to believe that National Socialism had saved Germany from political chaos, economic decline, social conflict, diplomatic ineffectualness, and military impotence. Nothing seemed to shake their confidence in the regime, not even its growing preference for partisan loyalty over professional expertise. They continued to reassure one another that their positions within the Nazi system were secure, that they were and would remain the allies and partners of the party. Some of them might have felt a twinge of apprehension, but they generally managed to suppress it by telling themselves that as long as they served the Third Reich faithfully and diligently, they would have nothing to fear.

Consider Ulrich von Hassell, who appeared to be the embodiment of the traditional German bureaucrat—conservative, patriotic, conscientious, and hardworking. The son of an army officer, born into a family of soldiers and landowners, he nevertheless decided shortly before World War I to enter the diplomatic service rather than seek a military career. A serious wound suffered in the Battle of the Marne forced him to retire temporarily and then to accept a succession of minor administrative positions. He reentered the foreign office under Weimar, however, rising rapidly through the ranks to the important post of ambassador to Italy. At no time did he try to disguise his monarchist and nationalist sympathies, but the republican regime, unlike its Nazi successor, respected the independence of the civil service. Most of the leading bureaucratic offices were therefore filled by men who, though skilled and experienced, did not share its ideals or approve its policies.

Hassell's attitude toward the Third Reich was far more favorable than it had been toward Weimar. Later some contemporaries claimed that he had never really been in sympathy with the Nazi regime, that he had been its secret opponent from the beginning. In February 1938, after he had been recalled from the ambassadorship in Rome, Count Galeazzo Ciano, the Italian foreign minister, noted in his diary: "Von Hassel [sic] . . . served his country and the cause of German-Italian friendship badly. Perhaps he tried to overcome his hostile attitude, but he did not succeed. He belongs, fatally and inexorably, to that world of the Junkers who cannot forget 1914 and, because they are at heart hostile to Nazism, have no feeling for the solidarity of the two regimes." Besides, he added, "von Hassel knew Dante too well. I distrust foreigners who know Dante. They try to screw us with their poetry."[8]

Six years later, in September 1944, at his trial for involvement in the plot against Hitler, Roland Freisler, the notorious hanging judge of the Third Reich, raised a similar charge of duplicity against Hassell. Why, he asked Hassell, did the latter agree to serve the "red government" of Weimar after World War I, although, judging by his avowed political principles, he was presumably "conservative"? Did this not suggest some dishonesty on his part?[9]

Hassell's reply appears to be a reasonably accurate summary of his political attitude during the preceding twenty-five years and how it changed in the course of time. He had indeed agreed to serve the republican regime, but only out of a "sense of national duty." He had not been in sympathy with the "Weimar system," and had therefore "welcomed National Socialism" in 1933. "Only gradually did a difference in outlook develop between him and the present government." Until then he had served the Third Reich honestly and loyally.[10]

Exactly when this "difference in outlook" between Hassell and the Nazi regime emerged is difficult to pinpoint, but it must have been well after his ambassadorship in Italy. Before then he would occasionally question a decision of his superiors or a policy of the government. But there is no evidence of any fundamental or systematic disagreement with the regime as such.

On the contrary, he seemed eager to demonstrate his fidelity to the new order, partly no doubt for reasons of expediency, but mostly out of inner conviction. As early as 1932, even before the establishment of the Third

Reich, he had confidently declared that Hitler sought equal rights for his nation and not revenge. Was that wrong? Was it unreasonable? In the fall of 1933, moreover, Hassell joined the National Socialist Party, in 1935 he participated in the commemoration of the failed Hitler putsch twelve years earlier, in 1936 and 1937 he attended the Nazi national congresses, and in 1937 he became brigade leader in the National Socialist Motor Vehicle Corps. None of this is proof of ardent support for the Third Reich. These were simply conventional displays of loyalty that the regime expected of those whom it entrusted with important bureaucratic posts. But neither do they suggest that Hassell was already at heart a principled opponent of National Socialism.[11]

Actually, he seemed to share many of the tenets and convictions of the new order. In September 1933 he urged the foreign office in Berlin to promote an understanding with Italy by the "unconditional recognition of the independence of Austria." But he did not favor blind acquiescence in the policies of the Dollfuss government in Vienna, he explained. "The first demand, which we are justified in making because the Germans in the Reich and in Austria are one people, [is] that every restriction on the National Socialist Party in Austria should be repealed." Hassell apparently accepted the Nazi contention that a common Germanic cultural heritage and racial character also meant a common Germanic political interest. His dispatch in the spring of 1937 describing conditions in Switzerland reflected the same view. He was pleased to find there "ethnic German sympathy combined with warm understanding for the Third Reich and a strongly anti-Communist attitude." Hassell, it seems, did not categorically reject the racism preached by the new order.[12]

He never descended to the vicious Jew-baiting in which many supporters of National Socialism engaged. He was too much the aristocrat, too much the gentleman of the old school, to engage in what he regarded as ethnic demagoguery and rabble-rousing. Yet at times he defended the Third Reich's racial policy, telling Mussolini in the summer of 1933 that the anti-Semitic measures adopted soon after Hitler's accession to power "had been portrayed quite falsely and exaggeratedly in the world press." He pointed to "the large number of Jewish lawyers who have been allowed to remain in their profession." Nor was Hassell above an occasional ethnic slur or stereotype. In October 1935, for example, he referred disparagingly to Maxim Litvinov, the Soviet commissar for foreign affairs, and to Tevfik Rüstü Aras, the Turkish foreign minister, as "completely Bolshevistic or half Bolshevistic Jews." Though he never became a confirmed anti-Semite, he was willing to tolerate and sometimes condone the anti-Semitism of those in power. He simply did not consider the issue important enough to justify the disavowal of a regime with which he was by and large still in agreement.[13]

What mattered much more, in his opinion, was the danger of Communism, not only to Germany but to Europe as a whole. In a lecture at the University of Cologne in January 1937, he maintained that "Bolshevism is by no means to be considered as only a political and social system which we consider false and dangerous." He saw in it also "an expression of an un-European form of thought that must inevitably poison and corrupt our innermost being." Indeed, "the contagious force of this doctrine" was so powerful that its "deadly germs" had already infected "the lifeblood of our nation." All of Western civilization in fact faced a terrible danger.

National Socialism in Germany and Fascism in Italy were the chief defenders of that civilization against the "influx of the un-European Bolshevik spirit." They had entered, Hassell maintained, on a long, difficult road leading out of "the contagion zone of the eastern, un-European way of thinking" toward a national consciousness "securely anchored in the European character." Such a national consciousness was "natural and salutary"; it would enable them to fulfill their "European mission" in the spirit of Dante and Goethe, Hassell's twin heroes. It would also require of them, however, "the exertion to the utmost of all spiritual forces" and "moral conduct on the part of self-reliant personalities." Hitler and Mussolini were trying to meet a dangerous but inspiring challenge. They were twin Saint Georges riding forth side by side to slay the Communist dragon.[14]

His removal from the ambassadorship to Italy a year later did not basically alter Hassell's view of the Third Reich. Personality clashes and tactical controversies, not any fundamental conflict of ideology, provoked the dismissal. It reflected in part the intensifying struggle between the experts and the ideologues in the German governmental system, between the professionals and the party insiders. But it was also in part the consequence of a difference of opinion regarding diplomatic policy. Hassell, like Goerdeler, was reluctant to oppose England and France to the point of risking a military confrontation. He would have preferred collaboration between the two leading dictatorships and the two leading democracies in Europe. The Nazi regime, however, began to rely more and more on the Rome-Berlin Axis, convinced that a united front of Germany and Italy could intimidate the British and the French. Hence the removal of Hassell represented a victory for the hard-liners in the Hitler government. But it did not result from a dispute regarding basic doctrines or ultimate goals. Hassell continued to believe that the Third Reich, despite occasional faults and mistakes, was in essence sound. He had not yet crossed the line separating tactical disagreement from principled opposition.

Popitz's position was by and large the same. Whereas Hassell was the polished diplomat among the bureaucratic resisters and Goerdeler the efficient administrator, Popitz was the respected financial expert—judicious, erudite, and sometimes oracular, abstruse, or simply pedantic. Though critical of Weimar, especially in its final years, he was also at first unimpressed by the National Socialist Party. Shortly before its victory he described those voting for it as "great landowners whose property is in difficulty, peasants and handicraftsmen, young people not overly capable of thinking, and worthy widows of government officials." The gains Hitler was making stemmed not only from "economic despair" but from the failure of the other parties, "especially the bourgeois parties," to deal effectively with the national question. The Nazis were, in his view, winning by default.

After the establishment of the Third Reich, however, he began to see possibilities and opportunities in National Socialism that had previously escaped him. Still, many questions remained unanswered. Would the "leader of the [Nazi] revolution" succeed in "also asserting his leadership with full authority in the task of reconstruction"? Popitz wondered in the spring of 1933. Would the "national enthusiasm" of the moment lead in the long run to "a new spiritual attitude" among the people of Germany? Or would the "materialistic outlook" prevail once again, using the new order as a screen "for the assertion of special interests and for the provision of security in state positions"? All in all, Popitz was hopeful. He thought that National Socialism might be able to resolve the crisis confronting Germany, that it might bring about the moral revival which was essential for national recovery. But he was not quite sure.

His doubts gradually diminished. For one thing, he too was impressed by the early achievements of the Third Reich. But there were also personal considerations. The new order seemed to appreciate Popitz's talents and accomplishments even more than the republic had. He was given the imposing though largely ceremonial position of Prussian minister of finance. More important, he became for a few years a close adviser of Hermann Göring. The latter hoped to enhance his reputation as a patron of learning, while the former sought to enlarge his political influence and prestige. Both were to be eventually disappointed. Yet for the time being Popitz became noticeably more favorable to the Nazi regime.

Thus in a lecture late in 1937 on his favorite subject, the taxation system, he compared "absolutistic forms of government," whose security was threatened by "the broad masses that are excluded from political power," with popular democracy, which represented "the domination of the masses," and with a "Führer state" resting on "the consent of the entire nation." Still diplomatic and circumspect, he did not say in so many words which of these was best. But there could really be little doubt about his preference.[15]

Goerdeler, Hassell, and Popitz belonged to the older generation of bureaucratic resisters. They were all born in the 1880s, within a few years of one another; they all reached maturity under the monarchical regime; they all remained loyal to the values and ideals of the imperial era. They supported the Third Reich basically because they hoped that it would bring about a return to the world of ideas in which they had grown up.

Fritz-Dietlof von der Schulenburg belonged to the new generation, born in the twentieth century, shaped by the postwar experience, and resolved to find a new solution to the problems of its society. For him the Hitler regime was not simply an updated version of the Wilhelmian state. It was a daring new experiment, an exciting attempt to create an entirely different social order, more courageous, more noble, more inspiring than any in German history. The older members of the bureaucratic resistance became supporters of the Third Reich out of expediency. But Schulenburg believed in it heart and soul; he was a convinced and ardent Nazi. His enthusiasm, moreover, seemed to increase with the increasing success of the Hitler dictatorship. And the Hitler dictatorship in turn knew how to reward such complete, unquestioning devotion. The relationship between the two soon became mutually beneficial.

On July 5, 1937, two weeks before he was appointed at the age of thirty-four to the position of deputy chief of the Berlin police, Schulenburg spoke in Stuttgart before a gathering of professional administrators about "the legacy of the Prussian state." He pronounced once again a ringing endorsement of the new order. The experiment in democracy after the war had led to the surrender of the "social order of the state" to "capitalism hiding behind the mask of Socialism." Special political and economic interests had undermined the "centralized strength" of the government. And the victor nations, by rendering the German army "weak and power-less," had enfeebled "the great school of discipline and spirit among the people." The republic had proved to be a disaster.

But National Socialism was bringing fundamental change. The regime was trying to "rejuvenate" the nation, rather than just the state, by turning to "the sources of [our collective] existence." It was seeking a "return of the nation to itself," rejecting the forces that had "alienated and enslaved the nation." The Nazi Party was the instrument by which the Führer would "fortify the state from within" and "unite the structure of the state with the people." In the Germany of the future "the people will express their essential nature and build their might so as to assert themselves in the struggle for existence of peoples and states." Schulenburg went on and on in this vein, rhapsodizing about the glorious destiny of the Third Reich.[16]

Adam von Trott zu Solz was roughly the same age. He too had been born in the twentieth century; he too remembered the chaos and demoralization of the postwar period; he too had witnessed the humiliation and ineffectualness of the Weimar regime in dealing with the great depression. But his political outlook was quite different from Schulenburg's. He belonged not to the Prussian nobility but to the more cosmopolitan and tolerant Hessian bureaucratic patriciate. His years of study and travel abroad, moreover, his enduring though vacillating sympathy with Socialism, and his friendship with many foreigners, some of them Jews, had made him distrustful of the doctrines espoused by the Third Reich. He stubbornly refused to join the Nazi Party; he did not even enter government service until after the outbreak of World War II. Trott was therefore someone who might have been expected to oppose the Hitler dictatorship, at least in private.

Yet he could not in fact bring himself to denounce the regime, least of all to his acquaintances abroad. He felt attracted, almost in spite of himself, to the populism and egalitarianism in National Socialism's rhetoric. He was also impressed by the new faith and enthusiasm he saw about him in Germany. But most important was his sense of national pride, his resentment of foreigners who presumed to lecture him about his country's wickedness. Who were they to preach to Germany about virtue and morality? What about the evils of British colonialism or French vindictiveness? Trott may have had his inner doubts about the Third Reich, but in the face of criticism from abroad he felt duty-bound to close ranks with his countrymen in defense of their government.

His indignation emerges clearly in his letter in the summer of 1937 to the British journalist Shiela Grant Duff dealing with the international situation. "The thing called for from you," he wrote in his usual convoluted style, "is not the falling back on nationalism and hypocritical virtues of your blessed government but on some firm and constructive vision of a cooperative and ordered international future by the standards of which you judge and criticise the present lack of one." He dismissed as supercilious her strictures regarding the Third Reich. "You haven't any right to denounce the policies of a country which is rather blindly and—I certainly admit—rather viciously groping for some economic outlet from the assumed moral superiority of a nation which has all she wants and has got it and maintains it with methods which are in many respects as blind and vicious."

Indeed, National Socialism with all its weaknesses and shortcomings might still be better than the effete and materialistic democracy of the West. "In many respects I feel that the internal development of Germany—if only the European peace can be kept—bears more promise in its potential social and economic working out and more honest and substantial bearing on a cooperative international future than the 'powers' that have let Spain and Abyssinia happen." Trott simply could not bring himself to desert the united front of all loyal, patriotic Germans against the calumnies of hypocritical foreigners.[17]

In sum, whatever may have eventually led to the emergence of a bureaucratic resistance against the Hitler dictatorship had not yet occurred during the period of the regime's consolidation. Those who later joined that resistance were still by and large obedient followers of the Third Reich. Some had become enthusiastic supporters, others were willing allies, and a few remained hesitant and uneasy fellow travelers. But none saw any alternative to the new order, and none believed that their nation should turn to some other form of government. Except for Goerdeler, none opposed National Socialism, not even inwardly, for its oppressiveness, ruthlessness, recklessness, or brutality. Only at the end of the decade did some of them rebel, and then more because of its methods and procedures than because of its principles and doctrines. They became resisters at last, but reluctant resisters, resisters for reasons of strategy and policy rather than ideology.

Carl Goerdeler as mayor of Leipzig delivering the welcoming address at a reception in the city hall in 1936. (Bilderdienst Süddeutscher Verlag)

A photograph of Henning von Tresckow during the war while he was serving on the Russian front. (Bilderdienst Süddeutscher Verlag)

12

The Conflict over Ecclesiastical Autonomy

The general support of the military and the bureaucracy for the Nazi regime did not begin to erode until the late 1930s. But almost from the outset another group voiced consistent criticism of some of the policies of the Third Reich. The soldiers and civil servants could not express their reservations about the government openly; their professional ethic made that impossible. They might offer dissenting expert advice or unfavorable technical appraisal, but only behind the scenes, only in confidence. In public they were expected to accept loyally the decisions of their superiors, whatever their private doubts or apprehensions. The churches, by contrast, had traditionally enjoyed a measure of autonomy denied to the armed forces or the administrative corps. The state acknowledged that spiritual authority was distinct from and independent of temporal authority. The two were expected to work together for the welfare of the community, but that each had a separate competence and jurisdiction was accepted by both, at least in theory. Only occasionally did they disagree over the line dividing one from the other, the precise boundary between the secular and the sacred.

It was over this issue that church and state began to clash after 1933. On the surface relations between them did not change in any significant way. The Nazi regime seemed to accept the traditional separation of power as unreservedly as the imperial or the republican regime had. But in fact it could not become reconciled to coexistence with another authority that, however sympathetic or conciliatory, claimed to exercise an independent jurisdiction. It could not, given its ideology, tolerate an autonomous religious establishment whose source of legitimacy was alleged to lie beyond the control of the government. It was prepared to recognize churchly independence only as a useful fiction disguising the reality of churchly subordination. As a result secular and spiritual power clashed in the most serious conflict of this kind in Germany since the *Kulturkampf* of the 1870s.

Still, its scope remained narrowly limited. The issues at stake were jurisdictional rather than moral or ideological in nature, because the opposing sides preferred not to raise fundamental questions of ethics and religion. They recognized that dwelling on their underlying philosophical differences would only intensify the conflict to the point where no compromise or retreat was possible. The religious leaders therefore argued with the political authorities mostly about such practical matters as the treatment of "non-Aryan" clergy and laity; the maintenance of confessional schools; the autonomy of Christian cultural, social, and occupational organizations; and the interference of Nazi youth activities with religious services and functions. Spokesmen for the government and the party complained in turn about political pronouncements from the pulpit hostile to the regime, about the divisiveness fostered by excessive denominationalism, about the ecumenicism and internationalism promoted by some ecclesiastics, and about the lack of enthusiasm for the Third Reich displayed by many churchmen. Each side had in fact more serious doubts about the other, but these remained generally unexpressed. To allow them to rise to the surface would have escalated the struggle beyond the point desired by either of the opponents.

The limited scope of the conflict helps account for the relatively small number of casualties. A list issued by the Protestant Church in August 1935 of disciplined clergymen in whose behalf prayers were being offered cited for the Berlin region 3 prohibitions by the authorities against speaking in public and 19 expulsions. In September 1937 the list included a total of 26 prohibitions and 33 expulsions as well as 120 arrests and 28 other punitive measures. Of those penalized, 12 came from Berlin. For the entire year 1937 there were 805 arrests, 120 of them involving Berlin clergymen. These arrests must have been generally of short duration, however, because the numbers appearing on the prayer lists on successive Sundays were considerably smaller. In any case, those who opposed the Nazi regime vigorously enough to incur a legal penalty could not have constituted more than 6 or 7 percent of the approximately 17,000 Protestant clergymen in Germany.[1]

Figures for the number of Catholic clergymen penalized for some form of opposition to the Third Reich are less detailed, but they suggest that the percentage was no greater and may well have been smaller. During the entire period of the Nazi dictatorship one bishop was expelled from his diocese, while another was sentenced to a short term in prison for involvement in currency smuggling. The number of Catholic priests incarcerated in the Dachau concentration camp has been variously estimated at 261 or 340. The total for imprisoned members of monastic orders was 133. The higher the rank of a churchman, moreover, the less likely was he to be punished for acts of civil disobedience. For example, the authorities made no attempt to silence Bishop Galen even after he became an outspoken critic of the government. Each side in the religious conflict sought to prevent the occasional forays and skirmishes from turning into an out-and-out war.[2]

On the part of the church leaders that entailed a deliberate effort to avoid involvement in any issue without direct bearing on some recognized ecclesiastical jurisdiction. They carefully refrained from saying anything about the suppression of freedom of thought, the punishment of ideological dissent, the politicization of learning and culture, or the persecution of Jews who were not converts to Christianity. Their silence did not mean that they approved of such policies, but it did reflect a continuing reluctance to risk a confrontation with the state regarding questions in which the church did not have clearly defined authority. Some clergyman might go beyond the boundaries of narrow legalism, thereby risking government reprisal. But most of them subordinated universal principle to parochial expediency. For them the most important duty was the defense of their communicants' denominational interests.

The state was equally reluctant to become involved in an all-out religious conflict. Behind the swagger and bravado of the Nazi regime was a recognition that organized religion commanded enough popular support to offer stubborn resistance against strong-arm tactics. It was one thing to imprison a few reputed left-wing sympathizers hostile to the new order. Their fate would interest only a handful of political radicals without following or influence. But the arrest of a clergyman might arouse a feeling of outrage among many members of his congregation; the incarceration of a bishop or archbishop might even lead to nationwide protests and demonstrations. Hence it would be best to avoid a direct confrontation with the ecclesiastical establishment. Both church and state thus sought to limit the scope and intensity of the religious conflict. Both helped to confine it to what was essentially a war of nerves.

Of the two major Christian denominations, Catholicism was the more accommodating. Its leaders felt no great sympathy for the regime, but they concluded that the interests of their church could be defended most effectively by a seeming acceptance of the Third Reich. Their strategy was to insist that they were not opponents but supporters of the government, that their criticism of its religious policy was motivated by sympathy rather than hostility. They merely tried to reinforce the Nazi regime, they claimed, by pointing out the mistakes that some of its overzealous followers committed in dealing with ecclesiastical affairs. Far from opposing the Third Reich, they hoped to make it stronger, to make it more popular and successful. How then could anyone accuse them of disloyalty?

There were some Catholic clergymen, to be sure, who refused to support or even appear to support the established system. A priest would occasionally speak out from the pulpit against some aspect of Nazi policy even though it did not affect the church directly, especially anti-Semitism, condemning it as cruel and unchristian, as an expression of "sinful racial pride" or "blind hatred." But such open expressions of dissent remained rare and confined to the lower ranks of the clergy. Members of the hierarchy almost never voiced them publicly, not because they were less sensitive to racial bigotry but because they believed that their duty as ecclesiastical leaders required them to avoid antagonizing the government over issues not immediately related to churchly interests. In their view, concrete institutional needs had to take precedence over abstract moral principles and theories.[3]

Bishop Galen exemplifies this strategy of trying to influence the Third Reich's religious policy from within. In the spring of 1936 he announced in a sermon preached at Gelsenkirchen his wholehearted support for the Führer's bold diplomacy, which was helping to restore a sense of pride and dignity to the German people. "There is an end [now] to the shameful state of affairs in which our nation, disarmed, had to bow to surrounding nations bristling with armaments, and in which a large part of our native country stood exposed and defenseless against the arbitrary incursion of hostile troops . . . into the heart of our industrial region." He prayed for divine support for Hitler's statecraft. "I ask almighty God to look on [the Führer's] work with favor, to bless it in its progress, and to give him the discernment and strength to overcome and avoid anything that might diminish or destroy that moral strength of our nation which is indeed the precondition and guarantee of the honorable character of any nation." There could seemingly be no question about the bishop's loyalty to the Third Reich.

Galen's public support for the regime, however, was designed in part to enable him to criticize its religious policy without appearing to be its opponent. He hoped to defend Catholic interests from within the system, as an adherent of National Socialism, as a believer in Hitler. Thereby his arguments would gain greater credibility and influence.

A combination of professed devotion and injured pride appears also in the draft of a pastoral letter that he composed late in December 1935. Here he declared that Catholics "wish with all their heart and pray to God daily for the success" of the "work of renewal of the German nation" that Hitler had undertaken. He praised the efforts of the government to restore "Germany's freedom, honor, and equality of rights" and to bring about "the end of the economic crisis and of unemployment." He added for good measure a denunciation of "so-called liberalism, which has always been condemned by the Church," assuring those in power that "we and the faithful whom we lead stand united behind the Führer."

Still, his loyalty to the new order, the bishop expostulated, only intensified his sorrow and indignation at the attempt of extremist elements in the Nazi Party to portray Catholicism as the enemy of the Third Reich. Could they not see that they harmed the cause they claimed to uphold? The sense of common purpose in Germany was being undermined by "the struggle unleashed against Christianity and [by] the countermeasures that we have adopted dutifully but with a heavy heart because of their unhappy consequences for the national community." Yet it was all so senseless, so unnecessary. "In the German Catholics loyal to the Church, the Führer will find at his disposal the most trustworthy supporters and loyal followers, as soon as the barriers are removed that keep us against our will from this support because of the unacceptable demand for the prior renunciation of our inherited Christian faith." If only the state would accept the hand of friendship being extended by the church.[4]

Catholic leaders advocated collaboration with the regime primarily in order to defend confessional schools, organizations, publications, and observances. They wanted to reach some compromise or accommodation with the government, some quid pro quo. In return for the preservation of a measure of ecclesiastical autonomy, they were prepared to accept and endorse National Socialism. They saw no reason why Catholicism should not be able to coexist with the Third Reich, as it had coexisted with the German Empire or the Weimar Republic. There were in fact some things in the Nazi ideology with which they were in wholehearted agreement: its rejection of secular liberalism, for example, as well as its opposition to the materialistic spirit and its condemnation of Marxist doctrine. Why then should not temporal and spiritual authority work together for the revival of Germany's power and greatness? All that was needed was a little more reasonableness and understanding, a little more restraint and moderation.

The reluctance to intensify the hostility of the regime toward the church also helped shape Cardinal Faulhaber's attitude toward ecclesiastical issues that he considered peripheral, for example, the treatment of Jews who converted to Catholicism. Writing in the fall of 1936 to Cardinal Adolf Bertram of Breslau, chairman of the Catholic Bishops' Conference, he tried to find a way of providing some protection for "non-Aryan" members of the church without openly defying the Nazi authorities. "The National Socialist view of the world condemns, in accordance with its principle based on blood and race that 'a Jew remains a Jew,' the baptized Jew as much as the unbaptized one." But for the Catholic bishops "the former Jew" becomes "a new creature" as a result of his baptism, "a true child of God's Church." He acquires the right "to be treated by the ecclesiastical authorities as a Christian and no longer as a Jew," and "not to be handed over to his anti-Semitic enemies." How then should the church respond to the request from the Ministry for Religious Affairs for information on the number of Jewish converts to Catholicism during the preceding thirty-five years?

Faulhaber understood the underlying reason for this request. "We have no illusions about the fact that the Ministry, which today is asking for the number of Jews baptized in individual years, will tomorrow also try to get the names of those baptized Jews." He recognized, moreover, that the information would be used to intensify the regime's campaign not only against Jews but against Catholics as well. "The bishops have surely no reason to provide material for a new inflammatory anti-Catholic article in the *Stürmer*." The cardinal feared that the spread of anti-Semitism would encourage the spread of anti-Catholicism. "The movement for a Germanic religion as well as many circles within the [Nazi] Party are as much opposed to the 'Oriental-Jewish-Roman religion' as to the old Jewish religion." There was no doubt in his mind that the position of the church was becoming increasingly dangerous.

Consequently, he remained reluctant to provoke a conflict with the government over the Jewish question. Perhaps some compromise could still be found, some way to retreat gracefully from an open confrontation. "As long as the demand of the Ministry for Religious Affairs and of the authorities behind it has a purely statistical purpose, we can and will comply with the request." Indeed, data on the number of Jewish converts might even prove useful as a source of information regarding church history. "When demands go beyond statistical purposes and . . . the inquiry has the objective of gathering material for new anti-Semitic measures, then, in my opinion, we can no longer participate in that." But why allow the dispute regarding baptized Jews to reach that point? Why not simply recognize and respect the traditional separate jurisdictions of church and state? Catholicism and National Socialism could then work together harmoniously for the welfare of the nation.

Faulhaber emphasized that his concern was restricted to converted Jews, that it did not extend to those who remained faithful to Judaism and certainly did not extend to those whose left-wing views threatened the stability of Germany. "The state has the right," he conceded in his letter to Bertram, "to take measures against the excesses of Jewry within its jurisdiction, especially when Jews who are Bolsheviks and Communists endanger the political order." But there could be no question about the loyalty of those who embraced Catholicism. The ecclesiastical leadership always made sure of that. "Regarding the Jews who join the Catholic Church, in whose case the pure intention of the conversion is always strictly examined by the Church authorities, the state can be confident and reassured that we are not dealing with Communists and Bolsheviks." Faulhaber wanted to make it clear that he was challenging not the government's anti-Semitic policy as such, but only the application of that policy to "non-Aryan" Catholics. He was willing to render unto Caesar the things which are Caesar's.[5]

Yet when dealing with issues he considered central in the defense of his religious community, the cardinal refused to compromise or retreat. The danger of open conflict with the regime could not deter him from performing what he regarded as his solemn pastoral duty. Here there could be no concession, no accommodation. Thus when the Nazi authorities in Upper Bavaria introduced a plan in the spring of 1937 to replace confessional schools with "common" schools attended by pupils from both major denominations, Faulhaber became a raging lion. This policy was altogether different from the government's treatment of a handful of Jewish converts. It threatened an educational right at the heart of Catholic ecclesiastical autonomy. It had to be resisted, whatever the cost.

The cardinal rejected out of hand the Nazi contention that the Third Reich was in fact the protector of Catholicism against persecutions such as the church had to endure in Russia and Spain. "Precisely because we do look at Russia and Spain, we oppose the erosion of the universal human right to profess one's faith and the universal right of parents to have their children educated in the faith of the parents." Even the secular and materialistic democracies of the West seemed to him to show greater respect for those universal human rights that he had been reluctant to invoke against the racial doctrines of National Socialism. "It would also be good," he declared indignantly, "if the statesmen [of Germany] looked at France, where indeed Jews and Freemasons sit in the government, but where parents are given the free choice to send their children to a confessional school even in a monastery or convent." On the issue of religious education, Faulhaber was willing to defy the regime.[6]

It was one of the few cases in which he or the other members of the hierarchy took an uncompromising stand. Although the struggle between Catholicism and National Socialism became at times very bitter, it remained as a rule limited in scope. It focused almost entirely on denominational schools, organizations, activities, and observances. It was deliberately compartmentalized, kept separate from broader questions of state authority or individual freedom. Each side hesitated to raise such underlying issues as legitimate power and political morality, civic duty and religious responsibility. To do so might have led to a confrontation from which there could be no retreat, a confrontation that both wanted to avoid. Hence the conflict remained restricted and disguised. On the surface there were mutual assurances of regard and loyalty, while beneath, the two adversaries sparred and maneuvered, advanced and retreated, made gains and suffered losses. The campaign went on endlessly and indecisively, because neither was willing to risk an all-out battle for ideals and principles.

The struggle of the Protestant Church against the Nazi regime was more open and therefore more bitter, in part because of disappointed hopes and expectations. When Hitler first came to power, many Catholics expected the worst; they feared repression, persecution, suffering, and martyrdom. Instead, they found a government that promised to respect their rights and traditions and that even concluded a generous concordat with the papacy. That early honeymoon soon gave way to quarrels and recriminations, but there was always the hope that, in spite of sharp differences, a reconciliation might eventually still be achieved. Most Protestants, however, had at first taken a favorable view of the Third Reich. Their leaders had hoped that the new order would turn from the secularism and materialism of Weimar to the spiritual values represented by the church. But their initial satisfaction turned to disappointment and resentment when they discovered that what the Nazi regime really sought was not partnership with but control over organized religion. Its ultimate purpose was the erosion rather than the protection of ecclesiastical autonomy.

The Protestant Church's apprehension was intensified by a profound sense of its vulnerability. Catholicism had international and supranational connections that strengthened its hand in dealing with the Nazi regime. But Protestantism, being purely national in structure, had to depend much more on the government for support and influence. Worse still, it faced not only the external pressure of the authorities but also the internal pressure of its many communicants who supported National Socialism. The struggle to defend its ecclesiastical autonomy was therefore more than a conflict between church and state; it was also a civil conflict within the church between opposing factions and loyalties.

In 1934 the Protestant opposition formed the Confessing Church, which sought to organize and represent those seeking to maintain the established form of ecclesiastical governance against the encroachments of the Nazi regime. Shortly after its founding, before government pressure and internal discord began to reduce its following, the Confessing Church included about a third of all Protestant clergymen in Germany. It was thus strong enough to express open disapproval of the Third Reich's religious policy. Yet though it proved more vocal and assertive than the Catholic opposition, the range of its criticism was equally narrow. It rarely ventured beyond arguments concerning the nature, the meaning, or the mission of Christianity. Some rare defender of religious autonomy, bolder than the rest, might cross the line between spiritual and secular opposition. But such excursions into systematic resistance against the Nazi regime were infrequent. Those seeking to protect German Protestantism against state encroachment usually went to great lengths to emphasize that they objected to the Third Reich's religious policies, not to its political goals or methods. Their opposition, they would reiterate, was not ideological but theological in nature.[7]

This deliberate isolation of the struggle to defend religious freedom can be seen, for example, in the Barmen Declaration of May 1934, which served as a statement of the basic beliefs and goals of the Confessing Church. "We reject the false doctrine that the state, going beyond its special mandate, should and could become the sole and entire order of human life and thereby also fulfill the vocation of the church." But the reverse was equally erroneous. "We reject the false doctrine that the church, going beyond its special mandate, should and could appropriate the nature, the tasks, and the dignity of the state and thereby become itself an organ of the state." These propositions simply restated the traditional doctrine of the two separate but complementary jurisdictions in the governance of the community, the temporal and the spiritual, each essential for the welfare of the whole. There was nothing here to challenge the ideological foundations of the Nazi regime.[8]

The Confessing Church sought in fact to make clear its desire to restore harmonious relations between secular and spiritual authority, which had in the past proved so beneficial to both. Thus at the synod in Augsburg in June 1935, it proclaimed its heartfelt wish for a reconciliation with the government. "We are waging the struggle, which has been forced on us, in defense of the truth of our creed, the freedom to preach, and the dignity of the Church for the sake of our nation as well." But this in no way meant disloyalty to the Third Reich. "Our prayer for our nation and its Führer comes from a sincere heart," the synod insisted.

Was it not therefore saddening that loyal members of the "German national community" were being treated as "enemies of the state, violators of its law, and disturbers of its order"? And yet "we are not justifying any real offense against the political system." The followers of the Confessing Church asked of the government only that it "not allow a gulf to open between Christianity and the national community." If German Protestantism were given the chance to perform "the service to our nation to which it is duty-bound before God and which it accepts with wholehearted devotion," it would soon prove a source of strength to the Third Reich.[9]

Occasionally some militant member of the religious opposition would go beyond the bounds of ecclesiastical controversy. Above the chorus of statements, resolutions, declarations, proclamations, and avowals of loyalty to the regime could be heard a rare voice emphasizing the connection between confessional autonomy and political freedom. Some of these expressions of dissent were remarkably bold in fact, despite the danger of reprisal by a dictatorial government. They went beyond the limits of nonconformity or opposition; they became a form of spiritual or theological resistance. Amid the popular intoxication with the Third Reich, disregarding the pervasive pressure for acceptance of the new order, a few followers of the Confessing Church remained defiant. Somehow they found the courage to look behind the facade of fanfares and parades at the dark reality of tyrannical rule.

Thus the memorandum "Concerning the Situation of the German Non-Aryans," drafted in the fall of 1935 under the direction of Martin Albertz, condemned the anti-Semitic program of the Hitler regime. It warned that the silence of German Protestantism regarding the persecution of the Jews was no better than Cain's reply to God's inquiry about his brother Abel. "And if the Church can in many cases do nothing for fear of its complete destruction, why does it not at least acknowledge its fault?" Should it not pray for those enduring "undeserved suffering and persecution?" Why were there no religious services seeking divine intercession for the victims of Nazi racism, "as there were for the imprisoned [Protestant] clergymen?" The church's silence "makes it very difficult for someone to defend it." How could there be Christians so self-righteous that they presumed to preach to the Jews about divine judgment despite their suffering, "for which we are responsible"? The memorandum was more than a pious injunction to treat others with charity, to love one's neighbor as oneself. It was an unequivocal denunciation of racial bigotry as a violation of God's law.[10]

A year later, in December 1936, Günter Jacob delivered a lecture at the synod of the Confessing Church in Breslau in which he offered a penetrating critical analysis of the ideology of the Third Reich. "We have characterized the National Socialist movement as a religion," he explained, because its claim to "unconditional validity" manifested an essentially religious outlook. Hence the state that "fanatically" promoted this outlook and was committed to its dogmas could be described as a "churchly state." It expressed "in demonic distortion" the summons of the New Testament to mankind to take a stand "for or against." In other words, this "dogmatically committed" state must by its nature require a "religious decision," it must demand "enthusiasm and fanaticism." It could not tolerate dissent or accept compromise. It could only recognize "followers and adversaries." Therefore any reservations, any doubts, must seem to it sacrilegious, as they had seemed sacrilegious to the Roman state that was "dogmatically committed to the cult of the emperor." Looking beyond the national enthusiasm aroused by Hitler's successes, Jacob beheld the irrational and totalitarian roots of the Nazi ideology. He did not seek negotiation or accommodation or reconciliation with it. He advocated, implicitly but unmistakably, its overthrow.[11]

And then there was always the most consistent and persistent religious opponent of National Socialism: Dietrich Bonhoeffer. From the very beginning, while most Protestant clergymen were still rejoicing at the fall of the "materialistic" republic, he had argued that the ideals of the new order were incompatible with Christian beliefs. Even before Hitler came to power, he had warned that "extreme elements" in Germany were exploiting popular resentment of Versailles for their own antidemocratic and ultranationalistic purposes. The Nazi Party, misusing the parliamentary system, was seeking the "establishment of a dictatorship." It was even gradually forcing its way into the church. Hence "responsible theological activity" faced the task of strengthening "that segment of the Germans and Christians in Germany who are fighting against Hitler." For if they failed, there would be "unforeseeable consequences" for "the whole world" as well as for the German people. All members of the church must oppose this danger by rejecting "a false nationalism" and "militarism" that "threaten the world with an unrest out of which a war could arise." The young theologian had sensed what the victory of National Socialism would mean.[12]

After the establishment of the Third Reich, Bonhoeffer had to be a little more careful in what he said, a little more restrained. But there could be no question about his views regarding the new order. In an article entitled "The Confessing Church and the Ecumene" published in the summer of 1935, he deplored the erosion of the sense of religious universality within German Protestantism. "The fact attested in the New Testament and in the symbolical books that the Church of Christ does not stop at national and racial boundaries but transcends them has been all too easily forgotten and denied under the assault of a new nationalism." There was no need for him to identify whom he held responsible for that assault.

Some five months later, in January 1936, his eulogy at the funeral of his grandmother became a bitter condemnation of the teachings of National Socialism. "With her a world is disappearing for us that we all somehow carry within us and want to carry within us," a world committed to "steadfastness in justice, the free speech of the free man, the observance of a promise once given, clarity and sobriety in discourse, and honesty and simplicity in personal and public life." The deceased could not endure seeing those principles ignored, seeing "the rights of a human being violated." Her last years were saddened, moreover, by "the great sorrow she felt regarding the fate of the Jews in our nation, a fate she shared and pitied." And yet that world of hers would not sink into the grave with her. "That legacy, for which we thank her, imposes a duty on us." Exactly what this duty was remained unspecified, but those listening to Bonhoeffer must have understood what he meant. There is still something very touching about this farewell to the dead and admonition to the living.

But the most eloquent, the most moving protest against the inhumanity of National Socialism was Bonhoeffer's sermon of July 11, 1937, concerning Psalm 58, the "Psalm of Vengeance." In it he lamented the "evil times" in which he lived, "when the world silently allows injustice to take place, when the oppression of the poor and wretched loudly cries out to Heaven and the judges and masters of the earth say nothing to that, and when the persecuted community in its greatest need calls on God for help and on men for righteousness and no word is heard on earth to provide it with justice." Bonhoeffer repeated the words of the biblical psalmist denouncing the acquiescence of society in wickedness. "Do ye indeed speak righteousness, O congregation? do ye judge uprightly, O ye sons of men?"

In his anguish he cried out that "those are human beings to whom injustice is being done." How could that be forgotten? He condemned Nazi bigotry without naming its victims. There was no need for that. It was enough that they were "human beings who are the creatures of God like you, who feel pain and misery like you, . . . who have their happiness and their hopes like you, who feel honor and disgrace like you, human beings who are sinners like you and who need God's compassion like you, your brothers." Yet those in power offered them only "pitiless and biased" words, judging them "not according to justice but according to the status of the person." Bonhoeffer had become an impassioned Old Testament prophet decrying the iniquity of the proud and the mighty.[13]

An even more remarkable expression of religious opposition to the Third Reich, remarkable not only for its boldness but also for its naïveté, was the confidential memorandum of May 28, 1936, which ten prominent militants in the Confessing Church submitted directly to Hitler. They decided not to publicize its contents, in part on the assumption that the government would find it easier to retreat from its position on ecclesiastical autonomy if it did not appear to be yielding to threats and pressures. They appealed in effect from the bad Hitler to the good Hitler, from the Führer misled by wicked advisers to the Führer guided by the Christian ethic. Their strategy revealed from the outset a fundamental misunderstanding of the totalitarian nature of the National Socialist ideology.

The memorandum began inoffensively enough with a ritualistic "respectful greeting to the Führer and Chancellor," adding even that the Protestant Church felt "closely attached" to the Third Reich "through the prayers, which it offers publicly as well as in private, for the nation, the state, and the government." But then came bitter protests and complaints. Precisely because they had expected so much from the new order, the authors were shocked to discover that "the struggle within the German nation against the Christian Church is more violent and determined than at any time since 1918." There was actually a danger that young people "might be kept from coming to him who is also the only Savior of German boys and girls." They directed a "simple question" to the leader of the nation, namely, "whether the attempt to dechristianize the German people, either with the continuing participation of responsible statesmen or merely with their looking on and doing nothing, is to become the official course of the government." The wording of the question was in itself a stern reproach to the Third Reich.

But the memorandum did not criticize only the regime's religious policy. It also condemned its racial doctrine as a violation of Christian morality, indeed as a transgression against God's commandment. Its authors, show-ing remarkable courage, minced no words. "If blood, race, nationality, and honor receive here the dignity of eternal values, then the Protestant Christian is compelled by the First Commandment to reject this valuation. While the Aryan man is being glorified, the word of God attests to the sinfulness of all human beings." And lest the Führer misunderstand its meaning, the memorandum explicitly rejected the central dogma of the Third Reich's racism. "If, within the framework of the National Socialist view of the world, an anti-Semitism that requires hatred of Jews is forced on a Christian, then the Christian commandment to love one's neighbor opposes that within him."

The memorandum even went beyond a denunciation of racism. It was one of the few statements of religious opposition to National Socialism that touched on state oppression and civil rights. "The Protestant conscience," it declared defiantly, "which also considers itself responsible for the nation and the government, is very heavily burdened by the fact that in Germany, which professes to be a state based on justice, there are still concentration camps and the measures taken by the secret police are exempt from judicial scrutiny." This issue was not an exclusive concern of secular authority; it had a religious dimension as well. "The Protestant Church perceives also in these things the danger that in our thinking about morality and justice an anti-Christian spirit will come to prevail." Here at last was a recognition of the essential inseparability of civic and religious freedom.[14]

There is no record of what Hitler said when he received the memoran-dum. He may have been angered by it or perhaps merely amused; he may have denounced its authors as traitors or dismissed them as fools. But the reaction of most members of the religious opposition is known, because a copy was smuggled out of Germany to Switzerland, where it was promptly leaked to the foreign press. The man believed responsible for this indiscre-tion was Friedrich Weissler, a "non-Aryan" lawyer who served as a legal adviser to the Confessing Church. The Nazi regime could now claim that those who had composed the memorandum were disloyal and unpatriotic, that they were collaborating with Germany's enemies. The ecclesiastical leaders, therefore, even those who had been critical of the Third Reich, rushed to dissociate themselves from the views expressed by the militants. They were intimidated by the charge of disloyalty, because their hope of influencing the regime's religious policy rested on their being perceived as its adherents, on their being accepted as loyalists and insiders. Yet ecclesi-astical extremists were undermining by their reckless language the confi-dence of the authorities that the moderates had been working so hard to cultivate. No wonder most church leaders anxiously disavowed the embarrassing memorandum.[15]

Their primary motive was expediency and conviction rather than fear. It had already become clear that the regime hesitated to take strong measures against religious critics of the Third Reich, even against outspoken and persistent critics, provided their opinions remained confidential or were expressed only to small groups of ecclesiastical malcontents. Although the police kept track of what was being said by the churchly opposition, no punitive action was taken against Martin Albertz or against Jacob and Bonhoeffer. As long as they did not seek to propagate or popularize their views, the danger of their being arrested was small. The authorities had no wish to make martyrs out of a handful of ineffectual ecclesiastical radicals.

Thus the reluctance of the Confessing Church to provoke an open break with the Third Reich could not have been based chiefly on a concern for the personal safety of its members. It reflected instead a belief that its goals could best be achieved by moderation and negotiation, not by defiance or resistance. Equally important, most Protestant leaders found themselves in essential agreement with much of the Third Reich's program. They too favored a revival of traditional values and loyalties, they too supported a more assertive stand in foreign relations, they too encouraged resistance against materialism and Marxism, they too preached the subordination of private or class interests to national needs and purposes. Why then provoke an open break with a regime that was essentially sound on so many important issues? It would be a mistake for either side to allow a dispute over religious policy to turn into a conflict over constitutional or political or racial policy.

This kind of reasoning can be discerned, for example, in the evolution of Niemöller's views and attitudes. No one could possibly accuse Niemöller of timidity. On the contrary, he displayed in the pulpit the same reckless courage that he had once exhibited as a wartime submarine commander. At first sympathetic toward National Socialism, which had seemed to him to share his own civic convictions, he soon became one of its boldest critics because of the government's efforts to restrict ecclesiastical autonomy. He even signed the memorandum to Hitler of May 28, 1936. This religious opposition to the Third Reich in turn had the effect of modifying his attitude on the racial question. Though in general still anti-Semitic, he began to take a more charitable view of those Jews who converted to Christianity. They deserved the full sympathy and support of the church, he gradually concluded.

Soon after Hitler came to power, Niemöller had written that the Germans had long suffered under the influence of the Jews. Still, the teachings of the church prohibited the exclusion of baptized Jews from ecclesiastical office, however difficult the acceptance of that prohibition might be. But "non-Aryan" Protestant ministers should at least behave with discretion, recognizing that it would be "ill-advised" for them to occupy a prominent position in churchly administration. Niemöller had even suggested that "non-Aryan" Christians might consider forming separate congregations of their own, although membership should be entirely voluntary. He was eager to find some way of avoiding a confrontation with the regime over the racial question without violating the principle of Christian universality.

In the course of the next few years, however, as he began increasingly to oppose the Third Reich's religious policy, Niemöller became more sensitive to the persecution that converted Jews had to endure. At the synod of the Prussian Protestant Church in September 1935 in the Steglitz district of Berlin, he demanded that more be done for "our baptized Christian brothers who are in their flesh Jews or half-Jews." He cited St. Paul's Epistle to the Galatians. "For ye are all the children of God by faith in Christ Jesus. For as many of you as have been baptized into Christ have put on Christ. There is neither Jew nor Greek, there is neither bond nor free, there is neither male nor female: for ye are all one in Christ Jesus." God's church must not simply admit Jews and then leave them to their fate under National Socialism. Its duty was to intercede for them, to speak, plead, and, if necessary, fight.[16]

Yet Niemöller's growing compassion toward a few thousand "non-Aryan" Christians did not basically alter his attitude toward the more than half a million "non-Aryan" Jews. In a sermon in August 1935 he reminded the members of his congregation that they must not add to the divine punishment of the Jews by their own hatred. Jesus had commanded them to "love your enemies." Still, there could be no denying that the Jewish people bore God's curse, and "because it rejected forgiveness," it carried with it "the unforgiven bloodguilt of its fathers as a terrible burden." Afterward Niemöller even admitted that "certain restrictions against the Jews seemed to me tolerable, considering the great aims the Nazis were driving at." The persecution of the Jewish community, though unjustified or at least excessive, did not seem to him to be properly the concern of a Christian clergyman.[17]

The religious opposition can thus be characterized as a resistance movement only in the sense that it engaged in an organized, systematic, overt, and consistent course of action against the Third Reich's ecclesiastical policy. It never sought to bring about a fundamental change in the nature of the Nazi regime. It was too narrow, too parochial in outlook to go beyond the bounds of denominational self-defense. Its major concern was churchly jurisdiction and administration. Only on the issue of religious governance did it disagree sharply with National Socialism. Otherwise it was prepared to tolerate or even support the Hitler dictatorship. It sought not to overthrow or even reform the established system but to find a secure and recognized place within it. Ultimately, its inability to rise above confessional expediency reflected the lack of an ideal expressing the transcendent moral responsibility of religious faith.

IV

The Beginnings of Resistance

Late in the afternoon on August 31, [1939,] I observed
Canaris coming down from upstairs. . . . The admiral took
me firmly by the arm, but he did not look at me. His gaze
was fixed sideways on the floor, absentmindedly and yet so
piercingly as if to bore deep through the building to its
foundations. [He said] to me in a voice choked with tears:
"This is the end of Germany."

HANS BERND GISEVIUS (1946)

13

Tightening the Totalitarian Grip

Were the men who tried to overthrow Hitler in the summer of 1944 motivated primarily by a concern for the welfare of Germany or by some broader moral principle above national interest? The answer to that question became a source of disagreement almost from the outset. Three years after the war Hans Rothfels, one of the first historians to deal with the resistance, concluded that its members were inspired by an ideal transcending the struggle against National Socialism. Their ultimate purpose was to free the world from a pitiless despotism. They were responding to impulses that were of universal validity. Though their coup failed, they deserve to be remembered as "standard bearers in the midst of chaos." What they did serves as a reminder that not all Germans succumbed to Hitler's spell.[1]

Rothfels, though himself a victim of National Socialism, never lost faith in that other Germany of humaneness and decency, which the members of the resistance seemed to him to embody. But some writers, especially in countries that had been forced to make heavy sacrifices to defeat the Third Reich, were less generous. In 1951, not long after Rothfels's eulogy of the participants in the uprising against the Nazi regime, the London *Times* offered a more critical evaluation. In an article entitled "Hitler's Victims," it suggested that "the conspirators of July, 1944, were not all . . . free from responsibility for the Nazi regime." Still, they were "the only Germans in all that time who, without prompting from abroad and by their own decision, rebelled against a Government which they had cause to recognize as both evil and ruinous." For this recognition, belated though it was, "they deserve honour" even more than for "their courage and self-sacrifice."

The democratic regime being built in Central Europe on the ruins of the Third Reich, the *Times* went on, should remember those who, though not entirely free of blame or complicity, eventually turned against National Socialism. "If the Germans defamed the memory of these men and reserved 'honour' only for those soldiers who to the very end meekly obeyed brutal and infamous orders, then indeed there would be faint hope for the German nation." The resisters, while seeking above all to save their own country, at least resisted.[2]

The two motivations thus ascribed to the resistance, the national and the supranational, are not mutually exclusive. Concern for the welfare of one's own country is not incompatible with concern for the welfare of all mankind. But what was the primary interest of those taking part in the coup against Hitler? What was their main consideration? In this regard the time when the resistance emerged is of major significance, not only for reasons of historical accuracy but for what it reveals about the purposes of the participants. By helping to identify the events and circumstances that transformed their support or acquiescence into a rejection of the Nazi regime, such a chronology provides insight into their beliefs and ideals. Its importance lies in what it says about the underlying attitude of the resisters toward the Hitler dictatorship.

Clearly, whatever turned them against National Socialism did not occur during the period of the new order's establishment, the period from roughly 1933 to 1935, when it devoted its energies primarily to the suppression of opposing forces and institutions. At that time the future resisters almost without exception more or less favored Nazi policies. Nor is there evidence of significant disapproval among them during the consolidation of the Third Reich from about 1935 to 1937, the high point of the authoritarian coalition, when the new elite and the old worked together for stability in domestic affairs and parity in foreign relations. The resistance did not begin until the regime's attempt to Nazify all forms of authority in Germany, beginning in 1938 and continuing until its collapse in 1945. Only after the decision of the new order to eliminate the distinction between state and party, between loyalty to the nation and loyalty to the government, did an organized movement for the overthrow of the Hitler dictatorship finally emerge.

The increased militancy of the Third Reich during the last prewar years became as apparent in international as in national policy. At home Nazification meant the progressive erosion of the autonomy enjoyed by the army and the bureaucracy, and their growing vulnerability to the pressure for ideological conformity. Abroad it took the form of a new aggressive diplomacy designed to alter the balance of power in Europe in favor of the Axis. The same strategy of combativeness resting on the threat of force was thus displayed in the regime's conduct of both domestic and foreign affairs.

The first manifestation of the new policy came early in 1938, when the relative immunity of the armed forces against political constraint in effect ended. The scandalous marriage of Field Marshal Werner von Blomberg, the minister of war, and the removal from office of General Werner von Fritsch, the army's chief of staff, on a false charge of homosexuality opened the way for the regime to assume greater control over the military. On February 4 Hitler announced that he was taking personal command of the armed forces, exercising his new authority through the compliant and obsequious General Wilhelm Keitel. The war ministry as a semi-independent agency mediating between the government and the army was thereby abolished. As if to show that he meant business, Hitler ordered sixteen senior generals relieved of their commands and forty-four others transferred to new assignments. Those who during the next few months went into retirement, at least temporarily, included several high-ranking officers who were to play a major role in the war beginning the following year, among them Gerd von Rundstedt, Wilhelm von Leeb, Günther von Kluge, and Erwin von Witzleben.

The extension of Nazi political and ideological control over the civil service was less dramatic but just as thorough. There had for some time been indications of an incipient estrangement between the regime and the more outspoken members of the bureaucracy. The resignation of Carl Goerdeler as mayor of Leipzig in the spring of 1937 was one sign; the resignation of Hjalmar Schacht as minister of economics eight months later was another. The decisive step, however, did not come until the following year, when the Third Reich put an end to the relative autonomy of the most exclusive and prestigious component of the bureaucracy, the diplomatic corps. Early in February Konstantin von Neurath, a conservative aristocrat of the old school, was replaced as minister of foreign affairs by the Nazi hundred-percenter Joachim von Ribbentrop. Loyalty to National Socialism had clearly become more important for advancement in the civil service than technical expertise or professional experience.

The extent of the politicization of the diplomatic corps could soon be seen in a series of important shifts in ambassadorial positions. Herbert von Dirksen, whose allegiance to the Nazi Party seemed beyond question, moved up from the embassy in Tokyo to the one in London. Franz von Papen, whose devotion to the Third Reich was a little suspect, continued his steady decline through the various gradations of governmental dignity, from chancellor in 1932 to vice-chancellor in 1933 to envoy to Austria in

1934 and finally to ambassador to Turkey in 1939. As for Ulrich von Hassell, who had long had his differences with Ribbentrop, he was peremptorily recalled from the embassy in Rome and forced into retirement while still in his fifties. All of this not only served but was intended to serve as a lesson to those who aspired to a career in the civil service.

The resolve of the Third Reich to bring about the Nazification of all aspects of national life also became evident in its intensified anti-Semitic policy. When first established, the new order insisted that measures directed against "non-Aryans" were necessary to reduce the excessive influence they had gradually managed to acquire. This argument seemed to possess a certain verisimilitude, because Jews did play a role in politics, finance, commerce, and culture disproportionate to their share in the population. But the essentially irrational basis of Nazi racism became apparent in the next few years, for as the Jewish community in Germany was progressively isolated, ostracized, humiliated, and persecuted, official hostility toward its members only increased. Their helplessness was perceived as merely a pretense, a sham. They were accused of secretly still conspiring with world Jewry to bring about the downfall of the Hitler government and thereby regain their dominant position. The psychological need of the National Socialists to see themselves as victims of Jewish plots and intrigues blinded them to the real consequences of their brutal, unrelenting racism.

This collective paranoia helps explain the decision of the regime in the fall of 1938 to take the next to final step in the solution of the Jewish question. The assassination of Ernst vom Rath, a junior member of the Third Reich's embassy staff in Paris, by a seventeen-year-old Polish Jew, Herschel Grynszpan, became the occasion for a nationwide pogrom in Germany orchestrated by the party authorities. On November 9, during the infamous *Kristallnacht,* the "night of broken glass," 267 synagogues were set on fire and 76 were destroyed. Mobs incited by Nazi storm troopers vandalized tens of thousands of Jewish shops and homes. In the aftermath more than thirty thousand Jews were arrested and sent to concentration camps, where about a thousand of them perished in the next few months. The Jewish community, moreover, was fined a billion marks for provoking those who had caused the damage. Jewish children were henceforth barred from attending German schools, and Jews were officially declared to be excluded from the economic life of the Third Reich. The way was now clear for the last phase in National Socialism's racial program, the phase of mass incarceration and genocide.

Yet the significance of the regime's new militancy at home was obscured by the effect of its new militancy abroad. In the course of the year and a half prior to the outbreak of the war, Hitler succeeded in bringing about a diplomatic revolution that altered dramatically the balance of power in Europe. By exploiting the fear of military conflict on the part of the Western democracies, he won a succession of impressive bloodless victories in international relations. The Anschluss of Austria in March 1938, the acquisition of the Sudeten region in September 1938, and the dismemberment of Czechoslovakia in March 1939 were the rich prizes in a game of brinkmanship played with consummate skill. Under his leadership Germany managed not only to overthrow the Versailles system but to achieve a territorial extent and diplomatic influence greater even than under the Hohenzollerns. Accomplishments of such magnitude seemed to most Germans well worth the subordination of the officer corps, the politicization of the civil service, and the persecution of an alien, unpopular racial minority.

During this roller coaster of alternating fears and celebrations, of alarming crises followed by exhilarating successes, the resistance against Hitler came into existence. But again, what was the basic motivation of its members? What led them to turn against the Third Reich at the moment of its greatest accomplishments in foreign policy? Was it concern regarding the Nazification of state and society, revulsion against the cruelty of the regime's anti-Semitism, a feeling that Hitler's diplomacy was going beyond the assertion of Germany's rightful place in Europe, or a fear that the government was moving toward a military conflict likely to end in catastrophe?

The evidence suggests that the tightening grip of the regime on national life was not a major factor in the emergence of a secret movement against the Hitler dictatorship. To be sure, there was grumbling and complaining among some members of the traditional social elite who saw their position threatened by the new radicalism of the right. The dissolution of the authoritarian coalition in particular and its replacement by an undisguised Nazi dominance left them bewildered and embittered. They began to feel that they had been tricked into contributing to their own downfall. Their growing antagonism toward a government they had once supported and served was thus fed by a sense of betrayal.

Especially the older members of the resistance felt this way. Hassell, for example, still resentful of his unceremonious dismissal from the diplomatic service, complained in his diary on September 17, 1938, that Hitler's speeches were "all demagogic, interspersed with sharp attacks against the entire upper stratum [of society]." His most recent speech before the Nazi Party congress had been delivered in "a wild, blustering tone." His "increased hatred for the upper stratum" was intensified, moreover, by "the warnings of the generals, with the exception of Keitel, against a war." Hassell felt that "the dislike for men of independent character is growing." Indeed, "whoever does not crawl is regarded as arrogant." That was the real reason for his own disfavor. "[The leader of the SS Reinhard] Heydrich said . . . explicitly that I am generally regarded by them as arrogant, and that Ribbentrop cannot stand me." Disappointed hopes, frustrated ambitions, political disagreements, and ideological differences all intermingled in his opposition to the Third Reich.[3]

Others shared Hassell's dislikes. Two weeks later, on September 29, his diary described a breakfast meeting at the Continental Hotel in Berlin at which Popitz sounded "very bitter," complaining that "they are proceeding with growing fury against the upper 'stratum,' as Hitler calls it." That was appalling. "Physical disgust will overcome any decent person . . . who hears speeches like the recent coarse speech by Hitler in the Sportpalast." Popitz feared that National Socialism was gradually undermining the traditional world of the German bureaucratic patriciate. And yet he could not bring himself to resign his ceremonial position as Prussian minister of finance in a government that, by his own statement, he found repugnant.[4]

Most members of the resistance, however, especially the younger ones, were more charitable in their view of the Third Reich. To them the subordination of the administrative system to the wishes of the Nazi Party seemed to make little difference. What really mattered was the success of the regime in defending the national interest, in regaining for Germany a position of strength in international affairs. Why worry about who was leading the foreign office or heading the embassy in Rome? The important thing was that the fatherland had regained confidence in its own destiny. And the credit had to go to National Socialism. About that there could be no doubt.

Schulenburg, for instance, though an aristocrat as much as Hassell and certainly more than Popitz, seemed indifferent to the Nazification of the bureaucracy. His faith in the new order remained unshaken; he continued to espouse its principles as if nothing had happened. In March 1938, a month after Neurath had been forced out of the foreign office, he once more lectured on his favorite topic, this time under the title "The Prussian Legacy and the National Socialist State," expounding the same apocalyptic views as in his lecture the previous July regarding "The Legacy of the Prussian State." His chief theme, expressed in almost identical terms, was again the historic mission of the Third Reich to strengthen and purify the national life of Germany.

National Socialism, Schulenburg remained convinced, was seeking "to free the life of our nation from all alien forces," allowing it to develop "in accordance with its own character." The new order was struggling "to awaken to new life" not only "the great national community" but also "all the other communities, of occupation, of family, and of municipality," that had been undermined by "the destructive forces of the French Revolution and the Enlightenment." It saw the state not as "an end in itself" but as "a means toward an end," specifically, as "the vital form of the nation" and of its collective might "organized for self-assertion in the struggle for existence as well as for the maintenance and development of its national-ity." Hence the need for the "segregation of Jews and descendants of Jews." Schulenburg was still the good, loyal Nazi.[5]

Trott's attitude toward the regime was different in theory but similar in practice. He was too much the liberal aristocrat with socialistic leanings to embrace the doctrines of National Socialism. But neither could he bring himself to oppose them unequivocally, especially not in discussions with foreigners. His national pride would not allow that. Instead, he tried to square the circle, to deprecate the Third Reich without condemning Germany, to be critical of the state without sounding disloyal to the nation. His strategy was to argue that while National Socialism had serious faults, Western democracy had faults too, perhaps even more serious ones.

Writing to a British friend in the fall of 1938, Trott suggested that "perhaps capitalist and imperialist democracy uses liberty as a smoke screen for definite coercive policies whereas some aspects of 'authoritarian' sys-tems may mean a more straightforward assertion of the rights of men in modern industrial society than its opponents realise." In other words, he contended, "the conflict of ideologies may really be quite unrepresentative or disguise the real nature of the conflict which may be based on rival but not different ambitions!" The argument that "the rival dynamic of the European Powers is ultimately incompatible and must result in the bloody victory of one ideology over the other" seemed to him simplistic. After all, England and France, like other states, had "definitely authoritarian ele-ments," and it would be "vicious" to ascribe that "merely to capitalist flirtation with fascism." Indeed, "every socialist state must be to some extent authoritarian, if it is to survive."

Conversely, every authoritarian state "must allow for the development of free individual personality to survive." Since that was true even of Nazi Germany, at least "to some extent," it became his duty "to try that out until I fail utterly." Trott conceded that he might fail, "because I have not the strength." But "I do not yet think it is impossible in principle." He

remained trapped between the opposing forces of nationalism and cos-
mopolitanism, liberalism and authoritarianism, paralyzed, unable either to
accept or reject the Third Reich.[6]

The armed forces responded to Hitler's assumption of direct military
command with equal indecision. Six years later, following the failed attempt against the Nazi regime, Schulenburg testified that the resistance
movement arose out of the army's disapproval of the breach of its traditional autonomy:

> The starting point is to be sought as early as the events of February 4, 1938
> (removal of Fritsch). On one side was arrayed a group of officers who followed
> the National Socialist leadership unconditionally. On the other side a group of
> officers formed the opposition, officers who considered the encroachment on
> the military to be a violation of its inner law, and who viewed the risks in the
> Führer's diplomatic and war policy as so great that they would in the long run
> exhaust the strength of the nation. Out of this split, which became visible on
> February 4, 1938, arose the designs for a putsch and then also the assassination
> plans directed against the Führer.[7]

Yet in fact there is no evidence of any significant opposition to the
extension of Nazi control over the armed forces early in 1938. The soldiers
seemed even more passive than the bureaucrats. There were no stubborn
insubordinates among them like Carl Goerdeler, not even grumblers and
complainers like Hassell or Popitz. Even those who had expressed private
disapproval of the blood purge of June 1934 remained noncommittal
during the bloodless purge of February 1938. Rommel, for example, had
been outraged by what happened in 1934, declaring, in confidence, that
"Hitler and his entire gang" should be outsted. And while Hans Oster did
not actually criticize the regime or its leadership, he did express alarm at
the growing influence of the SS. In 1938, however, both men, like almost
all other military officers, remained silent. Yet the suppression of the
brownshirts had been advantageous to the army, whereas the reorganization of its command structure was clearly a threat. The meek acquiescence
of the armed forces is still something of a puzzle.[8]

The best explanation seems to lie in a combination of factors. For one
thing, the Nazi regime was much stronger now than before, much more
popular and confident. To oppose its decision to assert greater control over
the armed forces might appear principled, but it was almost certain to
prove futile. The only likely result would be to reinforce the regime's
determination to dominate and subordinate the officer corps.

Besides, the military revival of Germany had come a long way since
1934. There were opportunities for reward, promotion, recognition, and

prestige that had earlier seemed unattainable. Should they be jeopardized for the sake of a doctrine of political noninvolvement based after all on precedent and tradition rather than formal law? The risk was too great and the prize too small. Acquiescence seemed the best course.

Finally, the new purge was carried out with much more skill and finesse than the old. Then, two senior officers, Schleicher and Bredow, had been murdered in cold blood, while close to two hundred other men and women, possibly many more, had been executed without so much as an indictment, trial, or sentence. But now two senior officers, Blomberg and Fritsch, were merely humiliated and dismissed, while a few dozen others were transferred or retired. There had been no violence, no bloodshed. Everything had been done in accordance with rules and regulations. How then could the armed forces be expected to object?

Barely a week after the Führer assumed direct command over the military, an article in the *New Statesman and Nation* in London expressed mock admiration for the smoothness with which the Nazi yoke had been imposed:

> Hitler's second purge shows an immense advance in poise and technique over his previous performance. It may have been ruthless but it was bloodless. When one read his two letters of thanks to his victims, that to Marshal von Blomberg generous and effusive, that to General von Fritsch cold and grudging, one had to realise that the Führer has acquired in five years some of the subtler arts of the governing man. Some critics have suggested that by leaving the fourteen generals alive, he showed a trace of weakness. On the contrary, this respectable moderation is a proof rather of self-confidence. The June massacre [of 1934] made an impression of panic: it was the act of a young and insecure despotism. Yet these generals whom Hitler has deposed represented a power incomparably more formidable than the storm-troop leaders whom he destroyed. [The latter] and their colleagues of the Nazi left were mere adventurers; a year before their end the average German citizen would have called them gangsters. The generals, on the other hand, were the hope, not merely of all that is Prussian and traditional in the army; they were the only spokesmen of the Junker caste who still carried their heads high. To get rid of them with such quiet efficiency was no small feat, for a former corporal and house-painter.

Turning to the likely outcome of the reorganization of the army's command system, the article changed its tone from ironic to monitory. "With this performance the Totalitarian State has achieved something approaching final perfection." The regime had already dissolved all rival political parties; it had crushed the trade unions, subjugated the press, and purged the universities. While the churches managed to preserve a measure of independence, they could offer little effective resistance. As for big business, "it grumbles inaudibly in luxurious corners and pours into sympathetic foreign ears its predictions of economic ruin." But it would not dream of organized opposition. "One rock alone stood erect above the Nazi flood. The army kept its traditions and the High Command retained the unyielding Junker outlook that had already survived fifteen years of the alien republican system." The military had been the only force in public life still outside the control of the Nazi movement.

That was precisely why the Third Reich was so determined to extend its authority over the armed forces. "For National Socialism is more than a system of obedience: it requires uniformity of thought." It could not tolerate a "neutral, nonpolitical" military establishment. "Its army must be, like every public institution on German soil, an extension and incarnation of its governing party." And now that it had achieved that goal, the regime would become more aggressive and ruthless in domestic as well as foreign affairs. "The outcome of this purge is unquestionably a victory for the extremer tendencies in Nazi policy."[9]

Could the officer corps in Germany have failed to recognize what was quite obvious to an observer in Great Britain? If so, it must have been because its members chose not to recognize it. They preferred to look the other way, to pretend that little had changed. A reorganization of the high command had taken place, that was all. There was nothing improper or even unusual in that. The regime would continue to pursue a vigorous and assertive foreign policy; it would continue to defend the nation's vital interests and to expand its armed forces. And the armed forces in turn would continue to gain strength, influence, recognition, and respect. Why jeopardize a partnership so clearly of mutual benefit?

Curiously enough, the aspect of the Nazification of public life arousing the greatest indignation was not the politicization of the foreign office or the subordination of the military leadership but the outburst of mass violence against the Jews during the *Kristallnacht*. Even some members of the officer corps who had appeared indifferent to Hitler's assumption of direct command over the armed forces expressed shock, at least in their private conversations, letters, and diaries, at the brutality of the anti-Semitic riots.

Claus von Stauffenberg, until then a loyal supporter of the Third Reich, began to have his first serious doubts as a result of the November pogrom. One of his fellow officers, Friedrich Wilhelm von Loeper, maintained after the war that it was above all the persecution of the Jews and the oppression of the churches that had turned Stauffenberg against National Socialism. Werner Reerink, another of his army comrades, recalled in the 1960s that the events of the *Kristallnacht* had led Stauffenberg, "who always championed justice, decency, and morality with special zeal," to express "a blunt condemnation of what had happened," deploring "the harm that would thereby be done to our fatherland throughout the world." Thereafter he began to criticize "people in the organizations of the National Socialist Party who, in light of their character and conduct, were a thorn in his side." He was taking the initial, hesitant steps on the road that would lead him to the resistance.[10]

The effect of the anti-Jewish riots on Helmuth Groscurth, one of the first soldiers to join the movement against the Nazi regime, can be ascertained more directly. A brief entry in his diary in the fall of 1938 expresses repugnance and outrage. "In November major activities against the Jews. The orders issued for the 'spontaneous' activities are kept separately. One has to feel ashamed of still being a German." That phrase, "one has to feel ashamed of still being a German," was to echo and reecho in varying forms in the political discourse of the resistance for the next six years.[11]

Some civilians in the resistance condemned the *Kristallnacht* even more strongly. Peter Yorck von Wartenburg, later included in the list of possible members of the provisional government to be established after the fall of the Nazi regime, testified in 1944 before the Gestapo that "in the course of the last few years an inward break with National Socialism has taken place within me." Among the chief reasons were "the National Socialist concept of justice" and "the extermination measures against Jewry, which went beyond the Nuremberg Laws." The anti-Semitic riots six years before had helped convert Yorck from a lukewarm supporter to an ardent opponent of the Hitler dictatorship.[12]

They also made a deep impression on Hans-Bernd von Haeften, the young diplomat who was among the first members of the resistance to be tried and executed after the failed attempt on the Führer's life. Writing in December 1938 to his friend Herbert Krimm, a Protestant minister, he expressed bitter disappointment at the failure of the clergy to condemn what had happened in Germany during the recent pogrom. "The passive attitude of the church toward that appears to me sometimes like a pastor in his clerical robe who, reading in the Gospel in a pious pose, . . . goes on his way and is so absorbed in his 'text' that he keeps on going. Or, if the misery lies so close in front of him that he stumbles over it, then he seeks refuge from this sight in a consoling Psalm and finds edification in it." Haeften could not understand how those who were supposedly the moral leaders of society could remain silent in the face of such a blatant violation of morality.[13]

But no one voiced greater abhorrence of the *Kristallnacht* than Hassell. The conservative aristocrat, still resentful of his unceremonious dismissal from the foreign service, increasingly distrustful of a regime he regarded as reckless and unprincipled, expressed shock in his diary on November 25, 1938, at what had happened two weeks earlier. He was appalled by the "vile persecution of the Jews." Indeed, "never since the world war have we lost so much credit in the world." Like many other members of the resistance, Hassell worried about the unfavorable impression that Nazi brutality was bound to make on public opinion in foreign countries. But more than that, "my chief concern is not the effect [of the anti-Semitic riots] abroad, in other words, any sort of reaction of a diplomatic nature, at least not for the moment. My really serious concern pertains to our inner life, which is being gripped ever more completely and tightly by a system capable of such things."

He had to agree with reluctance that the criticism of Germany in other countries was valid. "There is indeed nothing in life more bitter than being forced to regard foreign attacks on one's own nation as justified." Hassell tried to console himself with the thought that public opinion abroad would recognize the difference between the "real people" of Germany, who opposed the pogrom, and the "element that did this thing." Still, there could be no denying that "the lowest instincts were stirred up." At least this time "indignation" at what had happened seemed to affect not only "the overwhelming majority of educated people" in the Third Reich but also "very broad circles of the population."[14]

Clearly, most of the resisters, like many other Germans, disapproved of the anti-Semitic riots in the fall of 1938. But why? What was it about the *Kristallnacht* that they found so repugnant? After all, they had for five years been witnessing without serious objection a less dramatic but more persistent persecution of the Jewish community. They had observed with seeming indifference its segregation, ostracism, oppression, and humiliation. They had not criticized, not even in private, the economic boycott of 1933 or the Nuremberg Laws of 1935 or the countless petty, cruel discriminations in everyday life that the Jews had to endure. Why then did the November pogrom arouse such indignation and revulsion?

The answer seems to be that the members of the resistance, or at least a majority among them, were opposed not to anti-Semitism as such but to the "extremes" or "excesses" of anti-Semitism. They generally agreed that the Germanic and the Jewish racial characters were so different that they could not coexist in a state of harmony. There had to be a separation between them. But that separation should be orderly, legal, deliberate, and, if possible, humane. The *Kristallnacht* therefore shocked them with its outburst of mob violence, its display of raw mass brutality. It was all so undisciplined, so lawless and chaotic. The shameful thing was not its purpose but its method. Pogroms might be expected of Russians or Ukrainians or Rumanians, but surely not of Germans. The resisters were generally prepared to tolerate legal measures designed to exclude "non-Aryans" from national life, but not rampaging, looting, burning, and beating. They were, to put it simply, moderates rather than extremists in their anti-Semitism.

A report of October 28, 1944, from the official government inquiry into the plot to overthrow the Nazi regime supports this conclusion. "In very many interrogations regarding their attitude toward National Socialism there is the repeated statement that they were indeed in general no friends of the Jews, but that the 'brutal,' 'excessive,' and 'overly harsh' way of proceeding in the Jewish question, the 'clinging to the crazy idea about Jews,' was the cause for arousing the hatred of the entire world against us." Those arrested also criticized occasionally the "propagandistic treatment of the Jewish question by the [violently anti-Semitic] *Stürmer*." They expressed the view, "which is still widespread in the liberal and reactionary strata of bourgeois society," that "the solution of the Jewish problem should have been undertaken much more calmly, soberly, and 'delicately.'" Above all, "the so-called 'decent Jew' should have been treated differently from the profiteer and the East European Jew." As for the "uncompromising enforcement of the racial laws of National Socialism," the prisoners appeared to be "completely devoid of understanding." Their anti-Semitism was too squeamish, too fastidious, for the ruthless ideologues of the Third Reich.[15]

Those members of the resistance who did not participate in the conspiracy against Hitler displayed by and large the same prejudices and the same scruples as those who did. Genteel anti-Semites, they opposed brutality and lawlessness but believed that the segregation of the Jewish community by legal means was justifiable. The events of the *Kristallnacht* did not change their basic attitude. On December 6, 1938, Bishop Wurm protested against the recent pogrom in a letter to Minister of Justice Franz Gürtner. But he hastened to add that he objected to the indiscipline and violence of the riots, not to their underlying goal. "I do not question in any way the right of the state to oppose Jewry as a dangerous element. I have ever since my youth considered the judgment of men like Heinrich von Treitschke and Adolf Stöcker regarding the disruptive influence of Jewry in the religious, moral, literary, economic, and political sphere to be valid." But could not that influence be countered with a little more judiciousness, a little more restraint?[16]

The evidence regarding Niemöller's views is somewhat more ambiguous. After conceding reluctantly in 1933 that "non-Aryan" Protestants could not be barred from holding churchly office, he had mellowed enough by 1935 to preach that "there is no license authorizing us to supplement God's curse [against unconverted Jews] with our hatred." His own struggle against the Nazi regime's religious policy appeared to make him a little more sensitive toward its racial victims.

But his attitude continued to change. At his trial in February 1938 he attested to his dislike of Jews. Then, nine months later, he shifted again. Finally, he remembered toward the end of his life, the events of the *Kristallnacht* had made it clear to him at last that "the Jews were to be eliminated not simply from the church but from human society." He had been shocked. That at least was the recollection of an old man in his eighties regarding events more than forty years earlier. What is indisputable, however, is that in September 1939, ten months after the anti-Semitic riots, he volunteered for service with the armed forces of the Third Reich. "If there is a war," he explained at a press conference following the collapse of Hitler's regime, "a German doesn't ask is it just or unjust, but he feels bound to join the ranks." Opposition to Nazi racism could not provide a dispensation from this patriotic duty.[17]

Goerdeler's attitude toward the intensification of the government's anti-Semitic program is clearer. A compulsive and indefatigable writer of memorandums, reports, notes, and drafts, he left a voluminous record of his views on virtually every aspect of public policy. It shows that he was never a Jew-hater. On the contrary, he tried to protect Jewish shopkeepers in Leipzig against plundering storm troopers in the days following Hitler's appointment to the chancellorship, and the immediate cause of his resignation as mayor of the city four years later was the removal by the Nazi authorities of a statue of Felix Mendelssohn, which stood in front of the orchestra hall. Yet he too believed that only separation, not assimilation or coexistence, could solve the Jewish question.

In January 1938, after a visit to the United States, he reported that the boycott of German goods organized there as a protest against the Third Reich's racial policy "has its main center in New York [and] grows weaker with the distance from New York." In most of America the attitude toward the Jews was not really very different from Germany's. "We must always bear in mind that there is hardly a club in the United States which accepts Jews, that in many hotels Jews are not admitted, and that indeed in all the universities the percentage of Jewish students is tacitly restricted." The Americans were simply more discreet about their prejudice. "They thus harbor a certain reserve, characteristic of the Anglo-Saxons, with regard to the Jews, but they do not like to talk about it." Goerdeler had perceived the prevalence of racial and ethnic bigotry beneath the egalitarian surface of American society.

It should not therefore prove difficult, he argued, to put an end to economic retaliation against the Third Reich. All the German government had to do was make clear that, although it remained committed to the "principle" of anti-Semitism, "the individual Jew is, within the framework of the law, not to be deprived by extraordinary means of every opportunity for a livelihood." Better still, if the Nazi regime were to try to find a "positive solution" to the Jewish question in consultation with other states, the tension created by its racial policy would quickly disappear, "even in the United States." After all, most countries shared Germany's eagerness to settle the problem of the Jews once and for all.

What that "positive solution" should be became clear to Goerdeler about a year and a half later, following a visit to Palestine. It was simple, like most of his solutions: the mass emigration of the Jews to their ancient homeland. That would free them from discrimination and oppression, while ridding the non-Jews of an alien and unassimilable minority. What could be more logical? "The region is capable of absorbing a substantial Jewish immigration," he wrote in his report in July 1939. "For the solution of the Jewish question throughout the world that would be clearly an advantage." From the point of view of "our fatherland," in particular, it would be desirable that "as many Jews as possible settle in Palestine." His search for an answer to the Jewish problem had made of Goerdeler a Zionist of sorts.[18]

Most other members of the resistance held similar views. Many of them, though shocked and outraged at the anti-Semitic riots of 1938, remained convinced that the segregation of the Jews was necessary for the protection of Germany's national character and culture. While a few expressed alarm at the regime's increasing politicization of the civil service, their disapproval rarely went beyond grumbling and muttering. Almost none of them seemed troubled by Hitler's assumption of direct command over the armed forces. In short, the progressive Nazification of public life during the years immediately preceding the outbreak of the war does not appear to have been the basic cause of the formation of an organized movement to overthrow the Third Reich. That cause has to be sought elsewhere.

14

The Diplomacy of Brinkmanship

On February 12, 1938, only a few days after Hitler's purge of the military leadership and the diplomatic corps, the *New Statesman and Nation* prophesied that the process of internal reorganization in Germany would prove to be the prelude to a policy of external aggression. The Third Reich would soon seek to shift the balance of power on the Continent in favor of the Rome-Berlin Axis. What happened represented the triumph of the "extremer tendencies" in the Nazi regime, which had now prevailed over "the caution of the soldiers," just as a few months earlier they had prevailed over "the economic orthodoxy" of Hjalmar Schacht. The removal from the foreign office of the "cautious, elderly" Neurath and his replacement by the "clumsy amateur" Ribbentrop signaled a major change in German diplomacy. Europe faced a period of growing tension and instability.

The general outline of the coming diplomatic struggle in Europe seemed quite clear:

> Taken together, these dismissals and nominations point to a resolute and unflinching pursuit of Nazi policy. . . . There will be no hesitations or ambiguities in its alliance with Rome. It will flinch from no course that weakens or threatens the Soviet Union. It may plunge a little deeper into the Spanish adventure. It will certainly continue to consolidate its power in Eastern Europe by grouping Belgrade, Athens and Bucharest round itself. How soon it will be ready for some more reckless move in Vienna or against Prague we do not pretend to know. What is clear is that some forces making for restraint have been removed.[1]

It was a penetrating analysis. Without knowing what Hitler had said ·to his generals at the meeting of November 5, 1937, without even knowing that such a meeting had taken place, the editors at the *New Statesman and*

Nation guessed that a new phase in the foreign policy of the Third Reich was about to begin. More than that, they recognized what the main goals of that new phase would be. According to the Hossbach memorandum, Hitler had told the military leaders that in the event of war the first objective of the nation's armed forces must be "to crush Czechoslovakia and at the same time Austria." He conceded that his foreign policy might be risky, but there was no other way of achieving "the solution to the German question." After all, "the struggles of Frederick the Great to gain Silesia and the wars of Bismarck against Austria and France had [also] involved unprecedented risks, and [only] the swiftness of the Prussian action in 1870 had kept Austria from entering the war." Should the Third Reich act less boldly and decisively?

Besides, the Führer believed that in all probability England and even France had already become tacitly reconciled to the dismemberment of Czechoslovakia. "The difficulties facing the empire and the prospect of becoming once again involved in a long-lasting European war would ensure the nonparticipation of England in a war against Germany." And England's stance would be bound to affect French policy. A declaration of war by France without the support of Great Britain seemed to Hitler "not very likely." Even if war did come, "an advance of France through Belgium and Holland without the help of England is likewise improbable." That was reassuring, because "during the execution of our attack against Czechoslovakia and Austria," a standstill in the west would be essential. Though confident of success, he admitted that the use of force in international relations "can never be without risk."[2]

All in all, Hitler's strategy cannot be dismissed as simply reckless. It rested on the shrewd perception that the democratic states sought desperately to avoid a new military conflict, that they would go to almost any length to preserve the peace. Their self-confidence shaken by the economic consequences of the depression, fearful of social instability and political unrest, they were prepared to make major diplomatic concessions to prevent the outbreak of war. Moreover, the parliamentary parties in France and England most hostile to National Socialism were also traditionally the ones most critical of the Versailles peace settlement and most opposed to any new military confrontation. Hitler recognized what the soldiers and diplomats in Germany generally failed to recognize, that the superior armaments of the nations defending the status quo in Europe masked profound psychological insecurities and doubts. He was confident that these could be exploited to the advantage of the Third Reich. Sooner or later a test of armed strength would be unavoidable. But first, important gains could be made peacefully, by a combination of threats, pressures, promises, and deceptions.

This strategy achieved a diplomatic revolution that by the end of the decade had completely altered the balance of power. Its first phase was the removal of the financial and military penalties imposed on Germany at Versailles. It began in the summer of 1932, even before Hitler became chancellor, with the cancellation by the Lausanne Conference of the remaining reparations payments. Then came the withdrawal of the Third Reich from the League of Nations in October 1933, followed in March 1935 by the unilateral rejection of the disarmament clauses of the peace treaty. The final step was taken soon afterward with the remilitarization of the Rhineland in March 1936. Within three years Hitler gained by his diplomacy of brinkmanship what the Weimar Republic had for fifteen years vainly tried to accomplish through compliance, cajolery, and humbleness.

The price of his success, however, was the isolation of Germany. Before the establishment of the Third Reich, Berlin had been slowly and painfully regaining a measure of influence in international affairs, still far behind Paris, London, or Rome, but making steady headway. That changed with Hitler's victory. Most European countries perceived the Nazi regime as a threat to peace and stability. After completing the repudiation of Versailles, therefore, the Führer turned to the establishment of a new balance of power in which the dominant coalition of victor states would be challenged by an opposing coalition of revisionist states.

In October 1936 the two major right-wing dictatorships, Italy and Germany, entered into an informal alliance, an alliance foreshadowed by their joint intervention in the Spanish civil war, which had begun that summer. A month later followed the signing of the Anti-Comintern Pact between Germany and Japan, ostensibly directed against the machinations of international Communism, but in fact initiating close diplomatic collaboration between several governments opposed to the postwar status quo. In November 1937 Mussolini joined the Anti-Comintern Pact, and in December he underscored his support for a policy of revisionism by withdrawing from the League of Nations. The Continent returned to the dualism that had characterized international relations before the world war, with two hostile coalitions confronting each other, both hoping to avoid an armed conflict, but each determined to defend its vital interests. On February 24, 1937, at the celebration in Munich of the eighteenth anniversary of the founding of the National Socialist Party, Hitler dwelt on "the wonderful experience of the first years of struggle," boasting that "today we have once again become a world power."[3]

But that was not enough for him. Hitler really wanted not equality but primacy, not parity but dominance. Germany was to be more than a world power; Germany was to be the world power. And that resolve led to the final phase in Hitler's diplomacy, the phase of territorial expansion achieved by the threat of force. Assuming that an armed conflict was in the long run unavoidable, he wanted it to come before 1943–1945 because, according to the Hossbach memorandum, "after that date only a change for the worse, from our point of view, can be expected." In the meantime, however, he planned to tip the scale in favor of the Rome-Berlin Axis by a constant test of nerves exploiting the insecurity of the democratic states. It was a daring strategy that rested ultimately on his willingness to accept the risk of war.[4]

The incorporation of Austria in March 1938 marked the first and easiest demonstration of the new diplomacy of intimidation. Its success was due not only to the Führer's boldness but also to the fact that the Austrian Republic, as one of the revisionist states, had remained outside the French alliance system. In addition, the establishment in the spring of 1933 of an authoritarian, semi-Fascist regime in Vienna had cost that country whatever sympathy it still enjoyed in Western Europe. Three years later Mussolini, who had long played the role of protector of Austria, conceded tacitly that the Anschluss was the price he would have to pay for the Rome-Berlin Axis.

Most important, what happened reflected sharp divisions among the Austrians themselves. Many of them, for a variety of ideological, political, and economic reasons, welcomed union with the Third Reich. Indeed, on April 10, four weeks after the Anschluss, a plebiscite showed that 99.73 percent of the voters in Austria, compared to 99.08 percent in Germany as a whole, favored the union of the two countries. Even allowing for inadvertent or deliberate irregularities in the counting of ballots, even allowing for the fact that no organized opposition was possible and that no real choice existed, the conclusion that a substantial majority of Austrians supported the Anschluss once it had taken place appears irrefutable.

The next crisis, from April to September 1938, was more complicated. It centered on the Sudeten region of Czechoslovakia. To be sure, the Germans living there were no less eager than the Austrians to become part of the Third Reich. A political, economic, and cultural elite in the days of the Habsburg monarchy, they found themselves after the world war in the position of a disliked and distrusted ethnic minority regarded with suspicion by the authorities in Prague as an inherently disaffected element of the nation's population. Thus the claim of many Sudeten Germans that they were the victims of discrimination by the Czechs, though no doubt exaggerated, had some foundation. In any case, they never became reconciled to the new Czechoslovak state. Especially after Hitler came to power, more and more of them began to feel that union with Germany was not only desirable but attainable.

Yet Czechoslovakia's alliance with both France and the Soviet Union made the situation dangerous. Any attempt of the Third Reich to settle the Sudeten question by the use of force was bound to create the risk of a major European conflict. Throughout that summer, however, Hitler provided a virtuoso display of his diplomacy of brinkmanship. At times he sounded threatening, at other times conciliatory; first he made preparations for war, then he submitted proposals for peace; he appeared almost simultaneously belligerent, moderate, violent, and restrained. France and Great Britain finally yielded at the Munich Conference late in September, persuaded or at least hopeful that this supreme act of appeasement would introduce a period of diplomatic stability on the Continent. The Third Reich incorporated the Sudeten region amid wild rejoicing on both sides of what had been the German-Czech frontier.

The crisis that followed in March 1939 ended with the last great victory of Hitler's statecraft by intimidation. The dismemberment of Czechoslovakia, through the annexation of Bohemia as a "protectorate" of the Third Reich and the establishment of an "independent" puppet Slovakia, revealed at last the futility of the policy of appeasement pursued by the democratic states. Until then Hitler had been able to justify his acquisitions by invoking the principle of national self-determination, the same principle on which the victors in the world war had claimed to act in fashioning the peace. But now it became clear that for him national self-determination was a right only of the Germans in Austria and the Sudeten region, not of the Czechs in Bohemia or the Poles in the Polish Corridor. Not even Neville Chamberlain or Edouard Daladier could any longer have illusions about his ultimate goal. A new war in Europe, which had been a distinct possibility before the spring of 1939, became a near certainty thereafter.

And what about the members of the resistance? How did they view the diplomatic revolution effected by the Third Reich? Like the great majority of their countrymen, they rejoiced in the rapid territorial expansion of Germany, though at times expressing apprehension that the means employed might lead to a military conflict for which the nation was not yet ready.

Of all Hitler's diplomatic achievements, the Anschluss aroused the most enthusiasm and the least concern among them. Here was the consummation of a union that had been approved in 1919 by democratically elected constituent assemblies in both countries, only to be frustrated at the peace conference by the vindictiveness of the Allies. Its realization at last by an authoritarian rather than a liberal government in no way diminished its legitimacy or significance. The unification of Germany and Austria represented for the resisters a triumph of the national will without regard for party or ideology.

Those most supportive of the Nazi regime were predictably also the ones most excited about the Anschluss. While Hitler engineered the incorporation of Austria, Schulenburg rhapsodized about the great and glorious mission of National Socialism. "The party exercises political leadership by virtue of the historic legitimation it acquired in the struggle against the Treaty of Versailles and against the alien [Weimar] leadership," he declaimed. "It is unquestionably and unequivocally the bearer of the political will of the nation, in accordance with the will of the Führer. Within it the political energies of the people are always to be formed anew, infusing people and state with new life." This revitalization was of the greatest importance, because "the coming decades will not give our people rest or tranquility. No, we will go through storms and conflicts." His words were even more prophetic than he imagined.[5]

The attitude of Canaris appears at first glance more ambiguous. Karl Heinz Abshagen, who had met him a few times, reported in 1950 that shortly after the Anschluss he expressed bitter disappointment to a member of the Austrian general staff. "It's all the fault of you Austrians. Why didn't you shoot?" But this report seems to be one of the many apocryphal stories circulating in Germany in the postwar years regarding anti-Nazi sentiments expressed by the resisters long before they became the resisters. Erwin Lahousen, who knew Canaris better than Abshagen, declared in 1954 that the Anschluss was in fact "one of the few actions in foreign policy for which Canaris (and unfortunately even leading British statesmen at that time) did not criticize Hitler." Canaris himself spoke enthusiastically on April 22, 1938, about the momentous events of the last few weeks. "All of us are still dazzled by the experience of the great German consolidation, which exalts all German hearts. It was longed for, worked for, and fought for, and [now] it has found its realization . . . under the slogan: one nation, one Reich, one Führer." He displayed nothing but approbation and admiration for what had taken place.[6]

Even those less favorable toward the Third Reich seemed impressed by the achievement of the Anschluss. Bishop Wurm had often disagreed with the Third Reich, sometimes loudly and bitterly. But the union of Germany and Austria met with his complete approval. "The Third Reich and its leader," he wrote on April 10, "have achieved a success that cannot be valued highly enough with regard to its political, economic, and moral aspect." Perhaps the time had finally come for a reconciliation between church and state. "In a moment such as this, the wish of the Protestant clergy and of loyal churchly circles for the end of all discord in the relations between the political movement and churchly work is naturally especially strong. Any sign that a relaxation of tension might take place will be greeted with joy." Why could not temporal and spiritual authority begin working together for the welfare of the nation? "The church has its clear, very important, and very urgent tasks, while the state and the [Nazi] movement have other but equally important and equally crucial tasks. If each concentrates strictly on its own task, then nothing untoward will happen." The bishop hoped that Hitler would now demonstrate in domestic affairs those same statesmanlike qualities he had just displayed in foreign affairs.[7]

Even Hassell, though still embittered by his humiliating dismissal from the diplomatic service, had to admit that achievement of the Anschluss was a major accomplishment. In the article "Bismarck as Master of Diplomacy," published in the spring of 1939, he defended the Iron Chancellor against the charge of bringing about the expulsion of Austria from Germany in order to promote the narrow political interests of the Prussian state. That was unfair, Hassell argued. Bismarck did what he had to do; there was no other way to achieve national unification. "The idea of a complete disintegration of Austria-Hungary and the incorporation of the German areas into the emerging German Empire could not even be conceived at that time, quite apart from its unfeasibility for international reasons." But now, seventy years later, the situation was entirely differently. "The destruction of the Danubian monarchy as a result of the world war opened the way for the mighty events by which the Führer put an end to a 'tragic development,' as he correctly describes it." The reunion of Germany and Austria had become a historic necessity, which Hitler's diplomacy helped realize.[8]

Occasionally some members of the resistance did express reservations about the Anschluss, but only about its practical execution or its incidental result, not about its inherent justification. That is, criticism could be heard here and there regarding the Third Reich's reliance on political pressure and military intimidation, or regarding the policies introduced by National Socialism in Austria, especially the brutality displayed toward political opponents and racial aliens. The country's absorption into the Third Reich, however, seemed to them essentially logical and defensible.

Eugen Ott recalled after the war, for example, that General Beck, who had previously been favorable to the Hitler government, gave the impression in 1938 of a "deeply concerned opponent of the movement." He spoke with "bitterest condemnation" about the treatment of Austria after the German troops marched in. "Behind the unsullied shield of the Wehrmacht," he told Ott, "came the vultures of the party." He was shocked by the rapacity and cruelty of the triumphant Nazi regime.

Still, he never wavered in the conviction that the union of Germany and Austria was historically and ethnically justified. After all, the two countries had a common language, a common culture, and a common ethnic or racial character. While some of the measures introduced by the Hitler government in Austria following the Anschluss might have been reprehensible, that did not vitiate the Anschluss as such. Besides, the Third Reich, with a growing population and limited resources, urgently needed more territory. Expansion had become a national necessity. "It is true," Beck wrote late in May 1938, more than two months after the Anschluss, "that Germany requires greater *Lebensraum,* and indeed in Europe as well as in the colonial area." Even after he finally turned against National Socialism, and even after the outbreak of war a year later, he continued to believe that the incorporation of Austria was warranted as well as irreversible. The transgressions of the Nazi regime in no way diminished the legitimacy of the Anschluss.[9]

Goerdeler held similar views. He too considered the Germans and the Austrians kindred peoples bound together by ties of history, culture, and national spirit. They had been one nation for more than a thousand years, and their brief separation in the nineteenth century was destined to end in the twentieth. He differed from the Hitler government primarily in the conviction that the Anschluss could best be achieved as part of a general political settlement between Germany and the Western democracies. Following a visit to the United States, he wrote at the beginning of 1938 that it was still possible to reach some agreement "that secures vital German interests and amounts to the annulment of the essential parts of the dictate of Versailles." American public opinion, he felt confident, "is no doubt prepared to permit Austria to enter into a free union [with the Third Reich]." All that was needed was moderation, restraint, judiciousness, and a willingness to compromise.

His attitude toward the Anschluss thus resembled Beck's. But whereas Beck deplored the misdeeds of the "vultures of the party" following the Anschluss, Goerdeler condemned the strategy employed to achieve it: the blustering and bullying, the strutting and posturing, and above all, the wasting of an opportunity to reach an accommodation with the democratic states. After his arrest in 1944, the security police reported, "Goerdeler himself declared that the union of Austria with the Reich was a necessary and welcome development that could not be stopped. The method used in its execution, however, had brought the first major deterioration in the diplomatic position of Germany." His objections to the Anschluss were similar to his objections to most other policies of the Third Reich: the ends were often good, while the means were usually bad.[10]

The crisis in the summer of 1938 over the Sudeten region turned the growing disgruntlement of the resisters into outright sedition. Yet they had no doubts about the justness of its incorporation into the Third Reich. The same linguistic, cultural, and historic ties sanctioning the incorporation of Austria appeared to sanction the absorption of the western rim of Bohemia. They regarded Czechoslovakia, moreover, as an artificial state created by the victors after the world war to keep Germany isolated, a hodgepodge of diverse and incompatible ethnic groups in which the dominant Czechs lorded it over subordinate minorities of Slovaks, Hungarians, Ruthenians, and, most important, Germans. Without historic foundation or cultural tradition, the country could not and indeed should not survive.

Beck expressed a view widely held in the Third Reich when he wrote at the end of May 1938: "It is true that Czechoslovakia in its [present] form imposed by the dictate of Versailles is unacceptable to Germany, and that a way must be found to eliminate it as a source of danger to Germany, even, if need be, by a military solution." The only question in his mind was whether "the stakes are also worth the prize." The use of armed force to acquire the Sudeten region, though for the moment perhaps inexpedient, seemed to him in principle justified.[11]

Goerdeler, however, doubted the need for any warlike measures against Czechoslovakia, because he continued to believe, as he did before the Anschluss, that a reconciliation with France and Great Britain could lead to a satisfactory settlement of the Third Reich's chief territorial demands. Why risk a major war for something that could be gained through peaceful diplomacy? On April 30, following a month-long trip in Western Europe, he reported that "it is possible to secure all of the vital national rights of Germany, even the acquisition of the territory of the Sudeten German region, by means of negotiation." He had used every opportunity while abroad to explain that "[mere] autonomy [for the Germans] in Czechoslovakia cannot bring peace to Europe." It would only create new insoluble problems. "I found that the English had complete understanding for this clear, cold logic, which is at the same time sensitive to the fatherland's needs. They will certainly not let peace founder on this point, if we strive for the maintenance of peace in the world as a whole through a general agreement."

Even six years later, as he faced the hangman's noose, Goerdeler remained convinced that the entire crisis of the summer of 1938 could have been avoided with a little more finesse and adroitness. "The incorporation of the Sudeten province into the Reich is also desirable," he told his interrogators, "and it must be the goal of our future foreign policy to have the Sudeten province remain permanently in the Reich. But here too the brusque manner of execution undermined confidence in Germany and thereby created the initial source of future tensions." If only the Nazi regime had listened to him, everything could have turned out so much better.[12]

What led to the emergence of a resistance movement in Germany during the Sudeten crisis was thus not disagreement over the avowed goals of Hitler's foreign policy. It was the fear that an attempt to use armed force against the Czechs to obtain territorial concessions would lead to the intervention of France and the outbreak of a major European military conflict. Had Germany's rearmament reached the point at which it could risk such a test of strength? Many of the soldiers and bureaucrats in the Third Reich feared the coming of a new war, a new defeat, a new revolution, and a new Versailles. That was what made them resisters.

During the summer of 1938 small groups of dissidents in the armed forces and the civil service began to meet informally, to grumble, criticize, and warn, and to make plans—some legal, some half-legal, and some illegal—to prevent a war for which the nation was not ready. Most of the participants were military men: Wilhelm Canaris, for instance, and Erwin von Witzelben, Erich von Brockdorff-Ahlefeld, Erich Hoepner, Helmut Groscurth, and Hans Oster. But there were also a number of civilians among them, people like Wolf Heinrich von Helldorf, Ewald von Kleist-Schmenzin, Hans Bernd Gisevius, and even Fritz-Dietlof von der Schulenburg. For the first time since Hitler's rise to power, some of those who had been his supporters and allies began to think seriously about opposing him not only with arguments and pleas but with force. A concrete, organized resistance against the Third Reich was finally coming into existence.

Its most prominent figure during the days of the Sudeten crisis was Ludwig Beck. As chief of staff, he would have had to assume major responsibility for military operations that Germany was, in his opinion, incapable of executing. He felt it his duty, therefore, to warn the leadership of the armed forces against involvement in war, because the odds would be so clearly on the other side. In a memorandum submitted on July 16 to General Walther von Brauchitsch, commander in chief of the army, he explained his position. An outbreak of hostilities now would end in disaster. "We face the fact that military action by Germany against Czechoslovakia will lead automatically to a European or a world war," he maintained. "That such a war, as far as human judgment can tell, will end not only in a military but a general catastrophe for Germany surely requires no further elaboration on my part." The continued existence of Germany as a political power in Europe, indeed, its very survival as a nation, depended on the preservation of peace, at least for the time being.[13]

This conviction led Beck far beyond any legally permissible remonstrance against the policy pursued by Hitler in the Sudeten crisis. He began to advocate—not in writing, to be sure, but certainly in speech—a strategy of passive resistance by the leaders of the armed forces against the government's preparations for war. He in effect proposed mutiny. His notes for a discussion with Brauchitsch that same day, July 16, leave room for no other interpretation:

> All upright and serious-minded German men in responsible positions in the state must feel summoned and obliged to use all conceivable ways and means, including the ultimate recourse, in order to avert a war against Czechoslovakia, a war that must lead in its consequences to a world war signifying the *finis Germaniae*. The most important leaders of the armed forces are above all others summoned and qualified for this task, because the armed forces are the means of exercising the power of the state leadership in waging war. Ultimate decisions regarding the survival of the nation are at stake here. History will pronounce those leaders guilty of bloodshed, if they do not act in accordance with their professional and political knowledge and conscience. Their soldierly obedience reaches its limit at the point where their knowledge, their conscience, and their responsibility forbid the execution of an order. If in such a situation their counsels and warnings find no hearing, then they have the right and the duty to their nation and to history to resign from their positions. If all of them act in this way in united resolve, then the execution of a warlike action will be impossible. They will have thereby protected their fatherland against the worst eventuality, against destruction. It would represent a lack of fortitude and of any understanding of his task, if a soldier in the highest position during times such as these were to see his obligations and tasks only in the narrow framework of his military instructions without an awareness of his highest responsibility to the entire nation. Extraordinary times demand extraordinary actions.

No German general had ever said anything so revolutionary in purpose or subversive in implication.[14]

A few days later, on July 19, Beck advocated the prevention of war by even more drastic means. In his notes for another conference with Brauchitsch he went beyond passive resistance to the possibility of a palace revolution. Resistance against the outbreak of a military conflict, he suggested, should be accompanied by "a confrontation with the SS and with the system of rule by the [party] bosses," a confrontation "necessary for the restoration of orderly legal conditions." For perhaps the last time there was now an opportunity "to free the German people and the Führer himself from the incubus of a Cheka and from the consequences of boss rule." The excesses of the Nazi radicals were undermining "the welfare of the Reich" and permitting "the revival of Communism." But opposition to the party extremists did not mean opposition to the Third Reich—far from it. "There can and should be no doubt," Beck cautioned, "that this struggle is being waged for the Führer." Indeed, "upstanding and sound men in the party" should be persuaded of the "seriousness of the situation" and of the "necessity for such a step." Above all, there ought not to be "even the slightest suggestion of anything resembling a conspiracy." Rather, the united support of the military leaders "must stand behind this step." The coup should under no circumstances appear to be a coup.

Beck's notes concluded with a series of phrases or slogans clearly rejecting the policies of the Nazi regime. "For the Führer! Against war! Against the system of rule by the bosses! Peace with the church! Free expression of opinion! An end to Cheka methods! Once again justice in the Reich! Reduction of all taxes by half! No construction of palaces! Construction of housing for the people! Prussian simplicity and honesty!" Out of the palace revolution organized by the generals would emerge a more compassionate and humane Hitler and a more liberal and tolerant Third Reich.[15]

Did Beck really believe that his proposal would serve the interests of the Führer, or did he merely pretend in order to make it more acceptable to the other military leaders? No conclusive answer is possible because it was never put into effect. Brauchitsch did not report the plan for a coup to the political authorities, as he should have done, strictly speaking, but neither did he endorse it. Most of the other generals were equally noncommittal; they would not denounce and they would not approve. That indeed remained their attitude for the next six years. And it left Beck with only one thing to do. On August 18, 1938, he resigned from his position as chief of staff of the German army.

Efforts to prevent war by a coup against the Nazi government did not cease, however. Small groups of resisters, civilian as well as military, continued for another six weeks to meet, collude, plan, and plot. What would have come of their schemes remains unknown, because on September 29 the Munich Conference, to the great relief of most of them, ended the Sudeten crisis with a major diplomatic victory for Hitler. Some began to wonder at this point whether they had not underrated the Führer, whether he was not actually much more skilled and talented than had been acknowledged. But others, now that the danger had passed, started displaying unexpected bravado. If only those weaklings leading the democratic states had not capitulated so easily, they insisted, the resisters would have succeeded in overthrowing the Nazi regime. Chamberlain and Daladier were really at fault for not having acted with greater courage, confidence, and determination.

Thus two weeks after Munich, Goerdeler expressed his bitter disappointment to an American acquaintance. "An excellent opportunity has been lost," he wrote. The German people had not wanted a military confrontation, and the army would have done anything to avoid one. "If only England and France had accepted the risk of war, Hitler would never have used force. And then he would have been the one disgraced, and not, as is now the case, the sound elements of my nation. It would have been the end of Hitler." Why could not the democracies have helped save Germany from itself?[16]

Hjalmar Schacht, who had been actively involved in the resistance during the Sudeten crisis, was equally critical of the British and French. If they had stood firm, he wrote in his memoirs ten years later, everything would have turned out differently. There would have been no war, no devastation of the Continent, no sacrifice of millions of innocent lives, and no partition of the fatherland. "It is apparent from the subsequent course of history that this first attempt at a coup d'état by Witzleben and me was the only one that would have brought about a turn in the fate of Germany. . . . The war had not yet begun, and a peaceful discussion with our European neighbors offered the best prospect [for success]." In the fall of 1938 it would still have been possible to deal with Hitler through legal channels. Thereafter assassination became the only recourse. "I too strove from 1940 on for an assassination, but I had at least the inner satisfaction of having prepared at the right time for a coup d'état rather than an assassination and of bringing it to the verge of success." Yet history had turned against him. "I was unable to take into account the intervention of the foreigners," those bumbling British and French politicians.[17]

Whether the members of the resistance had in fact been in a position to challenge Hitler successfully during the Sudeten crisis seems highly questionable, however. They had no clear plan, no effective organization, little military backing, and even less political influence. Worst of all, they had no popular support. Most Germans, though alarmed at the prospect of war, were not yet ready to turn against the regime. Thus England and France could not count on any significant secret help or sympathy within the opposing camp. Only a succession of military reverses might have aroused serious opposition against National Socialism among the masses of the Third Reich. To most foreign statesmen this conclusion seemed inescapable.

Sir Neville Henderson, for example, the British ambassador in Berlin, remained skeptical when he learned that an unnamed informant, probably a German army officer hostile to the Nazi government, had expressed the view that "if by firm action abroad Herr Hitler can be forced at the eleventh hour to renounce his present intentions, he will be unable to survive the blow." Even "if it comes to war, immediate intervention by France and England will . . . bring about the downfall of the regime," the informant claimed. Still, the ambassador was unimpressed. "We already know Herr X.'s attitude," he reported to London on August 21, 1938, "and his pronouncements are clearly biased and largely propaganda." The assurances and exhortations of the resistance were, in his opinion, not to be taken at face value.[18]

Foreigners were not the only ones to express doubt about the chances for success of the plan to overthrow Hitler. General Georg Thomas, one of the participants, voiced the same doubt shortly after the collapse of the Third Reich. In retrospect, he did not blame the English and the French for failing to take advantage of a historic opportunity. The fault, he conceded, rested on the resisters themselves. "The execution of the venture miscarried, unfortunately, because, according to the view of the military commander chosen for the venture [Erwin von Witzleben], the young officers did not prove to be reliable for a political action of this sort." Dissension and indecision at home, not timidity abroad, doomed the plan.[19]

These differences of opinion regarding the feasibility of a coup during the Sudeten crisis remain unresolved, because they rest to a large extent on guesswork, conjecture, predisposition, and wishful thinking. What is clear, however, is that Hitler's diplomatic triumph at Munich had the effect of demoralizing and weakening the resistance. Many of its supporters, especially the skittish sympathizers and apprehensive fellow travelers, began to have second thoughts about the Nazi regime. Could they have been mistaken in their judgment? Did the government in fact possess greater wisdom and understanding than they had believed? Might the Führer have been right in insisting that the key to success was determination and steadfastness? They found it hard to oppose victory.

Even those who remained unreconciled to the Third Reich succumbed to a feeling of discouragement and hopelessness. In the months following the settlement of the Sudeten dispute, they continued to sulk and brood. The regime appeared invincible even to them, at least for the time being. When Robert Holtzmann, one of Beck's old acquaintances, visited him in November 1938, he found the former chief of staff still embittered. He no longer drew a distinction between the moderate, reasonable Hitler and the party radicals. Instead, while conceding that the Führer was "talented above the average, in art, for example," he also described Hitler as a "psychopath" who had established an "elite of inferiors." He had the "manners and behavior of a member of a soldiers' council." As for Beck himself, he was "greatly relieved" that it did not come to a military conflict. "I have since May pursued only one idea, How do I avoid a war? . . . I have warned." But in the end he found himself "alone," deserted by those on whose support he had counted. He could only reflect now in sorrow on what might have been.[20]

Even Goerdeler, usually so resilient and optimistic, so full of easy solutions to difficult problems, sounded close to despair. Was any way left now to oppose the "growing dangers to our Christian world" posed by the Nazi regime? One possibility, he wrote in October, would be "that I continue my work in the same way, that I remain in Germany and maintain contact as hitherto with political friends in other countries." Or "I shall come to America and from there proclaim to all the truth that we must be ready to defend with weapons our ideals of justice, Christianity, and humaneness." Given Goerdeler's natural buoyancy and his ardent patriotism, there was little doubt what he would eventually decide to do. But the discouragement felt by the opponents of the Third Reich after Munich must have been considerable for him even to contemplate emigration.[21]

This sense of discouragement helps account for the passive attitude of the resistance during the Czech crisis of March 1939, which ended with the annexation of Bohemia and Moravia by the Third Reich. France and England, surprised by the violation of Hitler's solemn assurances given only six months earlier, made no attempt to intervene, and the Third Reich won the last of its bloodless diplomatic victories. National Socialism appeared to have found the secret of perpetual success in international relations. How then could the members of the resistance be expected to undertake a coup against their government without either foreign encouragement or domestic support? They remained silent because they really had no choice.

Some still had doubts regarding Hitler's destruction of Czechoslovakia. The official report on the failed attempt to overthrow the Nazi regime in the summer of 1944 says that "the men belonging to the circle of conspirators considered our entry into the Protectorate [of Bohemia and Moravia] a . . . mistake and the source of the irreconcilable attitude of the Western powers during the war." But to many of them it was a mistake for reasons of expediency rather than principle. Goerdeler, for instance, judged the occupation of Prague "unnecessary and harmful." It was unnecessary because "the remnant of the Czech state would in any case have been viable only in close dependence on Germany, and its absorption, militarily, economically, and culturally, into the German sphere would in the course of time have occurred on its own." And it was harmful because "our entry into the Protectorate had represented a clear violation of the Munich Agreement. From that point on it was obvious that none of the Western powers would any longer enter into negotiations with Hitler." Here again, the fatal flaw was not in the ends but the means.[22]

The passivity of the opponents of the Nazi regime during the crisis of March 1939 is understandable. The resistance had emerged a year earlier in response to the risk of war, and once the risk diminished, the resistance diminished as well. The political and racial oppressiveness of the Third Reich had not relented, to be sure. If anything, it had intensified. But the harsh domestic program of the Hitler government was never the prime motivation of most of the resisters. Admittedly, they did not as a rule approve of that program. They often deplored and condemned it in private conversation, in strict confidence. Yet it took the danger of war to transform individual disapproval into collective opposition during the Sudeten crisis. Once that danger receded, they relapsed into criticizing and complaining. It would take an even more serious threat to the future of Germany to revive an organized, coherent movement against the doctrines and policies of National Socialism.

15

The March toward Armageddon

Diplomatic developments during the months following the destruction of Czechoslovakia succeeded one another with a relentless logic. There was something predictable and almost inevitable about them. Once the troops of the Third Reich marched into Prague, it became obvious what Hitler's next objective would be. No territorial provision of the peace settlement of 1919, not the loss of Alsace-Lorraine nor the prohibition of union with Austria nor the inclusion of the Sudeten region in the new Czech state, aroused as much resentment and bitterness in Germany as the creation of the Polish Corridor. Not only did it separate East Prussia geographically from the rest of the nation, but more than a million Germans were abandoned to the hateful rule of Poland. And to make matters worse, the Allies had insisted that Danzig, with an indisputably German population, become a quasi-independent "free city." To the Nazi regime the most intolerable part of an intolerable treaty was the boundary separating Germany from Poland.

Accordingly, no one was surprised when Hitler, as soon as he completed the dismemberment of the Czechoslovak Republic, began to prepare for the dismemberment of the Polish Republic. All the usual signs of an impending diplomatic campaign by the Third Reich for territorial expansion started appearing. The German press suddenly overflowed with stories about the shameful treatment of a defenseless minority by those heartless politicians in Warsaw. They featured piteous "eyewitness accounts," some of them not entirely without foundation, of the brutal behavior of the Poles. These in turn led to protests and demonstrations in Germany against the persecution of innocent kinsmen on the other side of the frontier. The Führer himself denounced the injustices that fellow Germans had to endure and vowed to do whatever was necessary to end them. It sounded quite familiar; everyone knew where it was leading.

Even Chamberlain and Daladier finally recognized the failure of their policy of appeasement. Hitler was simply unappeasable. More important, public opinion in the democratic states, which had been prepared to pay almost any price to avoid war, concluded with considerable reluctance that armed force was the only alternative to an endless succession of demands from Berlin and Rome followed by concessions in London and Paris. As a result, the Allies adopted a new strategy of diplomatic resistance against the Axis. On March 31 England and France gave Poland a guarantee of support in the event of an attack by the Third Reich. On April 13 they committed themselves to defend the independence of Romania and Greece. The network of anti-Axis agreements was completed on May 12 with an Anglo-Turkish treaty of mutual assistance, and on June 23 with a Franco-Turkish nonaggression pact. To emphasize their determination to resist further German expansion, Chamberlain introduced peacetime conscription for the first time in British history, while Daladier used the power to govern by decree, which parliament had recently given him, to accelerate French rearmament and order partial mobilization. This time there would be no Munich.

But Hitler was not easily intimidated. He knew better than they how to play the game of nerves, the game of diplomatic warnings and military threats. On April 28 he denounced the German-Polish nonaggression treaty of 1934 and the Anglo-German naval agreement of 1935. A month later, on May 22, he transformed the vague and amorphous Rome-Berlin Axis into a "Pact of Steel," a hard-and-fast military alliance. He too wanted to make it clear that his mind was made up. He would not retreat or compromise, no matter what.

Hitler in fact was not bluffing; he was ready to risk war to achieve his objective. This resolve appears in his assessment of the international situation before the military leaders of the Third Reich on May 23, the day after the conclusion of the treaty with Italy. Here he declared that the hour of reckoning with the Poles was approaching. "Poland will always be on the side of our opponents," he insisted, according to the notes of his adjutant, Lieutenant Colonel Rudolf Schmundt. "Despite treaties of friendship, the intention has always existed in Poland to use every opportunity against us." Hence the German government had no choice but "to attack Poland at the first suitable opportunity. . . . We cannot count on a repetition of Czechoslovakia. It will come to a fight."

Though still hopeful that the Western democracies would not intervene, Hitler seemed prepared for the worst. If they did intervene, then "the struggle should be waged above all against England and France." The British in particular were the sworn enemies of Germany, so that a "life-and-death" battle against them was in all probability unavoidable. Accordingly, "the Dutch and Belgian air bases must be occupied by military means. No consideration can be given to declarations of neutrality." The Führer had no illusions about the seriousness of the crisis facing him. "The view that we can get out of this cheaply is dangerous. That possibility does not exist. We should then burn our bridges behind us. It is no longer a question of right or wrong, but of the existence or nonexistence of 80 million people."[1]

The one consideration that still deterred him was the attitude of the Soviet Union. What would Stalin do? On the face of it, the two dictators were irreconcilable enemies, ideologically at least. Each saw in the other the leader of an evil regime based on treachery and deceit. Yet they also shared important interests and objectives. Both condemned the peace settlement of 1919, both opposed the policy of the victor nations in the interwar period, and both were hostile to the new Polish state. The Western democracies hesitated to enlist Moscow's support against the Third Reich, because that would mean allowing Soviet troops to be stationed in Poland. And once they got in, would they ever get out? No such concerns troubled Hitler. At the meeting with his military commanders on May 23, he observed in passing: "It is not out of the question that Russia will prove to be indifferent to the destruction of Poland." Even earlier, at the end of March or beginning of April, according to Hans Oster of the counterintelligence service, he had told Brauchitsch in a rare show of playfulness: "Do you know what my next step will be? You better sit down before I tell you. A state visit to Moscow."[2]

Hitler himself never got to Moscow, but late that summer his foreign minister, Joachim von Ribbentrop, did. On August 23 he was in the Kremlin to conclude a nonaggression pact obliging the Third Reich and the Soviet Union to remain neutral if either was attacked by another state or coalition of states. In a secret "additional protocol" signed at the same time, moreover, they agreed on their respective spheres of influence "in the event of a territorial and political rearrangement" in Eastern Europe. The Führer could now plan for the destruction of Poland without fear of a two-front war.

The signing of the German-Soviet treaty removed the last obstacle to the outbreak of hostilities. Hitler believed that the western democracies alone would not do much to assist the Poles. They might not even try. On August 22, the day before Ribbentrop concluded the pact in Moscow, Hitler assured his generals that "England does not really want to support Poland," indeed, "England thus cannot in fact help Poland." Hence the coming conflict was bound to be short. "If Herr v. Brauchitsch had told me that I would need four years to conquer Poland, then I would have answered: 'then it won't work.' [But] it is nonsense to say that England wants to wage a long war. . . . No one believes that the war will be of long duration." The Führer sounded quite confident.[3]

His mood changed a few days later, however. He had assumed that in all probability public opinion in Western Europe would oppose involvement in a major war, that Chamberlain and Daladier would be forced to resign, and that new cabinets in England and France would then bow to his demands as gracefully as they could. But none of that happened. Actually, a formal Anglo-Polish alliance was concluded in London as a clear sign that the English had no intention of yielding. This new alliance shook Hitler's confidence. He began to wonder whether he might not have been mistaken, whether the other side was not more determined than he had assumed, whether the coming war might not turn out to be long and exhausting after all. On the evening of August 25 he countermanded the order issued a few hours earlier to begin the attack against Poland the following day.

The military resisters, observing these signs of indecision on the part of the Führer, were overjoyed. The government would have to retreat, the myth of the regime's infallibility would be destroyed, and popular confidence in National Socialism would soon erode. It was the beginning of the end of the Third Reich. Hans Bernd Gisevius remembered Oster saying something like "the Führer is finished," while Canaris beamed: "He will never recover from this blow. Peace has been preserved for twenty years." But their celebration proved premature. Hitler gradually regained his nerve, resolving to go ahead with his plans for territorial expansion, whatever the cost. He issued a new order for the attack against Poland, and on September 1 the troops of the Third Reich crossed the eastern frontier. The twenty years' armistice in Europe had ended.[4]

The approach of war produced the same effect on the members of the resistance in the summer of 1939 as it had in the summer of 1938. They started once again to plan, collude, plot, and conspire to find some way of avoiding a military conflict that, they were convinced, must end in defeat for their nation. Their primary motive for seeking the overthrow of the Nazi regime was the patriotic resolve to save their country from the disastrous consequences of Hitler's foreign policy. Yet in a few cases the ideological basis of their rejection of the Third Reich broadened, transcending the limits of national or ethnic self-interest. Some of them began to speak not only about protecting the welfare and security of Germany but about defending vital moral principles and universal spiritual values. Their condemnation of National Socialism gradually shifted from criticism of its recklessness or willfulness to denunciation of its essential immorality.

Thus Goerdeler—the ardent patriot, the harsh critic of Weimar and the "dictate" of Versailles—changed the focus of his condemnation of the Nazi regime from its ineptness to its wickedness. He had in the past dwelt chiefly on the government's inflexibility, its unwillingness to negotiate or compromise, its risky financial strategy, and its refusal to seek some accommodation with the democratic states that would safeguard Germany's vital interests. But after the Munich Agreement his emphasis altered, at least temporarily: "As a German, I should actually be very pleased [with the acquisition of the Sudeten region]," he wrote to an acquaintance abroad. "I know, however, that these dictators are nothing but criminals." The Third Reich's economic policy would inevitably lead to "Bolshevism." Yet that was not the worst of it. Goerdeler's voice gradually assumed a new tone of moral indignation. "Hitlerism is poison for the German soul. Hitler is determined to destroy Christianity. He cannot bear the thought that Christ is guiding our ethical existence. Hitler would like to be the sole master of all of human existence."

The future looked bleak, because behind the impressive diplomatic achievements of the Third Reich lurked moral decline and spiritual decay. "The entire development [of recent months]," Goerdeler predicted, "which may appear to the outsider to be of great advantage to the German people, will end in the elimination of Christianity." Since the leaders of the Third Reich were "destroyers" willing to use any method to achieve their objective, the "period of suffering" of the German people under "brutal tyranny and medieval methods" would continue indefinitely. "It is not justice, reason, and decency that will shape the future of the world but brutal power."

No other conclusion seemed possible. "Hitler and his bandits" were working day by day for "the destruction of every incentive to private enterprise, the destruction of private capital and of all moral values." Their ultimate purpose, however, appeared to Goerdeler to be "the complete destruction of Christian culture and of the spiritual life of the individual, in other words, an extremely dangerous Bolshevism. Such is the reality." Still, his pessimism did not last long. Soon he was again busily drafting plans, outlines, programs, and proposals for preserving peace in Europe by some reasonable compromise between the Third Reich and the democratic states. But thereafter the conviction that National Socialism rested on oppression, ruthlessness, and immorality never left him.[5]

Hassell's attitude toward the Third Reich changed as well. His condemnation of its policies no longer expressed simply the injured pride of an aristocratic diplomat humiliated by the zealots and doctrinaires in power in Germany. Nor did it merely reflect the fears of a grand seigneur threatened by Nazi populism and egalitarianism. Like Goerdeler, he began to formulate a more systematic critique of the doctrines of National Socialism. In the summer of 1939 Hassell submitted for anonymous publication in one of the Swiss newspapers an article entitled "The Struggle for the State of the Future," which presented a critical analysis of the principles espoused by the Third Reich. The reluctance of the press in Switzerland to antagonize a powerful neighbor and the momentous international developments culminating in the outbreak of war prevented its appearance at that time. Only twenty-five years later was it finally published. It provides, however, an interesting insight into Hassell's views regarding the Nazi regime, which led him to participate in the resistance.

The purpose of the article, he emphasized, was not to examine the many economic mistakes of the Third Reich but to express his own "very serious doubts concerning the ability of National Socialism to develop the state and the political man of the future." Those doubts reflected in part the old-school conservatism that Hassell had long embraced, apparent in his complaint about "the lack of [the concept of] an organic structure of the state" in the Nazi ideology. But more important were his reservations regarding the totalitarian nature of the Hitler dictatorship, specifically, "the demoralizing overemphasis on the totality [of the state], which destroys the spirit," and "the lack of any sort of control in political life." The destructive forces inherent in the Third Reich, forces he had ignored or overlooked during his years of diplomatic service, finally became clear to him. He was never to lose sight of them again.

The intoxication of power, he now maintained, had led National Socialism to the distortion and corruption of whatever sound ideas it borrowed from the older, more traditional conservative movement. "Out of the healthy concept of the nation there emerges more and more a primitive idolatry of one's own blood." Those leading the state as well as those being led had neglected "the manifold manifestations of life and culture." Indeed, the regime sought to undermine the achievements of "millennia of development and human spiritual labor," thereby separating German life from "all non-German connections and associations." An aesthete genuinely devoted to the common cultural heritage of Europe, Hassell felt repelled by the ethnic exclusivity that National Socialism preached.

The sophisticated, cosmopolitan aristocrat was alarmed, moreover, at the spread of poisonous anti-Semitism in Germany. In truth, he himself had not always been above an occasional flirtation with racial bigotry. But the growing obsession of the Nazi ideologues with the "Jewish peril," especially the excesses of the pogrom of the previous November, became for him signs of a dehumanization of public life. He felt that he had to speak out. "Certain groups in the party displayed an absolutely bestial barbarity [during the *Kristallnacht*]," he wrote, still appalled. Their cruelties had been a symptom of even worse things to come. The nation was witnessing the "sadistic destruction of all means of existence for the Jews," motivated in part by prospects for self-enrichment. "The brutalization of the harmless individual member of this ethnic group" was bound not only to erode "the moral credit of the Third Reich" abroad but, worse still, to arouse "base passions" at home whose effect might prove "demoralizing in terrible ways." That was the destructive legacy of National Socialism. "What must be the inner nature of an ideology that requires such methods in order to prevail!"

The corrupting influence of the Nazi regime was apparent not only in its treatment of Jews. It could be seen in all aspects of national life, Hassell maintained. He complained about the spread of a "professionally incompetent, tyrannical caciquism." Untrained and unqualified members of the party, "often with a dubious past," were being given important administrative posts, while experienced civil servants, "outstanding but allegedly uncommitted to the [official] ideology," were being pushed aside. He also cited the ubiquitous Gestapo, "free from any control, shunning the light, and [employing] brutal and unscrupulous methods." The chief victims of the Third Reich were its own citizens.

A foreign diplomat had recently observed, according to Hassell, that the Boche had now triumphed over the German. "This police system and organized domestic espionage" had created an atmosphere in which no one dared utter even the mildest word of criticism against the state or the party without making sure that "doors and windows are closed [and] telephones covered." The regime fostered the "worst sort of hypocrisy," while destroying all vestiges of "civic courage." The individual citizen was therefore succumbing more and more to the temptation of winning favor in high places by "a servility that had hardly existed during the worst periods of Byzantinism" or by the denunciation of alleged opponents of the new order. National Socialism, in short, represented the same disease, the same danger to state and society, as Marxian "revolutionary socialism."

What was to be done? Hassell concluded that "the leading personalities in the party [are not even] remotely aware of what the problem is." They were incapable therefore of bringing about an "organic development of the state." They failed to see the importance of some "independent control" over the activities of the government. They appeared unaware of the need to prevent "spiritual and moral death" by opposing the excesses of totalitarianism. Yet there could be no doubt that "all existing ethical values" were being destroyed, leaving the way open for what the Third Reich had sworn to oppose, namely, "the lifeless mechanism of the Bolshevik sort."

Was there no hope then that "the foundations of a state of the future" would emerge out of National Socialism? That would depend on the quality of the men who had assumed control of Germany's destiny, Hassell maintained, on whether they were "great and farsighted enough" to recognize their own mistakes. Most important, it would depend on whether some of them had sufficient strength "to turn the rudder completely around at the last hour and, working hand in hand with the most valuable and politically gifted elements in the nation, proceed to a new beginning." Hassell was advocating, indirectly but unmistakably, the end of the Nazi regime.[6]

Yet such systematic critiques of the program and ideology of the Third Reich were rare. Occasionally some of the other resisters would voice an incidental, impulsive disapproval of one aspect or another of official policy. Late in 1938, for example, following a visit to the recently annexed Sudeten region, Peter Yorck von Wartenburg sounded deeply troubled by the government's aggressive expansionism. "This is driving us absolutely toward imperialistic thinking," his friend Otto Ehrensberger remembered him saying. "This must be opposed as soon as possible." Even oblique or equivocal criticism of this sort was infrequent. What motivated the members of the resistance primarily and almost exclusively in the summer of 1939 was what had motivated them in the summer of 1938: the fear that Hitler was dragging Germany into a war for which it was militarily unprepared. They did not as a rule question the justification for annexing the Polish Corridor any more than they had questioned the justification for annexing the Sudeten region. They questioned its feasibility.[7]

Still, while their motives remained the same, their circumstances had changed. Before the Munich Conference they had found significant support in the armed forces and the civil service because of a widespread belief that Hitler's diplomacy was amateurish. It would invite disaster. But that view changed with his dramatic successes in acquiring the Sudeten region and dismembering Czechoslovakia. Many of those who had initially considered him a reckless adventurer began to have second thoughts. They were much less willing now to contemplate the forcible overthrow of the Nazi regime. And that reluctance compelled the remaining resisters to change not only their tactics but their strategy as well.

They still hoped that they might persuade the Führer to postpone his plans for an attack against Poland by emphasizing the unpreparedness of the German armed forces. At the same time they continued to explore the possibility of a coup d'état by the generals, which would lead to the establishment of a more responsible government in Berlin. Finally, since the chances of overthrowing Hitler from the inside seemed remote, they began to seek help from the outside. In the months preceding the outbreak of hostilities they embarked on several unofficial, covert diplomatic missions designed to enlist support among the Western democracies. Sometimes they tried to persuade the British and French to offer the Third Reich some compromise that would preserve the peace if the Führer accepted or would turn the army against him if he did not. At other times they urged England and France to stand firm in the hope that Hitler would back down at the last minute, thereby undermining his credibility among the Germans. In either case, their basic objective was the prevention of a war which the nation was likely to lose.

A group of resisters including Popitz, Goerdeler, Beck, Hassell, Schacht, Oster, and Gisevius attempted the first of these tactics, open remonstrance or expostulation. Their chief spokesman, General Georg Thomas, head of the Economics and Supply Section of the supreme command of the armed forces, shared the view that everything must be done, as he put it, "to prevent the outbreak of war and spare the German people a new bloodbath." In the middle of August he submitted to Keitel a memorandum arguing that a campaign against Poland would lead to a world war, that such a war would be decided by the availability of economic resources, and that the Third Reich could not win because of the insufficiency of raw materials and foodstuffs. "Since a lost war would mean the destruction of Germany, the war must not take place."

But Keitel refused to listen. He assured Thomas that Hitler would never start a world war. The French, in the Führer's view, were a "demoralized, pacifist people," the British were "much too decadent" to help Poland, and America would never again send even a single soldier to Europe "to pull the chestnuts out of the fire for England and certainly not for Poland." He accused Thomas of being under the influence of "those pacifist men who did not want to recognize Hitler's greatness." He did not even report Thomas's views to the Führer.

Thomas did not become discouraged, however. Later that month, only a few days before hostilities began, he submitted to Keitel detailed statistical tables and charts designed to show Germany's economic inferiority to the other great powers. This time Keitel presented Thomas's conclusions to Hitler, who promptly dismissed them as baseless and fainthearted. There would be no world war, Keitel reported Hitler as saying, especially now that the Soviet Union was on his side. "The agreement with Russia is the greatest political achievement by German government leaders in decades." Thomas wondered whether Hitler actually believed that England would stay out of the war or whether Keitel had deliberately misrepresented the Führer's views. In any case, his remonstrances, like those of Beck a year earlier, failed to shake Hitler's resolve.[8]

Efforts at subversion accompanied therefore the efforts at persuasion. Once again, as during the Sudeten crisis, the resisters planned, schemed, plotted, and conspired to prevent war by overthrowing the Nazi regime through a military coup d'état. But the chances of success were even slimmer than those of the year before. Hitler's victories in the war of nerves with the democratic states had dispelled many of the earlier doubts regarding his skill as a diplomat. Even his opponents now hesitated to risk a palace revolution. The trouble was that those who had the will lacked the opportunity, whereas those who had the opportunity lacked the will. Kurt von Hammerstein-Equord, for instance, who had been commander in chief of the army until his retirement in 1934, remained an uncompromising opponent of the Nazi regime. On the eve of the war Heinrich Brüning, the exiled former chancellor, recommended him to the resistance as a man "without nerves" who, if it came to a coup, "would light up a Brazil cigar, seat himself in his easy chair, and give the order to fire." When this characterization was communicated to Hammerstein, he smiled grimly. "Just give me some troops," he told the anti-Nazi journalist Rudolf Pechel, "and I won't fail."[9]

But that was precisely the point. He had no troops, and those who did refused to use them for a military uprising. When Schacht tried in August to see General Brauchitsch and General Franz Halder, the new chief of staff, to remind them that under the constitution no declaration of war was valid without the approval of the Reichstag, they informed him that such a visit would be unwelcome. And when he persisted in his efforts, he was warned that he would be arrested if he tried to enter the headquarters of the armed forces. The leading officers, whatever their private reservations, had no intention of becoming involved in any plot to overthrow the Nazi regime.[10]

Beck's views admittedly elicited greater respect. He was after all still a soldier, a soldier who had held one of the highest positions in the army. He could not be simply dismissed as a meddling outsider, even though his opposition to Hitler had in fact intensified since his retirement as chief of staff. He had become more convinced than ever that the Führer's diplomacy would lead Germany into a military conflict that must end in disaster. In an essay written in the fall of 1938, for obvious reasons not intended for publication, he had warned of the consequences of the aggressive foreign policy being pursued by the Third Reich. "A war that Germany starts will immediately draw toward the battlefield states other than the one being attacked. In a war against a world coalition Germany will be defeated and will in the end be left at the mercy of such a coalition." Now, some nine months later, Beck's gloomy prophecy seemed on the point of realization. The nation faced catastrophe. He felt therefore that he must do everything possible to prevent the outbreak of hostilities, and that included appealing to his old comrades-in-arms.

First he wrote to Brauchitsch. Though dubious about the character and moral courage of the commander in chief, he hoped that the gravity of the situation might overcome the general's habitual indecisiveness. But Brauchitsch would not even reply. He was not loyal enough to the Nazi regime to betray Beck, but not hostile enough to support him. He did what he had done the year before during the Sudeten crisis: he remained silent. Soldierly duty became for him the rationalization for inaction in the face of the growing threat to his country.

Beck had somewhat better luck with Halder. The new chief of staff, still cordial and respectful toward his predecessor, accepted an invitation to meet with him to discuss the critical international situation. During their conversation Halder even agreed that the tyranny of the Gestapo had become intolerable, that a new world war would mean the end of Germany, and that there could be no peace in Europe until Hitler was overthrown. But then came reservations, hesitations, and counterarguments. The boundary between Poland and the Third Reich did seem unfair, Danzig was after all a German city, the British were unlikely to intervene militarily in Eastern Europe, and the Führer would no doubt succeed in preventing the outbreak of a global conflict. Why not let him win another few easy victories in foreign affairs? Then there would be time enough to overthrow him. The two men argued and debated without reaching any common conclusion. They parted still on friendly terms, shaking hands, but in profound disagreement. "What Halder lacked," in Gisevius's opinion, "was not intelligence nor awareness of his position nor patriotism. He lacked will."[11]

The refusal of the senior generals to take part in a palace revolution forced the resisters to rely on the methods of secret diplomacy to prevent the coming of war. Specifically, they tried to use their personal contacts in the Western democracies to encourage either a compromise solution to the problem of the Polish Corridor, or a stand against Hitler firm and un-equivocal enough to deter him from an attack against the Poles, or a combination of the two. During the spring and summer of 1939 a number of them, including Carl Goerdeler, Adam von Trott zu Solz, Helmuth James von Moltke, Fabian von Schlabrendorff, and Rudolf Pechel, visited England for the purpose of urging the British to be both tough and flexible in dealing with the Third Reich. They hoped, more out of desperation than sober judgment, that the right mixture of resolve and reasonableness might stop Hitler and preserve the peace.

The most ardent advocate of compromise among them was Goerdeler. Quickly recovering from the discouragement to which he had succumbed after Munich, he began to worry less about the moral threat and more about the military threat facing Germany. Soon he was again drafting plans and proposals for solving the international crisis. The avoidance of war remained in his opinion essential for the protection of the national interest. But the Third Reich acted with terrible recklessness, constantly challenging and provoking the democratic states, confident that they were too weak and divided to respond.

"Any assumption that England and France are neither able nor willing to engage in a struggle would prove to be a fatal mistake," Goerdeler warned in April 1939. Besides, there was really no need for a struggle. "Our critical vital rights can be secured by a peaceful understanding, and . . . all our future opportunities, all of them, depend on a prolonged period of calm, peaceful labor." Under conditions of international stability the "German talent for accomplishment" would prove most effective, whereas the difficulties confronting the other states would then "emerge most rapidly and clearly." By maintaining the peace, Germany could in all probability rise to "the leading position in the world," provided "we learn never to talk about it and to exercise restraint so that we never abuse that position." Why use violence to get something that could be attained through nonviolence?

That remained his position throughout the months between the Munich Agreement and the attack on Poland. In December he submitted to the

British foreign office the outline of an international agreement designed to preserve the peace while assuring free scope to the "German talent for accomplishment." The Polish Corridor was to be returned to the Third Reich, while the Poles would obtain access to the sea in some other form. A satisfactory settlement of German colonial claims would have to be reached as well. With regard to the Soviet Union, an effort should be made, though without the use of armed force, to reestablish there some "reasonable order," so that "Russia [could] gradually [be drawn] into a European collective structure." Finally, a free international monetary system was to be established with the help of a substantial loan to Germany. In return Germany would abandon all claims to hegemony in southeastern Europe, agree to the status quo in the Mediterranean, support the restoration of the position of England and France in East Asia, accept a general reduction in armaments, and join a new league of nations. Everyone would win, nobody would lose.

The same ideas appeared in a somewhat different form in another memorandum composed by Goerdeler in the spring of 1939. Here he wrote again about solving the problem of the "so-called Polish Corridor" by peaceful agreement, about the German need for overseas colonial possessions, which must be "as large and as capable of development as possible," and about the importance of an international loan of four to six billion marks to insure the stability of the German currency. In return he repeated the offer to renounce German ambitions for a dominant role in southeastern Europe, to accept the Mediterranean status quo, to help restore "the economic property rights of whites" in East Asia, and to participate in negotiations for a reduction in international armaments. Goerdeler even added the possibility of reestablishing Czechoslovakia as a permanently neutral state within the boundaries agreed to in Munich. He saw himself in those months as a peacemaker, a reasonable compromiser, skillfully steering a safe middle course amid the opposing destructive forces of national ambition.[12]

The British diplomats viewed him differently, however. To many of them he was just another German nationalist hoping to obtain through the rhetoric of conciliation what Hitler was trying to achieve through the threat of force. They found him unsubtle and heavy-handed. "I have known Dr Goerdeler personally and for some time," wrote Sir Robert Vansittart, diplomatic adviser of the Chamberlain government, to his colleagues in the foreign office. "I have also for some time suspected that he was merely a stalking-horse for German military expansion, and by military expansion I mean the expansionist ideas of the German army as contrasted with those of the Nazi Party. There is really very little difference between them. The same sort of ambitions are sponsored by a different body of men, and that is about all." Although Goerdeler might be able from time to time "to furnish interesting pieces of information on the internal situation in Germany," he was "not only worthless but suspect as an intermediary for 'settlement.'" In this respect he looked "very much like every other German expansionist."

Vansittart, a longtime opponent of the policy of appeasement, regarded "with consternation" Goerdeler's ideas concerning an Anglo-German rapprochement. To accept them would be "plain suicide," he maintained. It would be Munich all over again. "Not content with having dismembered Czechoslovakia, the Germans now wish to do the same to Poland and wish us to connive officially at their ambitions by double-crossing the Poles beforehand. Such an attitude is impossible for any honourable nation to adopt and the sooner it is dismissed the better." Even a new partition of Poland did not seem to be enough for people like Goerdeler. They also wanted "substantial colonial concessions" and a sizable loan from Great Britain. "These concessions on our part would all be irrevocable. What do we get from the German side? The answer is 'Nothing that is not obviously revocable at any moment.'" Vansittart remained profoundly suspicious of Germans bearing gifts.

He was not the only one. William Strang, head of the Central Department of the Foreign Office, had serious doubts as well about Goerdeler's proposals. He saw in them "a familiar likeness to other plans sponsored by the so-called 'moderates' in Germany, of which we have seen several of late." While the English government was being asked to make major concessions to the Third Reich, it would receive little in return beyond "the debased currency of mere undertakings." He felt strongly that "we ought to have nothing to do with this." The British diplomatic service included many others like him who, feeling betrayed by Hitler's dismemberment of Czechoslovakia after all his promises at Munich, were determined this time to resist German blandishments that merely provided a screen for German designs.[13]

The other would-be peacemakers in the resistance were generally more subtle than Goerdeler. But as often as not, they differed from him in nuance and emphasis rather than substance. They too hoped to prevent the outbreak of war by some compromise, some conciliatory gesture that would satisfy Hitler's ambition without destroying Chamberlain's credibility. Trott, for example, sent early in June on a fact-finding mission to England, reported to the German foreign office a private conversation he had with Lord Lothian, the well-known Liberal politician, during a week-end stay at Cliveden. The two men found themselves in close agreement, so close in fact that at times the views described in the dispatch appear to be Trott's as much as Lothian's. They shared above all the conviction that the outbreak of war could and should be prevented by an honorable compromise of the differences between their countries.

To start with, Lothian showed "an instinctively correct appreciation of the greatness of our Führer," Trott wrote, knowing that his report might be submitted to Hitler. "He sees in him not a hostile threat but an empire builder . . . like Cecil Rhodes." Not only that, "Lothian . . . has a feeling for the inner relationship of the German and the British claims to supremacy in the world, and he still half believes in their constructive reconcilability." Nevertheless, some conciliatory gesture on the part of the Third Reich was essential. The English statesman suggested therefore the same symbolic concession proposed by Goerdeler a few weeks earlier. If the German government agreed to the reestablishment of a Czech state, independent but disarmed and economically subordinate, that would have "a profoundly revolutionary effect on British public opinion." Hitler would thereby not only "disarm his bitterest opponents abroad" but also "restore confidence within Europe" and strengthen "the British desire for an understanding." Ultimately, "the gradual elimination of all material and moral differences still existing between Germany and England" would result.

The advantages for the Third Reich would be considerable. Lothian had conceded, according to Trott's report, that "the German *Lebensraum* would naturally have to extend economically far beyond the present boundaries." The problem of the Polish Corridor would also find its "obvious solution," once the Poles were no longer able to argue convincingly that increased economic dependence on Germany meant "national subjection." British distrust of German economic expansion to the southeast, moreover, would soon disappear. "If Germany led but did not dominate Central and Eastern Europe, the West European nations could also feel reassured about their own political position." In short, "nothing would stand any longer in the way of a brilliant rise of Germany in the world. . . . England-America . . . and Germany, as the only real great powers, could then jointly shape and guarantee the future political order of the world." It was a tempting, exciting prospect.

In the conclusion of the dispatch Trott openly expressed his support for the ideas advanced by Lothian. "The consistent rejection by the Führer of any halfhearted understanding with England" had produced in that country "a far more genuine revival of the desire for a total understanding as the only alternative to war." The present moment was especially propitious for an Anglo-German settlement because of the apprehension weighing on the British people and the burden of military preparedness. "To prevent [war, England] is today probably all the more ready to make concessions." Trott's argument was in essence the same as Goerdeler's. Why use military force to get something that could be obtained through peaceful negotiation?[14]

Not all of the resisters favored a policy of compromise. Some urged the British not to yield, hoping that a firm stand by the democratic states would force Hitler to back down, weakening his popular support, or that it would at least persuade the military that only a coup against the Nazi regime could avert war. Yet almost all of them, compromisers and non-compromisers alike, were motivated primarily by the fear that an armed conflict would end in disastrous defeat for Germany. They undeniably opposed National Socialism as well. But only the conviction that the Third Reich was unprepared for a test of military strength can explain the contrast between their total passivity prior to the dismemberment of Czechoslovakia and their feverish activity prior to the invasion of Poland.

Only that conviction, moreover, accounts for the feeling of despair to which many of them succumbed when it became apparent that their efforts to preserve the peace had failed. For Hitler could not be swayed; he could not be either appeased or intimidated. After hesitating for a few days, he gave the order to begin the attack against the Poles on September 1. Most of the resisters saw this order as an appalling tragedy. On the eve of the outbreak of hostilities Canaris appeared to be completely crushed. "This is the end of Germany," he said to Gisevius in a voice choked with tears. Nothing could now save the nation from catastrophe.[15]

Yet once the die was cast, the military resisters rallied behind the war effort. The same concerns that had led them to oppose the government's policy before the coming of the conflict led them to support it afterward. The defense of the fatherland became for them the sacred duty of all patriotic Germans regardless of politics or ideology. Their ultimate purpose after all seemed the same as that of the Third Reich: safeguarding the national interest. Since their disagreements with the regime had so far pertained more to means than to ends, the outbreak of war made those disagreements appear much less important. In fact, some of them looked forward to settling accounts with the Poles, those enemies and oppressors of the Germans. Groscurth, for instance, greeted with enthusiasm Hitler's address of April 28 denouncing the German-Polish nonaggression treaty.

"The Führer's great speech to the Reichstag now frees our work against Poland," he wrote in his diary. "That is good; it was high time." The reacquisition of the Polish Corridor had been the goal of German diplomacy for the last twenty years. And now it was finally about to be achieved.[16]

The churchly resisters supported the war effort just as strongly. When the nation was in danger, how could its spiritual leaders withhold their encouragement and blessing? On September 14 Bishop Galen, putting aside his differences with National Socialism, voiced unqualified approval of the German cause:

> The war, which was outwardly ended in 1919 by a coerced peace of violence, has broken out anew and has drawn our people and fatherland within its orbit. Once again our men and youths are in large part called to arms, standing guard at our frontiers in bloody struggle or in firm resolve to protect the fatherland and, at the risk of their lives, to win a peace of freedom and justice for our nation. And those who are left behind are summoned and determined, each in his place, selflessly dedicating his person, his strength, and all his means of assistance, to help our nation survive the test and soon enjoy again the fruits of peace.

The bishop bestowed his benediction on those defending the nation in its hour of greatest need.[17]

Niemöller went even further. He wrote to Admiral Raeder from the Sachsenhausen concentration camp asking to be released so that he might return to active duty with the navy. Raeder refused to reply, but several months later General Keitel informed Niemöller that his request could not be granted. As for his reasons for volunteering to serve the Third Reich, Niemöller offered several explanations after the war. Two of his sons were already in the armed forces and the third was about to become a soldier as well. How could he then remain indifferent to the war effort? His lawyers, moreover, had advised him to seek reinstatement in the officer corps. Besides, "we Christians in Germany were aware of the fact that we had a people and a mother country that we loved."

But then Niemöller came to the heart of the matter in a long letter he wrote in 1945 to George Bell, bishop of Chichester. When the war began, he saw only two possibilities. "1) Should Hitler win the war, Germany would be lost as Hitler was the murderer of her soul long before he became a mass-slaughterer of huge proportions. 2) Should Hitler lose the war, Germany would be lost because the other powers would tread us down completely and would not treat us as they did in 1918." He found both of those possibilities frightening. "In this dilemma there seemed to me, as for thousands of other Germans who loved their country, no other hope, considering the war had actually broken out, but that through a new government we might come to a negotiated peace." Hence for the time being there was really no choice but to defend the fatherland. "I could see no other way for myself, either as a Christian or a German."[18]

The dilemma confronting Niemöller also confronted the other members of the resistance. Most of them contemplated and weighed and pondered that dilemma; they agonized over it and grappled with it, without being able to resolve it. They continued to cling to the belief that a distinction could still be maintained between state and regime, between Germany and the Third Reich. They went on hoping that the gains made by Hitler might be retained without retaining Hitler. They refused to recognize that the defeat of National Socialism could be achieved only through the defeat of the German nation. Caught between patriotic duty and moral imperative, between national loyalty and humanitarian instinct, they wrestled with their conscience all the way to the scaffold. Like the prince of Denmark, they were unable to decide whether to be or not to be.

Only a few resisters, Bonhoeffer among them, rejected the Nazi regime without prolonged inner struggle. For him the Hitler dictatorship had always been inherently and ineradicably evil; his opposition to it was based on deep-rooted spiritual conviction rather than compelling national interest. On a visit to the United States in the summer of 1939, he decided to return to Germany to face the war, to resist National Socialism, and to share in the terrible punishment that awaited his countrymen for succumbing to the temptations of power. He made his position clear in a letter reportedly written to the American theologian Reinhold Niebuhr:

> I have had the time to think and to pray about my situation and that of my nation and to have God's will for me clarified. I have come to the conclusion that I have made a mistake in coming to America. I must live through this difficult period of our national history with the Christian people of Germany. I will have no right to participate in the reconstruction of Christian life in Germany after the war, if I do not share the trials of this time with my people. My brothers in the Confessional Synod wanted me to go. They may have been right in urging me to do so; but I was wrong in going. Such a decision each man must make for himself. Christians in Germany will face the terrible alternative of either willing the defeat of their nation in order that Christian civilization may survive, or willing the victory of their nation and thereby destroying our civilization. I know which of these alternatives I must choose; but I cannot make that choice in security.[19]

The authenticity of this letter may be questioned, since the original has not been found. Perhaps it expresses therefore not what Bonhoeffer actually said but what he might have said or could have said or should have said. The important point is that he was one of only a handful among the leading members of the resistance to oppose the Third Reich purely out of universal humanitarian faith, without regard for national allegiance or patriotic duty. He did what he did for the sake of all of mankind. As for the others, they generally went on weighing and pondering, wavering and agonizing, while about them the world of which they were part was sinking into ruins.

A photographic portrait of Ludwig Beck taken when he was chief of staff of the
German army between 1935 and 1938. (Ullstein Bilderdienst)

Ulrich von Hassell in a picture taken in the fall of 1937, a few months
before his removal from the position of German ambassador to Italy.
(UPI/Corbis-Bettmann)

V

Between the Threat of Victory and the Danger of Defeat

All of us have incurred so much guilt—for we are indeed responsible as well—that I see in this approaching doom only a just atonement for all the shameful deeds that we Germans have committed or tolerated in recent years. At heart I find it satisfying to discover that there is a retributive justice in the world after all. . . . I am tired of this endless horror.

HELMUTH STIEFF (1942)

16

German Successes or Nazi Triumphs?

The outbreak of war changed temporarily the perception of the resistance among many of its sympathizers and allies. Until then it had seemed to be a patriotic movement inspired by the resolve to prevent a military conflict likely to end in the defeat of Germany. Thereafter its activities began to appear treasonable not only in the legal but also in the moral sense. Even some of those who continued to criticize the ideas and policies of National Socialism decided that ideological differences must be put aside until the war was over. Then there would be time enough to deal with Hitler. For now all loyal Germans, whatever their political convictions, should rally to the defense of the fatherland. The resistance, which had expanded during the Sudeten crisis, contracted after the regime's success at Munich, and expanded again during the dispute over the Polish Corridor, contracted once more after hostilities began. For the time being, the demands of the struggle for victory overcame doubts regarding the Third Reich.

To those few who remained consistently loyal to the resistance, however, the coming of war did not obviate the need to protect the national interest by opposing the Nazi regime. Before the military conflict began, they had felt that Germany's security and welfare required the preservation of peace. Afterward they continued to argue that the timely termination of hostilities was the only way of saving the fatherland from catastrophe. Thus their basic attitude toward Hitler's foreign policy did not change with the outbreak of hostilities. They remained convinced that a war against the Western democracies was likely to end in the defeat of Germany. Indeed, the longer the war, the more likely the defeat. Their immediate purpose became therefore the reestablishment of peace through negotiation and compromise.

The fall of 1939 seemed an opportune time for international reconciliation. Although the swift defeat of Poland had strengthened Hitler's hand,
he appeared outwardly reluctant to jeopardize his victory in the east by an
offensive in the west. The British and the French displayed even less
enthusiasm for a major campaign. There were raids, skirmishes, and forays
along the Rhine, but little bloodshed and few casualties. The war had
seemingly reached a stalemate. Then why not agree on terms that could
satisfy Germany's legitimate demands without offending the pride and
self-respect of the Allies? Danzig would obviously have to become once
again part of the Reich, Posen and West Prussia would be reincorporated
as well, and the million Germans under the Polish yoke would finally rejoin
their kinsmen to the west. But as for the rest, what harm could there be in
a rump Poland, isolated, defenseless, and subservient? Such views regarding
a negotiated peace preoccupied the resisters during the months between
the fall of Warsaw and the invasion of Norway and Denmark.

They did not seem unrealistic. On both sides of the conflict there were
hints and suggestions, some of them quite explicit, that a compromise
settlement would not be unwelcome. On the evening of September 4, only
a day after the British declaration of war, Chamberlain broadcast in German a message to the citizens of the Third Reich declaring that the military
struggle resulted only from Hitler's false assurances and pledges:

> He gave his word that he would respect the Locarno Treaty; he broke it. He
> gave his word that he neither wished nor intended to annex Austria; he broke
> it. He declared that he would not incorporate the Czechs in the Reich; he did
> so. He gave his word after Munich that he had no further territorial demands
> in Europe; he broke it. He gave his word that he wanted no Polish provinces;
> he broke it. He has sworn to you for years that he was the mortal enemy of
> Bolshevism; he is now its ally.

How could anyone trust a statesman so duplicitous?

The British prime minister wanted to make it clear that the struggle was
being waged not against a nation but a government, not against a state but
an ideology. "In this war we are not fighting against you, the German
people, for whom we have no bitter feeling," he announced at the end of
his address, "but against a tyrannous and forsworn régime which has
betrayed not only its own people but the whole of Western civilization and
all that you and we hold dear." Only an unscrupulous man and his despotic
exercise of authority stood in the way of a just peace.[1]

Hitler was also eager to play the reluctant warrior, the reasonable,
moderate statesman. But he chose to wait until his main objective, the

overthrow of Poland, had been achieved. Only then, knowing that he now held the trump cards, did he extend the olive branch to the Allies. In a long, rambling speech to the Reichstag on October 6, he talked of his efforts to improve relations with France. The return of the Saar region to Germany, accomplished in 1935, was the only demand he had considered a "nonnegotiable condition for a Franco-German understanding." He had no other claims; he did not even want to raise the question of Alsace-Lorraine. He hoped simply "to bury the old enmity for all time and help the two great nations . . . find a way to each other." He would go on trying to eradicate among the Germans "the idea of an immutable hereditary enmity," encouraging instead "respect for the great achievements of the French people and for their history." All the French had to do was acquiesce in the destruction of Poland.

The Führer sounded equally conciliatory toward the British. He had always sought more than "Anglo-German understanding"; he had wanted "Anglo-German friendship." At no time and in no place had he ever opposed British interests. "I have in fact considered it a goal in my life to bring both nations closer together not only in their perceptions but in their feelings." If he had failed in that regard, that was a result of "hostility on the part of a group of British statesmen and journalists" who wanted "to initiate once again a struggle against Germany at the first available opportunity." Their motives, disguised in "empty phrases and assertions," remained for Hitler "inexplicable." But they would not deter him from pursuing his quest for peace. "I still believe even today that there can be real stability in Europe and the world only when Germany and England reach an understanding." He would continue to extend his hand in friendship. All the British had to do was take it.[2]

Four days later, on October 10, the Führer reiterated his willingness to conclude peace at a great public rally in the Berlin Sportpalast. The nation was prepared, if need be, to fight to the bitter end, he insisted. "No power in the world will again be able to overcome this Germany. They will not defeat us militarily or destroy us economically, and they will certainly not crush us psychologically. Under no circumstances will they witness in the future any kind of German surrender." But why talk of defeating or destroying or crushing? There was no longer any need to continue the war; the fall of Poland had removed the last obstacle to ending hostilities. "I have expressed our readiness for peace. Germany has no reason whatever for waging war against our western opponents." The opportunity to reach a reasonable settlement of all outstanding differences had arrived. It was now up to the English and the French to seize it.[3]

Hitler could afford to play the peacemaker. He had gotten what he wanted by armed force, and his only task at the negotiating table would be to win international approval for retaining the spoils of victory. It was easy for him to sound conciliatory. The Western statesmen, by contrast, knew that to acquiesce in the dismemberment of Poland would destroy whatever credibility they still retained. It would leave them even more vulnerable to future demands, future threats, and future retreats and humiliations. They had to stand firm; they had no choice.

On October 12 Chamberlain, replying in the House of Commons to Hitler's suggestions for peace, rejected them as inadequate and disingenuous. "It is after this wanton act of aggression which has cost so many Polish and German lives, sacrificed to satisfy his own insistence on the use of force, that the German Chancellor now puts forward his proposals." Hitler had made no attempt to make amends for "this grievous crime against humanity." He was merely trying to gain "recognition of his conquests and of his right to do what he pleases with the conquered." Great Britain could not negotiate with him without "forfeiting her honour" and "abandoning her claim that international disputes should be settled by discussion and not by force." Then the prime minister came to the "fundamental difficulty" in dealing with the Führer. "The plain truth is that, after our past experience, it is no longer possible to rely upon the unsupported word of the present German Government." There would be no more Munichs. The risk of violated pledges and broken promises was too great.

After this declaration of unshakable purpose, however, the prime minister softened his tone. He returned to the theme on which he had touched five weeks earlier in his radio broadcast to the German people following the declaration of war. "It is no part of our policy to exclude from her rightful place in Europe a Germany which will live in amity and confidence with other nations," he announced reassuringly. "On the contrary, we believe that no effective remedy can be found for the world's ills that does not take account of the just claims and needs of all countries, and whenever the time may come to draw the lines of a new peace settlement, His Majesty's Government would feel that the future would hold little hope unless such a settlement could be reached through the method of negotiation and agreement." In modern warfare, Chamberlain warned, both victor and vanquished must suffer cruel, devastating losses. And yet to yield to wrongdoing would mean "the extinction of all hope"; it would mean "the annihilation of all those values of life which have through centuries been at once the mark and the inspiration of human progress." Great Britain had to defend those values at all costs.

There was no reason, however, why the war should go on to the bitter end. There was room, the prime minister emphasized, for negotiation and compromise, but only between trustworthy governments. There could be no reconciliation with political leaders for whom solemn pledges were only tricks and stratagems. He repeated that "we seek no material advantage for ourselves; we desire nothing from the German people which should offend their self-respect." What the English wanted was more important than victory. They wanted the establishment of "a better international system which will mean that war is not to be the inevitable lot of every succeeding generation."

Chamberlain expressed confidence that men of good will, whether British or German, still yearned for international harmony. "I am certain that all the peoples of Europe, including the people of Germany, long for peace, a peace which will enable them to live their lives without fear, and to devote their energies and their gifts to the development of their culture, the pursuit of their ideals and the improvement of their material prosperity." All that stood in their way was a ruthless statesman and an evil system. The prime minister was implicitly calling for an end to the Nazi regime.[4]

Public opinion on both sides found a glimmer of hope in these declarations of purpose by the opposing political leaders. Perhaps a way out could still be found, perhaps some compromise could still be reached, maybe an international conference would be convoked, maybe an agreement might be patched together. In Germany in particular there was an almost desperate eagerness to believe that, now that Poland had fallen, peace could be restored and the mass slaughter of the previous world conflict avoided. It was easier to yield to wishful thinking than to face the awful prospect of total war. Millions continued to hope for a settlement, because not to hope seemed unbearable.

But Hitler himself had few illusions. He recognized that the Allies would refuse to negotiate with Germany as long as he remained in power. And he certainly had no intention of resigning in order to spare his nation devastation and bloodshed. The conflict would have to go on until one side or the other achieved victory. On October 9, a day before his public declaration in the Sportpalast that "Germany has no reason whatever for waging war against our western opponents," he composed a long memorandum for his military commanders describing the reason for waging precisely such a war. His purpose in announcing twenty-four hours later his "readiness for peace" was simply to persuade the German public that the responsibility for prolonging the conflict was not his but that of those warmongers in London and Paris.

"It is the goal of the British-French conduct of the war," according to Hitler's secret memorandum, "to dissolve or destroy once again the German state of 80 million people in order to reestablish the European balance in their own interest, that is, a condition of equality of power. This struggle must therefore be waged by the German nation once and for all, in one way or another." He conceded that victory over the Poles had strengthened the Third Reich "psychologically and materially" to the point where the Allies might be willing to sign a peace recognizing its gains in the east. But that was unlikely. His memorandum therefore dealt with "the unavoidable continuation of the struggle." The war would have to go on to preserve the Nazi regime.[5]

The members of the resistance disagreed. They could no longer see any justification for continuing the armed conflict. At the beginning of September they had rallied behind the government out of loyalty to their nation. A month later they turned against it once again for the same reason. All the legitimate aims of the war had now been attained. Why then go on fighting? The Allies had indicated their willingness to negotiate a reasonable settlement with a new, responsible government in Berlin. They would no doubt insist on some symbolic concessions, some superficial compromises. Yet the essential demands of Germany would be met. There would no longer be a Polish Corridor, a "free state" of Danzig, a disputed Silesian boundary, or an oppressed German minority. The last remaining injustices of Versailles would be eliminated. If that took the removal of Hitler from power, it did not seem an excessive price to pay.

But how? That was the question preoccupying the resisters throughout the months between the fall of Poland and the fall of France. To some of the hotspurs among them the answer seemed simple: seize Hitler, deprive him of power either by judicial procedure or summary execution, and proclaim the end of the Third Reich. Hammerstein-Equord, though now in his sixties, was one of those who felt that only boldness and determination were required. Recalled to active duty at the outbreak of the war, he was given command of an army group headquartered in Cologne. No sooner had he assumed his new duties, than he invited Hitler to come and inspect his troops to underscore to the Allies Germany's resolve to defend the western frontier. But the Führer, after briefly contemplating such a visit, declined the invitation, and shortly thereafter Hammerstein was again placed on the inactive list. Hitler had been saved, according to Pechel, by "the special sense he had that warned him of personal danger." He "must have gotten the feeling" that something was wrong. In any case, whether through premonition or chance, he managed to escape the planned *coup de main*.[6]

Whatever the reason, more than luck and a superannuated general would have been needed to overthrow the Nazi regime. Even if things had turned out differently, even if Hammerstein had succeeded in seizing and executing Hitler, it is doubtful that the Third Reich would have fallen. The government was too strongly entrenched to be defeated by some local mutiny; it enjoyed too much support, it commanded too much loyalty. That was the basic difference between 1918 and 1939. The death of Hitler would have simply meant his replacement by one of his lieutenants. The political system would have continued under a new Führer. Only an uprising supported by a substantial part of the army leadership could bring about the end of National Socialism. Hence the efforts of the resistance during the autumn and winter months concentrated primarily on persuading prominent generals that with the fall of Warsaw victory had been achieved, and now the only obstacle to a peace safeguarding the interests of Germany was Hitler. His historic role as destroyer of the Versailles system had been played out. He had ceased to be an instrument of national revival and become an impediment. He should be removed.

Such was the reasoning that led Groscurth, once the Poles had been defeated, to embark on a mission of subversion along the Rhine. He sought to convince some of the army leaders that the time had come to turn against the Nazi regime. An entry in his diary for December 21 refers to a "brief report to [General Gerd von] Rundstedt" in Koblenz regarding "the situation in the east." Two days earlier he had presented a similar report to General Wilhelm von Leeb. He also talked in Godesberg to General Hans von Salmuth, "who is at first disinclined, but then is successfully influenced by me." And finally he met in Cologne with General Kurt Brennecke, again "successfully." Groscurth was pleased with the results of his trip. "We have thus incited the most important parts of the western front to rebellion. With success, I hope!—We will continue!"[7]

There were limits, however, to how much influence a recently promoted lieutenant colonel could exert over the senior generals of the Wehrmacht. They were more likely to listen to someone of higher rank, someone with greater status and authority. That was why late in November General Thomas approached the chief of staff, Franz Halder, pleading with him to act boldly to prevent the defeat of Germany before it was too late. "I described to him the views of my friends," Thomas recalled afterward, "and asked him to persuade [the army commander in chief] Brauchitsch to avert a world war and, if need be, arrest Hitler." Halder declined; he was no Hammerstein-Equord. But his refusal, like so much of what he told members of the resistance, was ambiguous enough to leave the impression that he was the weak link in the chain of military command. They felt that he could and should be worked on.[8]

Beck therefore decided to seek another meeting with his successor as chief of staff. His views regarding the likely outcome of a war between the Third Reich and the Western democracies had not changed since his resignation in the summer of 1938. If anything, he felt even more strongly that his nation faced defeat. In a memorandum dated November 20, 1939, he argued that the victory in Poland had not significantly altered the balance of power between the two camps. "Contrary to a view expressed earlier, the military and political prospects regarding the outcome of the Second World War have changed quickly and indeed exclusively to the disadvantage of Germany." A review of the international situation had persuaded him "not only that Germany stands alone and will probably continue to stand alone, but that it also invites the risk, if things go on in this way, of increasing the number of its adversaries and becoming entangled in an increasingly difficult position." All this seemed to point to a grim conclusion. "A situation has developed that, after a sober examination of all its political and military aspects, leads even more urgently than before to a demand for ending—the sooner, the better—a world war that has from the outset been hopeless."

But how could the war be ended, when Hitler had stubbornly resolved to continue fighting until victory had been won? For Beck the answer was clear. He returned to the idea he had first advanced more than a year before during the Sudeten crisis. The highest responsibility of the soldier is not to his government but to his nation. If the policy of the government threatens the security of the nation, his duty demands that he oppose the government. From a strictly legal point of view that might be construed as subversive or even treasonable. But a higher morality rejected blind obedience to orders endangering Germany's survival as a great power. The armed conflict provoked by Hitler's insatiable ambition was one of those occasions when resistance against established authority became a supreme military virtue.

"The course that the responsible military leaders should follow today is clearly indicated," Beck argued in his memorandum of November 20. "The limits of their responsibility, however, especially in the case of the highest military leaders, are determined in days of greatest crisis by their own conscience, by their shared responsibility to the army and the nation, and by the anticipated verdict of history." Their duty now was to oppose the Nazi regime, whatever the cost.

Beck elaborated on this theme a few weeks later in another memorandum, this one dated January 2, 1940. He and the other resisters, like "all of us," wanted a "strong, consolidated Germany." But there was no compelling reason for the nation to become involved in a "struggle for existence." Neither the German people as a whole nor any substantial part of the German people had wanted a European war. Nor had the British and French in any way threatened Germany's security or provoked the present conflict. Therefore, to drag Germany into a military contest leading to "a possible, indeed, a probable catastrophe" was simply "beyond words." It defied all the rational laws of politics and strategy. "In such a situation there arises for those who are responsible and informed the right and the duty to subordinate every other consideration to the supreme demand for the self-preservation of the nation," in other words, the overthrow of the Third Reich.[9]

The situation demanded, moreover, prompt action, he maintained. Once Hitler launched his planned offensive in the west, the Allies would be less willing to agree to a negotiated peace. Reflecting late in October on the assurances of the British that they had no war aims incompatible with German honor and self-respect, Beck felt encouraged. "Since things will now no doubt move quickly," he commented, "we face a great decision." It was important to maintain the strength of the army, because "as soon as we become weak, we will have to deal with those people from the east." But an understanding with England and France should also be sought as soon as possible. "After a new violation of neutrality [by Germany, the Allies] will no longer be willing to conclude a 'peace without vengeance' even with [the leaders of the resistance]." Thus a coup had to take place before the stalemate in the west was broken.[10]

The need to act promptly led to a new meeting between Beck and Halder on January 16. But this time, to make sure the secret police could not overhear them, they exchanged their views in the course of a stroll through the half-deserted streets of Berlin. They mostly repeated what they had said five months earlier. Once again Beck argued that Germany could not win the war, that America would soon enter the conflict on the side of the British, that victory over Poland could not affect the final outcome, and that Hitler had lost all credibility among the neutral states. Once again Halder voiced his doubts and reservations. He too opposed Hitler, according to his protestations, but he did after all hold a responsible position in the armed forces. How could he be expected to take the lead in a coup? What if a civil war broke out? What if the army collapsed? He went on repeating all his old concerns, scruples, worries, and fears. Both men advanced essentially the same arguments they had advanced the previous summer, and with essentially the same inconclusive results. They parted still disappointed, still embittered, and still in disagreement.[11]

The resisters did not allow themselves to become discouraged, however. They continued trying to convince senior members of the officer corps that Hitler was leading the nation to disaster. His assertiveness and aggressiveness, according to their argument, may have won important successes in the past, but now he had overplayed his hand. He had provoked an unwinnable armed conflict. Germany faced once again a war of attrition, an exhausting stalemate in which the odds heavily favored the enemy. Or worse still, the Allies, supported perhaps by the United States, would soon launch an all-out offensive culminating in the defeat and occupation of Germany. The only way to avoid national catastrophe was to overthrow the Nazi regime.

But the rejection of Hitler's diplomacy did not mean the rejection of the gains achieved by that diplomacy. The members of the resistance had no intention of going back to the territorial boundaries of 1933, 1935, or even 1938. After all, the revision of Versailles had been a goal of all patriotic Germans long before the Third Reich. National Socialism had helped attain that goal by putting an end to the ineffectual republic and pursuing a more forceful foreign policy. Its historic function had now been fulfilled, however. It would therefore have to go, but its diplomatic achievements should not be abandoned. The resisters wanted in fact to secure and legitimize those achievements by a statecraft of moderation leading to peaceful coexistence with the Western democracies.

That was essentially Beck's position. Even before the war he had believed that the German sphere of influence should be expanded through the annexation of Austria and the reacquisition of the Polish Corridor. As for the "Czech aircraft carrier," which posed a constant threat to Germany's military defenses, it would have to be neutralized one way or another. The outbreak of hostilities only confirmed and strengthened his convictions. Not only Austria but the Sudeten region as well would have to remain a permanent part of Germany. What was left of Czechoslovakia, moreover, must inevitably become a client state of its powerful western neighbor. The fate of a rump Poland would be similar. It too must remain under German tutelage as long as the Soviet Union continued to pose a danger to the rest of Europe. Thus the main difference between the avowed territorial revisions sought by Hitler and by Beck was that the latter hoped to bring them about through agreement among the great powers. Believing that Germany could not prevail against England, France, and in all probability the United States, he favored a settlement in Europe that, while peaceful, would be "just and honorable."[12]

The civilians in the resistance sounded as expansionist as the soldiers. They too believed that though the diplomatic means employed by Hitler

were often dishonest and unscrupulous, his diplomatic ends were historically justified. They objected to his methods, not his proclaimed goals. In
October Goerdeler described to Hassell the terms on which Germany
should agree to end hostilities, thereby avoiding the danger of military
defeat. To start with, it was important to display a "readiness to make peace
on a basis of moderation." This meant "German parts of Poland to us,
independent [Polish] remnant state, [and] new arrangement for Czechoslovakia." But Germany would first have to become "a state based on
justice." In addition, an international reduction in armaments should be
initiated, including even "controls over the [German] construction of
airplanes and submarines," and there must be a "reestablishment of the
world economy," long one of Goerdeler's pet ideas. Above all, the Third
Reich would have to be replaced by a new political system capable of
making peace on such a basis.

Hassell was a little dubious. He feared that the Allies might insist on a
voice in the reconstruction of Germany. He felt uneasy, moreover, about
the proposed restrictions on the level of German armaments. But Goerdeler dismissed his qualms, confident that "the people would greet such a
peace with enormous relief." He even wondered whether Hermann
Göring might not be persuaded to help remove Hitler from power and end
the war on terms such as he was proposing.[13]

Hassell's own ideas regarding a settlement with the Allies were basically
similar. At a secret meeting in Switzerland on February 22 and 23, 1940,
with an intermediary from England referred to in his diary as "Mr. X"—
actually J. Lonsdale Bryans, who was in contact with Lord Halifax, the
British foreign minister—Hassell submitted a statement outlining his proposals for peace. In his translation of this document into English he spoke
of the need "to stop this mad war as soon as possible," for "the danger of
a complete destruction and particularly a bolshevization of Europe" was
growing rapidly. For him the Continent was not simply "a chess-board of
political or military action" but a common fatherland in which "a healthy
Germany in sound conditions of life" was "an indispensable factor." In
accordance with this view, the purpose of any peace treaty should be "a
permanent pacification and reestablishment of Europe on a solid base."

He meant specifically that "the union of Austria and the Sudeten [re-
gion] with the Reich" would have to be accepted without discussion. The
same would apply to Germany's western frontier, that is, Alsace-Lorraine
would remain French. "On the other hand, the German-Polish frontier will
have to be more or less identical with the German frontier in 1914." The
price for peace, in other words, would be paid mostly by the Poles.

Hassell concluded his statement with an enumeration of "certain principles which will have to be universally accepted" as a basis for the peace treaty and the reconstruction of Europe. First, he named "the principle of nationality," but "with certain modifications deriving from history." That involved the "reestablishment of an independent Poland and of a Czech Republic," though their boundaries would obviously be drastically reduced from those of 1919. Then came "general reductions of armaments" and Goerdeler's familiar "reestablishment of free international economical cooperation." Finally, a series of vague but unexceptionable "leading ideas" to be embraced by all European states: "a. The principles of Christian ethics. b. Justice and law as fundamental elements of public life. c. Social welfare as leitmotiv. d. Effective control of the executive power of state by the people, [but] adapted to the special character of every nation. [And] e. Liberty of thought, conscience, and intellectual activity." Like most of the resisters, Hassell envisioned the establishment of a peaceful and stable international order in which Germany would play a major, indeed, a decisive role.[14]

Still, the attempt to justify Hitler's overthrow with essentially diplomatic or military arguments rather than moral or ideological ones was risky. It seemed at the time to make sense, no doubt. How else could the commanders of the armed forces be persuaded to turn against the Nazi regime? Were they likely to be swayed by appeals for a more humane exercise of power or a greater tolerance for dissent or a broader understanding of the plight of "non-Aryans"? Clearly, the best way to enlist their support was through warnings against the danger of a long stalemate on the western front, an eventual collapse of the army, a new left-wing revolution, and ultimately another Versailles. Yet by basing their rejection of the Third Reich largely on its ineptness rather than its immorality, the leading resisters were staking everything on Germany's military defeat. A victory would mean the frustration of all their hopes and calculations. In that event, their subordination of moral principle to political expediency would have disastrous consequences.

That was why the remarkable successes of the Wehrmacht in 1940—the invasion of Denmark and Norway in April, the occupation of the Low Countries in May, and the surrender of France in June—signified the temporary disintegration of the resistance. They seemed to prove that those who had doubted the Führer were merely whiners and defeatists. Indeed, the year roughly between the capitulation of Paris and the attack against the Soviet Union marked the zenith of the popularity of the Third Reich. Not only was the German public dazzled by Hitler's triumphs, but the generals, who had only recently been grumbling about his recklessness, were now ready to concede his extraordinary talent as well. Even many of the resisters were forced to concede, often reluctantly and grudgingly, that they might have underestimated the Führer. Perhaps he did in fact have greater intelligence, insight, judgment, and discernment than they had given him credit for.

There were a few, however, who refused to succumb to the intoxication of success. The mass jubilation at the military triumphs of the Third Reich did not blind them to its essential immorality. Helmuth James von Moltke was among them. Never one of the hard-core activists in the resistance, he remained essentially a man of ideas rather than deeds, a theorist more than a pragmatist. He was morally too fastidious and temperamentally too squeamish for anything as messy as plots and conspiracies, assassinations and executions. And yet on June 17, 1940, three days after the fall of Paris, while everyone around him was rejoicing at the extraordinary victory of German arms, Moltke spoke in a letter to a friend about the "triumph of evil." He had been prepared to endure "every sorrow and misfortune," but something much worse awaited him now. He would have to wade through a "swamp of outward success, ease, and well-being." Defeat on the battlefield would have been far preferable to this progressive corruption of the national soul.

Even so, Moltke could not bring himself to consider concrete measures for overthrowing a government he feared and loathed. He lapsed instead into the contemplation of what a future post-Nazi regime should be like. Civic justice, he expatiated, meant that "every individual can unfold and develop fully within the framework of the totality of the state." The power of that totality had its limits, however. The government had no right, for example, "to dominate men and restrain them by force or by fear of the application of force"; it had no right "to transform men into wild beasts or machines"; it had no right "to demand of man unconditional obedience or blind faith." Moltke arrived in the end at the unimpeachable but bland conclusion that "the ultimate vocation of the state is therefore to be the protector of the freedom of the individual." Speculations of this sort did not pose much of a threat to the Third Reich.[15]

While the more militant resisters continued to plan for an eventual coup against the Hitler dictatorship, for the time being, as long as the Wehrmacht was winning victory after victory, there was little they could do but grumble. Besides, they too were impressed, without always admitting it, by the magnitude of the German military successes. Basically, what they would have liked, though they did not say it in so many words, was to keep Hitler's territorial gains without keeping Hitler.

Their ambivalence can be heard in Popitz's lecture to the Mittwochs-Gesellschaft late in 1940, delivered in his best professorial style—a little ponderous, a little orotund, but clearly expressing satisfaction at his nation's new dominant position on the Continent. The expansion of its sphere of influence beyond the German frontiers, he contended, could be assured by "treaties of an economic nature steadily increasing in scope," but especially by "the might and authority of Germany." It would of course be inadvisable to advertise to those states that "need our protection or are economically dependent" the full extent of their "loss of political power." Nevertheless, the present struggle for a "new concept of the Reich" must reveal and clarify for the German nation "its mission in the Central European area." That mission could obviously be fulfilled only by a "powerful state, that is, a complete state which firmly controls all the essential elements of civic life," and by a "nationally homogeneous people, the entire German people, imbued with a sense of community." Above all, the government should avoid not only the "egalitarianism imposed by a sterile centralization of the administrative system," but also "all federalistic and particularistic institutions." Did this tortuous rhetoric express veiled criticism of the Third Reich or constructive advice? It is hard to tell.[16]

Goerdeler seemed equally ambivalent, torn between an acceptance of the regime's gains and accomplishments and a rejection of its policies and methods. In a long memorandum composed early in 1941, he emphasized the shifts and inconsistencies of German foreign policy. First the government concluded a nonaggression treaty with Poland, and then a few years later it proceeded to destroy Poland. In 1939 it guaranteed the neutrality of the Low Countries, only to violate that neutrality in 1940. In 1933 it summoned the German people to a struggle against Bolshevism, in 1940 it received Russian delegations with full state honors, and now it was preparing to invade the Soviet Union. While extolling the virtues of the "Nordic race," it was sacrificing "white interests in East Asia to yellow interests." Clearly, the Nazi political system rested on duplicity.

A few months later, however, in a peace plan of May 30, 1941, which was transmitted to the British government, Goerdeler revealed that he was anxious to retain a substantial part of the territorial expansion which that duplicity had helped make possible. A comparison of his new proposals with those he discussed with Hassell in October 1939 reveals the extent to which victory over France had raised his expectations. No longer did retaining Austria, the Sudeten region, and the Polish Corridor satisfy him. Now the Memel district would have to remain German as well. In addition, he sought the "reestablishment of the boundaries of Germany as of 1914 with Belgium, France, and Poland," as well as the "restoration of the German colonies or of colonial areas of equal value." In return Goerdeler was prepared to participate in the creation of an international system of collective security. He spoke about the need to establish state boundaries on the basis of "the right of national self-determination," the "development of a method for international arbitration," a "general limitation and reduction of armaments," and "international control over armaments and armaments industries." Still, there could be no doubt about which nation would play the leading role in the postwar new order he envisioned.[17]

The triumphs of the Wehrmacht whetted Hassell's appetite as well. At first he lamented the end of his hopes for an imminent overthrow of the Third Reich. An entry in his diary of June 24, 1940, immediately after the surrender of France, insisted that victory must not be allowed to obscure the fundamental immorality of National Socialism. "No one can deny the magnitude of the success achieved by Hitler," he acknowledged. "But that does not change in any way the intrinsic character of his actions and the horrible dangers to which all higher values are now exposed. A demonic Spartacus can have only a destructive effect, unless an opposing force intervenes in time." Hassell added mournfully, "One could despair at the tragic situation of being unable to rejoice in the [German] successes." His loyalty to those "higher values" threatened by the victorious Nazi regime seemed unshakable.

In the course of the next year and a half, however, Hassell became increasingly reconciled to the Wehrmacht's conquests. He remained an opponent of the Third Reich, to be sure, but many of its gains in foreign affairs began to appear to him legitimate and justifiable. As a result of the Anschluss, he now maintained, Germany had inherited "the legacy of Prince Eugene" in southeastern Europe; it had assumed "the task of bringing peace and prosperity to the peoples of the Danube and the Balkans." Not only that, "the organization of the Baltic region has at present become a German mission," because its southern shore was under the control of a nation that, "measured by its numbers and economic importance, far surpasses all other Baltic nations." It could be argued, in fact, that the Baltic Sea was "essentially a Germanic Mediterranean." Hence the victories of the Third Reich, though admittedly motivated by an unjust purpose, might help to establish ultimately a just and stable order in Europe.[18]

The progressive acceptance by the resisters of the territorial gains achieved through Hitler's foreign policy reached its high point in the summer of 1941 with the invasion of the Soviet Union. This acceptance resulted not only from the remarkable initial successes of the German army: the daily advances of twenty-five miles and more, the hundreds of thousands of enemy soldiers taken prisoner, the capitulation of mighty fortresses, and the occupation of vast and rich provinces. It reflected also the feeling that the Third Reich had regained its sense of purpose, its consciousness of mission and commitment. Even many of those who had previously maintained that the Nazi regime had become corrupted by victory and power declared their support for the great crusade against materialism, godlessness, and Bolshevism. Until then they had sometimes deplored the war being waged against France, Belgium, Norway, and the Netherlands, kindred nations that belonged to the same culture and civilization as Germany. But the struggle against international Communism was a different story. It represented a revival of that idealism which had characterized the early years of the National Socialist Party. It was selfless and virtuous; it was a just war to defend the fundamental values of the Western world.

Most of the senior officers of the Wehrmacht, including those in the resistance, shared the feeling that they were marching into battle to defend morality and idealism. They were participating in an apocalyptic conflict between the forces of good and evil. Early in May 1941, almost two months before the invasion of the Soviet Union, Erich Hoepner approved a directive to his troops describing the lofty mission they were being summoned to fulfill. "The war against Russia is an essential part of the struggle for existence of the German nation," he exhorted. "It is the old struggle of the Germanic peoples against Slavdom, the defense of European culture against the Muscovite Asiatic flood." As if that were not enough, he added: "Bolshevism is the mortal enemy of the National Socialist German nation. Germany's struggle is directed against this destructive ideology and its supporters." Hoepner's opposition to Hitler did not in any way weaken his commitment to the great crusade against Communism.[19]

Hellmuth Stieff sounded equally convinced of the righteousness of the war against the Soviet Union. Writing to his sister late in August from army headquarters, he acknowledged that the resistance of the Russian troops was more stubborn than any the Wehrmacht had so far encountered. But that only proved the timeliness of the German attack. "The course of the campaign shows that it was indeed high time to eliminate this danger threatening all of Europe. Whether that would have been possible later for a weakened Europe is highly doubtful. But there is nothing doubtful about the intention of the Soviets to impose the world revolution on the West through the use of force at a time that appeared to them opportune." European civilization had had a narrow escape. "It would have been unbelievably gruesome and frightful, if this [Communist plan] had been realized." Stieff saw himself as a Siegfried confronting the Bolshevik dragon.[20]

Many of the bureaucratic resisters shared this enthusiasm, and no one more than Schulenburg. For him the attack against the Soviet Union marked the return of National Socialism to its early ideals of faith, dedication, courage, and sacrifice. There had been nothing selfish about the German decision to go to war. It was motivated in part at least by a desire to free the Russian people from Communism, he wrote in his diary early in July. Two months later he elaborated on this theme in another entry. Germany was carrying out a "mission imposed by destiny," namely, the "obliteration of Bolshevism." More than that, it was seeking to achieve "a Reich and a greater economic sphere in Europe with eastern areas for development, the dissolution of Russia, and the replacement of parasitic capitalism with a new order based on community." And what rival ideas did the "Anglo-Saxon powers" have to offer? "Nothing but fig leaves of obsolete capitalism and imperialism." There was little difference between the views of Schulenburg and those of the Nazi stalwarts regarding the war in the east.[21]

As for the religious leaders of Germany, how could they withhold their benediction from a struggle in defense of Christian beliefs and values? For more than twenty years they had been preaching against the dangers of atheism and materialism emanating from Moscow. Now their nation had embarked on a crusade against the forces undermining the moral foundations of the West. Even those churchmen who opposed the Third Reich on questions of denominational jurisdiction and autonomy felt obliged to support its campaign against godless Communism.

Bishop Galen, for example, endorsed in a pastoral letter of September 14 the resistance of the Hitler government against "Moscow's attempt to impose the Bolshevistic false doctrine and oppressive rule on Germany and Western Europe." The soldiers of the Wehrmacht, who had been guarding "the coast of the Atlantic Ocean and the shores of the Mediterranean Sea," were now marching against "the Bolshevik opponent in the east." Could any Christian clergyman remain indifferent to this struggle? "Our thoughts are day and night with our brave soldiers," the bishop declared, "and our prayers rise to heaven that God's support may remain with them in the future for the effective protection of our people and country against the Bolshevik threat." The differences between church and state had to be subordinated for the time being to the overriding need to defend morality and religion.[22]

As the troops of the Third Reich advanced farther and farther eastward, the resistance appeared to be in a state of disintegration. Not only had its skittish sympathizers and fair-weather friends largely abandoned the cause. Even its hard-core supporters were succumbing to doubts and misgivings. They remained convinced that the Nazi regime was ruthless and oppressive. But could anyone deny that the territorial gains it had won would permanently secure for Germany a leading role in Europe? And besides, was it really right to engage in conspiracy and subversion during wartime? Would it not be better to postpone the attempt to overthrow Hitler until peace had returned? Was not the defense of the fatherland more important than partisan disputes or ideological differences? Military victory had gradually forced the resistance to the brink of collapse. The only thing that could save it now was military defeat.

Claus von Stauffenberg (left) and his friend and fellow resister Albrecht Mertz von Quirnheim at German headquarters in Vinnitsa in the Ukraine in 1942. (Ullstein Bilderdienst)

Clemens August von Galen, the bishop of Münster, officiating at a religious ceremony conducted during the war. (Corbis-Bettmann)

17

The Moral Dilemmas of Hegemony

When in the winter of 1941 Claus von Stauffenberg, who three years later almost succeeded in assassinating Hitler, was invited to join the resistance, he declined. His brother Berthold, who acted as intermediary and recruiter, reported to the others: "I have spoken with Claus. He says that first we must win the war. Things of this sort should not be done during a war, especially not during a war against Bolshevism. But then, when we come home, we will get rid of the brown pestilence." His reply typified the attitude of many opponents of the Nazi regime who put the defense of the national interest above all other concerns. They disapproved and condemned the brutalities of the Third Reich, but they could not bring themselves to jeopardize the war effort by conspiring to end them. They consoled themselves with the thought that once victory had been achieved, they would turn against the Hitler dictatorship and set everything right.[1]

Stauffenberg remained reluctant to enter the resistance until the defeats suffered by the Wehrmacht on the eastern front persuaded him that the war was or at least might be unwinnable. But even many of those who joined long before him were motivated by essentially similar loyalties and concerns. They too strove to defend the national interest at all costs. The question was, What would best serve the national interest? As long as the choice seemed to be between victory and resistance, they opted as a rule for victory. Only after it began to appear that the choice might actually be between defeat and resistance did they join or rejoin the resistance. Both the decline of the anti-Nazi movement during the period of German military successes from 1939 to 1941 and its revival during the period of German military reverses from 1942 to 1944 reflected the primary concern of most of the resisters for the security of their nation.

It would nevertheless be unfair to charge them with indifference to the excesses of National Socialism. More than aware of them, the resisters often deplored and abhorred those excesses. But they faced a crisis of conscience, a spiritual dilemma that forced them to choose between national allegiance and moral imperative. As a rule, they decided to subordinate ethical principles to patriotic loyalties. Yet even while serving the Third Reich, many of them continued to grapple with doubts and scruples, with conflicting emotions and opposing convictions. The early victories of the Wehrmacht depleted the ranks of the resistance, but those who remained and even those who left, including those who later rejoined, often expressed privately bitter resentment toward a regime that forced them to sacrifice moral conviction for civic duty.

Their criticism focused above all on the domestic policies of the Third Reich, on its resolve to reshape the national character, to blur the distinction between private belief and public conduct, and to bring about the integration of the Nazi Party and the German state. The outbreak of the war enabled the regime to demand even greater conformity than before, even greater devotion to the established system and the official ideology. The early victories of the Wehrmacht, moreover, helped to reinforce the government's contention that all forms of criticism and dissent, regardless of motivation, were signs of disloyalty. The military conflict thus encouraged the Third Reich to strive for a more rapid Nazification of all aspects of German life.

Most of the resisters found this attempt to transform society and culture alarming. Hassell, for instance, always the proud aristocrat, was deeply troubled by what he perceived as the regime's doctrinaire social egalitarianism, its hostility toward traditional distinctions of class and education, and its advocacy of a mobocracy fed on bread and circuses. "According to all indications," he wrote in his diary in October 1939, "the hatred of the party for the nobility and the so-called intellectuals is growing ever stronger. While young noblemen are dying [in battle] in large numbers, [Nazi agitators and ideologues] are with impunity inciting the rabble . . . against the nobility. It is no wonder that more and more people, like Goerdeler, for example, are firmly convinced that Hitler basically wants to exterminate the nobility and the intellectuals."

In May 1940, while the German armies rapidly advanced toward Paris, Hassell worried about the effect of victory on the structure of German society. He foresaw "the coming to power of socialism in a Hitlerite form, the disintegration of the upper classes, the transformation of the churches into meaningless sects, etc." Since National Socialism "lacks any soul," since its "real credo" had become nothing but power, "we will have nature without God, and a soulless, cultureless Germany, and perhaps Europe as well, conscienceless and brutal." Whatever good the Third Reich may once have represented "has now been stifled by its negative quality."

The surrender of France a month later could not dispel Hassell's gloomy presentiments. The military successes of the Third Reich, he feared, would only intensify its determination to undermine the inherited values and institutions of German society. Why could not others recognize the danger? "Among the masses there is a surprisingly obtuse indifference, for they have for seven years been deafened by the drumbeat of loudspeakers." Yet even he was not quite sure what should be done. In October 1940, with the Continent largely under the domination of the Third Reich, he grappled once again with that terrible dilemma confronting most of the members of the resistance. "There is no doubt that if this system triumphs, Germany and Europe will face terrible times. But if it leads Germany to defeat, then the consequences will be unthinkable as well." Hassell continued to worry and agonize.[2]

Goerdeler was less gloomy. Indeed, he sounded at times almost optimistic. Sanguine and a little glib, he saw in National Socialism an expression of the demagoguery characterizing German politics since the fall of the old empire. It represented, he wrote early in 1941, "a mixture of fanatical idealism and unrestrained materialism." Lacking any sense of self-discipline or accountability, it had gradually imposed on the nation an unjust and oppressive system of government.

But whose fault was that? For Goerdeler the ultimate responsibility for the Hitler dictatorship rested on the Weimar Republic. The parliamentary regime itself might perhaps have proved tolerable or even acceptable. But the introduction of proportional representation, though "theoretically the fairest," transformed the constitutional structure into a "machine" incapable of producing an "organic suffrage." Those who voted and those who were elected no longer had any "organic connection." The only thing uniting them was "a temporary and more or less fragile community of interest." The outcome of such a "suffrage of the logarithmic table" was foreseeable. The mechanistic democracy of the republican system led directly to the doctrinaire authoritarianism of the Nazi dictatorship. One was simply the mirror image of the other.

Still, Goerdeler remained resolutely hopeful. A golden mean might still be found between the extremes of "fanatical idealism" and "unrestrained materialism." After all, both idealism and materialism were "natural and vital." Each had been tried in turn, first in an excess of democracy and then in a ruthless despotism. The time had come to reconcile them through a policy of "moderation." Germany needed a "foundation of reason, justice, a sense of order, an awareness of responsibility, decency, and experience as well as love of the people and of the fatherland." Goerdeler remained convinced that the Nazi dictatorship would sooner or later be replaced by some traditional, conservative form of government, paternalistic in nature but reasonable and restrained, such as he had advocated during the last years of the republic.[3]

The most trenchant criticism of the Third Reich, all the more remarkable because it was overt, came from some of the religious leaders. To be sure, it was easier for them than for the military or bureaucratic resisters to voice disagreement with the regime. Since they enjoyed considerable popular support among their communicants, the government was reluctant to move against them for fear of provoking public unrest. They could claim, moreover, that they were simply carrying out their churchly duties. They were not trying to interfere in affairs of state but to look after the spiritual welfare of those entrusted to their pastoral care. Yet what they had to say was at times so critical of the central doctrines of National Socialism that to say it required great boldness. They too became in a sense resisters, though usually without realizing it.

Questions of denominational governance and ecclesiastical authority remained at issue. But there were also new concerns about the euthanasia program that the government had introduced to rid the nation of the physically and mentally disabled. Not only did this program accord with the theories of National Socialism regarding the importance of eugenics. It also had the practical advantage of removing from the German population those who, because of their disabilities, were incapable of contributing to the war effort. They could indeed be regarded as an impediment to victory. Many of the religious leaders, however, saw this view as incompatible with Christian teachings regarding the sanctity of life. To God there was no such thing as a useless human being. All his creatures were precious, the weak as much as the strong, the sick as much as the healthy. To put any of them to death solely because of some incapacity would be a violation of divine commandment. Most churchmen therefore opposed the euthanasia program, usually in private, but occasionally even publicly.

The most outspoken among the Protestant leaders was Bishop Wurm. In a letter to Minister of the Interior Wilhelm Frick on July 19, 1940, while the victory over France was still being celebrated throughout the Third Reich, he condemned the destruction of human life for reasons of expediency. He rejected the contention that since "the hundreds of thousands of physically and mentally disabled are, from the economic and financial point of view, too heavy a burden for the German people," putting them to death was justifiable. Nor did he accept the argument that the families of soldiers who had fallen in battle were making an even greater sacrifice. He found all of that irrelevant. A nation's struggle for existence, he maintained, in which every citizen has to be prepared to risk his life, could be accepted as something decreed by the divine will. "But that the life of the weak and defenseless is destroyed, not because they are a danger to us but because we are tired of feeding and caring for them, that is against God's commandment."

Wurm contrasted what he believed to be the chivalrous behavior of the German soldiers with the morally indefensible policy of their government. Members of the Wehrmacht, once they had defeated the enemy, protected defenseless civilians, "especially women, children, the wounded, and the sick," without considering the burden they were thereby imposing on their own nation. They could have understandably taken stern measures against the French people, "who have done us so much harm." But that "would have been worthy of a Clemenceau, not of a German." How then could the Third Reich be harsher in dealing with its own disabled citizens than with its defeated foreign foes?[4]

On the Catholic side, Bishop Galen went even further, criticizing the regime for its disregard of the personal rights and liberties of the German people as well as for its violation of the sanctity of life. His immediate concern was the arrest of insubordinate clergymen and the expropriation of ecclesiastical property. But in a sermon preached in Münster on July 13, 1941, amid the patriotic exuberance inspired by the steady eastward advance of the German troops, he spoke of the moral danger threatening the nation because of the violation of basic human rights. The conservative prelate, a lifelong opponent of individualism and democracy, had found the courage to denounce his government publicly for its lawless exercise of power. Those gathered in the Lamberti Church that Sunday heard an Elijah in the pulpit condemning evildoers in positions of authority.

Galen began by describing the hardships suffered by his own church. He spoke of the arrest of innocent Catholics "without the possibility of defense and a judicial verdict," the imprisonment of clergymen, the suppression of monasteries, and the expulsion of members of religious orders, "our brothers and sisters." All this led him to invoke the "old and unshakable" principle: "*Iustitia est fundamentum regnorum!* Justice is the only firm foundation of any political system." In its treatment of his coreligionists, the Third Reich was violating that principle.

Then Galen expanded his argument beyond the boundaries of denominational self-interest. "The right to life, to inviolability, and to freedom is an indispensable part of any moral social order," he declared. The state might indeed be justified in restricting those rights as a form of punishment, but only in dealing with violators of the law whose guilt was proven in impartial court proceedings. "The state that transgresses this limitation . . . and permits or causes the punishment of the innocent undermines its own authority and respect for its sovereignty within the conscience of its citizens."

Did the bishop realize that what he was saying could be applied not only to his own coreligionists but to all persons regardless of faith or origin, to non-Christians as well as Christians, non-Germans as well as Germans, and non-Aryans as well as Aryans? He never said so, yet his words suggest that he must have been at least partly aware of the broader implications of his argument. He stated explicitly that he was dealing not with "a denominational Catholic problem" but "a Christian problem, indeed, a general human and national religious problem." His fight for justice, he maintained, was motivated by more than a concern for "the rights of the church." Besides demonstrating his "love for our nation," he was also trying to protect "the rights of the human personality." For could anyone doubt that without justice the moral foundations of the state would be endangered? Galen could not have remained altogether blind to the underlying significance of his bold, defiant sermon.[5]

Although the resisters as a rule directed their criticism primarily at what the Third Reich was doing to Germany, they were not indifferent to the hardships it was inflicting on occupied Europe. Indeed, they regarded those hardships as manifestations of the same brutal exercise of power displayed by the Nazi regime at home. They frequently expressed considerable sympathy for the victims of the German conquests, for the vanquished forced to endure humiliation and oppression at the hands of the victors. In particular, the harsh treatment of the civilian population of Eastern Europe, of Poles, Russians, and especially Jews, aroused among them indignation and sometimes outrage. This aspect of the resistance must not be overlooked.

Among the private letters, diaries, and reports of the military members are numerous references, many of them based on eyewitness accounts, to excesses committed under the German administration of the occupied areas. In his memorandum of November 20, 1939, Beck spoke of "the dreadful moral effect on the rest of the world of the German conduct of the war in Poland, and especially of the subsequent German policy toward the Polish population." Three months later he described a confidential report he had seen regarding conditions in Poland that exceeded even the "worst expectations." For example, "the SS forced 1,500 Jews, among them many women and children, to ride around in open freight cars until they all died. Then they had 200 peasants dig huge mass graves and later shot all the people who had worked on them." Beck was appalled.[6]

So was Canaris. According to a letter from Groscurth dated October 10, 1939, "C. talked about Warsaw and other matters. Horrible! . . . Very serious problems among the troops in the east regarding plundering. No wonder, after the training they have been receiving for years! But everything is now being condoned." Even prominent generals like Johannes Blaskowitz and Gerd von Rundstedt, though by and large loyal to the government, complained bitterly about "the lack of discipline and the plundering by troops under the leadership of officers." The occupation policies of the Third Reich seemed to many soldiers of the old school in clear violation of the rules of military conduct they had learned in the imperial army.[7]

Age alone, however, did not determine the attitude of the resisters toward the treatment of conquered Europe. The younger officers, who had embarked on their military careers under the republic, were generally as critical as the older ones, who had started out under the monarchy. No one was more outraged by Nazi brutality in Poland, for instance, than Stieff. After visiting "the ruins of Warsaw," he wrote in November 1939: "One walks there not as a conqueror but as someone burdened by guilt. I am not the only one to feel this way. The gentlemen who must live there experience it too." This feeling of complicity was intensified by "all the incredible things happening there on the side, which we must watch with folded arms." It was a terrible shock to him.

Stieff then launched into a passionate denunciation of the regime responsible for the brutalities committed against a defenseless civilian population:

> The wildest fantasies of atrocity propaganda grow pale in comparison with the things being perpetrated by an organized gang of murderers, robbers, and plunderers, presumably with the knowledge of the highest authority. We can no longer talk under these circumstances about "justified outrage at the crimes [formerly] committed against Germans [under Polish rule]." This extermination of entire families with women and children is possible only for a subhuman species that no longer deserves the name of German. I am ashamed of being a German. This minority, which is sullying the German name by murdering, plundering, and ravaging, will be the undoing of the entire Ger-

man nation, if we do not put a stop to their actions soon. For the things that have been described and demonstrated to me on the spot by the most reliable sources must arouse an avenging nemesis. Otherwise this gang will some day turn against us decent people as well and will terrorize its own nation with its pathological rage.

Amid the devastation of the Polish capital, Stieff had a frightening presentiment of the fate awaiting him and the other members of the resistance.[8]

The invasion of the Soviet Union two years later was accompanied by even worse atrocities against the conquered population and even louder protests among some of the military opponents of the Nazi regime. Early in June 1941, before the war actually began, Henning von Tresckow saw for the first time the secret orders that had been issued relaxing the penalties for crimes against civilians in the forthcoming campaign and calling for the summary execution of captured political commissars. Appalled, he decided to protest—in vain, as it turned out—to his commander, Field Marshal Fedor von Bock. On the way to headquarters, he told an accompanying officer, Rudolf-Christoph von Gersdorff: "If we do not succeed in persuading the Field Marshal to fly to Hitler immediately and bring about the revocation of these orders, then a burden of guilt will descend on the German nation that the world will not forget for hundreds of years." That burden would rest not only on the leaders of the Nazi regime, he feared, but "on you and me, on your wife and my wife, on your children and my children, on the old woman who is going into a store over there, on the man who is just now riding past us on his bicycle, and on the small child there playing with his ball."[9]

Whether those were Tresckow's precise words may be questioned. Gersdorff did not report them until long after the end of the war. In any case, they accurately reflected his revulsion at the brutalities of the Third Reich.

Stieff shared that revulsion. In a letter of September 5, 1941, he lamented that "sometimes it is almost too much for me." He felt "burdens imposed by the system" that once again made him "ashamed of [my] decent German background." The situation on the eastern front seemed to him so bad that "Poland was nothing by comparison." At the siege of Leningrad, for example, "they ordered, despite all remonstrances, the starving out [of the city] with all its inhabitants regardless of offers to surrender, which are alleged to be only tricks." Even women and children trying to get out were to be shot. "When a real devil in human form does something that would make a Genghis Khan green with envy, then of course one loses faith and confidence in the justice of the cause for which one is supposed to fight and work." Stieff was beside himself with indignation.[10]

The civilians in the resistance usually exhibited greater restraint. They had fewer opportunities to observe firsthand the excesses committed under the German occupation of the Continent. They had to rely to a considerable extent on rumor, speculation, and guesswork for their information. But they too often expressed shocked disapproval of the ruthlessness with which the Third Reich was treating the conquered populations. Moltke, who as legal advisor to the high command of the armed forces knew more than most of them, spoke in August 1941 about "hecatombs of corpses [resting] on our shoulders." There were reports "that in the shipments of prisoners of war and Jews only 20 percent arrive [alive], that hunger rages in the prisoner-of-war camps, [and] that typhus and all other epidemics bred by privation have broken out." He worried about "the bloodguilt that cannot be expiated in our lifetime and can never be forgotten." The nation was bound to lose the war, of that he was sure. But would it afterward produce men "capable of finding repentance and remorse in this punishment, thereby also gradually finding new vital forces? Or will everything disintegrate into chaos?" In either case, Germany would have to pay a terrible price for a terrible crime.[11]

Hassell was not as oracular. He sounded quite sober, almost matter-of-fact. But there could be no mistaking his underlying sense of outrage at the brutalities of the Nazi regime. As early as October 1939, barely a month after the outbreak of the war, he complained in his diary about "the disgrace with which the conduct of the war in Poland . . . has sullied the German name," especially "the frightful bestialities of the SS." A year later he rejected the view encouraged by the authorities that the humiliations being inflicted on the Polish population were justified, because "a decent Pole is as rare as a decent Jew." He discovered that young officers, government officials, and even some SS men were trying to avoid duty in the occupied countries, feeling "ashamed of being German." But many National Socialists stationed in Poland had abandoned their "ethical standards" and their "initially critical point of view," and now "think only of their own advantage, whether in the form of a job or of personal enrichment." Worse still, the Hitler regime had launched a "satanic campaign against the Polish intelligentsia with the avowed purpose of destroying it." The situation in Western Europe was not much better. "They are stealing on a grand scale, starting with [Göring]," not to mention "the juggling of figures between 'public' and 'private' thefts." Where would it all end?[12]

Goerdeler seemed to believe that it would end with the overthrow of the Nazi regime. He was not sure how or when that would happen, but there was no doubt in his mind about what must be done once it happened. The brutal and venal satraps of the Third Reich in the occupied countries should at once be replaced by honest and experienced civil servants, by men with administrative talent and managerial skill, men like Goerdeler himself. That would be the first and most urgent step.

He outlined what he had in mind in a long memorandum entitled "The Goal," which he composed early in 1941. As soon as a new German government was formed, the administration of the conquered territories must be entrusted to military governors assisted by "experienced and reliable civil servants and representatives of the foreign ministry." A "single center of responsibility" would thus replace the confusion of competing authorities and conflicting jurisdictions. "Unjustified interference in the administration of these territories and in the lives of their citizens is to end immediately," and to achieve that aim, "organizations and institutions formed by the National Socialist Party and its subdivisions are to be immediately eliminated." The result would be a more humane system of authority in subjugated Europe. "The self-administration of these territories will be restored as soon as possible and to the extent compatible with the requirements of German security." Goerdeler sought not the immediate end of Germany's domination of the Continent but a reasonable and responsible exercise of that domination.[13]

The resisters expressed special concern regarding the most pitiable and tragic victims of the Third Reich. For the Jews of Europe the period between the *Kristallnacht* of November 1938 and the invasion of the Soviet Union in June 1941 was the next to last stage in the Nazi solution of the "racial problem." During those three years their position deteriorated steadily from disfranchisement to segregation, ghettoization, and sporadic mass murder. Only one step remained to be taken for the final victory of National Socialism's anti-Semitic crusade: systematic extermination. And that step was now only a few weeks away. Although the resisters generally shared the view that under Weimar the Jewish community had acquired too much influence over national life, especially politics, finance, and culture, the growing brutality of the Hitler dictatorship became too much for them. By the time the war started they were repeatedly voicing their condemnation of the murderous racism of the Third Reich.

Shortly after the fall of Warsaw, for instance, Hassell spoke about the atrocities being committed by the SS, "especially against the Jews." It was a national disgrace. "When [our] people shoot down with revolvers Jews who have been driven into a synagogue, one can only feel ashamed." A month later Stieff wrote about the "extermination of entire families" referring to the anti-Semitic mass murders being committed in Poland.

Early the following year Beck spoke with revulsion about an account he had read of how more than a thousand Jews had been packed into freight cars in the dead of winter and shipped back and forth until they perished from cold and privation. Many other resisters expressed dismay as well at the atrocities being perpetrated against the Jewish population of the occupied countries.[14]

No one, however, with the exception perhaps of Bonhoeffer, was as sensitive to the inherent inhumaneness of racial persecution as Moltke. He was by nature too delicate, too squeamish, to countenance the violence and bloodshed needed to overthrow the Nazi regime. But there was no doubt in his mind that the brutalities of the Third Reich must end even at the cost of his own nation's defeat. Hence the beginning of the deportation of Berlin Jews to the ghettos of Eastern Europe in October 1941 produced in him an outburst of despair and self-reproach. "They want to spare us the knowledge that they will simply let [the Jews] perish from hunger and cold, and so they do it in Lodz and Smolensk," he wrote. "How can anyone know about something like that and still walk around freely? By what right? Is it not inevitable that some day it will be his own turn and that he too will be kicked into the gutter? All these things are only a flash of lightning, for the storm is still to come." A terrible fate awaited the nation that had witnessed such cruelty and done nothing.

In an agonizing admission of personal responsibility and guilt, he asked whether he himself was really much better than the others. "If I could only free myself from the terrible feeling that I have let myself be corrupted, that I no longer respond resolutely enough to things like that, and that they torment me without producing any spontaneous response. I have become perverted, because even in things like that I respond only with my brain. I think about the possible consequences instead of acting." The cry of anguish came from a sensitive, decent man torn between conscience and self-preservation.[15]

Goerdeler was the opposite of Moltke in temperament and outlook. Moltke, preoccupied with the moral dilemmas of power, could not deal with the practical problems of seizing and exercising it. He was overwhelmed by his own intellectuality. Goerdeler, by contrast, seemed to believe that most spiritual quandaries could be resolved through administrative expertise and managerial skill. He suffered from too much practicality. He objected to the policies more than the principles of National Socialism, to the methods more than the goals. He agreed in general that the Jews were an alien element in German national life, an element that should be isolated and removed. But there was no need for brutality or persecution. Would it not be better to try to solve the Jewish question by moderate, reasonable means?

"A new arrangement regarding the position of the Jews seems necessary throughout the world," he wrote in "The Goal." A failure to recognize that necessity would lead to "injustices, cruelties, and at the least to an unsatisfactory state of confusion." Something had to be done. "That the Jewish people belong to a different race is common knowledge." This knowledge pointed to a solution Goerdeler had first broached before the war. "The world will have peace only when the Jewish people are given a real opportunity to establish and maintain their own state," perhaps "in parts of Canada or South America." The creation of such a state would place most German Jews in the category of resident aliens, still entitled to own property and practice an occupation, but barred from the civil service and the franchise. As for the anti-Semitic Nuremberg Laws, they ought to be repealed, so that the problem of "racial mixture" through intermarriage could be left to "the sound common sense of the people."

Goerdeler conceded that "a wrong has undoubtedly been committed on a large scale in recent years through the expropriation, destruction, etc. of Jewish property and life in Germany," a wrong that could not be justified "before our conscience and before history." The nation should therefore seek, "in view of our position in the world and of our own conscience," to heal the wounds that had been inflicted. It should "detoxify" public opinion, reestablish "German self-respect," and act in accordance with its own "sense of justice." Accordingly, all restrictions imposed on the Jews with regard to nourishment, housing, communication, cultural activity, health care, and the choice of names must be removed. But more than that, "the ghettos in the occupied areas are to be organized humanely, [and] their future fate is to be decided by the appropriate local authorities with the approval of the military governors, because the Poles, for example, take a different position on this question than the Dutch." Segregation followed by expatriation, but without hostility or brutality—that seemed to be the gist of Goerdeler's solution to the Jewish question.[16]

The attitude of some of the other resisters was even more ambivalent. Consider the enigmatic Canaris. Never a rabid anti-Semite, he in fact tried on a few occasions to help the victims of Nazi bigotry at considerable risk to himself. In the spring of 1941, for instance, he approved a plan to send some five hundred Dutch Jews abroad, ostensibly as a means of "infiltrating secret agents into South America." This incident contributed to his temporary suspension from the position of head of military counterintelligence. Undeterred, he became involved in a still more hazardous venture a year later. In the summer of 1942 he arranged for permission for about a dozen elderly Berlin Jews to leave Germany so that, according to the official explanation, they might provide confidential information regarding conditions in the United States. "Hitler once wanted the Jews shipped abroad," Canaris remarked to a subordinate with a broad wink. "I have interpreted that as an order." He was not easily intimidated.

Yet he too was willing at times to make his own position more secure by outwardly supporting the regime's anti-Semitic measures and even advocating their intensification. Thus after the invasion of the Soviet Union he endorsed a plan requiring the Jews of Berlin to wear a distinguishing arm band, as those in occupied Poland had been doing for two years, and to move to the eastern part of the city so that they could be kept more easily under surveillance. The ostensible reason was that Jewish families had been entertaining Swedish, Swiss, and American journalists, and some of them had even been engaging in espionage and sabotage. It was important therefore to identify and segregate them. The plan was ultimately rejected because of the concern of Minister of Propaganda Joseph Goebbels that it might arouse sympathy for the Jewish community among the residents of the capital as well as abroad. But Canaris had made his point; he had demonstrated his loyalty to the regime. Still, could he have really believed that the Berlin Jews, isolated, scorned, and persecuted, were a threat to the German war effort? In all probability he was simply pandering to the anti-Semitic prejudices of National Socialism.[17]

As for Schulenburg, he appeared largely indifferent to the fate of the Jews. His biographer Ulrich Heinemann maintained fifty years later that he was "surely full of abhorrence and condemnation" regarding the anti-Semitic atrocities of the extermination squads. Yet the tone of the entries in his diary during the invasion of the Soviet Union is detached and matter-of-fact. "On the horizon [can be seen] the red glow of the flames of burning Białystok," he wrote in an entry dated June 26 and 27, 1941. "As we move through Białystok, dead Jews lie in the streets. The SS has used the opportunity to organize a hunt for Jews." A day later, on June 28, "we are told that, as is so often the case, they drove the Jews into the synagogue and then set it on fire." Compared to the outrage expressed by Stieff at roughly the same time, Schulenburg sounded self-possessed.

Whatever his true feelings, the atrocities accompanying the German advance did not alter his conviction that the war against the Soviet Union was justified. As for the brutality with which it was being waged, that was a tragic but inescapable consequence of any conflict of ideologies. "We come as liberators of the Russian people from Bolshevism," he insisted shortly after the invasion began. Two months later, on August 27, he was still confident that "we can as yet administer here creatively. . . . In a land that has just been freed from Bolshevism, we can rule only in accordance with principles that are opposed to Bolshevist principles. Property, personal freedom, and freedom of opinion and religion are the inalienable elements of policy." His belief that the Third Reich might govern Eastern Europe in keeping with those principles seemed unshaken by the accounts he had heard of Jews driven into their synagogues to be burned alive.[18]

Finally, there were a few resisters who accepted the anti-Semitic teachings of National Socialism not out of expediency or acquiescence but conviction. They genuinely believed that the machinations of world Jewry were behind the spread of materialism, capitalism, Communism, and atheism. Western civilization faced a terrible danger that, in their opinion, had to be crushed. On May 5, 1941, General Hoepner reminded the soldiers under his command that the struggle in Eastern Europe in which they were about to engage had as one of its main objectives "defense against Jewish Bolshevism." It would require of them "ruthless and forceful action against Bolshevist agitators, guerrillas, saboteurs, and Jews, and the total suppression of all active or passive resistance." He pointed out that the Soviet Union did not comprise "a single nationality," but included "a large number of Slavic, Caucasian, and Asiatic nationalities." Nor should they forget that "Jewry is strongly represented in the USSR." That made the coming war all the more important for the protection of Europe.[19]

General Carl-Heinrich von Stülpnagel was another member of the resistance who was quite conscious of the Jewish peril. In the early years of the Third Reich, his son testified after the war, he had objected to the erection near his home of a monument to the racist writer Theodor Fritsch. Yet not long afterward, as commander of the German Seventeenth Army on the Russian front, he expressed views that Fritsch would have heartily approved. On July 30, 1941, he issued an order that reprisals for actions by the civilian population against the invading forces should be directed, if necessary, against members of Russian youth organizations. But above all, "the Jewish Komsomols are to be regarded as the instigators of sabotage and of the formation of bands of young [guerrillas]." Three weeks later, on August 21, he submitted to the propaganda section of the Wehrmacht a demand for an "intensified struggle against Jewry." He was not motivated primarily by self-interest, by some calculated desire to demonstrate his loyalty to the ideology of the Third Reich. He genuinely believed that the struggle against the Jews was a struggle for the defense of European civilization.[20]

Hoepner and Stülpnagel were exceptions, to be sure. Most of the resisters felt sympathy in varying degrees for the victims of Nazi oppression, abroad as well as at home. But they kept telling themselves that for the time being the most important thing was to win the war. Once peace had been restored, they would replace the Hitler dictatorship with a more responsible and humane form of government. They failed to recognize, because they did not really want to, that the successes of the Wehrmacht were successes for National Socialism, that a victory for Germany would be a victory for the Third Reich. They preferred to believe otherwise. And so, while the brutalities of National Socialism grew and spread, the resistance continued to languish and dwindle. The fate of the Germans seemed to most of its members, understandably, no doubt, more important than the fate of the Poles or the French or the Russians or the Jews. They had to go on contending therefore with implacable moral dilemmas that could be neither ignored nor resolved. Defending the fatherland at any cost imposed on them a heavy, unrelenting psychological burden.

18

The Ebbing Tide of Conquest

What led to the revival of the resistance after the winter of 1941 was precisely what had led to its decline before, namely, the course of the war. Until then the final victory of Germany had seemed within grasp. The Wehrmacht's series of remarkable military successes had created a widespread belief that it was only a question of a few months, perhaps only a few weeks, before terms of peace would be dictated in Berlin. A coup against the government at such a time would no doubt be perceived by most Germans as an act of sabotage, indeed, as treason. The conclusion seemed inescapable. Any attempt to overthrow the Third Reich would have to be postponed until the return of peace. Did the resisters want to be labeled as back stabbers and traitors, like the November revolutionaries twenty years before?

The situation changed, however, after the attack against the Soviet Union. The Wehrmacht's long succession of victories was followed by an even longer succession of defeats. The fortunes of war suddenly shifted. Not only did the eastward advance of the German troops come to a halt on the outskirts of Moscow in December 1941, but they were forced for the first time into a long, costly retreat. The entry of the United States into the conflict at about the same time fundamentally altered the balance of power between the opposing sides. The outcome of the war, which had only recently seemed so predictable, became doubtful once again.

The Wehrmacht did return to the offensive in the spring of 1942, pushing deep into southern Russia and advancing in North Africa to within seventy miles of Alexandria. But then came a series of disastrous blows: the surrender of the Sixth Army at Stalingrad in February 1943, the capitulation of the Axis forces in Tunisia in May, the invasion of Sicily followed by the fall of Mussolini in July, and Italy's conclusion of an armistice with the Allies in September. Most damaging to public morale were the mounting air attacks by the Americans and the British against the cities of the Third Reich. They demonstrated even more dramatically than the bad news from distant fronts that the war was turning against the Germans.

The German public, which had euphorically assumed that the war was almost won, began gradually to succumb to a mood of pessimism and a sense of foreboding. The conflict would go on after all, the losses would continue to grow, the casualties would multiply and the bombings increase. Where would it all end? For the first time since the early months of the war, the possibility of defeat became an unspoken but constant source of concern in Germany. And with that concern came another, hitherto ignored or repressed, but now increasingly persistent. The misfortunes that the nation was experiencing represented perhaps more than military reverses or economic deficiencies. Maybe they were the signs of providential displeasure, of divine retribution. Maybe God was punishing Germany for the Third Reich's transgressions.

This feeling, irrational yet irrepressible, started to spread amid the growing devastation of Berlin, Hamburg, Munich, and Cologne. It fostered the belief that the hardships the Germans were enduring were a heavenly retaliation for the Nazi regime's cruelties, which they had silently witnessed and tolerated. The sense of complicity and guilt produced in turn a new feeling of compassion for the victims of the Third Reich. The fate of the Jews in particular became a frequent subject of private and sometimes even public debate in Germany.

Bishop Wurm, for example, wrote in a letter of August 9, 1943, to the Protestant clergy of Stuttgart about the connection, undemonstrable but undeniable, between his country's military reverses and its moral transgressions. "Our German nation," he declared, "has also assumed a heavy burden of guilt through the way in which the struggle against the members of other races and nations was conducted before the war and during the war. How many people who were personally innocent have had to atone for the sin and injustice of their countrymen?" The Germans were learning at last that wrongdoing inevitably invited retribution. "Can we be surprised that we are now also experiencing that? And even though we did not approve of it, yet we often remained silent when we should have and ought to have spoken out." The nation would have to pay a heavy price for its acquiescence in evil.[1]

The mounting defeats of the Wehrmacht also helped revive the resistance, which had declined and languished during the years of victory. Some of the religious leaders began to criticize the policies of the government with new boldness. The focus of their concern was no longer the familiar conflict between spiritual and secular authority. It even extended beyond the regime's euthanasia program or its violation of the civil rights of the citizens of the Third Reich. For the first time the anti-Semitic program embraced by National Socialism became the source of open dissent on the part of at least a few of the prominent churchmen.

This issue arose partly as a result of the growing feeling that Hitler was leading the nation to disaster. But it also reflected a moral revulsion against the decision of the government early in 1942 to approve formally the "final solution" of the Jewish question, in other words, genocide. The new policy, nominally secret but in fact widely known, overcame occasionally the reluctance of leading clergymen to speak out on questions that did not directly affect their communicants. Even those who had in the past condemned what they perceived as the unhealthy influence of the Jewish community in national life were shocked by a program of organized, systematic extermination. The most anti-Semitic among them felt that genocide was not a morally acceptable means of racial purification. And here and there some even found the courage to say so openly.

Curiously, those members of the Catholic hierarchy who had previously been most outspoken in criticizing other aspects of the regime's program were generally not the ones now opposing its policy of racial mass murder. Galen, for instance, had little to say on the subject of genocide. He had not become timid; he certainly displayed no hesitation in condemning those government measures that seemed to violate the principles of Christian morality. His opposition to the euthanasia program, to take one issue, remained unbending. "Once we concede that human beings have the right to kill their 'unproductive' fellow human beings," he preached in August 1941, "even though for the time being that affects only poor and defenseless mental patients, then we allow in principle the murder of all unproductive human beings such as the incurably sick, the cripples who cannot work, and the invalids disabled at work or in war. Then we allow the murder of all of us, once we become old and feeble and therefore unproductive." There was nothing fainthearted about the bishop's opposition to the destruction of some categories of innocent life.

His silence on the subject of anti-Semitism could not have therefore reflected fear for his personal safety. He was simply reluctant to challenge the authorities on a question that did not directly affect the confessional interests of his church. Besides, Galen was unwilling to say anything that might weaken popular support for the war effort or expose his coreligionists to the charge of political disloyalty. In July 1943 he thanked from the pulpit the soldiers of the Wehrmacht for their resolve "to defeat the attack by our enemies against the fatherland" and for their "achievements and sacrifices." He hoped that, "as Christians and decent human beings," they would continue to wage the struggle "decently and chivalrously." Their only goal should be to win an honorable peace for their nation. They should not let themselves be misled by "base feelings of vengeance and the ignoble demand to inflict on the members of the enemy nation, in order simply to retaliate, the same unnecessary destruction and bitter pain that . . . have been inflicted on us." Thoughts of retribution were unworthy of "Christians and Germans." The final solution, which must have been known to Galen, at least in broad outline, did not seem to shake his confidence that the Third Reich could still achieve a victory of justice and reconciliation.[2]

Although Cardinal Faulhaber was more sensitive to the cruelties the Jews had to endure, he remained too narrow in outlook, too expedient, to challenge the government on the issue of genocide. He felt that the interests of the Catholic Church should not be jeopardized for the sake of an alien and unpopular ethnic minority. Still, the brutality of Nazi anti-Semitism, clearly shocked him. On November 13, 1941, he wrote to Cardinal Adolf Bertram of Breslau, chairman of the Catholic Bishops' Conference, to express indignation at the inhumane methods employed in the deportation to Poland of "non-Aryans" living in Munich. Although the roundups were being conducted mostly at night, he had learned that "scenes are occurring which will hereafter be compared in the history of our time with the transports of the African slave traders." Some laymen were even asking him whether the bishops could not do something. But Faulhaber doubted that appeals on behalf of the Jews in general would find much sympathy among the authorities, who "blindly accept racial principles." Should not an effort be made, however, to help at least "those non-Aryans who have through conversion become . . . children of the Catholic Church and have thereby come under the protection of their diocesan bishops?"

The leaders of the church could of course request better treatment for all Jews "out of general humane considerations, [though these] will certainly not be acknowledged by the racial fanatics, and out of consideration for the honor of the German name in history." It would be more practical, however, to concentrate on the converts, since they were "real Catholics and members of the church." In any case, the bishops might try to mitigate the worst hardships inflicted on the "non-Aryans," hardships "that may some day rebound against our own people."

But Bertram was even more circumspect than Faulhaber. What good would it do to protest? "We are dealing here," he replied a few days later, "with the application of a basic principle of an ideology which has completely abandoned supernatural faith, and . . . which apparently believes that it has to apply this basic principle even in ways violating the bounds of common human feeling." Besides, the episcopate had other responsibilities. It should save its "limited opportunities to exert influence" for issues "that are more important and far-reaching from the point of view of the church," particularly, "how to counter effectively an influence hostile to Christianity and the church in the education of Catholic youth."

Faulhaber let himself be easily persuaded. Little would be gained by protesting against the treatment even of "non-Aryan" Catholics, he conceded to Bertram, given "the attitude of the office making these decisions." The government had finally agreed that converts would in general be excluded from the transports, subject to the approval of the local authorities handling the deportations. There was nothing more to be done. "Now we can at least say that the episcopate tried to mitigate the situation of Christian non-Aryans." And that was the last time the cardinal mentioned the subject in his correspondence.[3]

Among the Catholic hierarchy Archbishop Joseph Frings of Cologne displayed the greatest courage in speaking out against the tragic fate of the Jews. Preoccupied with the administrative and pastoral duties of his office, he had until then played a relatively minor part in the struggle between spiritual and temporal authority. But the treatment of occupied Europe by the Nazi regime and especially the final solution of the Jewish question led him at last to deal with the subject that most religious leaders had been reluctant to mention. On December 12, 1942, while the extermination camps in Poland were working day and night at their murderous task, he issued a pastoral letter to be read at Sunday services in all the parishes of his diocese. In it he referred to "ultimate principles of justice," principles independent of "temporal circumstances," which could not be regarded as an "expression of a unique national character" and which should not therefore become the "privilege of a single nation."

These "inherent rights," Frings declared, including "the right to life, to inviolability, to freedom, to property, and to a marriage whose validity does not depend on the arbitrary will of the state," must not be denied even to someone "who is not of our blood or does not speak our language." The temptation to violate them was especially great in time of war, when opposing armies confronted one another in bloody conflict. But without justice there could be "no better future, no just peace." The Germans must always remember that "a denial of these rights or indeed the inhumane treatment of our fellow human beings is an injustice not only against a foreign people but against our own people as well." Those who heard the archbishop's statement knew exactly what and whom he meant by "the inhumane treatment of our fellow human beings."[4]

Frings's boldness encouraged the other members of the Catholic episcopate to publish a collective condemnation of genocide, diplomatic in tone but unmistakable in intent. On August 8, 1943, they issued a pastoral letter concerning "The Ten Commandments as the Vital Law of Nations." It emphasized in particular the divine prohibition against murder. "Killing is bad in itself, even when committed allegedly in the interest of the common welfare." That was true whether the victims were "guiltless and defenseless" mental patients, incurable invalids, the mortally wounded, the newborn who were "genetically impaired and incapable of surviving," innocent hostages, disarmed prisoners of war, convicts, or "human beings of alien races and origin." All came under God's protection. "Even the supreme secular authority can and is permitted to punish by death only criminals who truly deserve death."

The bishops then invoked Saint Matthew. "Thou shalt love the Lord thy God with all thy heart, and with all thy soul, and with all thy mind," they quoted. "This is the first and great commandment. And the second is like unto it, Thou shalt love thy neighbour as thyself." From the Evangelist's injunction it was only a short step to their own exhortation on behalf of "those who can help themselves least." They included not only young people "in need of proper religious leadership and attention," but also "the innocent human beings who are not of our nation and blood" as well as deportees, prisoners, and foreign workers, all of whom had a right "to humane treatment and to both moral and religious ministration." Although the Nazi authorities could not have been pleased by this appeal, they took no action against the authors of the pastoral letter. They simply went on patiently and methodically with the task of racial improvement through mass murder.[5]

The Protestants were on the whole more outspoken than the Catholics in condemning genocide. Sometimes, rather than rely on circumlocutions like "members of other races" or "non-Aryans," they would even use the simple and unadorned "Jews." Their greater boldness reflected in considerable measure their greater security. They were not a beleaguered and distrusted minority like the Catholics. They were not as likely to be charged with disloyalty or lack of patriotism. They could afford to be more daring.

The most defiant among the prominent Protestant leaders was Wurm. Though at first favorable toward the Third Reich as a bulwark against materialism and Communism, he became increasingly critical in the course of the war. He found most objectionable the government's adoption of mass extermination as an instrument of policy, particularly the euthanasia program and the campaign against the Jews. But not only the regime was guilty of mass murder. Those who remained silent in the face of the regime's misdeeds bore the guilt as well. The Germans collectively had incurred a heavy burden of complicity, Wurm warned in a sermon on October 17, 1943, by failing to speak out against the moral transgressions of those in power. "Did we not look on while infirm life, the so-called life not worth living, was sacrificed, and must we not now witness how those among us who deserved life the most and were the most kind have fallen abroad? Did we not see the houses of worship of the others go up in flames, and must we not now witness our own houses of worship being burned down?" Instead of bewailing its losses, the nation should repent and atone for its sins.[6]

The bishop did not confine his criticism of the regime to religious sermons or pastoral letters. He wrote tirelessly to important government officials urging changes in policy, especially concerning genocide. On January 28, 1943, he submitted a letter to the Württemberg state ministry of the interior protesting "the way in which the struggle against other races and nations is being waged." Soldiers on furlough were reporting to the civilian population at home "what is happening in the occupied areas with regard to the systematic murder of Jews and Poles." Even those who had formerly deplored "the domination of Jewry in the most diverse areas of public life,"—Wurm included himself in this category—during the days when "almost the entire press was philo-Semitic in sympathy," could not now accept the view that one people had the right to exterminate another by measures applied against every individual "regardless of personal guilt." To put human beings to death without judicial verdict, simply because they belonged to "another nationality" or because of their "sick condition," violated God's commandment and shamed a "cultured people." Was it pure coincidence that since the adoption of the policy of genocide the fortunes of war had turned against Germany?[7]

Wurm continued to protest and argue vigorously with the leaders of the Third Reich. On February 8 he wrote to Wilhelm Murr, the governor of Württemberg, that "all measures by which human beings belonging to other nations or races are being put to death without a judicial verdict by a civilian or military court, merely because of their national or racial origin," should be halted. Such measures as well as the program to "eliminate" the mentally ill, being in violation of the divine commandment, "could bring a terrible retribution against our nation."

A month later, on March 12, the bishop sent a letter to Minister for Church Affairs Hanns Kerrl in Berlin maintaining that anti-Jewish policies, "especially insofar as they are being applied outside the laws in force," had long troubled the conscience of many Germans. The Christian churches hesitated to protest, knowing that their objections could be used by the foreign enemy for propaganda purposes. But there was a widespread popular feeling that the nation had assumed a heavy burden of guilt because "human beings have been deprived of their native country, their occupation, and their life without sentence by a civilian or military court."

On July 16 Wurm even wrote directly to Hitler, asking him, "in the name of God and for the sake of the German nation," to halt "the persecution and destruction to which many men and women in the German sphere of authority have been subjected without a judicial verdict." The "non-Aryans" in territories under the control of the Third Reich had now been "largely eliminated." Still, the extermination measures taken against them directly violated God's commandment and undermined the foundation of all Western thought and life, namely, "the God-given basic right to human existence and human dignity in general." They disgraced the German name.[8]

The Führer did not reply. He had other things on his mind in the summer of 1943. But Wurm went on, unremittingly though unsuccessfully, exhorting, preaching, arguing, and protesting.

Nevertheless, he insisted over and over again that he was motivated not by hostility but sympathy toward the Third Reich. He was its supporter and adherent, not its opponent. He intended his criticisms to strengthen the regime by making it aware of its own mistakes. This contention reflected partly a tactical consideration, the need to gain a favorable hearing from the political leadership. But it also expressed partly a sincere conviction. The bishop continued to share many of the ideas and ideals of the National Socialist Party. What he objected to were the excesses accompanying the effort to realize those ideas and ideals. He never became a principled opponent of Hitler's government. He sought rather to make it more acceptable by making it less arbitrary, dogmatic, and cruel.

Wurm's own formulation of his protests against the policy of racial extermination points to this conclusion. He made repeated declarations of support for the Third Reich. Writing to Murr early in 1942, he spoke of his sympathetic attitude toward National Socialism even before its rise to power, an attitude that had not really changed. "Despite developments in the ecclesiastical sphere that brought me temporarily into opposition to the measures adopted by the state concerning ecclesiastical policy, my loyalty to the nation, the state, and the Führer as well as my approval of the original National Socialist political program had remained unaltered." Even now he was at heart faithful to the regime.

That assurance appeared again in the letter he wrote in the summer of 1943 to Hans Lammers, chief of the chancellor's office. He admitted that the "ideological struggle which has unfortunately come to accompany the healthy program of National Socialism" seemed to him the basic cause of the military reverses of the last two years. The blessing of God, "so often entreated by the Führer himself," was being denied to the German nation and to "our brave and incomparable army" because the Third Reich no longer recognized God's holiness and the validity of his laws. This would have to change. Still, the purpose of the bishop's letter was "not to create difficulties for the leadership of our nation, but to help it." He insisted that he remained as loyal as ever to his country and to its government.[9]

He also declared repeatedly that his criticism of the Nazi regime's anti-Semitic policy was motivated by a concern not for the Jews but for the Germans. Mass extermination was turning public opinion abroad against the Third Reich. "Who are the only ones," he asked Goebbels in a letter of November 10, 1941, "who can find any satisfaction in the so-called systematic measures for the elimination of the mentally ill and the theft of ecclesiastical property, in all the measures against the church and clergy that have followed one another since the beginning of the war, and in the hard measures against the non-Aryans?" The answer was obvious. "Only Mr. Roosevelt and his accomplices! . . . We are continually providing material for the most malicious and mendacious enemies of the German nation, material they need to raise the crusading spirit [in their countries] to the boiling point." National Socialism should become more humane, if for no other reason than self-interest.

This argument appears and reappears in a variety of forms in Wurm's letters to leading bureaucrats. He reminded Hanns Kerrl that he had long warned against the "disastrous effect on [German] foreign policy" of the government's anti-Semitic program. "The extraordinarily important role of Jewry abroad in the spread and conduct of the war by the enemy powers completely confirms these warnings." At least some moderation of Nazi racism was clearly desirable. Similarly, Wurm urged Minister of the Interior Wilhelm Frick to support "a change in the entire Jewish policy," hastening to add that he was acting "not out of special liking for Jewry," but because of the conviction that genocide "violates God's commandments." When writing to Lammers to condemn "this policy of extermination directed against Jewry" as an "injustice," he emphasized once more that he was protesting not from any "philo-Semitic inclinations," but "simply out of religious and ethical sensibility."

Even in his correspondence with ecclesiastical administrators rather than government officials, he made it clear that he had little sympathy for Jews. "No Protestant church has questioned the right of the state to adopt racial legislation for the purpose of maintaining the purity of the German nation," he wrote to the Protestant Church Chancellery in Berlin in January 1942. Indeed, "leading men in the Protestant Church"—Wurm mentioned Adolf Stöcker and his followers in the days of the old empire— "were once the first ones to point out the dangers threatening the German nation as a result of alien Jewish control over economic, political, and cultural affairs." A resolve to avert those dangers still seemed to him fully justified.[10]

Thus Wurm opposed excessive, brutal, or murderous anti-Semitism, not anti-Semitism itself. He continued to maintain that the role of the Jews in German national life had to be restricted. He went on believing that the underlying ideals and principles of National Socialism were essentially sound. And he remained persuaded that the duty of the church toward the state was above all to help it correct any mistakes it may have made. Like almost all the other official religious leaders, he never crossed the line between criticism and rejection of the Third Reich. He did not stop protesting, pleading, and arguing, but he always did so from within the system.

The handful of churchmen for whom religious conviction became the basis for ideological resistance could be found almost entirely in the marginal dissenting groups within German Protestantism. The Confessing Church, for example, had in the course of the preceding decade become much smaller in size but much bolder in speech. In October 1943 its synod representing the eastern provinces of Prussia issued an "Interpretation of the Fifth Commandment" going far beyond anything that the mainstream religious organizations were prepared to risk. "The divine order," it pronounced defiantly, "does not recognize concepts like 'elimination,' 'liquidation,' and 'worthless life.' The extermination of human beings merely because they are related to a criminal or because they are old or mentally ill or belong to another race is not a [proper] exercise of the power that has been given to the authorities by God." It is an abuse and violation of that power.

The declaration did not stop even at that point. It urged the faithful to extend their help to "old people [as well as the] incurably sick, feeble-minded, and mentally ill." No "public decision" concerning such cases was morally binding on the true Christian, because "the person closest to him is always the one who is helpless and needs him especially without regard for race, nation, and religion." Even "the life of the people of Israel" should be sacred to him. To be sure, Israel had rejected Jesus, "but we human beings or even we Christians are not called on to punish Israel's unbelief." God's commandment to love one's neighbor did not admit any exceptions. No secular authority could override the moral imperative of religious faith.[11]

The most moving expression of spiritual resistance was the petition submitted by members of the Protestant community in Munich to their bishop, Hans Meiser, at Easter 1943. Emboldened perhaps by their ano-nymity, the petitioners denounced not only the official policy of anti-Semi-tism, but also by implication the regime which had approved that policy. "We can as Christians no longer bear it that the church in Germany remains silent regarding the persecutions of the Jews." They confessed themselves "guilty as well" for that silence. But now the time had come for the church to protest against the government's violation of the Ten Commandments, "thereby doing at last what it should have done long ago." The petitioners were simply obeying Jesus' commandment to love all human beings, whether or not they belonged to a particular faith, race, or nationality. Every "non-Aryan"—the word appeared in quotation marks in the original—was like the man in the parable in the Gospels who "fell among thieves." The question before all Germans was whether they would treat him as did the priest and the Levite or as the Samaritan did. No talk about the "Jewish question"—again in quotation marks—could free the Christian from the obligation to face his responsibility.

The duty of the church, the petition argued, was to attest that "the Jewish question is primarily an evangelical and not a political question." The "politically irregular and singular existence and identity of the Jews" derived from the fact that God had chosen them as the instrument of his revelation. The church must bear witness to this fact by assisting the Jews who "fell among thieves" under the Third Reich. It must by the same token oppose "that 'Christian' anti-Semitism" which speaks of "the 'de-served' curse against Israel." Even more important, it must denounce the attempt by the state to "solve" the Jewish question in accordance with its own "homemade political gospel," that is, "to destroy Judaism." The church should proclaim that it is indissolubly bound to Judaism "in guilt and promise." It should no longer seek shelter from the assault directed against Israel. It should attest instead that "along with Israel, it and its Lord Jesus Christ himself are being attacked." The fate of the Jews was inseparable from the fate of the Christians.[12]

The petition of the Munich Protestants is the most remarkable document produced by the religious resistance. It exhibits a touching conjunction of artless faith with indomitable courage. It had no effect on the Nazi policy of genocide, but neither did the authorities make any effort to identify and punish its supporters. It did not seem to them important enough. And yet in its devotion to the ethical and moral imperatives of Christian belief, it stands far above the expedient silence of Galen and Faulhaber or even the loyal opposition of Frings and Wurm. It remains a lasting reminder that spiritual faith can at times withstand even the most intense political intimidation or psychological pressure.

The military reverses suffered by the Third Reich also had the effect of reviving the secular resistance. Defeat freed the soldiers and bureaucrats hostile to the Nazi regime from the dilemma with which they had been grappling for a year and a half. They no longer had to choose between patriotic loyalty and ethical principle. What had before seemed treason now became duty. By seeking to overthrow Hitler they would be saving the nation from defeat rather than depriving it of victory. The Wehrmacht's misfortunes thus led to a renewal of plans, plots, and conspiracies against a government that appeared to be leading Germany to catastrophe. As in the months immediately preceding and immediately following the outbreak of the war, the secular resistance began to prepare for a coup against the Third Reich. The national interest no longer seemed to call for acquiescence. It now demanded subversion.

The reemergence of the movement to overthrow the Nazi regime can be measured by the increased numbers and activities of the resisters. First, there was a sudden influx of new recruits. The most important among them proved to be Claus von Stauffenberg, who finally decided that it might be a mistake to wait until victory had been won before removing Hitler from power. The German defeat before Moscow, and America's entry into the war, helped persuade him that in fact victory would remain unattainable as long as the Third Reich retained authority. Even after its overthrow only a compromise peace would be possible. Stauffenberg resolved therefore sometime in the second half of 1942 to join the resistance.

In addition, those who before the fall of France supported a coup, but then lapsed into acquiescence while victory appeared imminent, finally became rebels once again when defeat reemerged as a distinct possibility.

Thus Schulenburg, at one time a loyal Nazi, reached the conclusion early in 1942 that only a successful coup against the Third Reich could prevent the collapse of Germany. Similarly, Adam von Trott zu Solz, who in 1939 tried to use his contacts in England and America first to help avert and then to help conclude the war, and who remained inactive for the next two years, secretly submitted in the spring of 1942 a memorandum to the British government urging a peace of moderation to be reached after the fall of Hitler. He was once more an active resister.

Finally, there reemerged those whose hostility toward the Third Reich had never abated, but who during the period of German victories had been unable to do more than complain. Beck and Goerdeler are the best examples. The succession of military reverses starting at the end of 1941 enabled them to go beyond futile grumbling. For the next two and a half years they were engrossed in various plots and conspiracies against the Third Reich, which did not end until their mortal failure. Ultimately, only death kept them from witnessing the realization of all their predictions regarding the disastrous consequences of National Socialism.

What motivated most of the resisters, whether new converts or old believers, was above all the fear that the Third Reich was dragging Germany into the abyss. Concern for the national welfare, which previously led them to accept the Nazi regime, now led them to reject it. But they remained what they had always been, ardent patriots determined to protect their country's interests at all costs. Only their perception of how best to protect those interests changed.

Many resisters said as much repeatedly. After the failure of the coup against Hitler, Berthold von Stauffenberg told his interrogators that by 1943 he and his brother Claus had concluded that the war could no longer be won. "We therefore saw the only possibility of reaching a more or less acceptable solution in a prompt conclusion of peace with our [foreign] opponents. It was clear to us that this was not possible under the existing regime. But a change in the system [of government] seemed to us conceivable only through the death of the Führer." They tried to overthrow the Third Reich for the same reason its supporters tried to maintain it, namely, for the welfare of the fatherland.[13]

In essence Henning von Tresckow and Rudolf-Christoph Gersdorff said the same thing to Field Marshal Günther von Kluge in the summer of 1943, when they tried to persuade him to join the resistance. "That man must be gotten rid of." But Kluge would not hear of doing "such a thing." Informed that in fact Gersdorff had only recently tried to assassinate Hitler, he sounded shocked. "Gersdorff, what did you do? How could you do something like that?" The answer was unequivocal. "Because, *Herr Feld-marschall,* we take the position that it is the only way to save the German nation from complete ruin." It was Germany or Hitler.[14]

At about the same time a meeting of several of the resisters in the home of General Friedrich Olbricht—among them Beck, Goerdeler, Schulen-burg, and Erich Fellgiebel of the army headquarters Communications Section—reached the same conclusion. According to the report of the security police a year later, Beck presented his "usual pessimistic picture of the military situation," urging an immediate retreat on all fronts, while Goerdeler maintained that Germany's national debt had grown so huge that "there is simply no longer any solution in this area." Shortly thereafter at another gathering, this one attended also by Hellmuth Stieff and Claus von Stauffenberg, the resisters agreed that "a meeting of the Russians, the English, and the Americans in Berlin and a devastation of Germany must be prevented, and indeed by a forcible coup."[15]

A resolve to save the fatherland from military disaster was thus the most common motive of the resisters. It was not the only one, however. In many cases a revulsion against the ruthlessness of National Socialism reinforced the concern for the national interest. The movement to overthrow the Third Reich, in other words, was not inspired solely by patriotism. The resisters also experienced a growing feeling that the regime had exceeded the bounds of a firm but just exercise of authority, that it had become despotic, fanatical, cruel, and corrupt. It no longer deserved the support of decent, honorable Germans. By violating the norms of political morality, it had forfeited its legitimate claim to power. For the sake not only of the nation but of all humanity, it should be overthrown.

After the failure of the coup, Popitz testified that while he acknowledged the need under some circumstances to restrict personal freedom, "a certain protection under the law in its simplest form would be appropriate even in drastic measures." Schacht declared that he could not accept "the pro-nouncement and execution of verdicts without a legally determined judicial decision." Schulenburg went even further. He deplored "the abandon-ment of the foundation of law and the development [of the Third Reich] into a pure police state," maintaining that "a sphere of freedom must be accorded to the individual, as indeed to every institution, within which he can act in keeping with his conscience." Views such as these clearly expressed more than patriotic loyalty.[16]

The resisters generally denied, however, that their basic convictions had altered since the days a decade earlier when they willingly accepted and served the Hitler government. It was not they but the Nazis who had changed. Hence their present rejection of the Third Reich was as justified as their former support. They had nothing to regret, nothing to apologize for. According to the report of the security police, "the same people frequently assert that despite their fundamental agreement with the chief objectives of the National Socialist Party, their favorable attitude gradually weakened because of the practical methods employed for the achievement [of those objectives]."

In fact, many of those arrested emphasized their rejection of the means but not the ends of the Nazi regime. Wolf Heinrich von Helldorf, chief of the Berlin police, testified that "today, however, I can no longer approve what appears to me to be the realization of National Socialism." Berthold von Stauffenberg was a little bolder. "Almost all of the basic ideas of National Socialism have in their application by the regime become transformed into their opposite." Goerdeler was more cautious. "I along with many of my old colleagues saw dark stains gradually developing in a self-contained ideology." And the aristocratic publicist Karl Ludwig von Guttenberg stood somewhere in between. He accepted National Socialism "as an idea and a program," but he explained that there were "currents and intellectual tendencies within the party" that had made it impossible for him to join it "with complete conviction." All maintained that the Nazis were actually the ones who had abandoned the original sound ideas and goals of the Third Reich.[17]

Accordingly, they did not propose to replace the National Socialist regime with a new experiment in popular democracy. The last thing they wanted was another Weimar Republic. They remained profoundly suspicious of any form of government dependent on the whims and caprices of the ignorant masses. They hoped for a system of rule based on principles extolled by the defenders of the conservative tradition in Central Europe: authority without despotism, obedience without servility, loyalty without fanaticism, and forcefulness without brutality.

Regarding the views of Claus von Stauffenberg, there is the testimony of Hans Bernd Gisevius, not always a reliable witness, to be sure, but one who knew him personally in the days when both were prominent members of the resistance. "To put it briefly, the nation should [in Stauffenberg's view] remain soldierly and become socialistic. . . . Stauffenberg wants the military dictatorship of the 'true' National Socialists. . . . He does not want to renounce either the totalitarian or the military element or Socialism." His brother Berthold sounded by contrast moderate and flexible. "The new regime," he argued, "must be oriented more toward the bourgeois middle and must place Christianity more clearly in the foreground."

While Schulenburg remained vague regarding the future government of Germany, he did insist that "we must become the standard-bearers against Bolshevism in domestic affairs as well." What he meant was that "we will get rid of everything internally that is incapable of representing this higher [political] order in its personnel and its institutions." Accordingly, the National Socialist Party and the SS would have to be replaced by more reliable and controllable instruments of authoritarian rule. Canaris, by contrast, had few ideological scruples. All he wanted was the removal of Hitler from power as the precondition for a negotiated peace with the Allies. He was prepared to accept a liberalized Nazi state under the leadership of Göring and even contemplated approaching Heinrich Himmler and the Gestapo for the purpose of executing a coup. All in all, the great majority of the resisters sought a traditional conservative regime, honest, responsible, dependable, and disciplined.[18]

Many of them had still another reason for overthrowing the Third Reich. They were repelled not only by its oppressive measures at home but by its harsh policies abroad. The brutality of the German administration of conquered Europe seemed to them reprehensible, partly because it was unwise, but mostly because it was immoral. They criticized the injustices and cruelties the Nazi authorities tolerated or initiated in the occupied countries. Their indignation at the conduct of the regime toward the foreign populations under its domination was expressed in numerous statements both before and after the failure of their coup. They cannot be fairly charged with indifference to the racial excesses of National Socialism.

Thus the police inquiry into the resistance following its collapse reported that "the problems of the administration of the occupied areas and of the treatment of other nationalities play a large part in the criticism of National Socialism." In the case of Cäsar von Hofacker, the dissident industrialist and mutinous soldier, this took the form of the contention that the inept policies of the occupation authorities had squandered away "critical opportunities to bring about a sound relationship with France." Now the German nation would have to pay a heavy price for that mistake.

Claus von Stauffenberg criticized the regime more severely. A document found by the security police after the failed coup, unsigned but ascribed to him, declared that "the beginning of the end of our entire military development came in the Russian campaign, which started with the order to kill all commissars and then continued with the starving of prisoners of war and the organizing of raids on people for the purpose of obtaining civilian workers." Hassell confided in his diary his feeling of revulsion at the brutal occupation policies of the Third Reich. "The SS continues to behave in

Poland in an unbelievably shameful way," he wrote. "Now as before, the Polish 'intelligentsia' is being systematically decimated." Yorck declared after his arrest that "some of the actions we took in the occupied areas . . . had alienated me completely from the National Socialist state." There are many other instances of condemnation by the resisters of the Nazi regime's treatment of conquered Europe.[19]

They were especially shocked by the extermination of the Jews. Here was evidence of a cruelty more hideous than any of which they had believed the Third Reich capable. Their abhorrence appears over and over again in their conversations and writings. Stieff expressed it frequently in his letters to his wife. "Every other day," he cried out with revulsion, "a train with Jews [leaves Germany] for Minsk and then [abandons] them to their fate. . . . All of that must some day exact a retribution from us, and justly so." Tresckow, one of his friends recalled years later, said that what had led him and the others to attempt the overthrow of the Hitler dictatorship was not primarily the war, which was after all an officer's business, but the extermination of "tens of thousands of Jews" in the "most horrible way." Claus von Stauffenberg did not go quite so far, but he did express outrage at a directive issued by Ernst Kaltenbrunner, head of the security police, "which orders 'special treatment' in Auschwitz for 40,000 or 42,000 Hungarian Jews." And Hassell reported, appalled, that "countless Jews are being gassed in buildings constructed especially for that purpose, at least 100,000." That seemed almost unbelievable.[20]

But none of the resisters was as deeply affected by the final solution as the young officer Axel von dem Bussche-Streithorst, one of the handful of survivors of the failed attempt on Hitler's life. Soon after the war he described how the pogroms he had witnessed in Poland and the Soviet Union turned him against the Nazi regime. Especially horrifying was the extermination of Jews in the town of Dubno in the Ukraine. He had seen how two to three thousand of them were forced to lie down in mass graves, one on top of the other in long rows, to be shot in the back of the neck by members of an SS death squad. Then came a hunt for the few who had managed to survive by hiding. "A woman begged me, literally on her knees, to save her life. I could not help her." The memory of that awful moment continued to haunt Bussche for the rest of his life.[21]

Yet what most of the resisters objected to was not anti-Semitism but genocide. In the days of Weimar they had generally shared the view that Jews were acquiring an excessive influence in the life of Germany. Something had to be done to restrict their role in government, economy, and culture. Many members of the resistance continued to believe that there was indeed a Jewish problem to be solved, but judiciously, legally, and humanely. Segregation and exclusion were among the acceptable means of dealing with it; extermination was not. What they found appalling, in other words, was the palpable, hideous reality of mass murder: the pleas, curses, groans, and screams, the shooting, gassing, bloodshed, and carnage.

The findings of the inquiry by the security police into the failed coup support this conclusion. Its report of October 28, 1944, states that "in very many interrogations regarding the attitude [of the resisters] toward National Socialism there is the repeated assertion that they were in general certainly no friends of the Jews, but the 'brutal,' 'excessive,' and 'extreme' actions regarding the Jewish question and the 'clinging to the crazy idea about Jews' were the reason for arousing the hatred of the entire world against us." In their opinion, "the solution to the Jewish problem should have been reached much more calmly, soberly, and 'properly,' and . . . especially the so-called 'decent Jew' should have been treated differently from the profiteer and the East European Jew." On the question of anti-Semitism, as on so many other policies of the Third Reich, the resisters objected most to the means, not the ends, the methods, not the goals.[22]

And that raises a broader question, a question which cannot be answered with any certainty, but which cannot be entirely ignored either. Would the resisters have been as ready to risk their lives to overthrow the Nazi regime, if, though oppressive and brutal, it had continued to be militarily successful? Would they have then been willing to endanger the security of their own country in the name of a transcendent or universal morality? Probably not. They were too committed to the traditional values of their class and society. They were too loyal to their inherited ideals of service to the state and sacrifice for the fatherland. Only their gradual recognition of the hopeless situation of the resistance freed them ultimately from the ideological yoke of patriotic duty and national allegiance.

19

Searching for a Negotiated Peace

As their country's military situation continued to deteriorate, many of the resisters became increasingly preoccupied with the problem of how to defeat the regime without defeating the state, how to destroy the Third Reich without destroying Germany. They agreed that victory on the battlefield was no longer possible, usually blaming Hitler for that. Yet they directed their criticism generally at the conduct rather than the aim of the war. After all, who could condemn an armed struggle being waged to reconquer Danzig, eliminate the Polish Corridor, and liberate fellow Germans from the harsh rule of Poland? The annexation of Alsace-Lorraine could be justified as well, both historically and strategically. Even the invasion of the Soviet Union, though poorly planned, no doubt, and needlessly brutal, was above all a crusade in defense of European civilization. The true source of the danger threatening the fatherland was the Führer's inept leadership. He was doctrinaire, stubborn, and ruthless. He refused to listen to the advice of trained and experienced soldiers. He remained convinced that all that was needed to win was the will to win. Only removing him from power, therefore, could save the nation from defeat.

That conviction was a decisive factor in persuading the resisters to undertake the coup of July 20, 1944. According to a memorandum by Claus von Stauffenberg, "a defeat and the destruction of the material and human resources [of Germany] are inevitable, if we continue on the present course." In fact, "the fate threatening us can be averted only through the removal of the present leadership, [which] was unable to avoid a two-front war. The current regime has no right to drag down the entire German nation in its own collapse." In private conversation he was even more blunt. "It is indeed unprecedented in the history of a nation," a secretary recalled him saying, "that its leader constantly issues orders which will bring his nation ever closer to collapse." By now the only way out for Germany was the overthrow of the Third Reich.[1]

Berthold von Stauffenberg, who survived the coup long enough to be interrogated by the security police, shared his brother's views. He too believed that Hitler's conduct of the war not only made a German victory impossible, but was also making a German defeat unavoidable. In a discussion with Lieutenant Colonel Robert Bernardis, he maintained that "the Führer can no longer master the situation. The war in its present form is militarily lost." And who was responsible for that? "The Führer has issued an order that every inch of ground must be held," he was reported telling Captain Alfred Kranzfelder of the German navy. "This will exhaust the last reserves of energy of the troops. It would be better to withdraw in time and offer new resistance in a more favorable position. . . . If things go on in this way, the eastern front will collapse." The conclusion was obvious. "The Führer would have to go."[2]

General Olbricht agreed completely. At a meeting in his office with Claus von Stauffenberg, General Hans-Günther von Rost, and First Lieutenant Heinz-Günther Albrecht, he declared that the military situation of Germany was "totally hopeless." The vital interests of the nation might still be protected, but there was no way of avoiding the "approaching catastrophe" except through a coup d'état. Saying that he knew very well what the consequences of the failure of such an attempt would be for him and his family, Olbricht pronounced himself ready "to risk his neck in spite of that." Clearly, although the Allies would never agree to negotiate with Hitler, they might be willing to consider a compromise settlement with an anti-Nazi government in Germany. Therefore the only hope of saving the nation from defeat, surrender, and occupation was the overthrow of the Third Reich.[3]

The resisters were admittedly motivated by more than patriotism and the desire to save their nation from the results of Hitler's reckless and ruthless foreign policy. They opposed as well his despotic rule at home, his brutal oppression abroad, and the shocking cruelty of his racial program. But the primary consideration in their willingness to risk their lives in a coup against the Nazi regime was in most cases the resolve to protect the fatherland against the consequences of military defeat.

"In the fall of last year it was already clear to my brother and me that the war cannot be won," Berthold von Stauffenberg told his interrogators after his arrest. The only chance of preventing the collapse of Germany was "a prompt conclusion of peace." But that would be impossible as long as the Nazi regime remained in power. Hence some sort of "change in the system" was essential, and that could be achieved only through Hitler's death. Assassination, in other words, became a patriotic duty, because only through assassination "would the executive power be taken over by the Wehrmacht."

But what then? What would happen once the Third Reich had been overthrown? Claus von Stauffenberg had a clear answer. "After a change in regime," he wrote, "the most important goal will be to ensure that Germany continues to be a significant power factor in the interaction of [diplomatic] forces, and especially that the Wehrmacht remains a useful instrument in the hands of its leaders." The nation still had "various political opportunities" for exploiting the ideological differences among the Allies, but those opportunities were shrinking with each successive military defeat. "Quick action is therefore necessary." As the official inquiry put it, "the longer they discussed it, the clearer it became to the [resisters] that any attempt to overthrow National Socialism in order to make the Reich 'acceptable' as a negotiating partner with the enemy side would have a chance of success only in the event of the death of the Führer." And the sooner the death, the better the chance.[4]

The task before the resisters was thus to replace the Hitler dictatorship with a form of political authority capable of inspiring confidence in Washington and London. That meant broadening the social and ideological basis of their movement by including anti-Nazi elements from the republican era and by adopting a program unequivocally rejecting the goals and doctrines of National Socialism. In pursuing this strategy they were not being disingenuous. They sincerely opposed the oppressiveness and brutality of the Third Reich. But they knew that how the opposition defined and expressed itself would have an important effect on their chances for a compromise peace.

Berthold von Stauffenberg argued that although the war was militarily lost, a satisfactory settlement could still be achieved by diplomatic means, with one precondition. "Opportunities to negotiate regarding issues of foreign policy would arise only if the present regime were replaced by another." Once that happened, the prospects for peace would become much brighter. "In what direction we should negotiate diplomatically must be determined by the situation, and indeed in such a way that the tensions which undoubtedly exist among our opponents are in some way exploited." The establishment of an anti-Nazi regime in Germany, he remained convinced, was bound to weaken the uneasy Allied coalition.

Claus von Stauffenberg agreed with his brother. That the war could no longer be won by armed force seemed clear to him. Still, "various political possibilities existed in the exploitation of the contradictions within the enemy camp." Those possibilities arose from the irreconcilable differences between middle-class democracy and lower-class radicalism. But the opportunity to derive advantage from those differences was shrinking with every new defeat of the Wehrmacht. A successful invasion of Western Europe by the Americans and the British would destroy it completely. "Swift action is therefore essential." Both Stauffenbergs believed, moreover, along with most other members of what the police report described as the "clique of traitors," that supreme authority in the state must shift from Hitler to the generals "in order to provide the basis for a negotiated peace."

The strategy of the resisters thus rested on the assumption that the Allies could be persuaded to conclude a peace of reconciliation with a German government repudiating the Third Reich. The police investigation into the failed coup described with disdain how "the clique of conspirators imagined that the enemy, after the elimination of National Socialism, would negotiate with the Reich on even terms. They counted heavily on the effect abroad of propaganda to this end." Everything depended, however, on the continuing military effectiveness of the Wehrmacht. The resisters feared above all that the Russian front might collapse before they succeeded in "pitting politically the eastern and the western enemy against each other." The Stauffenbergs in particular argued that any hope of reaching a separate agreement with one or another member of the enemy coalition could be realized only as long as "the fronts remain intact," a condition that was proving increasingly difficult. "A two-front war is becoming in the long run unsustainable." A coup would therefore have to be undertaken promptly, while there was still something to negotiate about.

Although the resisters often talked about the need to reach an understanding "with one of the two opponents," there was no question which one they preferred. The Soviet Union remained for them the embodiment of radicalism and materialism, which they had always opposed. They had therefore been troubled by Hitler's pact with Stalin in 1939, however advantageous militarily. Should they now follow the Führer's example? Should they too subordinate principle to expediency? Their distrust of the Kremlin reflected their political, economic, and social—as well as ideological—convictions. They recognized that a major expansion of the Kremlin's influence in Europe would pose a serious threat to their own class and society. It would promote ideas and policies even more dangerous for them than those of National Socialism. They would be exchanging one form of tyranny for another. An understanding with Russia was therefore only a last resort, a measure of utter desperation. "They did not think at that time about the possibility of negotiating with the Soviet Union," according to the inquiry into the coup. "The danger of Bolshevism was such that coming to terms with the Soviet Union would be synonymous with ruin."

An agreement with the Western democracies seemed much more logical to the resisters. Not only did they have common beliefs regarding state, economy, and society, but they had common fears regarding the spread of Communism. Berthold von Stauffenberg, for example, felt sure that "negotiations with England can be arranged, because it cannot afford to hand over Europe to the Soviets." Admittedly, the British would have nothing to do with Germany as long as Hitler remained at the helm. But once he was removed, there should be no difficulty in reaching an understanding. "Stauffenberg was at that time of the opinion that we would be acceptable in an alliance only as long as the Reich can effectively oppose Bolshevism." The coup against the Nazi regime thus had to take place while the German army was still strong enough "to provide the basis for a negotiated peace."[5]

The resisters did not regard military effectiveness, however, as the only requirement for successful negotiations with the Western democracies. They also had to demonstrate that they had substantial popular support, that they were more than a small conspiratorial group of dissident soldiers and bureaucrats. Their political credibility would be greatly enhanced if they could persuade Washington and London that they represented a broad-based coalition of important interests and forces in German society. As leaders of a united front of various anti-Nazi groups, they would probably prove acceptable to the Allies. As an isolated faction of old-school conservatives who had supported Hitler in the high noon of his success and then turned against him in the twilight of defeat, they were likely to be rejected. The resisters thus had to claim greater social and ideological diversity than they in fact possessed.

That need is reflected in the secret letter, written in English, that Adam von Trott zu Solz gave at the end of April 1942 to Willem Adolph Visser't Hooft, general secretary of the World Council of Churches in Geneva, for transmittal to the British government. He conceded, at least by implication, that the attitude of the resisters toward the Third Reich had not always been above reproach. Perhaps they should have been less complacent, less shortsighted, less timid. "We do not intend to justify our own position, we are ready to accept our due share of responsibility and of guilt." But now the time had come for "responsible groups in the West" to extend support to "those forces in Germany which have consistently fought against Nihilism and its national socialist manifestations." Trott explained that "for obvious reasons" he could not provide in his letter the names of those who had joined the resistance. Nevertheless, "it can be said here that our support is drawn from the following groups: (1) Substantial parts of the working class (2) Influential circles in the army and bureaucracy (3) The militant groups in the churches." Trott meant to convey the impression that the movement to overthrow the Third Reich had a broad social and ideological foundation.[6]

Yet he himself must have known better. The claim that the resistance included "influential circles in the army and bureaucracy" was accurate enough, though he preferred not to elaborate on the size of their membership. But the statement that "the militant groups in the churches" supported it as well, while technically correct, was at least misleading. No prominent Catholic churchmen had joined those plotting against Hitler, and as for the Protestants, only a few fringe groups in the Confessing Church went much beyond occasional sermons condemning euthanasia and genocide. Finally, the assertion that "substantial parts of the working class" supported the resistance was at best wishful thinking and more likely deliberate overstatement. To be sure, most of the leaders of the Socialist trade unions under Weimar remained at heart opponents of National Socialism; some of them were eventually even recruited into the resistance. But there is no evidence that the rank and file of the old labor movement shared their sympathies and hopes. Trott's letter was in fact not a sober assessment of political opinion in Germany but a calculated attempt to win diplomatic support in Britain.

Similar considerations influenced the resisters in planning for the provisional government they intended to establish after Hitler's overthrow. At first the problem seemed simple. Once the Third Reich had fallen, the Wehrmacht would assume political authority in Germany until peace with the Allies could be concluded. But as their plans matured, they recognized that to win popular support at home and diplomatic acceptance abroad, the provisional government would have to include representatives of the old anti-Nazi parliamentary parties, especially the largest of those parties, the Social Democrats. This conclusion did not come easily to some of them. They had long been critical of the Weimar Republic, whose weaknesses they considered to be the basic cause of the rise of National Socialism. But they could see no alternative. According to the police investigation, "Goerdeler considered it essential that, going beyond a connection to the trade unions, contact with circles of the former Social

Democratic Party must be made." How else were they to create the appearance of a broad political coalition?[7]

A comparison of the lists of possible members of the provisional government prepared in January 1943, August 1943, January 1944, and July 1944, as well as an undated list found by the Gestapo after the failed attempt on Hitler's life, reveal that the resisters envisioned a one-sided partnership dominated by traditional conservatives, with the Socialists providing a facade of democratic and reformist respectability. Beck was to be the head of state, while the chancellorship would go to Goerdeler. Wilhelm Leuschner, the former leader of the Socialist trade unions, was proposed as vice-chancellor, with Peter Yorck von Wartenburg serving as his undersecretary, advising him, guiding him, and keeping him out of mischief. Similarly, while Julius Leber, who had been a Social Democratic member of the Reichstag until 1933, was to become minister of the interior, his undersecretary would be Fritz-Dietlof von der Schulenburg, who had once belonged to the National Socialist Party.

The other leading positions in the provisional government were all assigned to tried, reliable conservatives. The foreign minister would be either Hassell or Friedrich Werner von der Schulenburg, the former German ambassador to Moscow; the finance minister, either Popitz or the nationalist businessman Ewald Loeser; the minister of war, General Hoepner or General Olbricht; and chief of police, Helldorf or Tresckow. There was little danger of a government such as that embarking on risky experiments in popular democracy.

The resisters considered a few members of other anti-Nazi groups for posts in the provisional government. On one of the lists appears the name of Kurt von Schuschnigg, the former chancellor of Austria, as nominee for the ministry of cultural and religious affairs. On another, Adam Stegerwald, who had been prominent in the Catholic labor movement under the Weimar Republic, was included as minister of transportation. Still, a handful of Socialists and a sprinkling of clericalists could not disguise the fact that the political outlook of most of the resisters was closer to Bismarck or Hindenburg than to republican statesmen like Friedrich Ebert or Matthias Erzberger. The composition of the proposed provisional government was broad enough to create the appearance of an anti-Nazi united front, but without the risk of a new venture into republicanism like the one that had failed a decade earlier.[8]

The incongruence between the image of ideological diversity and the reality of ideological uniformity helps account for the reluctance of the resisters to prepare a detailed blueprint of the form of government with which to replace the Third Reich. To try to do so would have revealed the incompatibility of their own political objectives with those of the democratic opponents of National Socialism at home and abroad. It would have led to disputes and divisions within the anti-Nazi coalition even before the struggle against the Hitler dictatorship had been won. Hence discussion of the ultimate objectives of the resistance had to be postponed until victory. And that restricted for the time being plans regarding the future of the nation to those few issues on which the various opponents of the Third Reich, conservatives as well as liberals, Germans as well as non-Germans, basically agreed.

The most obvious was the need to put an end to the lawless and brutal methods employed by the Nazi regime. On this subject no difference of opinion existed among the resisters. The official inquiry into the coup reported that "within the reactionary circle of conspirators there was either an absolute lack of understanding regarding the forms and extent of the activity of the state police or a view that was deliberately distorted for purposes of agitation." Those arrested actually had the temerity to "impute directly" that the Gestapo "is exercising arbitrary rule and is acting in fact out of personal rather than objective motives." The SS officer preparing the report seemed shocked by accusations that appeared to him obviously unfair and unfounded.

Yet the resisters did in fact consider the Hitler government to be tyrannical. Among Goerdeler's papers seized by the police was the draft of a proclamation to the German people charging the Third Reich with brutality against its own citizens. "Countless Germans have for years been languishing in concentration camps, exposed to the greatest torments and often subjected to terrible torture." Nikolaus von Üxkull-Gyllenbrand, an uncle of the Stauffenbergs, testified after his arrest that he believed that "the future government must be entirely different from the present regime precisely in the administration of justice, and no feelings of personal malice or antipathy should play a part." As for those accused of crimes against the state, in his opinion "arrests and incarceration in concentration camps should under no circumstances take place in the same form and to the same extent as at the present time." None of the resisters would have quarreled with that view. Some might actually have thought it too restrained or too cautious or even too calculating.[9]

They agreed, moreover, that it was not enough to put an end to the crimes being committed by the Third Reich. The men responsible for those crimes had to be punished as well. The resisters insisted that the new government to be established after Hitler's overthrow must bring to justice all officials guilty of sanctioning brutalities and atrocities. They were to be tried, condemned, and imprisoned or executed. Nothing less could expiate the sins of the Nazi regime.

The Kreisau Circle, the most liberal group within the resistance, concluded at a meeting in June 1943 that punishment by due process of law for those responsible for the criminal activities of National Socialism had become a solemn moral obligation. It was of the utmost importance for the German nation to impose "on its own initiative" an "appropriate punishment for the violation of justice." The adoption of a "retroactive German penal provision" was therefore essential for the pronouncement through established legal procedures of a "prison sentence or death penalty" against "the violator of the law." This measure would apply to anyone who knowingly disregarded the "essential principles of divine or natural law, the law of nations, or the positive law generally agreed upon in the community of nations." Nor could an accused claim immunity from prosecution because he was obeying orders, unless evidence showed "a direct threat to [his] person or life, or unless some other form of coercion was exerted." The legal principles enunciated here resembled those adopted two years later by the victorious Allies for the postwar trials of war criminals.[10]

The other members of the resistance approved of them as well. On this point little difference existed between the liberal and the conservative wing of the anti-Nazi movement. Üxkull-Gyllenbrand declared matter-of-factly that "the personages of the present National Socialist regime should be tried by an established legal procedure." Goerdeler was much more vehement, in part because he was expressing his views not like Üxkull-Gyllenbrand in prison before a police interrogator, but in the secret draft of an address composed in 1942, which was to be read over the radio only after Hitler's fall. At least there can be no question about the sincerity of his statement:

> The sword of justice must pitilessly strike those who have made of our fatherland a travesty of a political system, who have banished justice and decency from the throne, who have tolerated and promoted corruption, who have shamelessly enriched themselves while the people suffered privation and bled and sacrificed their sons, who have, in committing horrible crimes against life, honor, and faith, tortured, mutilated, and destroyed human beings created in God's image just as we are, who have abused the power of the state, and who, while protecting themselves and their miserable gang, have sacrificed almost three million Germans in the bloody battles of this accursed war. . . . Therefore, in order to reestablish law, justice, and decency, in order to regain

that sense of security which can be gained only when everyone knows that he is responsible for his actions and omissions, we should examine the responsibility of all those in leading positions who received and executed without objection orders that they knew were contrary to law, conscience, or experience.

Goerdeler's radio address, though destined never to be delivered, remains one of the most forceful and eloquent indictments by the resistance of the inhumanity of the Third Reich.[11]

Declarations of sympathy for the Nazi regime's victims often accompanied expressions of outrage at its pitilessness. The resisters did not restrict their commiseration to Germans who were being persecuted because of suspicions regarding their loyalty or patriotism. They included as well foreigners suffering under the ruthlessness and exploitation of the Third Reich's occupation authorities. All those oppressed by National Socialism, regardless of nationality or race, were to be liberated, all were to be vindicated, all were to be avenged. The men seeking the overthrow of the Hitler dictatorship insisted over and over again on this sworn intention.

For example, the government declaration they proposed to issue after seizing power stated unequivocally that "the decent treatment of all human beings is necessary for the maintenance of justice and decency." National Socialism had violated that principle, however. "We consider it a profound dishonor to the German name that in the occupied areas, behind the back of the fighting troops and through the abuse of their protection, crimes of all sorts have been committed. The honor of our fallen soldiers has thereby been besmirched." And this had occurred under a regime that never tired of preaching about national pride and dignity.

The new anti-Nazi government would know how to deal with those who had disgraced their country by their rapacity and corruption. "Whoever has used the period of the war to fill his pockets abroad or has in any other way deviated a single inch from the path of honor will be held accountable." Officials who persisted in abusing their authority in the territories under German occupation would soon discover how different the new regime was from the old. "Punishment will be especially severe for those who from this moment on are caught in any sort of violation of the general rules of international law or of the laws of humaneness." The cruel methods of administration employed by the Third Reich would no longer be tolerated.

In the draft of his undelivered radio address, Goerdeler sounded equally stern. "We will also hold responsible those who, while abroad, have been guilty of any sort of violation of international law, honor, and the duty of a decent human being." As for the victims of Nazi tyranny, they must be immediately restored to their rights and freedoms. "The foreign workers who are in Germany will at once be given full equality in every respect with the German worker. Our nation must show that it abhors the exploitation and plundering of other nations which the Hitler dictatorship has practiced, and that it is ready to assuage their violated sense of honor and restore their violated rights." Those who had been conscripted for forced labor in the Third Reich would be free to return to their native countries, provided their repatriation could be carried out in an orderly fashion and the prior approval of their home governments could be obtained. At all events, the exploitation of the conquered Continent by the Nazi regime would come to an end.[12]

The resisters were especially sensitive to the atrocities committed against the Jews. Their condemnation of those atrocities cannot be ascribed to calculation or expediency. It expressed a heartfelt, sincere conviction. The "government declaration" found among their papers by the Nazi authorities states outright that "in past years an injustice was undoubtedly committed in Germany on a large scale through the expropriation, destruction, etc., of Jewish property and life, an injustice that we cannot defend before our conscience and before history." Those responsible for it should be punished. "Whoever thought he could enrich himself with Jewish property will learn that it is a disgrace for any German to seek such dishonest gain. In truth, the German people want to have nothing to do with the pillagers and hyenas among the human beings created by God." The resisters disavowed the Nazi regime's anti-Semitic policy unequivocally.

Indeed, the police official preparing the report on the failed coup could hardly believe what he was reading. "It is not the Jews but the Germans who are meant" by the "pillagers and hyenas," he noted incredulously. As for the implications of the declaration, "this means in practice the return of former Jewish property to the Jews, and the condemnation or punishment of Germans who have taken over parts of the former property of Jews." How could anyone in good faith defend claims to possessions that had been acquired through Semitic cunning and rapacity?[13]

The most persistent critic among the resisters of National Socialism's racial program was Goerdeler. The conservative bureaucrat who had once been the supporter and ally of the Third Reich, who had once advised Hitler on how to practice bigotry unobtrusively, how to be an anti-Semite without appearing to be one, emerged as an uncompromising opponent of the regime's policy of genocide. Perhaps he felt uneasy or even guilty about having contributed to the rise to power of a political system capable of organized mass murder. Whatever the reason, no one in the resistance displayed greater concern regarding the tragic fate of European Jewry.

As in the case of many of the resisters, the decisive factor shaping his attitude was not the abstract injustice of racial bigotry, but the direct, palpable experience of anti-Semitic brutality. His account of the deportation of the Leipzig Jews in January 1942 to the death camps of Eastern Europe reveals the inner revulsion of a man suddenly realizing the full horrors of genocide. The victims—men, women, and children alike—were transported in open trucks and cattle cars in the dead of winter to the killing fields of Poland. Among them was an elderly lady "whose brother, formerly a university professor here, had been seriously wounded in the last war and had received the Iron Cross, First Class." How many perished during the terrible journey eastward was unknown. "But horror fills the soul, when one thinks of the feelings of fathers and mothers seeing their children freezing and starving before their eyes." Nothing in the history of mankind could compare with this brutality, except perhaps "the persecution of the Christians under Diocletian."

Goerdeler's sense of abhorrence grew with the increasingly murderous application of the final solution. Eighteen months later, in July 1943, he described in the draft of a letter to Field Marshal Günther von Kluge a report he had heard from an SS soldier, barely eighteen years old and "formerly a decent fellow," who calmly declared that it was "not exactly nice to spray with a machine gun ditches filled with thousands of Jews and then to throw earth on the still twitching corpses." To Goerdeler that seemed so hideous as to be almost beyond belief. "What have they done to the proud army of the Wars of Liberation and of Emperor Wilhelm I!" he cried out. Of all the crimes committed by National Socialism, racial mass murder appalled him the most.[14]

The immediate changes in government policy that the resisters planned to introduce are thus clear. The oppressive rule of the Nazi regime would come to an end; those responsible for the atrocities it had perpetrated would be tried and punished; the countries conquered by the Wehrmacht would receive a greater measure of self-determination; and the program of anti-Semitic genocide would not only be abandoned but condemned and denounced. But what then? What would the future political structure of Germany look like?

Here the evidence is not nearly as conclusive. The members of the resistance preferred not to discuss in detail the form of political authority that should ultimately replace the Third Reich. For one thing, they were too preoccupied with plans and preparations for the overthrow of the

Hitler dictatorship. Yet, even more important, they recognized that any attempt to define the civic principles the new regime should embrace would have a divisive effect. It was not only likely to alienate important groups and interests in German society, but it might arouse the suspicions and criticisms of Allied statesmen with whom they hoped to negotiate a peace of reconciliation. All in all, it seemed best to avoid debate regarding the future constitution of the nation.

The small liberal faction within the resistance did consider this question from time to time, but its conclusions rarely went beyond ringing pronouncements or broad, amorphous principles. In his letter of April 1942 to the British government, for example, Trott spoke of the need for "self-government and decentralization within Germany." That meant, he explained somewhat ambiguously, "breaking up of the masses by the creation of smaller and greater units of local self-administration," as well as the "application of modern socialist principles in all sectors of political and economic life."

The proclamation expressing the views of the Kreisau Circle, which the Hessian Socialist Carlo Mierendorff drafted in the summer of 1943, was almost equally vague. It referred to a "socialist regulation of the economy" designed to realize "human dignity and political freedom," and to ensure a "secure existence for the clerical employees and workers in industry and agriculture and for the peasant on his land." This was an essential precondition for "social justice and freedom." In addition, the "expropriation of key enterprises in heavy industry" would end the "pernicious abuse of the political power of big business." The economy as a whole should be reorganized on the principle of self-administration with "equal participation for the working population as the fundamental element in a socialist order." The new regime, moreover, would protect agriculture against the danger of becoming "the plaything of capitalistic interests." Finally, the general welfare of the nation required a "reduction in bureaucratic centralism" and an "organic reconstruction of the Reich based on the member states."

What did all this mean? The proclamation included not a single word about the scope of the authority of the head of government, nothing about the establishment of a legislative assembly, nothing about the franchise or the system of voting, nothing about civil rights and freedoms. Even the use of the word "socialist" was ambiguous. Did it denote public ownership of the means of production and transportation or simply greater social equality and closer state supervision of the economy? It is hard to tell.[15]

The views of the conservative majority in the resistance were still more obscure. Even the police authorities investigating the failed coup, despite repeated interrogations and cross-examinations of the prisoners, remained unsure about their intentions regarding the future political system. "Whether the form of government was to be monarchical or nonmonarchical is unclear on the basis of the inquiries conducted so far," the official report concluded. "The question was left open by the clique of conspirators, and was only to be clarified later." Still, the class origin of the "leading personalities" among the resisters, their "family and social ties" to the former ruling dynasties, their "basic political attitude," and their use of terms like "imperial regent" or "general viceroy" seemed to suggest that ultimately "the establishment of a monarchy was envisioned." That was as far as those conducting the investigation were prepared to go.[16]

Their confusion is understandable. Not only were the members of the resistance reluctant to engage in debate about the future government of Germany, but what little they had to say was often in language so cryptic or recondite or mystical as to be almost incomprehensible. Claus von Stauffenberg, according to Gisevius, sought "the salvation of Germany through political officers who reject corruption and mismanagement, who strive for an orderly military leadership, and who can inspire the nation to make a last stand." The state should be both "soldierly" and "socialistic," both "totalitarian" and "military," rescuing the "betrayed cause" while at the same time maintaining a dictatorship of "'true' National Socialists." What did all this impenetrable rhetoric mean? Schulenburg sounded still more rapturous. If the resistance should fail to overthrow the Nazi regime, then its members "must take an oath and form an 'order,'" so that even under foreign occupation "a group of men who know one another and who, without external ties, are firmly devoted to the fatherland" would remain united in unshakable patriotic loyalty. The words echoed that abstruse, exalted discourse often heard in conservative nationalist circles during the last days of Weimar.[17]

These scattered bits and pieces of evidence point to the conclusion that if the coup against Hitler had succeeded, the resisters would in all probability have established a traditional conservative regime, honest and responsible, but elitist and hierarchical, resembling the old empire, though without an emperor, or, better still, resembling the presidential semidictatorship of the period immediately preceding the Third Reich. Clearly, they would not have agreed to a republican form of government like that of the 1920s, no matter how much more efficient or bold or effective. Most of them remained convinced that popular democracy must sooner or later lead to the rise of unscrupulous demagogues and rabble-rousers. The experience of the last twenty years only strengthened them in that conviction. They essentially wanted a return to the old, traditional virtues of German political life: selflessness, responsibility, duty, sacrifice, and obedience.

Would a new regime in Berlin representing those old virtues have been acceptable to the Allies? The resisters thought so. They reasoned, not altogether without foundation, that what the opposing side wanted to see established in Germany was a government that was clearly anti-Nazi but not necessarily anti-authoritarian. After all, the Soviet Union was hardly a model of democracy. And if Stalin could promote the formation of a "National Committee for a Free Germany" made up largely of conservative and aristocratic Wehrmacht officers who had been taken prisoner by the Red Army, were Roosevelt and Churchill likely to prove less flexible, less pragmatic? As for the demand for unconditional surrender issued by the Allies at the Casablanca Conference in January 1943, the resisters did not regard it as unalterable. There might still be room for negotiation, for compromise, for give-and-take. The important thing was to get rid of Hitler as soon as possible, while Germany still had something of value with which to bargain and barter.

A few members of the resistance did believe that an Allied military victory was not only inevitable but desirable. How else could the crimes of the Third Reich be expiated? In a memorandum of December 1943 intended for Roosevelt, Moltke announced his agreement with the views of the American president. Overcome by horror at the Nazi atrocities, filled with guilt and contrition, he wrote that "the [Kreisau Circle] considers an indisputable military defeat and an occupation of Germany absolutely essential for moral and political reasons." Hence the demand of the Allies for unconditional surrender was "justified," whereas "negotiations regarding peace terms are out of the question." He and the others were "pro–Anglo-Saxon" because "there is far-reaching agreement between our group and the Allies on the ideals that underlie our view of the world and on our basic views and goals regarding the future of the world, of Europe, and of Germany." The interests of "a future free and democratic Germany" coincided with those of the Allies, so that "a productive collaboration [between them] must and will of necessity result."[18]

There is no record that Roosevelt ever saw this memorandum, but if he did, he must have been pleased. Most resisters, however, would have found Moltke's views almost as reprehensible as most Nazis would have. For the resisters insisted to the end on a clear distinction between the unpardonable political crimes of the Third Reich and the justifiable territorial demands of Germany. Indeed, the rejection of the demands had led to the commission of the crimes. The need for a revision of the nation's frontiers emerged long before Hitler came to power and would continue long after he fell, unless a new peace treaty established boundaries more equitable than those dictated at Versailles. The resisters in fact intended the overthrow of the Nazi regime to facilitate the attainment of that objective.

The civilians among them were generally more explicit than the soldiers regarding the peace terms they hoped to obtain. The latter were too busy waging war and preparing a coup to worry about territorial disputes or frontier rectifications. But from time to time one or another would make some casual remark, some offhand observation, some brief allusion indicating that the plan to overthrow the Nazi regime did not in any way signify a willingness to return to the boundaries that had existed before its establishment. As late as the spring of 1944, according to the report of the police investigation, Claus von Stauffenberg had not only given the British government the names of the future German peace negotiators and asked that the trials of war criminals be left to the new anti-Nazi regime in Berlin. He had also expressed "the wish that Austria should remain part of the Reich." After all, the same principle of national self-determination that the Allies invoked to condemn the destruction of Czechoslovakia and Poland sanctioned the union of Germany and Austria.[19]

Hassell shared Stauffenberg's opinion, but he went far beyond the mere preservation of the Anschluss. In an article published in 1942, he spoke scornfully about the efforts of England and France during the interwar period to keep Austria, the "sick man on the Danube," artificially alive by "all sorts of injections." Now that those efforts had failed, Germany was being summoned to the task of "bringing peace and prosperity" to the Danubian and the Balkan peoples, a task imposed by the legacy it had inherited from the old Habsburg empire.

According to Hassell, Germany should also seek to expand its influence in another part of Europe. "Only that nation could be destined to become the bearer of a new principle of order in the Baltic confusion that emerged as the strongest force on the basis of its historical development as well as its natural qualifications, namely, the German nation," Hassell wrote that same year. Could anyone doubt that? "This southern border region of the Baltic," he repeated for emphasis, "includes a nation that in size and in economic significance exceeds by far all other Baltic nations." Should it not then logically play a dominant role among them? Hassell considered the denunciation of Nazi political ruthlessness perfectly compatible with the advocacy of German territorial expansion.[20]

The most ardent irredentist or annexationist among the resisters, however, was Goerdeler. He was certainly the most prolific, tirelessly grinding
out notes, memorandums, proposals, and programs, all designed to extend
Germany's prewar frontiers. In September 1943, despite the defeat of the
Wehrmacht in North Africa, despite the withdrawal of Italy from the Axis,
and in the midst of a successful Soviet offensive in the Ukraine, he was still
assuring Field Marshal Kluge that the British would no doubt agree to a
generous peace with a new anti-Nazi regime in Berlin. "In the east the
boundary of 1914, . . . Austria and the Sudeten region remain German,
the southern Tirol up to Bolzano-Merano becomes German again, Eupen-
Malmedy remain German, [and] there are to be direct negotiations between Germany and France regarding Alsace-Lorraine."

As late as May 1944, with American and English troops poised to invade
France and the Red Army already across the Romanian frontier, Goerdeler
continued to insist that the German demands in any peace negotiations
include "the Reich boundary of 1914 in the east, the retention by the
Reich of Austria and the Sudeten region, the autonomy of Alsace-Lorraine,
and the acquisition of the Tirol up to Bolzano and Merano." Three
months later he was in prison awaiting the executioner, but composed and
unafraid, sustained by an indomitable faith in his country and his God.[21]

To conclude from all this that he and the other resisters were motivated
exclusively by a desire to escape the consequences of military defeat would
nevertheless be a mistake. They genuinely believed that the Nazi regime
had come to embody the most corruptive and destructive forces in German
political life. It had to be overthrown at all costs. But they refused to
separate rejection of the Third Reich from defense of the national interest.
One did not motivate the other; the two were mutually dependent and
complementary. Still, by the summer of 1944 it was also clear to the
resisters that the effect of the fall of the Hitler dictatorship on the peace
terms Germany could expect was diminishing "with every new military
reverse," as Claus von Stauffenberg warned. It would prove negligible,
once a successful Allied invasion of France had taken place. The coup could
therefore no longer be delayed. For the resistance it had at last become
now or never.[22]

This photograph of Fritz-Dietlof von der Schulenburg is undated,
but it was probably taken around the time of the attempt to
assassinate Hitler in the summer of 1944.
(Ullstein Bilderdienst)

A picture of Helmuth James von Moltke at his trial in January 1945 for involvement in the resistance movement against the Third Reich. (Bilderdienst Süddeutscher Verlag)

VI

Death and Transfiguration

At a time when the German armies are engaged in a most difficult struggle, a very small group has now emerged in Germany . . . which believed that it could stab [the nation] in the back, as happened in 1918. But this time it made a serious mistake. . . . The circle that these usurpers represent is extremely small. It has nothing to do with the German armed forces and certainly nothing to do with the German army. It is a very small gang of criminal elements, who are now being mercilessly exterminated.

ADOLF HITLER (1944)

20

On the Brink of Redemption

The changing fortunes of war, which made the moment seem favorable for attaining the immediate goal of the coup, made achieving its ultimate purpose impossible. That is, an attempt to assassinate Hitler, even a successful attempt, was not likely to lead to an overthrow of the Nazi regime as long as the Wehrmacht remained victorious or at least capable of defending the nation. Under such circumstances, would the generals have been willing to assume power or would they have instead chosen to accept a new Führer appointed by the Nationalist Socialist Party? Would public opinion in Germany have regarded an uprising against the Third Reich as a means of liberation or as an act of treason? And what of the resisters themselves? Were they prepared to abandon the extensive military conquests in east and west, conquests won by so much effort and sacrifice, in order to put an end to a cruel dictatorship? Most of them remained convinced that a successful coup would be possible only after the Nazi regime could be charged with defeat and failure as well as corruption and oppression. To expect the nation to renounce victory for the sake of principle would be asking too much.

That was why the summer of 1944 seemed so propitious to the resisters. To be sure, there had been various schemes and plots earlier in the war to remove Hitler from power. But they had generally been the work of isolated individuals or small groups of conspirators—foolhardy, uncoordinated, desperate, and hopeless. They could have at best led to the assassination of the Führer; they could not have overthrown his system of government. But by the time Claus von Stauffenberg placed his bomb in the conference room at Hitler's headquarters in East Prussia, the situation had changed dramatically. The Red Army had crossed the prewar frontiers of the Soviet Union and was advancing into Poland, the Americans and the British had launched a successful invasion of France, and the Third Reich's fair-weather friends, Finland and Romania in particular, were preparing to change sides. Never before had the chances for a coup appeared so favorable, because never before had the regime appeared so inept. To more and more Germans an attempt to overthrow the Third Reich no longer meant a choice between national interest and moral principle; it meant a defense of national interest through moral principle.

Nevertheless, the reverses suffered by the Wehrmacht, reverses that made the resisters more anxious to reach an accommodation with the Allies, made the Allies less willing to accommodate the resisters. Why should they make concessions when victory was nearly in their grasp? As long as the German armed forces dominated the Continent, the resistance had seemed almost nonexistent. But now that the defeat of the Third Reich appeared imminent, there were suddenly urgent messages about the need to deliberate and compromise, to negotiate a just settlement, to establish fair boundaries, and to make territorial arrangements promoting a free and peace-loving Germany. To the Allied statesmen the new tack looked like a last-minute attempt to escape the consequences of Hitler's reckless foreign policy. Can anyone blame them? They were being asked to sacrifice advantages won in long years of deadly combat in order to make a new anti-Nazi government more palatable to the Germans. It was unrealistic to expect them to agree. It would have required more restraint, moderation, and selflessness than they could politically afford. They continued to cling, stubbornly but understandably, to the demand for unconditional surrender.

That stance helped engender a mood of gloomy resignation in Germany, a feeling of fatalism or inevitability. The military effort was sustained by its own momentum or sheer inertia, rather than by any hope of victory. Those who still retained faith in the Nazi regime gradually diminished to a small, fanatical group of true believers. But what was the alternative? The lost war continued because the prospective peace appeared to most Germans equally bad, perhaps even worse. The familiar perils seemed preferable to the unfamiliar ones.

This erosion of hope contributed to the reluctance of many opponents of the Third Reich to support its overthrow. Why add civil strife to the nation's miseries merely to hasten the victory of the Russians, the Americans, and the British? Whatever their form of government, the fate awaiting the Germans would be the same: defeat, occupation, and military government. The bitter quip "Enjoy the war because the peace will be awful" reflected the widespread sense of approaching but unavoidable disaster.

Most religious leaders shared this feeling. Some of them, especially after the military situation began to deteriorate, openly condemned the government's policies, starting with ecclesiastical supervision and churchly governance and ending with euthanasia and genocide. Yet they could not bring themselves to cross the boundary between criticism and resistance. Their hesitation stemmed in part from their conviction that a clear line of demarcation separated secular from spiritual authority, political from religious affairs. But it also expressed their reluctance to contribute to the impending foreign domination of their country, to alien ascendancy and oppression and exploitation. The Allied insistence on unconditional surrender made them unwilling to become accomplices in Germany's defeat. Not even their growing recognition of the immoral nature of the Third Reich could overcome their dread of being labeled traitors.

Wurm's papers contain the draft of a pastoral statement, unsigned and undated but apparently written shortly after the Allied invasion of France, in which the bishop described the increasing apprehension of the German people regarding the outcome of the war and recommended measures to be taken to prevent a total military defeat. Not even the "best sermons and lectures," he expounded, could overcome the basic causes of the sense of hopelessness spreading through the nation. The first of those causes was popular disappointment at "so many broken promises," from the government's assurances in the fall of 1941 that the Soviet Union had been defeated once and for all to its more recent guarantees regarding the impregnability of the fortifications guarding the Atlantic coast and the destruction of any Allied army invading France. Second, fear of revenge by the enemy forces, "especially by Jewry," had become widespread. Finally, many people were concerned that "the suppression of justice and personal freedom in Germany could become permanent." The situation was so serious that a drastic change in official policy was needed to reawaken popular support for the war effort.

Wurm maintained that only a "great national uprising" might still reenlist the energies of the people in a last desperate effort to repel the Allies. But such an uprising was "inconceivable and impossible" under a continuation of "present political methods." There was one way to inspire the masses, one way to arouse among them "new enthusiasm for the fatherland." That was "a solemn declaration that the fundamental rights of personal freedom and equal protection under the law, which were suspended . . . in February 1933, are being restored, that the secret police is accordingly being abolished, the independence of the judiciary is being restored, [and] freedom of opinion is being reestablished to the extent possible in wartime." Only the end of dictatorial rule could prevent the military collapse of Germany.

Wurm was not content with suggesting ways to save the nation from defeat. He also criticized the system of government that had invited the danger of defeat. There was nothing timid in his censure of the Nazi regime. "Unity and justice and freedom," he declared, "are pillars of the national welfare." Yet they had been undermined by the "present form of the state," so that now they could be strengthened only through a "noble-minded act of political leadership." In the "awful situation" confronting the nation, a situation created in large part by the "serious blunders of a military, political, and cultural nature" that the government had committed, "those in leading positions" had a duty to rally the people behind the struggle for an "ultimate victory." But the people would respond only if they felt that the reward for their heroic sacrifices would be "not enslavement under a privileged caste" but "freedom at home and abroad." Then they would renew their efforts in the "struggle against Bolshevism." Then they would fight against the enemy to the last. Then they would prove invincible.[1]

Did Wurm actually believe all that? Did he actually believe that National Socialism could become denazified, humanized, and liberalized? Did he believe that the Third Reich could be transformed into a defender of personal freedom and impartial justice? Or was he saying those things merely in order to play the critic of the regime without being perceived as its enemy? There is always the possibility, moreover, that, recognizing an "ultimate victory" as highly unlikely, he wanted to be seen after his nation's defeat as opposed to Nazism but loyal to Germany. In any case, he carefully kept himself from crossing the line between dissent and resistance.

On the Catholic side, Frings took a similar position. He too had in the past frequently expressed his disagreement with the government's policies, especially its treatment of the Jews. In a sermon delivered on Christmas Day 1943, he denounced once again the adoption of genocide by National Socialism as an instrument of state policy. "Whoever intentionally kills innocents and noncombatants, whether from the air or in any other way," the archbishop preached, "whoever deprives them of life merely because they belong to a foreign nationality, to a foreign race, that person sins against God's commandment: 'Thou shalt not kill.'" The argument seemed irrefutable.

In a pastoral address on March 12, 1944, Frings broadened his condemnation of racial murder to include other violations of civil rights and liberties. He demanded that "no citizen be deprived of his freedom without an opportunity to defend himself and to be heard by a regular or special court of law." For him the central issue, however, remained racial oppression and extermination. It was of the greatest moral importance that "no one who is innocent should be robbed of his possessions and especially not of his life, simply because he belongs to a foreign race." A violation of this principle must be regarded as "an injustice crying out to heaven." Therefore any government that tolerated such an injustice risked forfeiting the allegiance and obedience of its citizens. The underlying significance of what was being said from the pulpit of Great Saint Martin's Church in Cologne that day must have been unmistakable.[2]

Still, Frings too avoided overstepping the line between secular and spiritual authority. He was willing to denounce the methods and policies of National Socialism, but not its principles and doctrines. Like other leading churchmen, he believed that his religious responsibility required him to oppose the government whenever it encroached on confessional rights and privileges. But to call for resistance against the legally established political system on the basis of some abstract ethical doctrine, some universal moral imperative, was more than he was prepared to risk. He might have been tempted to go beyond reproaches and admonitions if he had felt that he could thereby save his nation from defeat and occupation. But to replace native oppressors with foreign oppressors, to substitute an alien dictatorship for an indigenous one, simply as a sign of penitence, as proof of contrition, that was too much for the archbishop. He chose instead to warn, reprove, exhort, and wait for the inevitable.

Faulhaber was even less inclined to provoke an open breach with the Nazi regime. When some of the resisters approached him with a tacit request for support or at least endorsement, the cardinal became very uneasy. Though still regarded on the strength of his Advent sermons a decade earlier as at heart an opponent of National Socialism, he had since then grown increasingly circumspect and wary. Those who tried to persuade him to approve an attempt to overthrow Hitler, if only by implication, misjudged their man. In private he would still criticize this or that policy of the Nazi regime, this or that injustice, this or that atrocity. But in public he did not even go as far as Frings or Galen. He had become a model of clerical discretion, diplomatic, prudent, correct, and extremely cautious.

Convinced that his overriding duty was to protect the confessional interests of his church, Faulhaber remained determined to avoid any provocation to the Nazi authorities that might expose those interests to attack. He recognized that the Third Reich harbored forces of evil and corruption;

privately he was even willing at times to condemn its principles and practices. But to advocate the overthrow of the government, even in strict confidence, that was too much for him. What if the attempt should fail? The regime would then renew all those old ugly charges about the Catholics being disloyal and subversive. Even if it succeeded, many Germans would still blame Catholicism for the hardships of defeat and occupation. Besides, would not the fall of the Third Reich open the gates to godless Bolshevism? The cardinal thought it best to avoid taking sides so as to ensure that his church could continue to fulfill its spiritual mission unimpeded in the coming postwar era.

Thus he became alarmed when Goerdeler approached him with a seemingly harmless inquiry: "whether it is possible that the Catholic Church in Germany could achieve greater independence under a German primate in dealing with the Curia, and in what ways it could work together with the Protestant Church." Goerdeler then casually added the question whether Faulhaber had by any chance "opportunities to exert influence in diplomatic affairs." The subsequent police investigation into the coup had little doubt about the real purpose of such queries. "The conversations, even if in their course the intention of altering the government was not mentioned directly, served as a preliminary exploration of the possibility of the assumption of power by the military and the subsequent civilian government."

Faulhaber must have reached the same conclusion. He recognized that Goerdeler was trying to ascertain not merely his opinion concerning collaboration between the two Christian denominations but his attitude toward an uprising against Hitler as well. His reply was therefore resolutely noncommittal. He intended not to sound unfriendly, but also not to arouse suspicion regarding his loyalty to the regime, especially not on the part of the Gestapo. He assured Goerdeler that he regarded the present time as more favorable than ever for cooperation between Catholics and Protestants. As for the other inquiry, "the cardinal has connections in diplomatic affairs only to the pope." The answer, though given in private, was designed to avoid offending, alarming, or antagonizing anyone in authority.[3]

Moltke had no better luck. According to his later testimony before the official inquiry, Faulhaber simply would not budge. "I happened to be in Munich when the cardinal was to preach in Saint Michael's Church. That interested me, and Father [Augustinus] Rösch got me a good seat in the church and told me that the cardinal would see me, if I wanted him to. I then visited him and we talked about the question of the position of the church within the state." But that was as far as it went. Faulhaber avoided discussing political issues with Moltke as resolutely as he did with Goerdeler. "The conversation was not very fruitful, because basically the cardinal could not be persuaded to go beyond talking about the concordat." He remained the cautious ecclesiastical diplomat to the end, prudent in speech, wary in policy, listening to divergent views, tolerant of opposing opinions, but determined not to subordinate concrete denominational needs to broad ethical imperatives.[4]

The stalwarts in the resistance were of course much bolder. They had long since crossed the Rubicon between criticism and rejection of the Third Reich. They had made an unshakable commitment to Hitler's overthrow. Yet they too became increasingly affected by the mood of glum fatalism spreading across Germany, the sense that no matter what they did, an inescapable tragic fate awaited their nation. As the time for initiating the coup approached, the coup for which they had been waiting so long and so impatiently, the dominant feeling among them was neither elation nor excitement but resignation in the face of probable failure. The Allies, their victory finally within reach, were not likely to retreat from the demand for unconditional surrender. And that made the outcome of the planned uprising highly dubious. Even if Hitler was assassinated, would the leaders of the Wehrmacht agree to serve an insurrectionary regime prepared to capitulate to the enemy? And what about public opinion? Were most Germans ready to accept a new government willing to submit to defeat and occupation? The prospects before the resistance were gloomy.

Not even its most resolute members could withstand the spreading mood of discouragement. Beck himself became despondent. Ever since the Sudeten crisis he had worked tirelessly to bring about the overthrow of a regime that was endangering Germany and oppressing Europe. Yet now that a coup was about to take place, he sounded strangely dispirited. The historian Friedrich Meinecke reported shortly after the war that at their last meeting in May 1944 Beck appeared to be prepared for failure. "It is no use," he sighed. "Nothing can save us. We must now drain the bitter cup of sorrow to the bitterest end." He meant, Meinecke surmised, that the plan for an uprising had been betrayed to the authorities and that the participants were about to be arrested. They had therefore resolved to make "a last attempt to save Germany," knowing that it was almost certain to fail. What actually troubled Beck, however, was not fear that the regime had found out about the impending coup. It was rather the realization that neither the leadership of the army nor the nation as a whole was likely to support a revolt whose immediate effect would be to hasten military defeat.[5]

Tresckow sounded discouraged as well. In June 1944, replying to a question whether the coup should still be undertaken, since the Allies had now invaded France and no diplomatic advantage could therefore be expected from a change of government in Berlin, he maintained that the effort should nevertheless be made, not in the hope of success but despite the probability of failure. "The attempt to assassinate Hitler must take place, whatever the cost. Even if it should not succeed, the coup d'état must be undertaken in spite of that. For what matters is no longer the practical goal, but to show the world and history that the German resistance movement dared to make a decisive move, risking the lives of its members. Anything else besides that is unimportant." He had come to accept the likelihood of defeat. For him the significance of the uprising would now lie in its symbolic meaning, in its demonstration that there were Germans ready to die opposing the moral evil embodied by the Third Reich.[6]

The Stauffenberg brothers shared this feeling. They too gradually recognized the unlikelihood of success. Even Hitler's assassination would probably not lead to the attainment of their original political objectives. It would not save their nation from military defeat or create a free German state or result in a peace of compromise or even establish a new independent government in Berlin. It was too late for that. And yet a coup had to be attempted in spite of its hopelessness, as a moral act, as a symbolic gesture, as a historic legacy to future generations. Berthold told his wife a few days before the uprising: "The most terrible thing is to know that it cannot succeed, and yet that we must do it for our country and for our children." Like Tresckow, he had come to view the attempt to overthrow the Nazi regime as a fulfillment of duty and an acceptance of martyrdom.[7]

His brother Claus was at first more optimistic. He continued to believe as late as the spring of 1944 that the coup had a 50 percent chance of success, his widow recalled afterward. He even thought that the Allies might be willing to allow Germany to retain some of the territorial gains achieved under Hitler. The invasion of Normandy by American and British forces early in June destroyed those illusions, however. Would a coup at this point have any significant effect on the outcome of the war? he wondered. He even began to ask himself whether "it still makes any sense now to stick to our plan, since a practical political goal is no longer attainable." The other members of the resistance persuaded him that the overthrow of the Nazi regime must be attempted regardless of the outcome. But he too came to feel that the uprising was likely to end in failure. Like his brother, he began therefore to emphasize the symbolic or moral significance of a coup. "To yield passively to infamy and paralyzing force is worse than a failure," he told his friend Urban Thiersch on July 1. "Only action is capable of gaining freedom, inwardly as well as outwardly." The important thing was not practical success but spiritual commitment.[8]

What was the ideological basis of this conviction, increasingly common among the members of the resistance, that the attempt to overthrow the Third Reich had to be made, whatever the odds? The obvious answer, correct though not complete, is patriotism. They were prepared to sacrifice themselves to protect their nation against the disaster threatening it as a result of Hitler's mistakes and crimes. However small the chance of success, the effort had to be made. Their duty to Germany demanded it.

In fact considerable evidence supports this contention. The resisters themselves repeatedly emphasized their love of country, their resolve to defend the fatherland against a terrible danger. On the evening of July 20, for example, shortly before his execution for treason, General Olbricht described what had led him and the others to seek the overthrow of the Nazi regime. "I don't know how posterity will later judge our deed or how it will judge me personally," his son-in-law Friedrich Georgi remembered him saying. "But I know with certainty that all of us acted free of any sort of personal motives, and that we dared attempt the ultimate only in a situation which was already desperate, in order to protect Germany against total destruction. I am convinced that posterity will some day recognize and understand that." His purpose, in other words, had been the same as that of all loyal and patriotic Germans: to save the nation.[9]

Three weeks later, at his trial for participating in the failed coup, Schulenburg told the court essentially the same thing. The proceedings were secret, but according to the testimony of a friend of his who had seen the official record, he too insisted that he had been motivated above all by devotion to his country. "We undertook this action in order to protect Germany against an unspeakable misery. It is clear to me that I will be hanged for that, but I do not regret my deed, and I hope that someone else will carry it out at a more opportune moment." He remained unshaken in the conviction that the overthrow of Hitler was essential for the salvation of Germany. What his accusers condemned as treason, he defended as patriotism.[10]

This feeling that an uprising against the Third Reich was essential for national survival motivated many of the other resisters on the eve of the coup. It dominated, for example, the important meeting of July 16 in the Berlin apartment of Berthold von Stauffenberg, a meeting attended by his brother Claus as well as Schulenburg, Trott, Yorck, Hofacker, Georg

Hansen, Albrecht Mertz von Quirnheim, and Ulrich Wilhelm von Schwerin-Schwanenfeld. The discussion centered on the justification, strategy, and objective of the coup, which was to take place in only a few days. Hofacker maintained that "neither a peace of victory nor a peace of compromise is possible." The only attainable objective was to make "the unavoidable defeat" as "tolerable as possible" and "liquidate politically the war that has been lost militarily." Hence the purpose of the uprising should be "a timely capitulation," so that Germany could retain in some measure a "tolerable position" in Central Europe during the postwar period. Only a "complete change in the system" and the "removal of the Führer" could achieve that end. The basic goal of the coup, in his view, should be the defense of the national interest.

Trott supported this position. Describing the impressions he had gathered during a trip to Sweden late in June, he even argued that there was still a chance of reaching a compromise peace with the Allies once Hitler was overthrown. "The people on the enemy side will be ready to negotiate as soon as the precondition for it, a complete change in the regime, has been achieved." He seemed confident that unconditional surrender could still be avoided, that room for maneuvering, bargaining, and trading still existed, provided a successful coup took place.[11]

Even Claus von Stauffenberg, though more of a realist, hoped that the overthrow of Hitler could still save Germany from the most serious consequences of a military collapse. It would certainly spare the nation needless bloodshed and devastation. In a memorandum found among his papers after the attempt to assassinate Hitler, he argued that a continuation of the war would inevitably lead to "a defeat and the destruction of the [nation's] material and human resources." That danger could be averted, in part at least, by "the removal of the present leadership." He made the same point in his conversation with Thiersch. Speaking about the "inescapably hopeless military situation," Stauffenberg conceded that "an overthrow [of the present government] would not change anything in that regard." Yet it would not be useless either. "A great deal of bloodshed could be prevented and terrible chaos at the end could be avoided." The nation might still be protected against some of the disastrous results of the approaching military collapse.[12]

There may have been an element of calculation in the arguments advanced by some of the resisters in support of the coup. They may have been trying in part to allay the doubts and fears of the waverers among them. Perhaps they were also hoping to justify their plan to commit an act of treason by invoking the primacy of the national interest. But their private conversations and letters, what they said to friends and relatives, often exhibit the same tone of ardent patriotism, the same avowal of devotion to the nation, and the same readiness to sacrifice their lives in defense of Germany. There can be little question about the centrality of nationalism in the decision to seek the overthrow of the Third Reich.

Thus shortly before his execution on August 10, Schulenburg wrote to his wife: "My professional life will remain only a fragment, but in the end history will judge us and find us not guilty. You know that love for the fatherland motivated me as well." Four weeks later, on September 8, Schwerin-Schwanenfeld said almost exactly the same thing in his farewell letter to his wife: "You know that my actions were always undertaken for the sake of Germany, in accordance with the traditions of our family and out of a burning love for the fatherland, which outweighed everything else. Other times will bring with them other customs and opinions, different in detail from ours. But love for the fatherland will forever remain the constituent part of life that predominates over everything else." The conviction that he was sacrificing himself for his country, that he had risked death so that his nation might live, gave him the strength to face the hangman.[13]

Patriotism accounted, moreover, for the desperate hope of many of the resisters that once Hitler had been removed from power, Germany might still be able to obtain tolerable peace terms. They refused to believe, because they did not really want to believe, that the Allies would insist on unconditional surrender even from an anti-Nazi government. Surely, there would be room for negotiation, for compromise, for give-and-take. There might in fact be an opportunity to retain under a new regime some of the gains achieved under the old. Even Claus von Stauffenberg, though generally practical and hardheaded, communicated to the British barely a month before the coup his wish for the maintenance of the union of Germany and Austria after the conclusion of peace.[14]

Goerdeler went much further than that. At the end of May he prepared a summary of the territorial acquisitions to be sought in negotiations with the Allies, a summary that sounded as if Germany were winning rather than losing the war. He wanted to retain not only Austria but the Sudeten region as well. He also envisaged a substantial eastward expansion at the expense of Poland, and the reacquisition of the southern Tirol. Even Alsace-Lorraine was to become an autonomous province. He must have realized that such a wish list would be totally unacceptable to the Allied statesmen. Still, by making far-reaching demands at the beginning, he apparently hoped to be able to make modest gains in the end. He was still thinking in terms of the old-style prewar diplomacy of bartering, finessing, and horse trading.[15]

Beck had fewer illusions. He recognized the futility of any hopes for retaining the territorial gains achieved under Hitler. The Allies were too bitter, too resentful, to allow that. They would insist at the least on a return to the boundaries of 1933. Yet perhaps further territorial losses could still be avoided. In any case, the overthrow of the Third Reich would undoubtedly help protect Germany against the danger of foreign occupation and military government. That was worth something. The new regime, however, would first have to convince the victors that it was genuinely opposed to the doctrines and policies of National Socialism. "After the final catastrophe awaiting us," Beck told Meinecke, "a united anti-Nazi party must be formed, extending from the extreme right to the Communists, for in fundamental national questions one can count on the reliability of the Communists."

He was not sure enough of that reliability to include any Communists in the list of members of the provisional government to be established after Hitler's overthrow. Still, a united front of the various political forces in Germany opposed to Nazism, including both leftists and rightists, would look good to the Allies, especially to the Soviets. It might help create a climate favorable to a peace of moderation. But there was no time to lose; the resisters must not wait for the inevitable military collapse. They must act and act promptly. "Immediately after [our] assumption of power," Beck maintained on July 11, "skilled negotiators should be sent to London and Moscow." Perhaps something could still be salvaged from the coming military debacle.[16]

There can thus be little doubt that in attempting their coup, most of the resisters hoped first and foremost to protect the national interest. Marie Vassiltchikov, a Russian émigré living in Berlin who knew some of them, wrote in her diary on July 19, the day before the coup, about the central role of nationalism in the thinking of the resisters:

> The trouble is that there is a fundamental difference in outlook between all of them and me: not being German, I have never attached much importance to what happens afterwards. Being patriots, they want to save their country from complete destruction by setting up some interim government; whereas I am concerned only with the elimination of the Devil. Besides, I have never believed that even such an interim government would be acceptable to the Allies, who refuse to distinguish between "good" Germans and "bad." This, of course, is a fatal mistake on their part and we will probably all pay a heavy price for it.

Her criticism of Allied policy may be open to challenge, but her characterization of the resisters as essentially patriots was on the whole sound.[17]

And yet there was more to it than that. For in the last few months before the attempt to assassinate Hitler, a new tone began to resound in the discourse of the resistance, a tone faintly and intermittently audible before, but now increasingly recurrent, increasingly persistent and insistent. Some of those involved in planning the coup started to suggest that the attempt to overthrow the Nazi regime must be made not primarily to save Germany but as an act of atonement or expiation. Even if it should fail, even if the fatherland should be conquered and occupied, the resistance must wage its struggle against National Socialism as a moral obligation, as a sacrifice for mankind, as an appeal for forgiveness and redemption. It no longer really mattered whether the nation could avoid military defeat, whether it could retain its old boundaries, or even whether it could maintain its sovereignty and independence. What mattered was proving to the world that at least some Germans, acting out of conscience and in accordance with universal moral values, were willing to sacrifice themselves to protect humanity against an unspeakable evil. The act of resistance assumed a symbolic meaning that transcended the practical outcome of an uprising.

Echoes of this new conviction could be heard even in some of the familiar arguments about the need to save Germany by destroying the Third Reich. Talking to Thiersch shortly before the coup, Claus von Stauffenberg declared defiantly, almost boastfully: "I am engaged in high treason with all the means at my disposal." He conceded that the removal of Hitler from power would not prevent a military defeat. Nevertheless, "the disgrace of the present government must be expunged." Practical success no longer mattered most. Rather, resistance against an evil system of authority, regardless of its outcome, would provide those who had dared embark on it with "freedom, inwardly as well as outwardly." By staking their lives on an attempt to destroy the Nazi regime, he and the others would be freed from a burden of guilt for having for years accepted and served that regime. The coup had become more than a weapon in defense of the national interest. It grew into a means of private atonement, a source of personal redemption.[18]

Similarly, Tresckow insisted that the attempt to assassinate Hitler should be carried out even though the Allies were unlikely to retreat from their demand for unconditional surrender. The probability of a failure of the coup could not deter him. "For what matters is no longer the practical goal," he maintained, "but to show the world and history that the German resistance movement dared make a decisive move, risking the lives of its members." He too had begun to talk about achieving "freedom, inwardly and outwardly." He too advocated resistance at all costs, to the end, as a form of individual and collective atonement, expiation, regeneration, and redemption.[19]

This shift in the justification of the struggle against National Socialism from patriotic duty to moral imperative is even more apparent in the case of Beck. Too much the realist to indulge in wishful thinking about the retention of any of the territorial gains acquired by Hitler, he nevertheless sounded at times hopeful that Germany might at least be able to avoid military collapse and foreign occupation. Hence he favored the formation of an anti-Nazi united front and the opening of peace negotiations with the enemy as soon as the Third Reich had fallen. But at other times he seemed resigned to failure, to probable failure in overthrowing the Third Reich and to certain failure in modifying the Allied demand for uncondi-tional surrender. It was all useless, he conceded two months before the coup. The nation could no longer be saved. "We must now drain the bitter cup of sorrow to the bitterest end."

Yet the struggle to destroy National Socialism had to go on despite its hopelessness. Beck remained unyielding on this point. He insisted that the moral significance of the coup transcended its practical result or political outcome. "The decisive question is not what will become of this or that individual personally," he tried to convince wavering members of the resistance. "The decisive question is not even what the consequence for the nation will be. What is decisive is the unbearable reality that for years and years crimes after crimes and murders after murders multiplied in the name of the German nation, and that it is our moral duty to put an end with all means at our disposal to those crimes committed in the usurped name of our nation." The man who had six years earlier helped organize the resistance in order to protect the national interest was now arguing that its highest purpose must be to express a universal morality.[20]

The conviction that the overthrow of the Third Reich had become an ethical imperative was also at the heart of the "government declaration" found by the secret police among Goerdeler's papers after the failed coup. This detailed statement of purpose, which the resisters hoped to broadcast after assuming power, culminated in a peroration emphasizing the spiritual and religious foundations of their movement. The nation's "most urgent task," regardless of what the future might bring "materially," was to cleanse the "much dishonored German name." For "God does not exist simply to be invoked as providence at every suitable opportunity." He demands rather that his commandments be strictly observed. It was thus a "terrible mistake" to assume that "our future could be built on the misfortune of other nations or on the suppression of and contempt for human dignity." The declaration urged the Germans to enter once again on "the path of justice, decency, and mutual respect." That was the spirit in which they would henceforth have to fulfill their moral obligation. "Let us scrupulously follow in all things God's commandments, which are inscribed on our conscience, even if we find them hard. Let us do everything to heal wounded souls and alleviate suffering." The ultimate goal of the struggle to overthrow the Nazi regime should be not political but moral regeneration, not a national but a spiritual rebirth.[21]

Not all of the resisters, nor even most of them, subscribed to this new view of their duty and mission. But a significant and growing number did. What led primarily to its acceptance varied from one case to another. For some the recognition that they were not likely to overthrow Hitler and even less likely to achieve a compromise peace fostered the conviction that the justification for what they were about to do had to be ethical rather than pragmatic in nature. For others the loss of life and the spread of privation in their own country engendered a greater sensitivity to the suffering that other countries had been forced to endure at the hands of the Third Reich. And for still others, though they almost never acknowledged personal responsibility, the attempt to assassinate Hitler was a form of vicarious atonement for their earlier support of his regime. In most cases, a combination in varying proportions of these attitudes and beliefs played the decisive role. What is clear in any event is that as its hour of decision approached, the resistance gradually began to undergo a significant shift in its underlying motive, purpose, vindication, and faith.

21

A Mortal Failure

The dramatic events of July 20 are too familiar to require lengthy retelling or reinterpreting. The central fact emerging from all the developments of that extraordinary day was the failure of Claus von Stauffenberg's bomb to kill Hitler. And that failure in turn, whether the result of cruel mischance, as his opponents believed, or of providential intervention, as some of his supporters maintained, meant the end of the resistance. The authorities were left with the simple task of rounding up those involved in the plot, interrogating them, pronouncing them guilty, and executing them with or without the benefit of a trial. The insurrectionary movement, which had begun in the late 1930s as an attempt to avert the danger of a new war, collapsed six years later during the final phase of that war.

Its failure produced an unending stream of speculations and conjectures about what might have been. What if the Führer's conference that afternoon had been held in his underground bunker rather than in a wooden hut where the shock of the explosion quickly dissipated? What if the briefcase containing the bomb had not been pushed so far under the heavy table, which absorbed much of its destructive force? Even though Hitler survived, might not things have still turned out differently if Beck and Witzleben had promptly broadcast to the country, especially to the armed forces, their support of the coup? And what if Field Marshal Günther von Kluge had ordered the troops under his command in France to turn against the Nazi regime? What if? And what then?

Even had the resisters met with better luck, however, even had they managed to assassinate Hitler, even had they displayed greater resolve or boldness in rallying the nation against the government, it is by no means clear that they would have succeeded. Many of the army leaders in the summer of 1944 remained reluctant to play the role that the Socialists had played in the fall of 1918. At least those who had overthrown the imperial regime thought they were protecting the fatherland against the worst consequences of military defeat. They believed, naively but sincerely, that the victors would prove more generous to a new democratic order in Germany than to the old authoritarian one. But now such expectations seemed illusory. The Allied statesmen had given no indication that they would be less harsh toward an anti-Nazi than a Nazi regime. There appeared to be no Woodrow Wilson among them preaching the Fourteen Points.

The leaders of the Wehrmacht generally recognized that by supporting the coup they might be shortening the war, they might be ending the bombing of their nation's cities and reducing its military and civilian casualties. But they would also be hastening its defeat and occupation. Worse still, they might later be reviled by their countrymen as weaklings, defeatists, traitors, and backstabbers. Even if Hitler had been killed, it remains an open question whether many of them would have been willing to assume that burden of responsibility. They might well have preferred to go on carrying out orders and waging a war they knew was lost.

There can be little doubt, however, about the attitude of the leading statesmen and of public opinion in the Allied countries. They almost unanimously considered the failed coup in Germany an attempt by those who had been the supporters and followers of the Nazi regime to avoid paying the price for their complicity. After using the Third Reich to preserve their traditional position in state and society, the resisters were now turning against it for the same reason. They hoped in 1944 to use the familiar strategy which had proved so successful in 1918 and in 1933. But this time it would not work. To the Allies the unsuccessful insurrection did not signify an ideological rejection of National Socialism but served as evidence of growing war-weariness and defeatism in Germany.

Hence the Allied statesmen were anxious not to let the attempt on Hitler's life weaken the popular resolve to wage the war until final victory. A day after the coup Secretary of State Cordell Hull announced in Washington that "the attacks on Hitler . . . clearly indicate that a realization of Germany's impending defeat is spreading in the Reich." The "frantic attempts" to restore the appearance of unity in the high command could not disguise sharp differences of opinion between the leaders of the Wehrmacht and the leaders of the Nazi Party resulting from the "steadily deteriorating military position of Germany." No amount of "internal reshuffling or repression by Himmler" could conceal from his countrymen the fact that "many German generals believe that Germany has lost the war."

But that did not mean, Hull warned sternly, that the American war effort could be relaxed. "We should not let these apparent developments give rise to overoptimism." That would be dangerous. "The fighting ahead will be hard and we should intensify our efforts here at home and make all the sooner and more certain the defeat of our enemies." The uprising against the Nazi regime would not be allowed to affect either the war aims or the peace terms of the Allies.[1]

Four days later, on July 25, Anthony Eden, the British foreign minister, said essentially the same thing in the House of Commons. He was more cautious than Hull in drawing conclusions from the attempted coup in the Third Reich. "The German government have . . . been at great pains to prevent information leaving the country. They have great experience and skill in the machinery of repression and secrecy and we are, therefore, for the present mainly dependent upon our assessment of the various and often contradictory public statements made during the last few days by the German leaders." He thus hesitated to comment on recent developments in the Third Reich. Yet, despite his reticence, he concluded with an exhortation similar to that of the American secretary of state. "While we may justly draw encouragement from the recent news, it should spur us to further activity—(cheers)—to ensure Germany's final defeat in the field at the earliest possible date. (Cheers)." What had happened the previous week at the Wolf's Lair, Hitler's headquarters in East Prussia, would have no effect on the conduct or outcome of the war.[2]

In the Soviet Union none of the prominent political figures would comment on the attempt by the resistance to overthrow the Nazi regime. To do so might arouse false hopes regarding an imminent end of the war; it might weaken the popular will to wage the struggle until the enemy's unconditional surrender. But on July 23 the journalist and novelist Ilya Ehrenburg, who had become an unofficial spokesman for the government, published a statement insisting that the fate of the Third Reich would have to be decided on the field of battle. "Hitlerite Germany will be driven to her knees not by insurgent officers, but by ourselves and our Allies." None of the Germans were to be trusted, "neither the intelligentsia nor the silly ones, neither the blind nor those who have recovered their sight." Only tanks and bullets were reliable. "Our troops move faster than the consciences of the Fritzies. It is to be expected that the Germans will understand everything when we reach the gates of Berlin."

Ehrenburg conceded that some of the Wehrmacht's generals had been involved in a plot to assassinate Hitler. But that did not make it a mass uprising. "People are needed for a people's movement," he expounded, whereas in Germany the only ones left were "Fritzies and Gretchens—a cowardly, greedy mass that can neither think nor feel." As for the senior officers who finally decided to revolt against the Nazi regime, they had for years served that regime loyally and obediently. Now they thought they could pose as its opponents by staging a coup. But they were mistaken. The war would go on until the German government, whatever its form or ideology, decided to surrender.[3]

Although there were differences of nuance and emphasis between the Soviet Union on one side and the United States and Britain on the other, all three agreed that the recent attempt to assassinate Hitler must not shake their determination to achieve complete victory. On July 22, therefore, the British Broadcasting Corporation transmitted a statement to occupied Europe expressing the official view of the Allied governments regarding the failed uprising. "The attitude of the Allies is simple and clear. We endorse the judgment of the [German] generals if not their motives. We would welcome a mass movement in Germany to end the war by capitulation and would accept capitulation from whoever is in a position to offer it and is prepared to carry it out." There would be no negotiations, however, no compromises, no concessions. The system of government in Berlin, whether Nazi or non-Nazi or anti-Nazi, would have no effect on the outcome of the armed conflict. The only question was whether the Germans would decide to prevent further loss of life and property by surrendering now or whether they would go on fighting and dying until forced to surrender later.[4]

Winston Churchill, the only one of the leading Allied statesmen to comment at length on the coup against Hitler, restated and elaborated this position on August 2. In a speech before the House of Commons, he emphasized once again the unyielding attitude of the coalition against the Third Reich:

> Not only are those once proud German armies being beaten back on every front and by every one of the many nations who are in fighting contact with them, every single one, but, in their homeland in Germany, tremendous events have occurred which must shake to their foundations the confidence of the people and the loyalty of the troops. The highest personalities in the German Reich are murdering one another, or trying to, while the avenging Armies of the Allies close upon the doomed and ever-narrowing circle of their power. We have never based ourselves on the strength of our enemy but only on the

righteousness of our cause. Therefore, potent as may be these manifestations of internal disease, decisive as they may be one of these days, it is not in them that we should put our trust, but in our own strong arm and the justice of our cause.

The war would go on until the victorious Allied troops finally met in Berlin.[5]

While the statesmen professed real or feigned indifference to the failed coup, the journalists and publicists studied it in minute detail, concluding almost unanimously that it was nothing more than an attempt by some of the leaders of the Wehrmacht to wriggle out of a hopeless military situation. It did not represent any change of heart, any admission of guilt. It was simply a trick, a ruse, a stratagem. On July 22 the London *Times* characterized it as "a move by a group of German generals and officers," members of a military establishment constituting one of the "main pillars of the State," who had recognized that "Germany's defeat was certain and that Hitler's policy and strategy were leading Germany to further disaster." They had decided therefore "to save what they could from the wreck" before the Allied armies invaded the Third Reich. But no one knew anything about their future plans, "whether to fight on under more prudent and abler generalship or whether to approach the allies for armistice terms." In either case, they had sought nothing more than "to end the present régime and the present military command." They had acted out of practical necessity, not out of moral conviction. Hence their failure was no cause for regret.[6]

Two days later the Stockholm correspondent for the *Times* described the coup as the result of a bitter dispute regarding ultimate authority in the Third Reich between two competing state institutions. It was "the outcome of the Nazi Party's struggle for effective control of the forces, particularly the army, at home and abroad." While an insurrectionary spirit had been gradually developing among the generals, it had not yet matured. Most of them had been unprepared for "concerted action." To be sure, "they had jealously resisted direct control by the party and, as professional soldiers, Hitler's dictation of strategy: but for the most part they resisted only passively, though in many cases so stubbornly that this led to resignations or dismissals." Their "innate and cultivated" sense of discipline had kept them from going further than that.

As a result, most of the senior officers were as surprised by the attempted coup as the Führer himself, according to the *Times* article. "No action has followed, it appears—organized or unorganized—against Hitler or his Government." Those who initiated the uprising had neither any force behind them nor any plan before them, "certainly an unthinkable method for any general." Their revolt was therefore easily smashed in a few hours. "The only essential change of organization that resulted was that the chief gangster of the Nazi Party, Himmler, was placed formally in command of the whole German armed forces in the homeland, with the immediate task of carrying out a thorough purge by ruthless shooting of disloyal officers." None of this should affect the Allies, however. Their task, now as before, was to continue the armed struggle until the Third Reich had been defeated totally and irrevocably.[7]

John W. Wheeler-Bennett, who a decade later was to publish one of the earliest systematic accounts of the resistance, critical in tone but carefully researched and generally persuasive, offered an even harsher assessment. Shortly after the attempt on Hitler's life, he maintained that its failure should not be simply a matter of indifference to the Allies. Rather, they should welcome it as serendipitously serving their needs and purposes. It was a piece of good luck:

> It may now be said with some definiteness that we are better off with things as they are today than if the plot of 20th July had succeeded and Hitler been assassinated. . . . The Gestapo and the SS have done us an appreciable service in removing a selection of those who would undoubtedly have posed as "good" Germans after the war, while preparing for a third World War. . . . It is to our advantage therefore that the purge should continue, since the killing of Germans by Germans will save us from future embarrassments of many kinds.

The defeat of the coup, in his opinion, would simplify the task of waging war and concluding peace. It would destroy once and for all any illusion on the part of the Allies regarding negotiations with "moderates" or "liberals" in the Third Reich. It was a blessing in disguise.[8]

American commentators were equally unbending. They too viewed the attempt to assassinate Hitler as simply a trick to avoid paying the penalty for collusion by those who had once been his collaborators and accomplices. It did not represent a change of heart; it was a deathbed conversion. The Nazi regime, by arresting and executing the resisters, was unintentionally helping the Allies achieve their goal.

On August 2 the *New York Herald Tribune* declared in an editorial that "if Hitlerism has begun its last stand by destroying the militarist tradition, then it has been doing a large part of the Allies' work for them." A week later, on August 9, it elaborated on this theme. "Americans as a whole will not feel sorry that the bomb spared Hitler for the liquidation of his

generals. They hold no brief for aristocrats as such, especially those given
to the goosestep and . . . to collaboration with low-born, mob-rousing
corporals." Why should they care who gained the upper hand in Germany?
"Let the generals kill the corporal or vice-versa, preferably both." As for
the failed coup, it was "just dandy" that Hitler, the "ethnological visionary," had finally turned against some of the senior officers in the armed
forces, those "chief exponents of his master race," the "personification of
German arrogance." A plague on both their houses.[9]

The *Nation* took a similar position. In an editorial appearing at the end
of July, it welcomed signs of a "deepening split" between the Wehrmacht
and the Nazis, the "twin pillars of German aggression." The two had
originally worked hand in glove. "The army could not have organized the
nation for war without the Nazis; the Nazis could not have gained power
without the backing of the army." But now that defeat approached, each
was trying to shift blame to the other. Hitler, knowing that the Allies
would never negotiate with him, wanted to fight on, waiting "in his mystic
way" for some miracle. The "Junker chiefs," however, realizing that they
could not win, hoped that by getting rid of Hitler they might save
themselves and their "caste." Basically, they were trying to preserve Germany from "that total defeat that would make a 'next time' impossible."
They hoped to persuade the Allies to come to some agreement with them,
thereby escaping the shameful burden of unconditional surrender. "[But]
we think they are fooling themselves; the Allied leaders certainly will not
consent to any terms that leave German militarism a chance to recover."
Indeed, they should not. "The signs of German disintegration are not an
opportunity to make deals; they are, rather, an inspiration to complete the
process of unrelenting pressure." Nineteen forty-four must not become
another 1918.[10]

A week later the military and economic historian Alfred Vagts, who had
emigrated from Germany in the 1920s, published his own interpretation
of the attempt to assassinate Hitler, an interpretation more moderate in
tone but equally stern in judgment. The "enforced harmony" between the
Wehrmacht and the SS, he explained, had become strained as a result of
the mounting military defeats of the Third Reich. Specifically, the Allied
invasion of Normandy had led to developments in Germany similar to
those produced in Italy a year earlier by the invasion of Sicily. "A considerable group of old officers, their names indicative of noble birth, 'lost
courage.'" They realized that their chances of survival as a "governing and
possessing" elite were threatened. In the "cold morning" of defeat, following an "orgy of blood" during the preceding decade, they suddenly

became "conservative" once again, concluding that only decisive action against the Nazi regime could save their position in German society. "These neo-conservatives, with affiliations in big business and big agriculture, made a salvage attempt." One of them, in fact, "a Graf von Stauffenberg," had agreed "to throw the bomb for them." But his attempt could not in any case have altered the outcome of the war. The Allies were resolutely determined to continue fighting until they achieved the unconditional surrender of the Third Reich.[11]

The *New Republic* advanced a somewhat more generous view. It questioned the interpretation suggested by "a number of newspaper and radio commentators" that the coup against the Nazi regime had been designed primarily to preserve the Wehrmacht's ability to wage a third world war. "According to this argument, the leaders hope to surrender now, keep the army intact, and fight us again after a few years or decades." Several of the officers involved in the uprising, perhaps even most of them, might indeed have been thinking along these lines. Still, "this is another of the too-smart interpretations which usually turn out to be wrong historically." There was a more plausible explanation for the coup. The professional soldiers were not only "patriotic and devoted men." They were also "realists." The Nazis, however, were "hysterical fanatics who care little about the death of other people, or even of themselves, in the Nazi cause." It was therefore quite possible that at least some of the resisters wanted to surrender for an obvious reason. "They are sure they will be defeated, hope to get better terms now than later, [and] want to spare the German people the additional misery of continued bombing and of seeing their land turned into a battlefield as the Allies advance from both East and West." Neither treacherous nor devious, they were simply pragmatists who had recognized that the war was lost.[12]

The journalist and author Karl O. Paetel had his doubts about this analysis. An expatriate like Vagts, but one who did not emigrate to the United States until after 1933, he reflected essentially the views of the German left in exile. What troubled him most about the abortive attempt to overthrow the Third Reich was that it did not represent a mass movement. "This was purely a struggle inside the army." The tight grip of the secret police might have accounted in part for the limited scope of the uprising. "But a more important reason is probably the fact that the German people, even if they knew what was going on, would see in it only a quarrel between two sets of masters." The officers participating in the assassination attempt did not oppose Hitler "on any sort of principle of morality." Many of them had in fact followed him for years. "They revolted against him because they thought he was now a bad leader and for no other reason." Most important, as far as "the masses of the people" were concerned, the failed coup had destroyed the official myth that the Germans were "all in the same boat." It had become clear that there was a mutiny on board. "Realization of this is a necessary prerequisite to a real revolution, the sort that is made only with the aid of the masses themselves, when the workers and peasants at home and the soldiers at the front begin to stir." Paetel saw the abortive July uprising as only the prelude to a new November revolt, like the one that had toppled the old imperial order twenty-six years before. But this one would be better planned and executed; it would be bolder, tougher, and surely more successful.[13]

Even those few foreigners who expressed some sympathy for the resistance did so cautiously and confidentially, basing their position on expediency at least as much as principle. Ralph C. Busser, for example, who had been the American consul in Leipzig before the war, wrote to Secretary of State Hull early in August to urge that an effort be made to help Goerdeler, at that time still in hiding from the Gestapo, escape to the Allied side. He spoke of Goerdeler's "courageous opposition to the sinister policies of the Nazi regime, his liberal and democratic principles, and his consistent friendliness toward the United States and Great Britain." As a longtime fighter for freedom, he deserved the support of all opponents of National Socialist tyranny.

Those who knew Goerdeler well, including probably Goerdeler himself, might have been surprised to hear him described as "liberal and democratic." He had never been called anything like that before. But Busser was interested in more than narrow, technical accuracy. He wanted above all to aid the American war effort and to hasten the victory of the Allies.

"From conversations I had with Dr. Goerdeler shortly before my departure from Leipzig in February, 1940," he assured Hull, "and from the contents of a letter he wrote sometime ago to an American friend, . . . I believe that Dr. Goerdeler, as a peace-loving German anxious to speed the termination of the war and the end of the loathsome Nazi regime, would be willing to broadcast to the world an important message concerning the true conditions in Germany at the present time." Such a message, Busser argued, could prove quite useful in the conduct of psychological warfare. "Acting as a spokesman for the anti-Nazis and the disillusioned German people in general, the propaganda effect of [a declaration by Goerdeler], and the response thereto in Europe and America, would probably hasten the internal collapse of Germany and encourage the revolt of the people in the territories still occupied by the armed forces of the Reich." The unsuccessful coup could still turn out to be helpful to the Allies by spreading demoralization and defeatism in the enemy camp.[14]

The indifference to the resistance displayed outside Germany contributed to its isolation within Germany. If its members had been able to hold out to their countrymen the prospect of some advantage, some concession, some benefit, the popular attitude toward their attempt to overthrow the Nazi regime might have been more favorable. But all they could offer was a choice between surrendering now and surrendering later. To surrender now would mean the cessation of aerial bombardment and the end of bloodshed on the battlefield, but it would also lead directly to occupation, partition, and the harsh vengeance of the victors. To surrender later would require the continuation of a hopeless military struggle. Still, was the familiar horror of the war much worse than the unfamiliar horror of the peace? Besides, there was always the chance that some new secret weapon might turn the tide, that some brilliant stroke of strategy would stop the enemy advance, that some change of government within the Allied coalition could make it more willing to negotiate with the Third Reich. What the resistance had to offer could not overcome the mood of gloomy resignation on the part of the German population.

The official attitude of the Nazi regime was of course much more sanguine. Many of Hitlers followers interpreted his narrow escape from the assassin's bomb as a sign that fate or providence or God would protect him until the fulfillment of his lofty destiny. He himself seemed to share this feeling. In his radio broadcast to the German nation on July 21, after denouncing the "very small clique of ambitious, unscrupulous, and at the same time criminally stupid officers" who had tried to kill him, he adopted an uncharacteristic tone of pious devotion. That he had emerged from his ordeal unhurt seemed to him "a confirmation of the task assigned to me by providence to continue to pursue the goal of my life as I have done until now." But as for those who had tried through conspiracy and assassination to keep him from pursuing that goal, for them there would be no forgiveness. They were "a very small gang of criminal elements, who are now being mercilessly exterminated." The Führer meant every word of that.[15]

The failure of the coup aroused an outpour of public declarations of loyalty to the Third Reich, some of them quite sincere, others partly sincere, still others a little insincere, and a few entirely mendacious. Party bosses, leading bureaucrats, prominent diplomats, and high-ranking officers, including some who had at one time or another flirted with the resistance, fell over each other in the sudden rush to announce their undying devotion to Hitler. Since everyone was in danger of being regarded as a suspect, everyone became eager to prove his innocence. The fate of those involved in the unsuccessful coup encouraged those who were not to proclaim their unshakable faith in National Socialism, their resolve to fight for the sacred cause to the last drop of blood, and their readiness to lay down their lives in the regime's defense. It was not an edifying spectacle.

But what about the attitude of the broad masses? The evidence is somewhat ambiguous, because the authorities were determined to make it appear that the average citizen of the Third Reich was as opposed to the attempt on Hitler's life as the leaders of the party. Still, even in their confidential correspondence defenders of the regime made no mention of any popular expressions of sympathy for the resistance, however indirect, however guarded. A summary prepared by the secret police on July 21 emphasized that "in all the reports there is unanimous agreement that the news about the attempted assassination has shocked the entire nation, arousing the greatest dismay and alarm as well as profound indignation and rage." From several cities, from Königsberg and Berlin, for example, came accounts of women in shops and on the streets breaking into tears and becoming in some instances "completely disconcerted." Joy over the failure of the attempted assassination was "extraordinarily great." People everywhere were breathing a sigh of relief. "Thank God, the Führer is alive."

All in all, "not a single word has so far been heard which would suggest that any citizen supported the plot." On the contrary, even those elements of the population that did not always endorse National Socialism unreservedly condemned the conspiracy to assassinate Hitler. The opinions expressed by workers in the northern part of Berlin, for example, "who formerly stood clearly on the opposing side," generally condemned the betrayal of the Führer in such a dastardly fashion as a "filthy attempt at murder." What would have happened if the plot had succeeded was described by all as "inconceivable." It would have meant defeat, ruin, and the destruction of the nation. "That would have been the end" was a view heard throughout Germany. What a stroke of luck it was that Hitler had survived.[16]

A week later, on July 28, a secret report by the security organization of the SS, though conceding that the failed coup was still causing some popular concern, insisted that public opinion remained loyal and steadfast. There may have been widespread discussion of the background and consequences of the attempted coup, but "a deterioration in morale, according to the accounts we have received, has not taken place." On the contrary,

"the population is relieved that the Führer did not fall victim to the plot."
Information received from Berlin, Frankfurt an der Oder, Innsbruck,
Kattowitz, and other cities suggested that "almost everywhere the feeling
of attachment to the Führer and confidence in our leadership have been
strengthened." The terrible events of the previous week had admittedly
caused a few disturbing signs of popular uneasiness. Here and there, in
Frankfurt am Main, for example, as well as in Innsbruck, Cologne, and
Linz, some people were expressing the fear that "the events of July 20
could weaken our political situation in dealing with foreign countries."
Worse still, there were occasional questions whether "our situation is so
bad that even men in the immediate entourage of the Führer have lost their
confidence in victory and their courage." But those were rare exceptions
to the overall steadfastness of public opinion. "In general, a rise in fighting
spirit and in the determination to stick it out at all costs has become
noticeable." The regime had nothing to worry about.[17]

Obviously, reports by the secret police and the SS should be read with
caution. Their authors, committed National Socialists, tried, sometimes
deliberately and sometimes subconsciously, to portray the situation of the
Third Reich as rosily as possible. Yet what they were saying was confidential, intended only for those unquestionably loyal to the Hitler government. They were not likely to suppress important information regarding
the state of public opinion merely because it was unfavorable or unwelcome. Their analyses may still be open to challenge on points of emphasis,
nuance, or interpretation. Perhaps only a handful of women actually became "completely disconcerted" in shops and on the streets after learning
of the attempt to assassinate the Führer. Perhaps some of the workers in
Berlin did not share the view that the coup was "a filthy attempt at
murder." There may even have been people who did not really feel that
the overthrow of the Third Reich "would have been the end." Still, if the
German public did not view the unsuccessful uprising with universal
abhorrence, neither did it show signs of significant support. Its attitude can
best be described as passive or indifferent. There were no riots, strikes,
marches, or demonstrations. To that extent, the reports of the police
authorities were essentially correct.

Even church leaders who had on previous occasions openly criticized the
measures and policies of the Nazi regime now thought it best to remain
silent. They raised no public appeals for clemency, no private expressions
of sympathy. They had been willing to condemn the government for
meddling in ecclesiastical governance, for introducing legalized euthanasia,
or for engaging in anti-Semitic genocide. But appearing to condone trea-

son was another matter. That would have meant violating the boundary between religion and politics, between theology and statecraft. The members of the churchly elite, Protestants and Catholics alike, studied and pondered that invisible boundary; they reflected and agonized over it. And yet they could not bring themselves to cross it. There were simply too many denominational interests at stake, too many confessional concerns. It seemed best to stop short of provoking an open confrontation with the government authorities.

Two months after the failed coup, Wurm in a private letter condemned the Nazi regime every bit as passionately as Beck or Goerdeler or Hassell. "Everyone knows or can know how the Third Reich has dealt with the Jews, especially since the night of November 9–10, 1938, and during the war, to the point of their complete extermination abroad in Poland and Russia." It was also common knowledge that "serious injustice has been committed in the occupied territories against entirely innocent people as a result of the reintroduction of the hostage system, which was common in the times of barbarism." Moreover, the Nazis had engaged in "the systematic murder of the mentally ill," they had introduced an "entire system" of secret police and concentration camps, and they had promoted the suppression of the last remnants of an "independent judiciary." To Wurm National Socialism had become the political embodiment of moral corruption.

The implications of his conviction were clear. "Can a devout Christian hope for divine blessing for a nation that has allowed all these things to happen, and for a political system that did all these things and allows no criticism of any sort regarding its measures?" Still, the tyrannical Nazi regime could not be overthrown by conspiracies, assassinations, and coups. A loyal member of the church, "if he loves his nation and deplores . . . injustice," must hope instead that "those responsible will arrive at a recognition of their monstrous guilt." Putting it another way, "a deliverance of the German nation is [impossible], unless its leadership acknowledges its injustice and atones for that injustice." In the meantime, all that a believer in the Christian faith could do was wait, trust, and pray. For only God might soften the hearts of the leaders of the Nazi regime. Only God could change the system of government established under the Third Reich. Besides—the thought must have occurred to the bishop, although he never said so—even if God did not change the Nazi system of government, the victorious Allies soon would.[18]

Faulhaber would not even go that far. He did not condemn any of the policies of National Socialism, not even in private, not its political and religious oppressiveness nor its bureaucratic and judicial despotism nor its eugenic and racial mass murder. He was too busy trying to extricate himself from the embarrassing discovery by the secret police that he had been in contact with Goerdeler and Moltke. Their conversations had, at the cardinal's insistence, never gone beyond a discussion of ecclesiastical questions. But would the Gestapo believe that? In the paranoid atmosphere of the weeks following the failed coup, everyone was a suspect or at least feared being one, including Faulhaber. He tried desperately to prove that he had nothing to do with the assassination plot. "The result of an interrogation of Cardinal Faulhaber regarding his conversation with former mayor Goerdeler is interesting," according to a report of the secret police at the end of August. "Faulhaber practically fell over himself in rejecting and condemning the plot of July 20 and in his declaration of loyalty toward the Führer." His eager abjectness aroused the scorn even of his inquisitors.

The authorities decided, however, not to pursue the matter. He did not appear to be implicated deeply enough to warrant further investigation. But Faulhaber could not be sure of that. He felt that he needed some additional form of insurance, some secondary line of defense. Among his papers there is the draft he composed of a statement to be issued by the Catholic episcopate condemning the attempt to assassinate Hitler. "The fearful crime of July 20 and its aftermath," the statement declared, "have persuaded us Catholic bishops to raise our voices once again in support of the sanctity of the Fifth Commandment, 'Thou shalt not kill,' and to keep telling our congregations . . . that the Fifth Commandment brands with the mark of Cain anyone who plans murder against a fellow human being or actually commits murder or participates by conspiring with others in preparations to commit murder."

Faulhaber did not invoke the Decalogue to condemn the SS or the Gestapo or the death squads busily exterminating "non-Aryans." The evildoers in his statement were those who had tried to put an end to the SS and the Gestapo and the death squads by assassinating Hitler. The statement did appeal to the Führer "in the holy name of God" to instruct the judiciary of the Third Reich that "every accused, whether a German national or a foreigner, should be tried in court in accordance with the laws of justice and humaneness to determine in each case whether a capital crime has actually been committed." The state had the duty "before God and the world," moreover, to exercise its right to impose the death penalty "without prejudice and without political predisposition." But the cardinal's emphasis rested above all on the obligation of the citizen to obey the established legitimate government. "Wherever authority exists, it is or-

dained by God. Whoever rebels against authority rebels against God's
order." To ensure his personal safety and to protect the interests of his
church, Faulhaber was prepared for the time being to play a defender of
National Socialism.[19]

Even some of the conservative opponents of the Third Reich disapproved of the plot to assassinate Hitler. It was one thing to criticize the
principles and objectives of the Nazi regime. But to instigate an uprising
in wartime, an uprising bound to hasten the nation's defeat, was something
altogether different. Niemöller was in the concentration camp at Dachau
at the time of the coup, imprisoned for his opposition to the government's
ecclesiastical policy. But after his release in the spring of 1945, he made a
statement at a press conference on June 5 that indirectly but unmistakably
repudiated the resistance. "If there is a war a German doesn't ask is it just
or unjust, but he feels bound to join the ranks." He himself had never
really disagreed with Hitler regarding questions of politics. He had opposed him solely because the Third Reich wanted not only "man's body
[but also his] soul." That and that alone had been the basis of his rejection
of National Socialism.[20]

The conservative intellectual Friedrich Percyval Reck-Malleczewen expressed greater vehemence. The son of an East Prussian landowner, he was
socially and ideologically close to the resistance. But the denunciation in
his diary of those involved in the attempt to kill Hitler was as harsh as any
by Ehrenburg in the Soviet Union or Wheeler-Bennett in Great Britain.
The would-be assassins had for years covered up the Nazi regime's "every
act of treason, every orgy of murder and rape," because Hitler enabled
them to play once again a prominent role in public affairs. They had
remained indifferent to "the misery of all the victims of the bombings [as
well as] the misery of the prisoners in the concentration camps," since any
change in government might have threatened their position. But now that
"the bankruptcy [of the system] can no longer be denied," they were
abandoning the cause they had so long defended "in order to provide a
political alibi for themselves." They were betraying the Third Reich, "just
as yesterday [they] betrayed the republic and the day before yesterday the
monarchy." It was a damning indictment.[21]

The small liberal fringe of the resistance represented by the Kreisau
Circle was more sympathetic. Still, its members remained critical of those
who had planned and organized the abortive coup, critical not only of their
principles but also of their methods. Moltke described Goerdeler's views
on the future of the nation as "bourgeois reactionary" and "dilettantish."
Theodor Steltzer, another democratic resister, secretly transmitted a

memorandum to the Allies a few days before the attempt on Hitler's life describing "the German opposition against National Socialism." In it he insisted that "except for us there is no circle based on groups independent of Hitlerism that would be in a position to embrace all forces willing to undertake the work of reconstruction." The resistance comprised various factions, especially "a conservative circle with decidedly activist aims." But those people "could not be taken seriously." They were so traditional in outlook, so devoted to the values of the past. They simply should not be entrusted with the task of building the new, free Germany.

Yet what the members of the Kreisau Circle objected to went beyond the conservative ideology of those plotting to assassinate Hitler. They were also reluctant in principle to employ force as an instrument of political change. They were too fastidious in their idealism to engage in anything as messy as bombing, maiming, and killing. That sort of dirty business should be left to others, preferably the Allies. Two weeks before his execution Moltke thanked providence for having saved him from the temptation to rely on violence in the overthrow of the Third Reich. "Just think how wonderfully God has molded this, his unworthy vessel," he wrote to his wife. "At a moment when the danger existed that I might be drawn into active preparations for a coup, . . . I was [arrested early in 1944], so that I am and remain free of any connection with the use of force." He was grateful for that.

Moltke remained the Hamlet of the resistance to the end, agonizing over the cruel dilemmas and exigencies of a time out of joint. Almost fifty years later his widow recalled that, though "not so much against murdering Hitler," he had serious "scruples" about it. He did not actually regard the deed as "impossible," but he kept wondering "how one could do it, whether one could do it." In any case, he was convinced that "Stauffenberg and his friends could not pull it off successfully." Nor could anyone else, for that matter. In any case, what difference would it make? "You don't have anyone who can do it right. And it won't help anyway. Everything's too far gone, and so horrendous. You can't change anything. We have to leave it to the Allies, whether you want to or not." It all seemed to him so hopeless. "We are dilettantes. It won't succeed for us." The more he thought about it, the more reasons he found for not doing it. After all, an unsuccessful uprising against the Nazi regime might "cost the lives of people needed to govern postwar Germany." And so it went. Moltke met the executioner still unable to decide whether to be or not to be.[22]

The uprising of July 20 ended in fact as he had predicted, in a disastrous defeat, a mortal failure. It was all over in less than twenty-four hours. The outcome was due in part to Hitler's luck in surviving the attempt to assassinate him. But even if he had not, it is doubtful that the final outcome would have been much different. The fatal weakness of the resistance was its isolation. It had no significant support, neither at home nor abroad, neither among liberals nor conservatives, neither among sympathizers nor critics of the regime, neither among the upper nor the lower classes. The movement initiated six years earlier to overthrow the Hitler dictatorship collapsed within a day because it had never become more than a conspiratorial attempt at a palace revolution.

Those involved in that attempt were finally forced to recognize the full extent of their isolation. Their response to it provides an insight into their guiding principles and ideals, their primary goals and motives. The way in which the first victims of the failed coup met their death is particularly significant, because its suddenness left little time for reflection or rationalization. Some of them seemed simply stunned. On the night of July 20 Beck, bewildered, tired, barely recovered from a serious cancer operation, tried to shoot himself but was too overwrought to carry out his purpose, even after two attempts. A soldier had to finish him off. His last words were an interrupted reminiscence about the old days.[23]

Friedrich Olbricht and Claus von Stauffenberg, both of whom were executed shortly afterward by a firing squad following a summary court-martial, remained more composed. Olbricht declared that while he did not know what judgment history would pass on the resistance or on his role in it, his conscience was clear regarding the cause he had tried to serve. "I know with certainty that all of us acted free of any sort of personal motives, and that we dared attempt the ultimate only in a situation that was already desperate, in order to protect Germany against total destruction." Future generations would surely recognize and acknowledge that.[24]

Stauffenberg was even more succinct. As he stood against the wall facing the firing squad, he shouted out: "Long live sacred Germany." That was his farewell. But he was saying essentially the same thing as Olbricht. Both voiced at the moment of death their love of country and their commitment to their nation. They were not blind to the injustices that others had been forced to endure at the hands of the Third Reich. Indeed, they deplored and condemned those injustices. Their primary allegiance, however, remained to their own state and their own people. They were above all patriots, not chauvinists, not jingoists, but patriots in the best sense of that disputed term.[25]

Yet the most moving statement by the resistance following its collapse did not come from someone who had been at the Wolf's Lair that fateful day or at the army high command on the Bendlerstrasse in Berlin. It came from far to the east, from the Russian front. Although Henning von Tresckow had long been an opponent of the Third Reich, he did not play a major role in the coup of July 20. He became, however, one of the first resisters to maintain that the struggle to overthrow the Nazi regime must be based on more than national duty or patriotic loyalty. It was a moral obligation to all mankind. On the day after the failure of the assassination attempt, he explained to a fellow officer the ultimate meaning of what had just taken place:

> Now the entire world will assail us and revile us. But I am now as before absolutely convinced that we acted properly. I consider Hitler to be not only the archenemy of Germany but also the archenemy of the world. When I stand in a few hours before God's judgment seat to give an account of my actions and omissions, I think that I will be able to defend in good conscience what I did in the struggle against Hitler. If God once promised Abraham that he would not destroy Sodom if only ten righteous men lived there, then I hope that because of us God will also not destroy Germany. . . . The moral worth of a human being begins only when he is ready to sacrifice his life for his conviction.

Tresckow then drove to the front lines and blew himself up with a hand grenade. Thus he sought to expiate his nation's acquiescence in a terrible moral evil, to admit guilt, do penance, and ask for forgiveness.[26]

22

The Passion of the German Resistance

As soon as the coup of July 20 was crushed, the Nazi regime launched a manhunt for those involved, which continued without interruption until the collapse of the Third Reich nine months later. That had been predictable. Hitler was in dead earnest when he declared in his radio address immediately after the suppression of the uprising that the resisters would be "mercilessly exterminated." Their punishment, however severe, would clearly have no bearing on the outcome of the war. There was no danger of any new insurrection against the government. Nor was the fate of those who had tried to assassinate the Führer likely to influence the policy of the Allies toward Germany either before or after their victory. Still, those responsible for the abortive coup had to be identified, arrested, and executed—for symbolic and psychological reasons. They had disobeyed orders, they had broken ranks. They had dared to state openly what almost everyone else was thinking secretly. Worst of all, they had tried to mitigate the consequences of the imminent military defeat by hastening the overthrow of the Third Reich.

The actual number of those punished for participating in the coup is hard to determine. Estimates vary widely and usually tend toward overstatement. It is often difficult to distinguish between penalties imposed for involvement in the events of July 20 and those for other acts of political protest or transgression. All in all, the number of those executed in connection with the uprising was probably less than two hundred, while the total of those arrested in all likelihood never reached a thousand. These figures, though more modest than some earlier calculations, suggest that almost everyone who was involved in the plot, and quite a few who were not, received some form of punishment by the authorities.[1]

The leaders of the resistance were in most cases tried in court proceedings that gave them an opportunity to defend themselves, although the final verdict was never really in doubt. The importance of those trials, however, does not lie in any new evidence regarding the plans or activities of the resisters. It is to be sought rather in what they reveal about the views and feelings of those involved in the failed coup as they faced the prospect of certain death. Confronting the implacable Roland Freisler, judge, prosecutor, and executioner in one, many of them remained calm and composed, displaying remarkable steadfastness and at times even bold defiance. Their courageous conduct in accepting the consequences of the failure of what they had hoped and sought for such a long time has become part of the martyrology of the German resistance.

There is the story, for example, that Field Marshal Erwin von Witzleben calmly said to Freisler at his trial: "You can hand us over to the hangman. Within three months the outraged and tormented people will call you to account and will drag you alive through the muck of the streets." Whether he actually said that may be questioned. The official record does not contain those words, although that does not prove that they were never actually spoken. In any case, at least Witzleben's composure at his trial seems established beyond doubt.

Some of the others were even bolder in their denunciation of the Nazi regime. Yorck von Wartenburg told the court, "the essential thing that ties all these questions together is the totalitarian claim of the state in dealing with the citizen without regard for his religious and moral obligations to God." Hans-Bernd von Haeften went still further. "According to the view I have of the role of the Führer in world history, I assume that he is a powerful instrument of evil." Ulrich Wilhelm von Schwerin-Schwanenfeld began to talk about "the many murders in Poland." Although the judge would not let him finish, his meaning was perfectly clear. To condemn the Third Reich to its face took real courage.

Not only did several of the resisters refuse to be intimidated by Freisler. A few even dared to bait and provoke him. Josef Wirmer, who would have become minister of justice if the coup had succeeded, taunted the judge about what awaited him after the Allied victory. "Although I will hang, it is not I but you who are afraid." And when Freisler jeered that "soon you will be in hell," Wirmer shot back: "It will be a pleasure for me, Your Honor, provided you soon follow me." General Erich Fellgiebel was equally defiant. He told the judge to hurry up with the hanging of the accused, or else he himself would hang before they did. There are other examples of the remarkable bravery with which many of the resisters faced defeat and death.[2]

Admittedly, the evidence on which these accounts rest is not always unimpeachable. It may have been occasionally embellished or inflated or surmised or even manufactured. The need to idealize and heroize the resisters in the new Germany of the postwar era became eventually so compelling that a critical, dispassionate examination of the hard facts often proved difficult and sometimes impossible. The wish became father to the thought. That was understandable and probably unavoidable. But even taking all this into account, there can be no denying that many of the men in the resistance faced the executioner calmly and courageously. Many of them, moreover, remained convinced that what they had tried to do was both just and justifiable. And many of them found solace in the thought that in the end history would award them the victory that life had denied them.

There were exceptions, however. Some resisters regarded what was happening to them with bewilderment and incomprehension. Especially those who had not been directly involved in the plot to assassinate Hitler could not understand why they were being condemned for a crime they had not committed or even contemplated. To be sure, they had criticized the doctrines and practices of National Socialism. But did that deserve hanging? After all, they had only theorized and debated; they had never actually done anything. They had simply discussed the possibility of a better Germany in the future, a freer, kinder, gentler, and nobler Germany than the present one. Did that justify capital punishment? They had too much faith in the essential goodness and reasonableness of mankind to grasp fully the malignity of the Nazi regime.

The best known among these perplexed nonviolent resisters was Moltke. A man of humane outlook and liberal conviction, he had become an opponent of the Nazi regime long before the would-be assassins of Hitler. While many of them were still pondering whether it might not be better to wait until the war was won before attempting to overthrow the Third Reich, whether it was not possible that those in power would sooner or later recognize the error of their ways, and whether the security of the nation did not outweigh the wickedness of the government, Moltke perceived from the outset the inherent immorality of the doctrines and policies of National Socialism. There could never be any question about the sincerity or consistency of his rejection of the Hitler dictatorship.

In a farewell letter to his sons written shortly before his execution, he tried to describe the principles that had shaped his political outlook. "I have throughout my life, as early as my school days, fought against the spirit of narrowness and violence, of arrogance, of intolerance, and of absolute, merciless consistency, the spirit that is prevalent among the

Germans." That spirit had ultimately found its fearful expression in the Third Reich. But Moltke continued to oppose it boldly and unconditionally, now as before. "I have also devoted myself to overcoming this spirit with its evil consequences such as excessive nationalism, racial persecution, lack of faith, and materialism." No idle contention, no last-minute attempt at self-exculpation or self-justification, the letter summarized the fundamental ethical beliefs behind his rejection of the Third Reich.[3]

Yet this very commitment to principle made it difficult for him to understand those who lacked such commitment. He assumed that his opponents acted on principle as well, different perhaps from his own, but principle nevertheless. Thus he could not see any reason for his condemnation or grasp the arbitrariness, the vengefulness, the sheer malevolence behind the death sentence imposed on him. He remained bewildered up to the moment of his execution. Less than two weeks before going to the gallows, he expressed this sense of disbelief to his wife:

> In the [court] proceedings all specific accusations were shown to be invalid, and they were therefore dropped. Nothing remained. That of which the Third Reich is so afraid that it must condemn 5 people . . . to death is in the end only the following: a private individual, namely yours truly, has been shown to have discussed with 2 clergymen of both denominations, with a Jesuit Provincial and a few bishops, without the intention of doing anything concrete, and that has been established, matters "which belong to the exclusive authority of the Führer." What we discussed were by no means questions of organization, by no means the structure of the Reich. . . . What we discussed were questions regarding the practical and ethical demands of Christianity. Nothing more. And only for that were we found guilty.

Moltke found some consolation, however, in the thought that he had at least remained aloof, methodologically as well as ideologically, from those who tried to overthrow the Third Reich by conspiracy and bloodshed. No one could accuse him of countenancing political violence. He would meet death with his principles unsullied and his convictions uncompromised. "We are, according to these [court] proceedings, untouched by the Goerdeler muck, we are untouched by any practical activity," he wrote with a feeling of moral satisfaction. "We are being hanged because we thought together." Perhaps it was better this way. "If we must indeed perish, then I am by all means in favor of dying for that reason." Being executed for thinking seemed preferable to being executed for trying to kill Hitler. At least he could go to his death with a clear conscience.[4]

While some of the resisters rejected the use of force against the Nazi regime for reasons of principle, others repented its use for reasons of conscience. They became penitents. Languishing in prison after the failure of the coup, facing certain death, they began to express doubts about the role they had played. Should they have participated in the uprising in the first place? Did not their resolve to change the form of government by conspiracy represent a form of moral arrogance, a display of self-righteousness and self-importance? Should not the nation's destiny have been left to God's divine will? And should not they themselves have followed orders, performed their duties, and hoped for the best, like the great majority of their countrymen? Such were the questions troubling these contrite members of the resistance in their last days and hours.

Hellmuth Stieff was one of them. A senior army officer who had for more than a year been involved in planning and preparing the coup against Hitler, he acknowledged after his arrest that his conduct had been indefensible. Indeed, it deserved the death penalty. In his last letter to his wife written just before his execution, he said as much. "The main [court] proceedings took place yesterday and today. The [prosecutor's] motion is for death, and it cannot be otherwise. It is just." He regretted the "pain and disgrace" that his traitorous conduct had caused her. Death, he declared, is not an end but "only a change." They would meet again in the afterlife, "once I have atoned for everything in which I erred in this life." That thought gave him strength. "I go calm and composed to my death, which I myself, burdened with guilt, have invited." He offered no excuses, no apologies, no explanations.

Stieff insisted only that his motives, even if wrong and presumptuous, had been honorable. He had not been driven by ambition or self-interest. His sole concern had been the welfare of his nation. "You know," he maintained to the end, "that I did not act as I did [out of] ill will, even if appearances are now against me. I made a mistake and I was at fault. It was wrong of me, a mere human being, to try arrogantly to interfere in God's work." And now he would have to pay the penalty for that mistake. Stieff died a few hours later, still overcome by a profound feeling of guilt and remorse.[5]

Some of the others had a change of heart as well. Albrecht von Hagen, who a few months earlier had helped provide the explosives intended to kill Hitler, was also overcome by contrition after his arrest. His farewell letter to his wife sounded very much like Stieff's. He too grieved over the hardships she would have to endure. "Now that I must leave you," he wrote, "I bitterly regret having caused you this terrible sorrow, and I ask you with all my heart to forgive me. The bitter fate I have thereby brought upon you is causing me deep concern, but the fact that I will no longer be able to help you in the difficult times ahead is the source of my greatest sorrow." The ultimate cause of his personal misfortune, however, was not the Nazi Party or the Third Reich or even the war. He alone was responsible. "I cannot quarrel with my fate," he concluded, "because I myself am guilty of having brought it on." He could only repent and die.[6]

Lieutenant Colonel Robert Bernardis, the liaison officer between the resisters in Berlin and those in Vienna, was not quite so hard on himself. He blamed unfortunate circumstances as much as personal failings for his impending execution. He spoke of "an unhappy chain of events" that had drawn him into the failed coup, something "for which I must now atone." He had placed too much confidence in an unnamed member of the resistance, a confidence "most bitterly disappointed." Nevertheless, his intentions had always been honorable. "I wanted only to do good. I never even dreamed of acting out of any ambitious or foolhardy motives." He would soon have to pay the price for his mistake, however. He too was "terribly sorry that I must cause [his wife] . . . this pain, [but] unfortunately I can no longer change that." If he had only known then what he knew now, things would have turned out much differently, much better. "I thought I would do good, but that was wrong." In retrospect, what happened seemed to him "an act of providence." That thought provided him in his last hours with a measure of consolation.[7]

General Erich Hoepner, briefer and more to the point, did not speculate about destiny or the divine will. He simply urged his family to "think of me with a little love, even though I am responsible for great sorrow." In contrast, Karl Friedrich Klausing, who had spent July 20 at the Berlin headquarters of the resistance helping direct the uprising, was now overcome with guilt and remorse. In his farewell letter to his parents he described the death sentence pronounced against him as "appropriate for what I did." Nothing less would have been suitable punishment for his act of treason. "Looking back, especially after seeing the ringleaders of the entire operation, I can only regard it as a sign of divine mercy that it prevented the coup's success, which would have meant chaos and the end of the German nation." This conviction enabled him to accept calmly "what awaits me." But while he could acknowledge his terrible mistake, he could not undo it or "wipe away the disgrace I have brought upon our name." Like the others, he declared that "my greatest regret is to be causing you this pain on top of all your other troubles." He went to the gallows later that same day, profoundly dejected and guilt-ridden.[8]

After the war some writers suggested that these statements of contrition were not really genuine, that they were obtained by the security police in return for promises of generous treatment for the families of the prisoners. But such contentions seem farfetched. For one thing, the tone of the various farewell letters sounds too authentic, too heartfelt, to have been coerced or extorted. They reveal too much personal pain and sorrow. For another, the remorse expressed by the condemned men appeared in private communications that were not meant to be published. They could not have been easily used by the authorities to shape or influence public opinion. Finally, to the ardent supporters of the Nazi regime the knowledge that the traitors had gone to their death incorrigibly obdurate would have been as welcome as the news that they had at the last moment become penitent and reconverted. There is simply no persuasive reason to question the sincerity of the remorse voiced by some of the resisters before their execution.

In any event, most of them did not plead or regret or apologize. They remained stubbornly unrepentant. They defied the regime, convinced to the end that the attempt to overthrow Hitler had been justified. Their bold conduct at the trials that condemned them to death has helped form the later popular view of the resistance. Posterity sees the men of July 20 as they stood in the dock, steadfast and composed, courageously facing the charges of treason directed against them. Hassell, still calm during the legal proceedings, still dignified, more the accuser than the accused; Hermann Maass refusing to make a final plea to the court in protest against the judge's constant malicious interruptions; Schulenburg treating with disdain and sarcasm Freisler's accusations of disloyalty to the nation; Haeften stating bluntly that "Adolf Hitler was the incarnation of evil"—such are the scenes that define the postwar image of the resisters.[9]

Yet there also are other important sources of information regarding their feelings and convictions after the failed uprising, sources not as dramatic as the statements made in court but more comprehensive and illuminating. The record of their interrogations in prison by the security police provides especially useful information. Extending over a considerable period of time, conducted in private, without the exchange of accusations and counteraccusations that characterized the summary trials of the prisoners, those interrogations shed light on the resisters' opinions, reflections, ideas, and emotions during the months and weeks preceding their execution. They constitute an invaluable historical source providing a more subtle and nuanced portrait of the resistance than the colorful but meager and superficial court records.

They reveal that while most of the participants in the coup did not regret their attempt to overthrow the Nazi regime, neither did they disavow their earlier acceptance and support of that regime. Even after their mortal failure, facing imminent execution, they remained generally persuaded of the soundness of many of the basic beliefs and ideals of National Socialism. What had turned them against the Third Reich was its abandonment of those beliefs and ideals. They regarded themselves as in a sense more loyal to the original ideology of the party than its own leaders. Success and power had corrupted the regime, seducing its supporters with temptations they found irresistible. Its opponents, meanwhile, had remained faithful to the doctrines of selfless service, moral responsibility, individual sacrifice, and collective duty. Who then were the true defenders of the national interest and who its betrayers? Who were the real renegades and who the real patriots?

According to one report by the security police, "a large number of those interrogated state that they had declared themselves by and large in agreement with the objectives of the National Socialist Party in 1933." Berthold von Stauffenberg, for example, had testified that "regarding domestic policy, we certainly approved by and large the basic ideas of National Socialism." Those ideas had seemed to him "healthy and forward-looking." They included "the concept of the leader" and "responsible and expert leadership," a "healthy hierarchical order" and a sense of "national community," the principle that "collective welfare takes precedence over individual welfare," the "struggle against corruption," an "emphasis on rural life and on the struggle against the spirit of the big cities," the "idea of race," and finally the resolve to create "a new legal system determined by the German character." Indeed, there appeared to be almost no part of the Nazi program in those early days of which Stauffenberg did not approve.[10]

Several of the other resisters expressed similar views. Some of them supported the original program of the Third Reich even more vigorously. Lieutenant Colonel Nikolaus von Üxküll-Gyllenband testified that "after the seizure of power [by the Nazis], I was an avowed supporter of the Führer, and I was also convinced that he would lead us to great achievements." Wolf Heinrich von Helldorf, former chief of the Berlin police, told his interrogators that "my personal view, today as always, is that I approve of National Socialism as it was understood and taught by us in the years of struggle [before 1933]." But no one surpassed Popitz in praise for the achievements of a government that was about to put him to death. "I approve of the National Socialist Party in every respect," he told the police authorities, "and I see in it the historical necessity, arising out of the internationalism and Judaization of the period of the [Weimar] system and out of the intolerable crises of the parliamentary parties, of uniting the German people within their total national boundaries and governing them in the only way in which they can be governed, considering their geographical situation." The officials reading these police reports must have been surprised at such avowals of loyalty to the ideology of the Nazi regime from those who only a few weeks earlier had tried so hard to overthrow it.[11]

Even Goerdeler, the chief civilian architect of the resistance, conceded that the Third Reich was not without its redeeming qualities. After his arrest for participating in the coup, he continued tirelessly turning out essays, memorandums, outlines, and proposals, most of them explaining the mistakes of the past and suggesting their rectification in the future. Writing helped him remain calm and composed, even sanguine at times.

In "Our Idea," one of the treatises composed in prison, he acknowledged that National Socialism had brought with it "two good things" that should be retained even after its fall by the future government of Germany. First, it recognized that "life is a struggle" requiring "work and accomplishment," but a struggle "ennobled by the observance of God's commandments." Second, it emphasized the principle that "we must help one another," or more concretely, that "the system of compensation for labor [should be] such that capital does not earn excessive profits." Moral commitment and social justice, those were still sound foundations for the future process of national recovery and regeneration.

Goerdeler could at times be even more generous in assessing the teachings of National Socialism. He stated at one of the interrogations that "the essential principles of the party," namely, "the fatherland above everything else, integrity in official conduct, honesty in administration, common welfare above individual welfare, and social justice," were lessons he had learned as a boy in the home of his parents. And those lessons had remained close to his heart throughout his life.

For that matter, Hitler's foreign policy did not seem to Goerdeler altogether unjustified. He testified before the security police that "the incorporation of Austria into the Reich was a necessary and welcome development that could not be stopped." The annexation of the Sudeten region under the Munich Agreement was "welcome" as well. Indeed, "it must be the goal of [German] foreign policy in the future to have the Sudeten region remain permanently part of the Reich." As for the outbreak of war less than a year after the annexation, that had its roots in the "dictate of Versailles," he insisted.

Goerdeler described in detail his views on the background of the military conflict and how it might have been avoided in "Thoughts of a Man

Condemned to Death," another of the essays composed during his six months in prison. Here he argued that a more skillful diplomacy could have prevented the outbreak of hostilities. Even the issue of the Polish Corridor, the problem in international relations that concerned him most, "could have been settled peacefully in the period 1932–39." The key would have been a decision to make the solution to the Sudeten question part of a general agreement among the great powers regarding all outstanding disputes. It would have been so simple, Goerdeler maintained with his usual easy optimism.

But the diplomats refused to see that. They remained obdurate and shortsighted. Poland even participated in the partition of Czechoslovakia. England and France, moreover, failed to propose, as they clearly should have, that the Sudeten question along with all other international problems be submitted to a general conference of the European states. If they had done so, the Germans would have been able to present the claims for territorial expansion that Goerdeler had long supported, claims not altogether different from those advanced by Hitler: "the [Polish] Corridor, Posen, the southern Tirol up to Bolzano and Merano, and colonies." Diplomatic preparations would have probably taken no more than six months, so that the conference could have opened early in 1939 under the slogan "European peace." Everything would have been settled by negotiation. Germany's legitimate demands would have been met, while "Poland could then be united with Lithuania and the border states to form a Baltic-Polish federation, economically strong, with harbors in Liepaya and Riga, forming a bulwark against Russia." But the British did not pursue this strategy, mostly because "they had lost their nerve." As a result, the war came a year later. And whose fault was that? Surely, Chamberlain and Daladier contributed by their timidity almost as much to the outbreak of hostilities as Hitler did by his recklessness.[12]

Could these declarations of agreement with many of the principles and some of the policies of the Third Reich have been inspired primarily by the hope of escaping the hangman? Not likely. The resisters must have realized that the Nazi regime had no choice but to impose the death penalty on anyone who attempted to assassinate Hitler. Their crime had been too serious, their guilt too great, to be mitigated by expressions of support, genuine or feigned, for the government's goals. Nothing could save them from the gallows, and they knew it. Nor can the trustworthiness of the official reports regarding the interrogation of the prisoners be seriously questioned. Those reports were not intended for public consumption; they were confidential communications submitted by Ernst Kaltenbrunner, chief of the security police, to Secretary to the Führer Martin Bormann. They were expected to be accurate and to the point, without embellishment or digression. There is no reason to challenge their general reliability. Indeed, what they reveal about the views of the resisters following their arrest is generally consistent with the views often expressed by them before their arrest. The reports thus cannot be dismissed as either spurious or misleading.

That assessment raises another question, however. If those involved in the attempt to overthrow the Third Reich stayed in many cases loyal to the original ideas and ideals of National Socialism, what led them to make that attempt in the first place? What changed them from supporters to opponents of the regime? The records of the security police provide an answer to that question as well. According to one of the reports, "the conduct of National Socialism in practice—and in this connection certain personal occurrences and experiences are cited from time to time—has [in the opinion of the resisters] often been in very stark contrast to its avowed principles." Another report also emphasized this point. "The same people generally maintain that despite their theoretical agreement with the main objectives of the National Socialist Party, they gradually began to waver in their favorable opinion because of the practical means employed to achieve [those objectives]." As Ferdinand von Lüninck put it, at first he and the others had nothing against National Socialism, but since then "a great deal of water diluted the wine of our initial enthusiasm."[13]

The reasons given for this growing disillusionment varied widely, but they all derived more or less from what those arrested described as "a lack of honesty" on the part of the Nazi regime. None of them conceded that they had been mistaken in their original favorable assessment of the party's ideology. Rather, its leaders had gradually become false to that ideology in their pursuit of power. Schulenburg complained about "the abandonment of the foundation of law and the development into a pure police state." He now recognized that "a sphere of freedom must be guaranteed to the individual, as well as to every institution, within which he can act in accordance with his conscience." Popitz acknowledged that restrictions on personal freedom were sometimes unavoidable, but they must not be allowed to deny the ordinary citizen "a measure of legal protection of the most elementary sort." Schacht said that he could not approve of "the issuance and execution of court sentences without a legally determined judicial decision." And Üxküll-Gyllenband insisted that the government had violated the principle that justice must be administered under all circumstances without "feelings of personal rancor or antipathy." These men considered the Third Reich's gradual drift into arbitrariness and despotism to be its fatal weakness.[14]

Others, according to the security police, focused on the regime's errors in foreign policy and its harsh treatment of the conquered territories and peoples. Their criticism ranged from "skepticism about whether we acted properly" to a "self-lacerating" condemnation of the ineptness of the German authorities in France. Hofacker in particular had become embittered by the failure of the government to establish "a lasting [friendly] relationship" with the French. That was a result of the "confusion and inconsistency" of its bureaucrats in Paris, who had constantly provided the losers in the war with an opportunity to exploit the mistakes of the German occupation.

Goerdeler emphasized the errors of the Third Reich's prewar diplomacy. He approved of the incorporation of Austria, but how it was done had led to "the first major deterioration in the international position of Germany." The same mistake marred the otherwise justifiable annexation of the Sudeten region. The regime's methods had seriously damaged foreign confidence in Germany, creating "the initial cause of future tensions." But the most obvious blunder had been the destruction of what was left of Czechoslovakia. After that it became clear that "none of the Western powers would any longer engage in negotiations with Hitler." And yet it was all so unnecessary. The diminished and defenseless Czech state would in any case have become dependent on Germany militarily, economically, and culturally. Why then needlessly antagonize England and France, making the outbreak of war after the next international crisis almost inevitable? All of the nation's legitimate diplomatic objectives could have been met without shedding a drop of blood.

Berthold von Stauffenberg directed his criticism at Hitler's foreign policy as well, but he addressed primarily the mistakes committed since the outbreak of hostilities. He pointed to the alliance with Japan, the conflict with England, and the influx into Germany of large numbers of foreign workers as examples of the violation by the Nazi regime of its own racial doctrines. "The concept of race has been fundamentally betrayed in this war, since precisely the best German blood is being irretrievably sacrificed, while at the same time Germany is being populated by millions of alien workers, who surely cannot be characterized as racially of great value." Was there any logic in that?[15]

Another aspect of Nazi racial policy troubled the resisters even more: the way in which the regime had dealt with the Jewish question. They did not deny as a rule that under Weimar the Jews had acquired too much influence in national life, but that influence should have been curbed less brutally, less ruthlessly. The adoption by the Third Reich of genocide as an instrument of statecraft represented a clear violation of the teachings of morality. Moreover, it helped arouse foreign hostility against Germany and the Germans. It was thus both inhumane and dangerous. It should never have been allowed to become part of the government's program.

"They were of the opinion," according to the police reports, "that the expropriation of the Jews could have been carried out in a form 'more worthy' of Germany." Although no friends of the Jews, they believed that brutal procedures adopted in dealing with the Jewish question had aroused the hostility of the entire world against Germany. Those interrogated seemed generally to agree that "the solution to the Jewish problem should have been undertaken much more calmly, soberly, and genteelly." Racial murder was in any case morally always reprehensible.

Those views appear with varying nuances and emphases in the testimony of several of the resisters. Heinrich von Lehndorff-Steinort declared discreetly that although he was an "opponent of the Jews," he had never entirely approved of the National Socialist concept of race "and especially not of its practical application." Berthold von Stauffenberg even more cautiously described how he and his brother Claus had indeed accepted the racial principles of National Socialism "as such," but had considered them "extreme and excessive." He would not elaborate.

Popitz explained his views at considerable length. He had certainly been of the opinion that "the Jews must vanish from political and economic life." But he had also generally recommended "a somewhat more gradual approach," especially "out of considerations of foreign policy." The exclusion of Jewry from political and economic life had been "unavoidable." Still, "the violent procedure leading to the destruction of property, to arbitrary arrests, and to the annihilation of life could not be reconciled with law and morality, and besides, it seemed dangerous to me because of the views that must have spread among our people regarding the value of property and human life." Popitz concluded by referring once again to the unfortunate effect of Nazi anti-Semitism on public opinion abroad. "At the same time I saw in our treatment of the Jewish question the great danger of intensifying international hostility toward Germany and its political system." The racial program of the regime had gradually become a threat to national security.

One of the few resisters to denounce the genocidal policy of the Third Reich unreservedly and unequivocally was Yorck. He did not claim to have been in principle opposed to excessive Jewish influence in public affairs; he did not explain that his objections applied only to the methods, not the purposes, of official racism; he did not even try to mitigate his criticism by references to public opinion at home or abroad. He made it clear to the security police that he opposed mass murder simply because it was wrong. Barely a week after the failure of the coup, he testified: "In the course of the last few years an inner break with National Socialism occurred within me. What alienated me completely from the National Socialist state were in particular the National Socialist concept of justice, the extermination measures against Jewry going beyond the Nuremberg Laws, and the procedures we adopted in part in the occupied territories." During another interrogation two months later, he was even more precise. "The extermination measures against Jewry, which go beyond justice and the law," the official report described him as saying, "had produced in him an inner break with National Socialism." He resolutely refused to moderate or extenuate his denunciation of genocide.[16]

Yet no one among the resisters devoted as much thought to the tragic fate of the Jews under the Third Reich, to its historical background and moral consequence, as Goerdeler. There is something touching about that man, the conservative Prussian bureaucrat alone in his prison cell, his plans defeated, his hopes shattered, facing imminent death, but still trying to prepare the way for some future reconciliation between Germans and Jews. His views and reflections during the last months of his life reveal the characteristic inner contradictions in his thinking: kindly benevolence side by side with surprising insensitivity, universal morality struggling uneasily against national loyalty, ethical responsibility in frequent conflict with patriotic duty. All those incompatible elements in Goerdeler's perception and outlook appear clearly in his final meditations on the Jewish question.

Now as before, he saw the only sound solution to that question not in coexistence or even assimilation but in a peaceful and friendly separation. He did acknowledge the need for reparation for the Third Reich's expropriation of property belonging to Jews. "Unjustifiable enrichment through the acquisition of Jewish wealth is an injustice and should be indemnified. Compensation to those injured who are still alive is essential." But restitution formed only a small part of Goerdeler's plan. Its keystone was his proposal that "a large or small territory (perhaps in Palestine or South America) will be declared a sovereign Jewish state." Jews throughout the world would become citizens of that state, entitled to its protection and subject to its taxation. In all other countries they would acquire the status of resident aliens, still free to practice certain occupations and own some businesses, but excluded from such rights of citizenship as holding office and voting. An arrangement of this sort would be fair to all the parties.

Goerdeler believed that by now the Jews as well as their non-Jewish friends had come to recognize the urgent need to solve the problem of international anti-Semitism once and for all. "It is a mistake to think that the Anglo-Saxons love the Jews," he maintained. "The opposite is the case." He recalled that during his visit to the United States in 1937 he saw hotels with signs, in Goerdeler's own English, "not for jewish people." In the American universities, moreover, no more than 3 percent of the students, "according to an unwritten law," could be Jewish. Was that really much different from conditions in Germany before the war? Goerdeler's plan would help solve this problem. As for mixed marriages between Jews and non-Jews, that should be left in the future to the "healthy sense of race and humanity" of those involved. Goerdeler concluded by condemning the genocidal policies of the Nazi regime, while arguing that the fault was not entirely one-sided. "We should not try to disguise what happened, but we must point out the great responsibility of the Jews, who had interfered in our public life in ways lacking any proper restraint." Jewish excesses under Weimar had, in his view, prepared the way for anti-Jewish excesses under the Third Reich.[17]

Having apportioned responsibility for the tragedy that had befallen European Jewry, Goerdeler could turn to ways of achieving a reconciliation between Jews and non-Jews. The two should let bygones be bygones, they should frankly admit their faults and then shake hands. The appeal he composed a few weeks after the coup against Hitler, while still in hiding from the police, is at once kindly, well-intentioned, sanguine, touching, clumsy, and naive:

> You Jews, don't stoke the fire. . . . You have a just claim to an independent state in which every Jew will have the rights of citizenship. But your farsighted men warned you already decades ago to stay out of the internal disputes of other nations. Now accept the hand of reconciliation and make this hour truly great. People will attest that I did what I could in Germany to protect you. Outrage in my heart at the inhumaneness with which Hitler persecuted and exterminated you drove me to my actions as much as pain at the abuse of my people. They are a good and hearty people, but completely unpolitical. They were provoked to the utmost by the dictate of Versailles. As a result of its effects they were forced to cope with very serious crises. Only in this soil could Hitler sow and reap his mischief. Until then you never experienced hard times in Germany, as [head of the World Zionist Organization] Dr. [Chaim] Weizmann has said. Let my people expiate the injustice they have committed with the terrible injustice they have suffered. If all of you think and act nobly in this way, you will be blessed and your labor will be fruitful.

Goerdeler remained convinced to the end that the bitter, tragic legacy of genocidal murder could be overcome by mutual understanding and a firm resolve not to repeat the mistakes of the past.[18]

The resisters risked their lives to overthrow the Nazi regime out of still another motive, at least as important as the despotic treatment of Germans or the brutal treatment of non-Germans. That motive appears only infrequently in the reports of the security police, but it comes out clearly in the farewell statements and letters of many of those executed for participating in the coup. It was the growing fear that Hitler's conduct of the war would lead the nation to defeat and disaster. Unless he was removed from power, Germany would be overwhelmed, occupied, and partitioned. In other words, a concern for national welfare and security, a sense of patriotic duty and allegiance, played a major role in persuading most of the resisters that they must be prepared to sacrifice their lives in an effort to save their country.

This conviction can be heard, for example, in Claus von Stauffenberg's invocation of "sacred Germany" as he faced the firing squad. It appears again in the message that a few hours before his execution Canaris communicated to a fellow prisoner by tapping in Morse code on his cell wall: "My time is up. I was no traitor to my country. I did my duty as a German." And it resounds in Schulenburg's last letter to his wife: "My professional life has remained only a fragment, but in the end history will judge us and declare us not guilty. You know that love for the fatherland motivated me as well." For these men and for many others, patriotism was an important factor, often the major factor, in their decision to support an uprising against the Third Reich.[19]

But what if Hitler had been winning the war? Would the resisters still have tried to overthrow the Nazi regime, knowing that to do so might jeopardize the chances of military victory? There is no way of deciding that question conclusively one way or the other. Nevertheless, there is considerable though scattered evidence, especially the close correlation between the fortunes of war and the size and militancy of the resistance, suggesting that the security of the nation predominated over the other considerations.

The issue is even more complicated than that, however. For a minority within the resistance, a small but significant minority, believed that the struggle against the Third Reich must transcend the boundaries of patriotic duty and national loyalty. What mattered to these dissenters most was not whether their country won or lost the war and whether the Allies did or did not accept Germany's "legitimate" demand for a revision of the Treaty of Versailles. What concerned them above all was the need to oppose, for the sake of humanity as a whole, the moral evil embodied by National Socialism. Although they did not as a rule play a leading part in organizing the coup against Hitler, their courageous summons to do battle against the forces of Nazi oppression and brutality remains the most eloquent ideological justification of the resistance.

Several of them have become well known in the martyrology of the movement to overthrow the Third Reich. Bonhoeffer, who had been an opponent of the Nazi regime from the outset, was arrested in the spring of 1943. Moltke, while ambivalent and undecided on some of the important issues confronting the resistance, never wavered in his condemnation of the Hitler tyranny. He too was arrested quite early, about nine months after Bonhoeffer. In addition, the handful of Socialists, men like Julius Leber, Wilhelm Leuschner, Carlo Mierendorff, and Theodor Haubach, who had been uncompromising opponents of National Socialism since the days of Weimar, paid the price for that opposition with long years in concentration camps.

Yet the most poignant expressions of guilt and remorse for the crimes committed under Hitler came from some of the lesser-known members of the resistance. Albrecht Haushofer had spent his life in the shadow of his famous father, one of the founders of geopolitics. But in his *Moabit Sonnets* composed in prison he voiced a courageous, moving, unsparing self-criticism for not having fought against the Nazi regime more promptly and more boldly:

> Yet I am guilty otherwise than you think,
> I should have recognized my duty sooner,
> more sharply named disaster as disaster—
> I withheld my judgement much too long. . . .
> Today I know what I was guilty of.[20]

Andreas Hermes, who had been prominently involved in Weimar politics as a member of the Center Party, was one of the few resisters to survive the Third Reich. After being condemned to death early in 1945 for his support of the coup, he too contemplated, in what he believed to be his farewell letter to his son, the heavy burden of collective moral responsibility resting on the German nation. "Our guilt is immeasurably great and cries out for expiation for the countless murdered human lives, for the justice a thousand times violated, for the demoralization of our people, especially our youth, and for the unspeakable sufferings and torments inflicted with inhumane pitilessness on our nation and on other nations." He called for a solemn rite of "self-purification," however, rather than the exaction of vengeance. "Not our opponents but we ourselves are being summoned to this act of purification." A moral revival was, in his view, the inescapable, the essential precondition for a national revival.[21]

Yorck was one of the few members of this group who played a significant role in directing the coup of July 20. Yet for him as for the others the ultimate significance of what they tried to do transcended national patriotism. In his last letter to his wife he did say that "I too am for my part dying for the fatherland." But what this signified, he hastened to explain, was that "my death will, I hope, be accepted as an expiation for all my sins and as an expiatory sacrifice for that which all of us collectively bear. May also the remoteness of our age from God be diminished somewhat as a result." The belief that he was atoning for the moral evil committed in the name of his nation helped him face the hangman.[22]

If, as Tresckow hoped before committing suicide, God would spare Germany, as he had once promised Abraham to spare Sodom, for the sake of a handful of the righteous, then surely Bonhoeffer, Moltke, Leber, Leuschner, Mierendorff, Haubach, Haushofer, Hermes, and Yorck belong among that handful. But what about the others? What about those who had at first accepted and served the Nazi regime, then turned against it out of patriotic loyalty at least as much as moral principle, and finally risked and lost their lives in the attempt to assassinate Hitler? What about Beck, Goerdeler, Hassell, the Stauffenbergs, Schulenburg, Canaris, Stieff, Popitz, and Tresckow himself? Should they also be included among the righteous for whose sake God would spare Germany? Possibly, perhaps even probably. But only God could be quite sure.

23

Through Martyrdom to Beatitude

Through a long tortuous process the resistance gradually evolved from an act of infamy under the Third Reich into a postwar symbol of an irrepressible longing for a free Germany. In the years immediately following the Nazi regime, the Germans were too preoccupied with the problems of day-to-day existence to reflect much on the abortive attempt to assassinate Hitler. And when they did, most of them saw little beyond a conspiratorial plot whose success would have merely hastened the day of national defeat and humiliation. What seemed to concern them most under the Allied occupation were the pervasive hardships of daily life, the unending shortages of food, housing, clothing, fuel, and transportation. They had to contend, moreover, with the bitter social consequences of those hardships: demoralization, discouragement, black-marketeering, pandering, and prostitution. Finally, the harsh behavior of the occupiers toward the occupied, not always authorized but often tolerated, aroused ill will among the Germans. Instances of exploitation, abuse, vandalism, theft, violence, and rape, especially in the early months of the occupation, seemed to confirm the predictions of the National Socialists regarding what would happen in the event of defeat. The prevailing mood of helplessness and desperation did not encourage sympathy for the participants in the resistance.

Less tangible irritations intensified the resentment of the vanquished. It soon became apparent that being German was not a prerequisite for feeling or behaving like a member of the master race. In their daily conduct some of the military and civilian representatives of the Allied powers did not seem very different from the representatives of the Third Reich in conquered Europe. They displayed the same haughtiness toward the defeated, the same assumption of moral superiority, the same indifference toward the suffering of the losers. On top of that, according to semiofficial doctrine, the Germans were held collectively responsible for the misdeeds committed by the Nazi regime, misdeeds reflecting their national history, character, and culture. Now they would have to undergo a long process of reeducation that would make them better, kinder, and nobler, more like the victors. It all seemed so humiliating.

There was not much they could do to show their resentment, however. The normal channels of public opinion—newspapers, periodicals, books, plays, and films—came under the control of the Allied authorities. But one important outlet remained for the expression of popular feeling in defeated Germany. Leading churchmen retained, at least in the western zones of occupation, a measure of freedom similar to that which they had enjoyed under the Third Reich. In the performance of their pastoral duties, they were often able to communicate their views on political and social questions with an openness that few of their compatriots could afford. The Allies might not like what some ecclesiastics had to say any more than the Nazis did, but they too hesitated to arouse popular protest at home and abroad by arresting prominent members of the German clergy. The opinions of the religious leaders thus became a rough but fairly accurate gauge of the state of mind in occupied Germany following unconditional surrender. They reflected the mood of a people bewildered and demoralized by a national catastrophe of unprecedented dimensions.

A feeling of collective humiliation arising out of total defeat pervaded the country, although few Germans regretted the fall of the Third Reich. By the end of the war most of them felt bitter toward the Nazi regime for having pursued policies leading to disaster. A military capitulation after so much sacrifice of life and property might perhaps have been acceptable if followed by the establishment of a responsible and humane national government. Yet the foreign conquest, occupation, and partition of their country seemed to culminate a succession of disasters they had been forced to endure ever since the battle at Stalingrad. The form of oppression might have become altered with the replacement of one kind of dictatorial rule by another, but the result was continuity rather than change.

This sense of wounded national pride could be heard in the Easter sermon Bishop Galen delivered in Sendenhorst near Münster on April 1, 1945, more than a month before unconditional surrender. Though in the past often critical of the Third Reich, he now viewed the prospect of the military collapse of his country with foreboding. "Yesterday the first troops of our opponents in the war marched through our town. . . . Yesterday's Holy Saturday will have been for each and every German, as it was for us, a shocking experience that will remain a sad memory: the sight of the troops of our opponents in the war marching here in our country, in the German land."

Galen chose not to dwell on how "bitter" the experience had been or how "our heart bleeds for the misery of our people." He had one thing to say publicly, however. He had heard that a lie was being deliberately spread that he had sought contact with the enemy troops and had even entered into negotiations with them. He was outraged. "I declare that whoever is asserting that or anything like that is telling an untruth. For I have neither sought nor had any sort of contact with anyone from the [Allied] ranks, nor have I spoken a word with anyone. Any assertion of this sort is a lie and a slander." The bishop was determined to make it clear that he would never seek an accommodation with the victors at the expense of the patriotic loyalties of his communicants.[1]

Soon more concrete issues began to appear in the public statements of the religious leaders. Complaints grew about the conduct of Allied soldiers and of the "displaced persons," mostly foreign workers who had been conscripted for wartime employment in Germany and who now found themselves freed from the restrictions imposed by the Third Reich. These workers were widely accused, not always without foundation, of engaging in acts of thievery and violence. The resentment by the Germans of real or alleged lawlessness on the part of Allied soldiers and foreign civilians was aggravated by a widespread belief that the occupation authorities were unofficially tolerating this lawlessness, that they were looking the other way. Many prominent churchmen shared this belief.

On May 18, barely a week after the end of the war, Bishop Wurm paid a courtesy call on the commanding general of the French troops in Stuttgart. The latter told his visitor that he had heard "how bravely you resisted the Nazi regime," assuring him that "the rights and properties which National Socialism took from you will today be restored to you." But that had not been the purpose of the bishop's visit. He launched into a bitter condemnation of the behavior of some of the conquerors. "We have, as a church and as a people, gone through difficult times," he began. "We have long seen this end coming; we waited for you as our liberators, in whispered tones and then in a loud voice." But those expectations had been disappointed. "How did you come? Never did a body of German troops enter a conquered city in this manner or allow itself such orgies." Wurm regretted having to be so blunt. "But it is my duty to raise my voice against any injustice, from whatever side it may come." He felt compelled to speak out; he had no choice.

Though at first taken aback, the French commander soon recovered and launched a counterattack. As a "devout Catholic," he assured his visitor, he too had found the behavior of his troops "painful." But whose fault was that? "In this regard the Germans bear the chief responsibility as well." For "they transported our young men capable of bearing arms from France to their labor camps, so that we had to recruit our army of liberation in North Africa without an opportunity to familiarize those wild Mohammedan tribes with Christian beliefs." He refused to discuss the matter any further. But the two of them, the French general and the German bishop, could at least commiserate about the misdeeds of those barbarians who had been enlisted out of sheer necessity in the defense of democracy.[2]

Galen had similar complaints, although his barbarians were different from the ones in Stuttgart. Among his papers are notes he prepared for the protest presented by him on April 13 to the head of the British military government in Westphalia. He started out with a general statement regarding the essential function of any system of government. "The authorities also assume, in addition to power, the duty and the task of securing public order and protecting life and property against needless violence, destruction, and plunder." But then he turned to the problem of the "foreign workers," who were stealing "out of need," he conceded, yet whose lawlessness should be curbed. To provide them with adequate food and housing might admittedly prove a "difficult problem." Still, as a temporary measure they could at least be forbidden, as were the Germans, to be on the streets during nighttime hours.

They were not the only lawbreakers, however. Worse still were members of the Allied armed forces. "The American soldiers" in particular, "they plunder out of wantonness (Negroes)." The bishop found it "incomprehensible" that they had "so little discipline and order," especially at night. Even churches had been desecrated. The only solution was to impose severe restrictions on the off-duty hours of military personnel.

Then Galen turned to a theme on which Wurm had touched. He too had hoped that the Allied victory would mean a return to liberty and the rule of law. But he had found only a different form of brutality and oppression. "We did not believe the German spokesmen who told us that in the east and even in the west rape and plunder are being tolerated or even encouraged. We believed the English radio, which said that they were coming to restore justice and freedom in Germany, which said that the population in the occupied areas would be treated decently." How bitter then was his disappointment. The victorious powers should realize before it was too late that their occupation policies must change. "If decisive action is not taken at once to put an end to the raping of women, the plundering, and the thievery, then we will have to believe what we were told. Our population is being taught hatred and retaliation . . . , it is being driven to despair and Bolshevism." Indeed, the danger existed that the nihilistic spirit of the last years of Weimar would reemerge in an even more destructive form.[3]

Many Germans had still other grievances against the Allied occupation, grievances psychological rather than material in nature, but almost as embittering as the lack of food or the shortage of housing. They resented the tone of superior virtue that the victors frequently adopted toward the vanquished. They rejected the glib assertion that, because of their tradition or culture or national character, they were the inveterate delinquents among the peoples of Europe. After all, were the crimes committed in the name of National Socialism so much worse than those committed in the name of democracy? Was Stalin—or Roosevelt and Churchill, for that matter—so superior to Hitler? Did the Allied statesmen never engage in deceit or oppression or warmongering? Did they never approve measures leading to the death of innocent civilians? An irritating self-righteousness on one side provoked a stubborn defensiveness on the other.

Many of the church leaders subscribed to this feeling, none more so than Cardinal Faulhaber. Always an ardent patriot, a staunch defender of Germany's honor, he found it insufferable that foreigners should treat his country as the pariah of the international community. That was not only an injustice; it was an outrage.

He poured his heart out in a letter of May 17 to Pope Pius XII, who, he assumed, would not prove altogether unsympathetic. The cardinal complained that "American journalism wants to create a world sensation out of the occurrences in the concentration camps, among them Dachau near Munich." Not only the surrounding villages but the German people as whole were being held responsible for what had taken place there. Admittedly, there could be no question that "atrocious crimes" had been committed, crimes "that we all abhor." But—here Faulhaber lapsed into a familiar locution of the postwar period—"none of us had any detailed information, and whoever uttered a word of criticism would have ended up in a camp himself." And then he invoked another defensive cliché of the occupation years: "If we could show in a film the corpses of people who had been buried alive and torn to pieces during an air attack by the Americans, the pictures would be no less horrifying." Who among the Allies had the right to cast the first stone?

In a pastoral directive to the Munich clergy late in June, the cardinal insisted once again on the moral equivalence of the cruelties committed by each side during the war. He maintained that after barely a month of the Allied occupation, "which thus does not have a 12-year history like Dachau," incidents had already taken place that deserved condemnation "from the viewpoint of the moral order." He was referring presumably to what had come to be called euphemistically "fraternization" between the occupiers and the occupied. But far worse, American journalists and soldiers were being brought to Dachau to film and display "to the entire world, down to the last Negro village," the "shame and disgrace of the German nation." Was that fair? What about "the corpses of the thousands and thousands of people who, buried or burned or torn to pieces by bombs dropped from airplanes, lay on the steps of cellars or in the streets," victims of "attacks by British and American fliers"? Would not the world be equally outraged by "this picture of horror"? In truth, the atrocities of the Third Reich were roughly counterbalanced by the atrocities of the Allied powers. Why then dwell on them?[4]

Closely related to this argument was the contention of many Germans that since they had known nothing about the crimes committed by the Nazi regime, they should not be held responsible for them. Let the guilty few be punished. But the great majority was innocent, and that innocence ought to be acknowledged and respected. Niemöller emerged from his imprisonment by the Third Reich declaring that he was "shocked and shattered" to learn what had been going on in the concentration camps. Yet he also insisted that most of his countrymen had known as little about that as he. He stated at an interview with American and British correspondents: "You are mistaken if you think any honest person in Germany will feel personally responsible for things like Dachau, Belsen, and Buchenwald. He will feel only that he was misled into believing in a regime that was led by criminals and murderers." Niemöller rejected categorically the concept of collective national guilt. "The world will be astonished," he predicted, "when it sees how many good people are left in Germany." Why punish the innocent many for the misdeeds of only a few?[5]

This view encouraged the widespread opposition to the policy of denazification adopted by the occupation authorities, especially in the American zone. To be sure, most Germans felt little sympathy for the former leaders of the Third Reich. They generally regarded the party bigwigs as blind ideologues or unscrupulous opportunists whose mistakes had brought the nation to disaster. But the imposition of penalties on ordinary Nazis, on the local schoolteacher or postmaster or policeman or town councilor, seemed to many people unfair. Those were after all acquaintances, friends, relatives. They may have once strutted and postured in their brown uniforms, they may have cheered at the mass rallies, they may have mouthed or even believed the slogans of National Socialism. But they had meant no harm, they had not really done anything bad. And they were now disillusioned, ready to admit their mistakes. Why not let bygones be bygones? By punishing them, by barring them from official positions and prestigious occupations, requiring them to perform menial labor, even jailing some of them, the Allies were being vindictive. Denazification, far from serving as an instrument of democracy, would only breed bitterness and resentment.

Long after the occupation ended Wurm expressed this view in his memoirs. He remained convinced that the American "reeducators" had made "ludicrous psychological mistakes" because they failed to recognize the difference between the "sentiments of the [German] population" and the "actual rule of the [Nazi] Party." The entire "monstrous apparatus" of denazification had been unnecessary. All that was needed to restore freedom and justice in Germany was "the return of orderly conditions, the reestablishment of a good food supply, and the removal from public office of evil and unreliable elements." That would have been quite enough.

The Americans, however, did the "exact opposite." They removed from positions of authority "people of proven merit, of unimpeachable character and broad professional experience," actually imprisoning many of them, and replaced them with "dubious people, with swindlers and adventurers." Some members of the military government did seek the advice of the Germans, but they could not prevail against those of their countrymen who blindly accepted the watchwords coined "on the other side of the ocean." Wurm concluded with an unflattering historical comparison. "The Americans after the occupation of Germany did not act one bit more sensibly than, for example, the Prussians in Alsace after 1870." The experiment in denazification had proved a dismal failure.[6]

This atmosphere of privation, bitterness, humiliation, and resentment left little room for reflection on the significance of the resistance. The problems of sheer physical survival were too pressing, too exhausting. The men who had almost succeeded in assassinating Hitler a few years earlier were largely forgotten amid the misery of the occupation. And when they were remembered, it was usually with disapproval. They appeared disaffected, disloyal. Why could they not have gone on fighting to the end like most of their compatriots? Could they not see that by trying to overthrow the government while hostilities were still in progress they were betraying the soldiers at the front? Even if their coup had succeeded, it would have merely hastened the defeat and occupation of their country. They seemed in retrospect shortsighted, misguided, perhaps even traitorous. Some fifty years later the British writer Anton Gill reported: "Several relatives of conspirators whose names are famous told me that to carry such a surname was a disadvantage in postwar Germany."[7]

The critical attitude toward the resisters persisted long after the occupation came to an end. Surveys of public opinion in the early years of the German Federal Republic revealed little nostalgia for the Third Reich but considerable ambivalence toward those who had tried to overthrow it. A poll conducted in November and December 1952 showed that sharp differences remained regarding the uprising against the Nazi regime. Thus in reply to a question whether someone who was convinced that "injustices and crimes" were being committed under the Hitler dictatorship would have been justified in resisting it, 41 percent of the respondents said yes, 36 percent gave "other answers," and 23 percent were undecided.

But what about wartime? Should a principled opponent of the Nazi regime have resisted while hostilities were still going on or should he have waited until the return of peace? Only 20 percent said that resistance during the war was defensible, 34 percent believed it would have been better to wait, 15 percent said that there should have been no resistance at any time, neither in war nor in peace, and 31 percent were undecided. As for the practical consequences of the coup, 14 percent answered yes to the question whether conditions in Germany would be better today if there had been no attempt to overthrow Hitler, another 14 percent believed that perhaps conditions would be better, 38 percent said that they would not be better, and 34 percent were undecided. Moreover, in reply to a question whether their country would have won the war if there had been no resistance, 21 percent thought so, 15 percent thought that it might perhaps have won, 45 percent said no, and 19 percent were not sure. The results show that three years after the establishment of a new democratic regime in West Germany, public opinion remained sharply divided regarding the movement against the Third Reich.[8]

The same ambivalence characterized the popular attitude toward the attempt to assassinate Hitler. The event itself had left a deep impression on the great majority of Germans. A poll conducted in June 1951 showed that 89 percent of the respondents still remembered what had happened on July 20, 1944. Only 11 percent reported that they "know nothing about it." But the replies were much more divided on the question "How should we in your opinion judge the men of July 20?" Here 40 percent expressed a favorable view of the resisters, 3 percent were "vacillating in their judgment," 30 percent were unfavorable, 16 percent had "no opinion, do not know," and 11 percent insisted that they had "no recollection of July 20."

The end of the occupation and the reestablishment of an independent German state had failed to dispel serious misgivings regarding the attempt to overthrow the Nazi regime.[9]

Still, by the early 1950s the prevailing view of the resistance had become more favorable, both inside and outside Germany. For one thing, the coming of the cold war changed the general attitude in the United States and Britain toward their recent enemy. The Germans ceased to be viewed as the perennial troublemakers and warmongers of Europe. The threat to peace now seemed to come from the Russians. And as the Western democracies prepared to meet this new threat, they began to see in the Germans potential recruits or even allies in an anti-Soviet coalition. This new attitude not only contributed to the establishment of the German Federal Republic but also led to a reappraisal of the resistance. The recollection of the movement to overthrow the Third Reich during the war seemed to offer support to the experiment in democracy in Germany after the war. It seemed to show that even under the Nazi regime some Germans were willing to risk their lives in defense of liberty and justice. Most important, it seemed to vindicate the decision of the United States and England to accept them as partners.

From the point of view of the German Federal Republic there were even more compelling reasons to embrace the resistance. The attempted coup against the Hitler dictatorship helped refute the concepts of collective responsibility and collective guilt. It seemed to demonstrate that there were good Germans as well as bad ones, that not all of them had been Nazis. Many had been anti-Nazis or at least non-Nazis. Thus the official attitude toward the resisters, an attitude that gradually helped shape public opinion, began to change. They became the symbols of an undying commitment to freedom in Germany, which could not be suppressed even in the darkest hours of the Third Reich. The men who had organized the uprising of July 20, 1944, most of them conservative and nationalistic, began to be perceived as the heroes and martyrs of a new democratic regime in their country. They assumed the role of mythic symbols of beliefs and values that they had not always shared in life. They became in effect German Nathan Hales or Lord Nelsons or Joans of Arc.

This shift in the perception of the resistance was noticeable first outside Germany. As early as 1948, while most Americans were still convinced that the attempt to assassinate Hitler had been the work of disgruntled army officers trying to escape the consequences of a lost war, Hans Rothfels argued that they had in fact been motivated by principles of "universal validity." He himself had never wavered in his loyalty to the nation of his birth. A German patriot, though not a jingoist, he had been seriously injured while serving as an officer in the imperial army during World War I. Politically he always remained a moderate conservative, defending the Bismarckian tradition, denouncing the Versailles peace settlement, and advocating a national policy of forceful diplomacy and social responsibility. But none of this could save him from the bigotry of the Nazis. After coming to power, they removed him from his professorship at the University of Königsberg and then forced him into exile because of his "non-Aryan" background. His faith in Germany remained unshaken, however. He continued to perceive Hitler as an aberration, as a subverter of the highest traditions and values of the German spirit. The men of the resistance however, had proved that those traditions and values could not be crushed even by the most cruel of totalitarian tyrannies.

This reevaluation was the central theme of his *German Opposition to Hitler,* which defiantly challenged the accepted view in the United States regarding the coup of July 20, 1944. Rothfels maintained that "the German resistance was part of a European resistance." Yet it also displayed unique features deriving from its special circumstances. "Elsewhere among the fighters for liberation—and this is not said for the purpose of criticism—there were undoubtedly rogues, attracted by opportunities of violence suitable to their taste. In the German opposition there were none of [these] 'underworld' elements." The resisters inside the Third Reich found themselves in an "exceptional position," forced to recognize that "to fight for liberation was to fight for defeat." And that recognition compelled them to embrace an ideal that transcended "the struggle against the Nazis or against external oppression," an ideal not confined to "locality or nationality." They fought for universal moral principles, for timeless spiritual values. They became "standard bearers in the midst of chaos." Rothfels was promoting revisionism with a vengeance in postwar America.[10]

The London *Times* reappraised the German resistance more cautiously. Gradually, hesitantly, even grudgingly, it too conceded by the fall of 1951 that the earlier dismissal by the Allies of the coup against Hitler had not been entirely justified. The resisters may not have been quite the heroes and idealists portrayed by Rothfels. They were in truth "not all democrats"; they were not even "all free from responsibility for the Nazi regime." Nevertheless, they were the only ones in the Third Reich who, "without prompting from abroad and by their own decision," rose against a government which they recognized as "both evil and ruinous." They deserved to be honored not only for their "courage and self-sacrifice," but also for their willingness to risk their lives in defense of justice and morality. They had

earned the respect of their countrymen more than the dutiful soldiers "who
to the very end meekly obeyed brutal and infamous orders." The true
heroes of Germany were not those who died defending the Third Reich
but those who died opposing it.[11]

Even Wheeler-Bennett relented a little. He was still no ardent admirer
of the uprising of July 20. In his masterly study of the military's role in
German politics during the twentieth century, he continued to insist that
"[the resistance] was certainly not an essentially democratic movement."
The one motive common to all its members was "a deep desire to save their
country from a catastrophe of cataclysmic proportions." Nevertheless,
Wheeler-Bennett conceded, it was "more than a mere military revolt or a
gesture of frustrated ambition." Nor could it be characterized as simply "a
hot-bed of militarist reaction." It even displayed at times "elements of
democracy." Admittedly, generals like Beck and Witzleben had acted in the
tradition of Yorck von Wartenburg in 1812 or Hindenburg in 1918. They
too "perceived Germany . . . to be in dire peril and sought to avert it by
extraordinary means." There could be no denying, however, that they were
also prompted by a loyalty higher than unquestioning obedience to a
regime or a leader.[12]

By this time the attitude in Germany toward the resistance was changing
more dramatically. The early political and economic successes of the Federal Republic encouraged a new favorable view of those who a decade
earlier had tried to overthrow the Third Reich. The German public may
still have had some reservations about the resistance, but the shapers and
molders of public opinion—government, journalism, scholarship, and culture—were starting to embrace its members as the martyred forerunners of
the new order. A complete turnaround in historical perception had begun.

In 1952 Eberhard Zeller published the first comprehensive account of
the diverse groups and circles involved in the movement against the Nazi
regime. Two years later a second edition appeared and two years after that
a third, each longer and more detailed than the previous one. In his
conclusion the author advanced what became the accepted, official interpretation of the resistance in West Germany. Its members had sought to
end a "terrible war" by some reasonable compromise that would enable
the opposing sides "to find once again their sense of community and once
again live together." Even more important, they had hoped to encourage
Germany "to undergo a process of purification by its own determined
resolve, thereby regaining the inner freedom to act and to grieve." Finally,
through their uprising they intended to prepare the way for "new forms of
political life and for the coexistence of nations." Those who only a few

years earlier had been regarded as defeatists and shirkers were now being enshrined as heroes and idealists.[13]

By the time of the tenth anniversary of the attempt to assassinate Hitler, the apotheosis of the resistance was virtually complete. In commemoration of that attempt, Annedore Leber, widow of the Socialist leader who had been executed for his participation in the anti-Nazi movement, published a collection of short reverential sketches of sixty-four men and women who had died opposing the Third Reich. She arranged them in several distinct categories designed to underscore the diversity of backgrounds and convictions represented by the resistance: young people, idealistic intellectuals, selfless humanitarians, defenders of justice, champions of tradition, devout Christians, and ardent libertarians. "Men and women, young and old," the author wrote, "people from all strata of the population and from all regions of the country, could not become reconciled to injustice. Sooner or later they came to oppose it." A "growing spiritual rebellion" drove them to the "liberating deed" of July 20. They were "true human beings, seeking, hoping, caring, struggling, suffering human beings." Within them, "as within each of us," struggled "the most contradictory forces." And yet they met the challenge before them, because "in a difficult hour of decision their conscience was strong enough." Could posterity remain indifferent to the ideals and aspirations that had inspired their act of ultimate self-sacrifice?[14]

For those Germans who still felt a little guilty because they had initially accepted the Third Reich, another close relative of a prominent member of the resistance offered consoling words. Alexander von Stauffenberg pointed out that many of those who lost their lives opposing Hitler had at first supported him, because it had by no means been clear that the destructive forces within National Socialism would ultimately prevail over its creative potentialities. He was no doubt thinking of his brothers Claus and Berthold and probably of himself as well. "A true picture of that time must be presented in many colors," he argued. "We should not repeat the frequent mistake of painting it in a crude black-and-white style. It is a gross misrepresentation to pretend today that the supporters of the Nazi system at that time had all been devils, while its opponents had been nothing but angels." The important point was that those opponents, regardless of when they turned against the Nazi regime, "sealed with their blood after July 20, 1944, the struggle against the satanic Antichrist under conditions of unspeakable menace and terror." The resistance against the Third Reich succeeded ultimately in transcending all differences of class, occupation, or ideology.[15]

But the official benediction was pronounced by President Theodor Heuss of the German Federal Republic. In an address on June 19, 1954, at the Free University of Berlin, the lifelong liberal saluted those who had tried to assassinate Hitler, most of them staunch conservatives, as forerunners and trailblazers of the new democratic order in Germany. "This hour should be an acknowledgment and an expression of thanks," he declared. It should attest to the idealism and sense of justice of those who had so heroically represented the "spirit of freedom." But more than that, it should voice profound gratitude for the legacy their "proud death" had left to "the life of our nation." For "the shame forced on us Germans by Hitler has been wiped away with their blood from the sullied German name." To him that was the enduring significance of the resistance. "The legacy is still in force, the obligation has still not been fulfilled." The symbolic or mythic function that had once been performed by Frederick the Great, Scharnhorst, Bismarck, and Moltke in the old imperial Germany was now being assigned in the new democratic one to Beck, Goerdeler, Stauffenberg, and Hassell.[16]

Not all of Germany accepted this reassessment, however. The Democratic Republic, which had been established in the former Soviet zone of occupation, embraced the resistance as well, but its concept of what the resistance was differed profoundly from that accepted in the Federal Republic. It had much more stringent requirements of class, occupation, and especially ideology. The real heroes of the struggle against the Third Reich were workers, peasants, left-wing intellectuals, and dedicated radicals. The ultimate test for distinguishing between true and spurious resisters was their attitude toward the Soviet Union. Those suspicious or hostile toward Moscow were dismissed as disaffected allies of National Socialism who had turned against it out of expediency rather than principle. The leaders of the Democratic Republic thus viewed the men participating in the coup of July 20, 1944, as opportunists and trimmers. These resisters belonged to the well-to-do classes in society, many of them to the aristocracy; they had faithfully served the Hitler dictatorship as soldiers and bureaucrats; worst of all, they had as a rule supported the Third Reich's crusade against Communism. How then could they be regarded as heroes in the new Germany being built on the ruins of the old?

That view became the accepted interpretation in the east even before the establishment of the Democratic Republic. As early as 1947, during the Allied military occupation, an article published in the *Weltbühne* in the Russian sector of Berlin maintained that those who had three years earlier tried to overthrow the Third Reich were not much better than those who had fought to defend it. The "rebellious generals" were "flesh of the flesh of German imperialism." They had tried to use the "old tactic" of "pitting the west against the east," hoping "to win subsequently the war in the east with the help, if at all possible, of the western countries." Nor were the generals the only ones to pursue this plan. "Goerdeler as well, a conservative friend of the monarchical form of government and a leading figure in bourgeois anti-Nazi opposition circles, accepted this platform." Even "a Social Democratic group belonging to the oppositional Kreisau Circle of Count Moltke" supported these schemes and intrigues. All the traditional opponents of the Communist movement—aristocracy, bourgeoisie, and reformist Socialism—had banded together to try at all costs to prevent a victory of the Soviet Union.[17]

For the next forty years the central thesis of the Democratic Republic's official historiography regarding the movement against the Third Reich remained unchanged. There were, according to this thesis, two resistances, one good, the other bad, one progressive, the other reactionary, one looking to the future, the other to the past. The attempt to overthrow the Nazi regime in the summer of 1944 belonged to the bad resistance, the reactionary one. An article published in the leading historical journal of East Germany on the tenth anniversary of the uprising declared that "what the leading men of July 20 intended to give the German people was not a peace treaty guaranteeing Germany's freedom and independence." They wanted rather "an Anglo-Saxon occupation and, if possible, the continuation of the war against Soviet Russia." What had changed since the days when they had faithfully served National Socialism was not their ideology but their strategy.

And that strategy was transparent. Some of the members of the "military caste," having bet on "Hitler and company" and recognizing that they were about to lose that bet, decided to place a wager on a more promising contestant, namely, "the armies of the Anglo-Americans." Thereby they hoped to avoid unconditional surrender and perhaps even retain Austria, the Sudeten region, and the Polish Corridor. But to achieve their goal, they had to act while they still held such "bargaining chips" as France, Holland, Belgium, Poland, Norway, and Denmark. Hence their haste in preparing the coup, a haste that contributed substantially to their failure. Still, there was no reason to regret the outcome of the uprising of July 20. "The conspirators did not seek a true democratization of Germany, but rather the maintenance of the dominant position of the monopolists, Junkers, and generals." They never intended to give the people any "active role" in deciding what the future of their nation should be. Why shed tears over their fate?[18]

As late as 1987, only two years before the fall of the Berlin wall, the historian Kurt Finker of the Karl Liebknecht School of Pedagogy in

Potsdam was still arguing that many of the soldiers and bureaucrats who had tried to overthrow the Third Reich pursued essentially the same ends as their opponents, only by different means. "Certain circles within German imperialism sought the removal of Hitler without, however, seriously trying to weaken the imperialistic system." The leading representatives of those circles were men like Goerdeler, Hassell, and Popitz. They wanted not only "the maintenance of the existing order" but also "an agreement with the Western powers that would enable them to retain as large a part as possible of the conquests in the east." They were no less expansionist, no less reactionary than the Nazis. "Anticommunism and fear of a revolution were an essential motive for the actions of those forces." The argument recalled on some points the one often heard among members of the anti-German coalition forty years before at the time of the July uprising.[19]

Yet little by little, especially after the intensity of the cold war began to abate, the official view of the resistance in the Democratic Republic softened. Most of its members were still regarded as incorrigible reactionaries, antirevolutionary in domestic policy and anti-Soviet in foreign affairs. But there were a few exceptions, especially Claus von Stauffenberg. What distinguished them from the others was not social background, occupational status, or political outlook. Stauffenberg after all seemed as aristocratic, militaristic, and conservative as any of the resisters. The decisive factor was their view of the Soviet Union. While most of the resisters were, like Goerdeler, deeply suspicious of Moscow, Stauffenberg was prepared to negotiate with the Communist underground in Germany and with Stalin's government in Russia. That was enough. It made him acceptable to a regime that viewed a favorable attitude toward the Kremlin as a requirement of heroism.

"Count Claus von Stauffenberg," wrote a journalist with the *Weltbühne* shortly after the war, "went far beyond the [ideological] framework of the other military men participating in the conspiracy." The latter wanted as a rule merely to preserve the Wehrmacht and use the occupied territories to help sow dissension among the Allies. They intended to give the armed forces time to catch their breath and to ensure a conservative form of government in Germany. "Stauffenberg had an entirely different conception." He rejected the "irresponsible game" of trying to organize a "united front between post-Hitler Germany and the Western powers directed against the Soviet Union." Instead, he favored the inclusion of the Communists in the "insurrectionary front," supported in this view by Julius Leber. Those two men, the aristocratic army officer and the Socialist politician, were the true heroes, indeed, the only heroes, of the July uprising.[20]

In the course of the following decade the Democratic Republic's view of the resistance became a little more generous. An article published in 1979 in East Berlin included not only Stauffenberg and Leber among the "anti-fascist heroes" of Germany, but also Adolf Reichwein, another Socialist member who had been willing to cooperate with the Communists. The chief villain, however, remained the same. "Goerdeler belongs to Bonn, Brussels, and Washington, but Stauffenberg to Berlin. By which is meant not the [fashionable] Kurfürstendamm [in the western part of the city], but the capital of the German Democratic Republic, in which everything good, decent, and noble in the history of the German people and in German politics has found a refuge—in the sense of Karl Marx, Karl Liebknecht, Ernst Thälmann, and Rudolf Breitscheid. But also in the sense of Count Claus Schenk von Stauffenberg." The soldierly aristocrat had now been officially admitted to the pantheon of Communist heroes.[21]

A prominent spokesman for the Communist regime confirmed his elevation. Kurt Hager, member of the Politburo and secretary of the Central Committee of the governing Socialist Unity Party, expounded at considerable length that "history offers examples of representatives of the exploiting classes who were able to retain or to achieve indirectly . . . a grasp of reality without going beyond the limits of perception determined by their class." Bismarck was a case in point. His realism enabled him to judge soberly, especially in questions of foreign policy, and "to argue for good relations with Russia." Other prominent figures in German history had also risen above their class interests and prejudices to serve the nation: "Yorck von Wartenburg, . . . Rathenau, Stauffenberg, and some individuals involved in the conspiracy of July 20, 1944." The gates of acceptability in the historiography of the Democratic Republic were gradually widening.[22]

By the end of the 1980s they had become half-open. Kurt Finker, the biographer of Stauffenberg and Moltke, conceded that the resistance included soldiers and politicians "who had or who acquired a realistic view of the situation," and who decided in the course of the war to seek "the violent overthrow of the Nazi regime." What made their resolve all the more impressive was that, with the exception of a handful of Socialists, "they either belonged to the ruling class themselves or served it as officials and officers." Despite that, "they had found their way to a decision." These good resisters included not only Stauffenberg but also "Tresckow, Stieff, Beck, and others" willing to face the consequences of an uprising against the Third Reich. Unfortunately, many officers who inwardly condemned National Socialism still felt bound by their oath of loyalty as soldiers. They were afraid of being accused later of perjury and treason. Only a few recognized that "honor" meant not "the formal fulfillment of their oath to Hitler" but rather the performance of their duty to "our people." The interpretations of the resistance in East and West Germany, though still far apart, had begun to converge.[23]

Would they have eventually met? Would they have arrived at a consensus regarding the proportions of Communists and anticommunists, proletarians and bourgeois, peasants and landowners among the heroes of the anti-Hitler movement? Probably not. The underlying ideological differences between them were too profound to be bridged by moderation, compromise, or concession. They did manage to reach some common conclusions regarding Stauffenberg, Tresckow, and Stieff. But as for Goerdeler, Hassell, Popitz, and the other anti-Soviet resisters, the differences could not in all probability have been reconciled. The question, however, soon proved academic. The end of the cold war, the collapse of the Democratic Republic, and the reunification in 1990 of the two Germanys, or rather the absorption of one by the other, meant that the view of the resistance commonly accepted in the West became the official national interpretation. To be sure, a growing number of scholarly revisionists continued to challenge the orthodox hagiography of the uprising of July 20. But in general those who participated in that uprising had become at last the official martyrs and heroes of a new, united, democratic Germany.

On the fiftieth anniversary of the attempt to overthrow the Third Reich, Chancellor Helmut Kohl reverentially invoked the memory of those who had died opposing Nazi tyranny. In a speech at the Bendlerstrasse in Berlin, in the courtyard where the first victims of Nazi vengeance were executed, he described what they had done as "an act of moral self-assertion." They had proclaimed to the world that "the dignity of each individual human being is more important than any political power and is superior to it." The resistance had united Germans "of the most diverse political convictions" in a common struggle against "the rule of criminality." Although they were "not many," they were undeniably "the best." The principal objective for most of them had been the reestablishment of law and justice and a return to "ethical values and standards." But their lasting legacy, according to the chancellor, was "the sense of community of the believers in democracy." The Federal Republic commemorated the failed coup with the same solemnity with which the Hohenzollern monarchy had once celebrated the anniversary of the founding of the German Empire.[24]

How would the resisters themselves have reacted to their enshrinement as the patron saints of the new order in Germany? Probably with bewilderment. Generally opposed to democracy, contemptuous of pacifism, and critical of the spirit of "materialism," they were not likely to have felt much sympathy for a regime committed to popular sovereignty, international peace, and material comfort. Conversely, the Federal Republic, having renounced the traditional civic attitudes and values of the German polity, may have seemed inconsistent or perhaps even faintly disingenuous in celebrating the memory of men who had embodied many of those attitudes and values. Yet its commemoration of them was more than a convenient fiction or spurious symbol. Admittedly, most members of the resistance, fallible, gullible, sometimes culpable, had at first accepted and served the Third Reich. Then, gradually, almost in spite of themselves, they began to rise above the limitations of their age, their class, and their ideology. They began to see, hesitantly, intermittently, reluctantly, and often only dimly, the terrible evil in the Nazi regime. And having seen it, they eventually decided to oppose it. Their motives may have been mixed, parochial and universal, expedient and selfless, patriotic and humanitarian, mean and noble. But in the end they risked and lost their lives fighting a brutal and tyrannical political system. Is that not enough? Posterity has perhaps no right to demand more from those it decides to anoint as its martyrs and heroes.

Notes

Introduction

1. *Hitler: Reden und Proklamationen, 1932–1945*, ed. Max Domarus, 2 vols. (Munich, 1965), 2:2128.
2. Great Britain, *Parliamentary Debates: House of Commons, 1943–44*, 5th ser., 402:1487.
3. *Bayern in der NS-Zeit*, ed. Martin Broszat, Elke Fröhlich, Falk Wiesemann, Anton Grossmann, and Hartmut Mehringer, 6 vols. (Munich and Vienna, 1977–1983), 1:11–12.
4. Hans Rothfels, *The German Opposition to Hitler* (Hinsdale, Ill., 1948), pp. 165–166.
5. Wolfgang Foerster, *Generaloberst Ludwig Beck: Sein Kampf gegen den Krieg* (Munich, 1953), p. 164.
6. Fabian v. Schlabrendorff, *Offiziere gegen Hitler*, ed. Gero v. S. Gaevernitz (Zurich, 1946), pp. 129, 153.
7. *Beck und Goerdeler: Gemeinschaftsdokumente für den Frieden, 1941–1944*, ed. Wilhelm von Schramm (Munich, 1965), p. 222.
8. Hans Karl Fritzsche, *Ein Leben im Schatten des Verrates: Erinnerungen eines Überlebenden an den 20. Juli 1944* (Freiburg, Basel, and Vienna, 1984), p. 81.
9. *Landesbischof D. Wurm und der nationalsozialistische Staat, 1940–1945*, ed. Gerhard Schäfer (Stuttgart, 1968), pp. 164–165.
10. Clemens August von Galen, *Akten, Briefe und Predigten, 1933–1946*, ed. Peter Löffler, 2 vols. (Mainz, 1988), 2:848.
11. John W. Wheeler-Bennett, *The Nemesis of Power: The German Army in Politics, 1918–1945* (London and New York, 1953), pp. 689–690.
12. Nicholas Reynolds, *Treason Was No Crime: Ludwig Beck, Chief of the German General Staff* (London, 1976), p. 38; Alexander von Falkenhausen, autobiographical report, November 15, 1946, pp. 7–8, National Archives (Washington, D.C.), Foreign Military Studies, MS B-289; Klaus-Jürgen Müller, *General Ludwig Beck: Studien und Dokumente zur politisch-militärischen Vorstellungswelt und Tätigkeit des Generalstabschefs des deutschen Heeres, 1933–1938* (Boppard am Rhein, 1980), p. 339.
13. Bodo Scheurig, *Henning von Tresckow*, 2d ed. (Oldenburg and Hamburg, 1973),

pp. 20, 44; Hans Bernd Gisevius, *Bis zum bittern Ende,* 2d ed., 2 vols (Zurich, 1946), 2:263.

14. Gerhard Ritter, *Carl Goerdeler und die deutsche Widerstandsbewegung* (Stuttgart, 1954), p. 62; Michael Krüger-Charlé, "Carl Goerdelers Versuche der Durchsetzung einer alternativen Politik 1933 bis 1937," in *Der Widerstand gegen den Nationalsozialismus: Die deutsche Gesellschaft und der Widerstand gegen Hitler,* ed. Jürgen Schmädeke and Peter Steinbach (Munich and Zurich, 1985), p. 385; Carl Goerdeler, memorandum of August 1934, p. 25, Bundesarchiv (Koblenz), NL Goerdeler, 12.

15. Fritz-Dietlof von der Schulenburg, "Partei und Beamtentum," *Deutschlands Erneuerung: Monatsschrift für das deutsche Volk,* 6 (1932), 347–348, 352; idem, "Neuaufbau des höheren Beamtentums," April 1933, pp. 3–4, and "Reichsreform," spring 1934, p. 1, Bundesarchiv (Koblenz), NL Schulenburg, 1.

16. *Die Evangelische Landeskirche in Württemberg und der Nationalsozialismus: Eine Dokumentation zum Kirchenkampf,* ed. Gerhard Schäfer, 6 vols. (Stuttgart, 1971–1986), 1:226, 228–229; *Allgemeine Evangelisch-Lutherische Kirchenzeitung* (Leipzig), March 24 and April 7, 1933.

17. Galen, *Akten, Briefe und Predigten,* 1:37, 96–97.

18. *"Spiegelbild einer Verschwörung": Die Opposition gegen Hitler und der Staatsstreich vom 20. Juli 1944 in der SD-Berichterstattung,* ed. Hans-Adolf Jacobsen (Stuttgart, 1984), pp. 168, 447–448.

19. Ibid.

20. Alexander von Stauffenberg, "Die deutsche Widerstandsbewegung und ihre geistige Bedeutung in der Gegenwart," in *Bekenntnis und Verpflichtung: Redenund Aufsätze zur zehnjährigen Wiederkehr des 20. Juli 1944* (Stuttgart, 1955), p. 161.

1. Opposition to Democracy

1. Wheeler-Bennett, *Nemesis of Power,* p. 689.

2. *"Spiegelbild einer Verschwörung,"* ed. Jacobsen, p. 302.

3. Müller, *Beck,* pp. 323–324.

4. *Die Reden gehalten in den öffentlichen und geschlossenen Versammlungen der 62. General-Versammlung der Katholiken Deutschlands zu München 27. bis 30. August 1922* (Würzburg, 1923), p. 4.

5. *Akten Kardinal Michael von Faulhabers 1917–1945,* ed. Ludwig Volk, 2 vols. (Mainz, 1975–1978), 1:278–279, 283.

6. *Der Tag* (Berlin), January 5, September 7, 1918.

7. Fritz-Dietlof von der Schulenburg, "Preussisches Beamtentum," March and June 1931, p. 6, Bundesarchiv (Koblenz), NL Schulenburg, l.

8. *Beck und Goerdeler,* ed. Schramm, pp. 147–148.

9. Müller, *Beck,* pp. 329–331.

10. Johannes Popitz, "Finanzausgleich," in *Handwörterbuch der Staatswissenschaften,* 4th ed., 9 vols. (Jena, 1923–1929), 3:1031.

11. Johannes Popitz, *Der Finanzausgleich und seine Bedeutung für die Finanzlage des Reichs, der Länder und Gemeinden* (Berlin, 1930), p. 8.

12. Carl Goerdeler, economic memorandum of 1930–31, pp. 3–4, Bundesarchiv (Koblenz), NL Goerdeler, 21.

13. *"Spiegelbild einer Verschwörung,"* ed. Jacobsen, p. 302.
14. Scheurig, *Tresckow,* p. 44.
15. Hellmuth Stieff, *Briefe,* ed. Horst Mühleisen (Berlin, 1991), p. 71.
16. *Kölnische Zeitung,* February 9, 1931.
17. Schulenburg, "Partei und Beamtentum," p. 347; Ulrich Heinemann, *Ein konservativer Rebell: Fritz-Dietlof Graf von der Schulenburg und der 20. Juli* (Berlin, 1990), p. 22.
18. *Evangelische Landeskirche in Würtzemberg,* ed. Schäfer, 1:228.
19. *Berliner Evangelisches Wochenblatt,* February 22, 1931.
20. Dietrich Bonhoeffer, *Gesammelte Schriften,* ed. Eberhard Bethge, 6 vols. (Munich, 1958–1974), 6:244.

2. Breaking the Shackles of Versailles

1. *Der Tag* (Berlin), November 24, 1918.
2. Müller, *Beck,* pp. 323, 327–328.
3. Bonhoeffer, *Gesammelte Schriften,* 6:243.
4. Martin Niemöller, *Vom U-Boot zur Kanzel* (Berlin, 1935), p. 147.
5. Ritter, *Goerdeler,* p. 23.
6. *"Spiegelbild einer Verschwörung,"* ed. Jacobsen, p. 302.
7. Müller, *Beck,* p. 330.
8. Ritter, *Goerdeler,* p. 27.
9. *Berliner Evangelisches Sonntagsblatt,* January 25, 1931.
10. Scheurig, *Tresckow,* p. 20.
11. *Berliner Evangelisches Sonntagsblatt,* January 25, 1931.
12. *Deutsches Volksblatt: Tageszeitung der Deutschen Jugoslawiens* (Novi Sad), February 23, 1932.
13. *"Spiegelbild einer Verschwörung,"* ed. Jacobsen, p. 302.
14. Georges Castellan, *Le réarmament clandestin du Reich, 1930–1935: Vu par le 2e Bureau de l'état-major français* (Paris, 1954), p. 442.
15. Frederick O. Bonkovsky, "The German State and Protestant Elites," in *The German Church Struggle and the Holocaust,* ed. Franklin H. Littell and Hubert G. Locke (Detroit, 1974), p. 129.
16. *Das Evangelische Deutschland: Kirchliche Rundschau für das Gesamtgebiet des Deutschen Evangelischen Kirchenbundes* (Berlin), March 26, 1933.

3. The Struggle against Materialism

1. Niemöller, *Vom U-Boot zur Kanzel,* pp. 179–180.
2. Stieff, *Briefe,* p. 64.
3. *Das Evangelische Deutschland: Kirchliche Rundschau für das Gesamtgebiet des Deutschen Evangelischen Kirchenbundes* (Berlin), March 26, 1933.
4. *Die Mittwochs-Gesellschaft: Protokolle aus dem geistigen Deutschland 1932 bis 1944,* ed. Klaus Scholder (Berlin, 1982), pp. 67–68.
5. *Evangelische Landeskirche in Württemberg,* ed. Schäfer, 1:228–229, 249, 365.
6. Galen, *Akten, Briefe und Predigten,* 1:37, 2:1185.

7. Michael von Faulhaber, *Judentum, Christentum, Germanentum: Adventspredigten gehalten in St. Michael zu München 1933* (Munich, 1934), p. 44.
8. *Berliner Evangelisches Wochenblatt,* April 5, 1931.
9. Galen, *Akten, Briefe und Predigten,* 1:96–97.
10. Ulrich von Hassell, *Deutschlands und Italiens europäische Sendung* (Cologne, 1937), pp. 18–19.
11. *Evangelische Landeskirche in Württemberg,* ed. Schäfer, 1:393.
12. *Akten Kardinal Faulhabers,* ed. Volk, 1:279, 806.
13. Galen, *Akten, Briefe und Predigten,* 2:902.
14. Fritz-Dietlof von der Schulenburg, "Reichsreform," spring 1934, p. 1, Bundesarchiv (Koblenz), NL Schulenburg, 1.
15. *Junge Kirche: Halbmonatschrift für reformatorisches Christentum,* 1 (1933), 222.
16. *Berliner Evangelisches Wochenblatt,* April 26, 1931; *Der Tag* (Berlin), March 26, 1933.
17. "*Spiegelbild einer Verschwörung,*" Jacobsen, pp. 447–448.

4. That Perennial "Jewish Question"

1. "*Spiegelbild einer Verschwörung,*" ed. Jacobsen, pp. 447–448.
2. Scheurig, *Tresckow,* p. 20; Wilhelm Canaris, "Politik und Wehrmacht," in *Wehrmacht und Partei,* ed. Richard Donnevert (Leipzig, 1938), p. 53.
3. "*Spiegelbild einer Verschwörung,*" ed. Jacobsen, p. 449.
4. Ritter, *Goerdeler,* p. 64; Carl Goerdeler, memorandum of August 1934, p. 29, Bundesarchiv (Koblenz), NL Goerdeler, 12.
5. Gregor Schöllgen, *Ulrich von Hassell, 1881–1944: Ein Konservativer in der Opposition* (Munich, 1990), p. 32; *Deutsche Parteiprogramme,* ed. Wolfgang Treue, 2d ed. (Berlin and Frankfurt, 1956), p. 112.
6. Fritz-Dietlof von der Schulenburg, "Preussisches Beamtentum," March and June 1931, p. 6, and "Neuaufbau des höheren Beamtentums," April 1933, p. 3, Bundesarchiv (Koblenz), NL Schulenburg, 1.
7. "Ein NS-Funktionär zum Niemöller-Prozess," *Vierteljahrshefte für Zeitgeschichte,* 4 (1956), 313.
8. James Bentley, *Martin Niemöller, 1892–1984* (New York, 1984), p. 65; Martin Niemöller, "Sätze zur Arierfrage in der Kirche," *Junge Kirche: Halbmonatschrift für reformatorisches Christentum,* 1 (1933), 269–270.
9. Evangelisches Zentralarchiv in Berlin, NL Dibelius, 50/R19.
10. *Berliner Evangelisches Sonntagsblatt,* April 9, 1933.
11. "Die katholische Kirche und die Judenfrage," *Eine heilige Kirche,* 16 (1934), 176.
12. Faulhaber, *Judentum, Christentum, Germanentum,* pp. 10, 18–19.
13. *Akten Kardinal Faulhabers,* ed. Volk, 1:705, 726; Ludwig Volk, *Der bayerische Episkopat und der Nationalsozialismus, 1930–1934* (Mainz, 1965), p. 78.
14. Faulhaber, *Judentum, Christentum, Germanentum,* pp. 10–11, 116.
15. *Akten Kardinal Faulhabers,* ed. Volk, 1:682–684, 705; Volk, *Der bayerische Episkopat,* p. 78.
16. Julius Leber, *Schriften, Reden, Briefe,* ed. Dorothea Beck and Wilfried F. Schoeller (Munich, 1976), pp. 232, 263.
17. Bonhoeffer, *Gesammelte Schriften,* 2:45, 50–51.

5. The Collapse of the Republican Regime

1. "Die Wahlen zum Reichstag am 4. Mai 1924 und am 7. Dezember 1924," *Statistik des Deutschen Reichs,* 315, no. 2 (1925), 4–5, and 315, no. 3 (1925), 6–7; "Die Wahlen zum Reichstag am 20. Mai 1928," ibid., 372, no. 2 (1930), 4–5.

2. "Die Wahlen zum Reichstag am 14. September 1930," ibid., 382, no. 1 (1932), 6–7; "Die Wahlen zum Reichstag am 31. Juli und 6. November 1932 und am 5. März 1933," ibid., 434 (1935), 8–12, 76–80.

3. Max Habermann, "Der Deutschnationale Handlungsgehilfen-Verband im Kampf um das Reich, 1918–1933: Ein Zeugnis seines Wollens und Wirkens," pp. 7, 73–74, 84, Deutscher Handels- und Industrieangestellten-Verband (Hamburg).

4. Werner Conze, Erich Kosthorst, and Elfriede Nebgen, *Jakob Kaiser,* 4 vols. (Stuttgart, Berlin, Cologne, and Mainz, 1967–1972), 1:147, 266.

5. Leber, *Schriften, Reden, Briefe,* pp. 245–246.

6. Bernhard Watzdorf, "Die getarnte Ausbildung von Generalstabsoffizieren der Reichswehr von 1932 bis 1935," *Zeitschrift für Militärgeschichte,* 2 (1963), 86.

7. Alexander von Falkenhausen, autobiographical report, November 15, 1946, pp. 7–8, National Archives (Washington D.C.), Foreign Military Studies, MS B-289; Eugen Ott, "Bemerkungen zu den Akten des Instituts für Zeitgeschichte," p. 2, Institut für Zeitgeschichte, (Munich), Zs 279; Müller, *Beck,* p. 339.

8. Heinz Höhne, *Canaris: Patriot im Zwielicht* (Munich, 1976), pp. 134–135; Gert Buchheit, *Soldatentum und Rebellion: Die Tragödie der deutschen Wehrmacht* (Rastatt, 1961), p. 224.

9. Watzdorf, "Die getarnte Ausbildung von Generalstabsoffizieren," p. 86; Stieff, *Briefe,* pp. 71, 76.

10. Hermann Foertsch, *Schuld und Verhängnis: Die Fritsch-Krise im Frühjahr 1938 als Wendepunkt in der Geschichte der nationalsozialistischen Zeit* (Stuttgart, 1951), p. 22; Christian Müller, *Oberst i. G. Stauffenberg* (Düsseldorf, 1970), pp. 97–100; Peter Hoffmann, *Claus Schenk Graf von Stauffenberg und seine Brüder* (Stuttgart, 1992), pp. 123–124, 507–509; Joachim Kramarz, *Claus Graf Stauffenberg, 15. November 1907–20. Juli 1944: Das Leben eines Offiziers* (Frankfurt am Main, 1965), pp. 46–48.

11. Carl Goerdeler, economic memorandum of 1930–31, pp. 3–4, 47–48, and "Unsere Idee," November 1944, pp. 5–6. Bundesarchiv (Koblenz), NL Goerdeler, 21, 26.

12. *Die Mittwochs-Gesellschaft,* ed. Scholder, pp. 67–69.

13. Fritz-Dietlof von der Schulenburg, "Preussisches Beamtentum," March and June 1931, p. 6, and "Reichsreform," spring 1934, p. 1, Bundesarchiv (Koblenz), NL Schulenburg, 1.

14. *Evangelische Landeskirche in Württemberg,* ed. Schäfer, 1:393.

15. "Ein NS-Funktionär zum Niemöller-Prozess," p. 312; Bonkovsky, "German State and Protestant Elites," pp. 136–137; Bentley, *Niemöller,* pp. 41, 43.

16. *Das Evangelische Deutschland: Kirchliche Rundschau für das Gesamtgebiet des Deutschen Evangelischen Kirchenbundes* (Berlin), March 26, 1933.

17. *Hitler: Reden und Proklamationen,* ed. Domarus, 1:232–233; *Akten Kardinal Faulhabers,* ed. Volk, 1:673.

18. "Die Wahlen zum Reichstag am 31. Juli und 6. November 1932 und am 5. März 1933," *Statistik des Deutschen Reichs,* 434 (1935), 142–143.

19. Ewald von Kleist-Schmenzin, "Eine Absage," *Mitteilungen des Hauptvereins der Konservativen,* (Berlin), March 1933, p. 3.
20. Bonhoeffer, *Gesammelte Schriften,* 6:244.

6. The Military and the Third Reich

1. *Trial of the Major War Criminals before the International Military Tribunal,* 42 vols. (Nuremberg: 1947–1949), 32:464.
2. Erich v. Manstein, *Aus einem Soldatenleben, 1887–1939* (Bonn, 1958), p. 275.
3. Watzdorf, "Die getarnte Ausbildung von Generalstabsoffizieren," p. 86.
4. Manstein, *Aus einem Soldatenleben,* pp. 274–275.
5. Reynolds, *Treason Was No Crime,* p. 46.
6. Castellan, *Le réarmament clandestin du Reich,* p. 442.
7. Müller, *Beck,* pp. 433, 437 n. 13.
8. Höhne, *Canaris,* p. 135; Buchheit, *Soldatentum und Rebellion,* pp. 228–229.
9. Scheurig, *Tresckow,* pp. 44–45; Gisevius, *Bis zum bittern Ende,* 2:263.
10. *"Spiegelbild einer Verschwörung,"* ed. Jacobsen, p. 302.
11. Watzdorf, "Die getarnte Ausbildung von Generalstabsoffizieren," p. 86.
12. Hans Speidel, *Invasion 1944: Ein Beitrag zu Rommels und des Reiches Schicksal* (Tübingen and Stuttgart, 1949), p. 182.
13. Hermann Graml, "Hans Oster," in *Der zwanzigste Juli: Alternative zu Hitler?* ed. Hans Jürgen Schultz (Stuttgart and Berlin, 1974), p. 134.
14. Speidel, *Invasion 1944,* p. 182.
15. Kramarz, *Stauffenberg,* p. 48.
16. Heinrich Büchler, *Carl-Heinrich Stülpnagel: Soldat, Philosoph, Verschwörer* (Berlin and Frankfurt am Main, 1989), p. 125.
17. Watzdorf, "Die getarnte Ausbildung von Generalstabsoffizieren," p. 86; *Trial of the Major War Criminals,* 33:305; Stieff, *Briefe,* pp. 87–88.
18. Höhne, *Canaris,* pp. 209–210.
19. Ibid., p. 135.

7. The Bureaucracy and the Third Reich

1. National Archives (Washington, D.C.), Department of State, MS 862.20200 Goerdeler, Karl (DR)/8-544, p. 6.
2. Carl Goerdeler, memorandum of August 1934, pp. 25, 31, Bundesarchiv (Koblenz), NL Goerdeler, 12.
3. Johannes Popitz, "Eugen Schiffer zur Kritik unserer Zeit," *Juristische Wochenschrift,* February 27, 1932, p. 619.
4. *Die Mittwochs-Gesellschaft,* ed. Scholder, pp. 67–68.
5. *"Spiegelbild einer Verschwörung,"* ed. Jacobsen, p. 448.
6. Fritz-Dietlof von der Schulenburg, "Reichsreform," spring 1934, pp. 1, 5, Bundesarchiv (Koblenz), NL Schulenburg, 1.
7. Goerdeler, memorandum of August 1934, p. 52, Bundesarchiv (Koblenz), NL Goerdeler, 12.
8. *Die Mittwochs-Gesellschaft,* ed. Scholder, pp. 67, 69.

9. *Deutsches Volksblatt: Tageszeitung der Deutschen Jugoslawiens* (Novi Sad), February 23, 1932.
10. Krüger-Charlé, "Carl Goerdelers Versuche," p. 394.
11. Leo Baeck Institute (New York), Julie Braun-Vogelstein Collection, part IV, box 28, folder 5 [Diana Hubback (Hopkinson)], unpublished manuscript on Adam von Trott zu Solz [1946], p. 43.
12. Fritz-Dietlof von der Schulenburg, "Neuaufbau des höheren Beamtentums," April 1933, pp. 2–3, Bundesarchiv (Koblenz), NL Schulenburg, 1.
13. *"Spiegelbild einer Vershwörung,"* ed. Jacobsen, pp. 448–449.
14. National Archives (Washington, D.C.), Department of State, MS 862.20200 Goerdeler, Karl (DR)/8-544, p. 6.
15. Ritter, *Goerdeler,* p. 64.
16. Carl Goerdeler, memorandum of August 1934, p. 29, Bundesarchiv (Koblenz), NL Goerdeler, 12.
17. *Manchester Guardian,* February 21, 1934.

8. The Catholics

1. *Hitler: Reden und Proklamationen,* ed. Domarus, 1:232–233; *Akten Kardinal Faulhabers,* ed. Volk, 1:673.
2. Galen, *Akten, Briefe und Predigten,* 1:37, 96–97, 333, 369–370.
3. *Katholische Kirche und Nationalsozialismus: Dokumente 1930–1935,* ed. Hans Müller (Munich, 1963), pp. 170–171.
4. *Akten Kardinal Faulhabers,* ed. Volk, 1:806.
5. Faulhaber, *Judentum, Christentum, Germanentum,* p. 44.
6. *Augsburger Postzeitung,* December 20, 1934.
7. *Katholische Kirche und Nationalsozialismus,* ed. Müller, pp. 170–171.
8. Galen, *Akten, Briefe und Predigten,* 1:333.
9. Guenter Lewy, *The Catholic Church and Nazi Germany* (New York, London, Sydney, and Toronto, 1964), pp. 283–284; "Die katholische Kirche und die Judenfrage," p. 176.
10. Galen, *Akten, Briefe und Predigten,* 1:46–47.
11. *Akten kardinal Faulhabers,* ed. Volk, 1:705, 726; Volk, *Der bayerische Episkopat,* p. 78.
12. Faulhaber, *Judentum, Christentum, Germanentum,* pp. 7–10, 18–20.
13. Ibid., pp. 10–11, 19, 116–117.
14. *Beilage zum Amtsblatt Nr. 20 d. Erzdiözese München u. Freising,* November 15, 1934.
15. *Akten Kardinal Faulhabers,* ed. Volk, 1:682–683.
16. Ibid., p. 705; Volk, *Der bayerische Episkopat,* p. 78.
17. *Akten Kardinal Faulhabers,* ed. Volk, 1:684, 705, 831; Volk, *Der bayerische Episkopat,* p. 78.

9. The Protestants

1. *Bayern in der NS-Zeit,* ed. Broszat et al., 1:406.
2. Theophil Wurm, *"Habt die Brüder lieb, fürchtet Gott, ehret den König!": Predigt*

am Sonntag Jubilate, 22. April 1934 über 1. Petri 2, 11–17 im Münster zu Ulm (Stuttgart, 1934), pp. 4–5.

3. Klaus Mammach, *Widerstand, 1933–1939: Geschichte der deutschen antifaschistischen Widerstandsbewegung im Inland und in der Emigration* (Berlin, 1984), p. 141.

4. *Deutschland-Berichte der Sozialdemokratischen Partei Deutschlands (Sopade), 1934–1940,* 7 vols. (Frankfurt am Main, 1980), 1:715–717.

5. *Das Evangelische Deutschland: Kirchliche Rundschau für das Gesamtgebiet des Deutschen Evangelischen Kirchenbundes* (Berlin), March 26, 1933.

6. *Der Tag* (Berlin), April 2, 1933.

7. Bentley, *Niemöller,* p. 43.

8. Martin Niemöller, . . . *dass wir an Ihm bleiben!: Sechzehn Dahlemer Predigten* (Berlin, 1935), pp. 17–20.

9. Ibid., p. 44.

10. Ibid., p. 51.

11. *Allgemeine Evangelisch-Lutherische Kirchenzeitung* (Leipzig), April 7, 1933.

12. *Das Evangelische Deutschland: Kirchliche Rundschau für das Gesamtgebiet des Deutschen Evangelischen Kirchenbundes* (Berlin), March 26, 1933; *Der Tag* (Berlin), April 9, 1933.

13. Bentley, *Niemöller,* pp. 78–79; "Ein NS-Funktionär zum Niemöller-Prozess," p. 313.

14. Wurm, *"Habt die Brüder lieb,"* p. 4.

15. *Das Evangelische Deutschland: Kirchliche Rundschau für das Gesamtgebiet des Deutschen Evangelischen Kirchenbundes* (Berlin), March 26, 1933; *Der Tag* (Berlin), March 26, 1933.

16. "Die nach Amerika gerichtete Rundfunkrede des Herrn Generalsuperintendenten Dibelius vom 4. April 1933," pp. 2–3, Evangelische Arbeitsgemeinschaft für kirchliche Zeitgeschichte (Munich).

17. Otto Dibelius, *Ein Christ ist immer im Dienst: Erlebnisse und Erfahrungen in einer Zeitenwende* (Stuttgart, 1961), p. 122.

18. Martin Niemöller, *Alles und in allen Christus!: Fünfzehn Dahlemer Predigten* (Berlin, 1935), p. 87.

19. Bentley, *Niemöller,* pp. 62–63, 67; Niemöller, "Sätze zur Arierfrage," pp. 269–270.

20. Eberhard Bethge, *Dietrich Bonhoeffer: Theologe, Christ, Zeitgenosse* (Munich, 1967), pp. 557–558.

21. Bonhoeffer, *Gesammelte Schriften,* 2:45, 50–51, 116–117, 4:459.

10. The Armed Forces under the Hitler Dictatorship

1. *Zwischen Widerspruch und Widerstand: Texte zur Denkschrift der Bekennenden Kirche an Hitler (1936),* ed. Martin Greschat (Munich, 1987), p. 240.

2. *Akten zur deutschen auswärtigen Politik, 1918–1945,* series D, 13 vols. (Baden-Baden, Frankfurt am Main, Bonn, and Göttingen, 1950–1970), 1:29–31.

3. Manstein, *Aus einem Soldatenleben,* p. 275.

4. *Trial of the Major War Criminals,* 32:464.

5. *Akten zur deutschen auswärtigen Politik,* series D, 1:32.

6. *Berliner Tageblatt,* October 17, 1935.
7. Hermann Teske, *Die silbernen Spiegel: Generalstabsdienst unter der Lupe* (Heidelberg, 1952), pp. 31–32.
8. Klaus-Jürgen Müller, *Das Heer und Hitler: Armee und nationalsozialistisches Regime, 1933–1940* (Stuttgart, 1969), p. 161.
9. Canaris, "Politik und Wehrmacht," pp. 48, 53–54.
10. "Niederschrift des Vortrags Konteradmiral Canaris bei der Ic-Besprechung im O.K.W. am 3.3.1938," pp. 4–7, National Archives (Washington, D.C.), T-77/Roll 808/Frames 5540874–5540885.
11. "Die nationalpolitische Stellung des Offiziers in der Deutschen Wehrmacht: Vortrag Vizeadmiral Canaris, Oberkommando der Wehrmacht, am 22. April 1938 in Wien," pp. 1–4, 6, 8, Institut für Zeitgeschichte (Munich), F6.
12. Höhne, *Canaris,* pp. 209–210; *Akten zur deutschen auswärtigen Politik,* series D, 5:761–762.
13. *"Spiegelbild einer Verschwörung,"* ed. Jacobsen, p. 118.
14. Müller, *Beck,* p. 37 n. 114.
15. Ibid., pp. 100, 433–434.
16. Foerster, *Beck,* p. 51.
17. Müller, *Beck,* pp. 496–497.
18. *Trial of the Major War Criminals,* 16:640–641.

11. Nazi Dominance and Bureaucratic Accommodation

1. *"Spiegelbild einer Verschwörung,"* ed. Jacobsen, p. 168.
2. Carl Goerdeler, economic memorandum of 1930–31, pp. 47–48, and memorandum of August 1934, pp. 25, 31, Bundesarchiv (Koblenz), NL Goerdeler, 21, 12.
3. Jeremy Noakes, "German Conservatives and the Third Reich: An Ambiguous Relationship," in *Fascists and Conservatives: The Radical Right and the Establishment in Twentieth-Century Europe,* ed. Martin Blinkhorn (London, 1990), pp. 87–89.
4. Carl Goerdeler, memorandum of August 1934, p. 29. Bundesarchiv (Koblenz), NL Goerdeler, 12; Hans Walz, "Meine Mitarbeit an der Aktion Goerdeler," November 1945, p. 3, Bundesarchiv (Koblenz), NL Gerhard Ritter, 131.
5. Carl Goerdeler, memorandum of July 9, 1937, p. 8, Bundesarchiv (Koblenz), NL Goerdeler, 12.
6. Carl Goerdeler, memorandum of August 1934, pp. 24–25, Bundesarchiv (Koblenz), NL Goerdeler, 12.
7. Carl Goerdeler, report on the United States, January 2, 1938, pp. 50–52, Bundesarchiv (Koblenz), NL Goerdeler, 22.
8. Galeazzo Ciano, *1937–1938 Diario* (Bologna, 1948), p. 121.
9. *Akten zur deutschen auswärtigen Politik, 1918–1945,* series E, 8 vols. (Göttingen, 1969–1979), 8:435–436.
10. Ibid., p. 436.
11. *Deutsches Volksblatt: Tageszeitung der Deutschen Jugoslawiens* (Novi Sad), February 23, 1932; Schöllgen, *Hassell,* p. 68.
12. *Akten zur deutschen auswärtigen Politik, 1918–1945,* series C, 6 vols. (Göttingen,

1971–1981), 1:827; Ger van Roon, *Widerstand im Dritten Reich,* 4th ed. (Munich, 1987), p. 127.

13. *Akten zur deutsche auswärtigen Politik,* series C, 1:546, 4:678.

14. Hassell, *Deutschlands und Italiens europäische Sendung,* pp. 18–19.

15. Popitz, "Eugen Schiffer," p. 619; *Die Mittwochs-Gesellschaft,* ed. Scholder, pp. 68, 178.

16. Fritz-Dietlof von der Schulenburg, "Das Erbe des Preussischen Staates," *Württembergische Verwaltungs-Zeitschrift,* 33 (1937), pp. 152–153.

17. *A Noble Combat: The Letters of Shiela Grant Duff and Adam von Trott zu Solz, 1932–1939,* ed. Klemens von Klemperer (Oxford, 1988), p. 259.

12. The Conflict over Ecclesiastical Autonomy

1. Friedrich Zipfel, *Kirchenkampf in Deutschland, 1933–1945: Religionsverfolgung und Selbstbehauptung der Kirchen in der nationalsozialistischen Zeit* (Berlin, 1965), p. 124.

2. J. S. Conway, *The Nazi Persecution of the Churches, 1933–45* (London, 1968), p. 175.

3. Lewy, *Catholic Church and Nazi Germany,* pp. 283–284; "Die katholische Kirche und die Judenfrage," p. 176.

4. Galen, *Akten, Briefe und Predigten* 1:333, 370.

5. *Akten Kardinal Faulhabers,* ed. Volk, 2:179–180.

6. Johann Neuhäusler, *Kreuz und Hakenkreuz: Der Kampf des Nationalsozialismus gegen die katholische Kirche und der kirchliche Widerstand,* 2d ed., 2 vols. (Munich, 1946), 2:244.

7. Zipfel, *Kirchenkampf in Deutschland,* p. 124.

8. *Kirche im Kampf: Dokumente des Widerstands und des Aufbaus in der Evangelischen Kirche Deutschlands von 1933 bis 1945,* ed. Heinrich Hermelink (Tübingen and Stuttgart, 1950), pp. 112–113.

9. Ibid., pp. 277–278.

10. Bethge, *Bonhoeffer,* pp. 557–558.

11. *Zwischen Widerspruch und Widerstand,* ed. Greschat, p. 240.

12. Bonhoeffer, *Gesammelte Schriften,* 6:243–244.

13. Ibid., 1:240–241, 4:415–416, 458–459.

14. *Zwischen Widerspruch und Widerstand,* ed. Greschat, pp. 104, 106–107, 113–114, 117–118.

15. Conway, *Nazi Persecution of the Churches,* pp. 163–164; Bentley, *Niemöller,* p. 120.

16. Niemöller, "Sätze zur Arierfrage," pp. 269–270; Bentley, *Niemöller,* pp. 62–63; *Die Synode zu Steglitz: Die dritte Bekenntnissynode der Evangelischen Kirche der Altpreussischen Union,* ed. Wilhelm Niemöller (Göttingen, 1970), p. 302.

17. Niemöller, *Alles und in allen Christus,* pp. 87–89; Leo Stein, *I Was in Hell with Niemöller* (New York, London, and Edinburgh, 1942), p. 120.

13. Tightening the Totalitarian Grip

1. Rothfels, *German Opposition,* pp. 165–166.

2. *Times* (London), October 4, 1951.

3. Ulrich von Hassell, *Vom andern Deutschland: Aus den nachgelassenen Tagebüchern, 1938–1944* (Zurich, 1946), p. 17.

4. Ibid., p. 21.

5. Heinemann, *Ein konservativer Rebell,* p. 202.

6. *A Noble Combat,* ed. Klemperer, p. 331.

7. *"Spiegelbild einer Verschwörung,"* ed. Jacobsen, p. 87.

8. Speidel, *Invasion 1944,* p. 182; Graml, "Oster," p. 134.

9. *New Statesman and Nation,* February 12, 1938, p. 236.

10. Kramarz, *Stauffenberg,* p. 72.

11. Helmuth Groscurth, *Tagebücher eines Abwehroffiziers 1938–1940,* ed. Helmut Krausnick, Harold C. Deutsch, and Hildegard von Kotze (Stuttgart, 1970), p. 157.

12. *"Spiegelbild einer Verschwörung,"* ed. Jacobsen, p. 110.

13. Gerhard Ringshausen, "Evangelische Kirche und Widerstand," in *Deutscher Widerstand—Demokratie heute: Kirche, Kreisauer Kreis, Ethik, Militär und Gewerkschaften,* ed. Huberta Engel (Bonn and Berlin, 1992), p. 89.

14. Hassell, *Vom andern Deutschland,* pp. 29–30.

15. *"Spiegelbild einer Verschwörung,"* ed. Jacobsen, p. 474.

16. Otto L. Elias, "Der evangelische Kirchenkampf und die Judenfrage," *Informationsblatt für die Gemeinden in den niederdeutschen lutherischen Landeskirchen,* 10 (1961), 217.

17. M. Niemöller, "Sätze zur Arierfrage," pp. 269–270; *Die Synode zu Steglitz,* ed. W. Niemöller, p. 302; M. Niemöller, *Alles und in allen Christus!* p. 87; "Ein NS-Funkionär zum Niemöller-Prozess," p. 313; Bentley, *Niemöller,* pp. 65–66, 147; *Time,* June 18, 1945, p. 26.

18. Carl Goerdeler, report on the United States, January 2, 1938, pp. 38–39, and "Reisebericht: Palästina," July 1939, pp. 5, 10, Bundesarchiv (Koblenz), NL Goerdeler, 22, 15.

14. The Diplomacy of Brinkmanship

1. *New Statesman and Nation,* February 12, 1938, pp. 236–237.

2. *Akten zur deutschen auswärtigen Politik,* series D, 1:29–30.

3. *Hitler: Reden und Proklamationen,* ed. Domarus, 1:681.

4. *Akten zur deutschen auswärtigen Politik,* series D, 1:29.

5. Heinemann, *Ein konservativer Rebell,* pp. 204–205.

6. Karl Heinz Abshagen, *Canaris: Patriot und Weltbürger* (Stuttgart, 1950), p. 183; Höhne, *Canaris,* p. 272; "Die nationalpolitische Stellung des Offiziers in der Deutschen Wehrmacht: Vortrag Vizeadmiral Canaris, Oberkommando der Wehrmacht, am 22. April 1938 in Wien," p. 1, Institut für Zeitgeschichte (Munich), F6.

7. *Kirche im Kampf,* ed. Hermelink, p. 445.

8. Ulrich von Hassell, "Bismarck als Meister der Diplomatie," *Die neue Rundschau,* 50., no. 1 (1939), 272.

9. Eugen Ott, "Bemerkungen zu den Akten des Instituts für Zeitgeschichte," p. 2, Institut für Zeitgeschichte (Munich), Zs 279; Müller, *Beck,* p. 521; Reynolds, *Treason Was No Crime,* pp. 177, 208–209.

10. Carl Goerdeler, report on the United States, January 2, 1938, p. 51, Bundesarchiv (Koblenz), NL Goerdeler, 22; *"Spiegelbild einer Verschwörung,"* ed. Jacobsen, p. 353.

11. Müller, *Beck,* p. 521.

12. Carl Goerdeler, report on England and France, April 30, 1938, p. 18, Bundesarchiv (Koblenz), NL Goerdeler, 14; *"Spiegelbild einer Verschwörung,"* ed. Jacobsen, p. 353.

13. Müller, *Beck,* p. 544.

14. Ibid., p. 552.

15. Ibid., pp. 554–556.

16. *Goerdelers politisches Testament: Dokumente des anderen Deutschland,* ed. Friedrich Krause (New York, 1945), pp. 57–58.

17. Hjalmar Schacht, *Abrechnung mit Hitler* (Hamburg and Stuttgart, 1948), p. 23.

18. *Documents on British Foreign Policy, 1919–1939,* 3d series, 10 vols. (London, 1949–1961), 2:125–126.

19. Georg Thomas, "Gedanken und Ereignisse," *Schweizer Monatshefte,* 25 (1945–46), 541.

20. Müller, *Beck,* pp. 102, 579–580.

21. *Goerdelers politisches Testament,* ed. Krause, p. 62.

22. *"Spiegelbild einer Verschwörung,"* Jacobsen, p. 353.

15. The March toward Armageddon

1. *Trial of the Major War Criminals,* 37:548–551.

2. Erich Kordt, *Nicht aus den Akten . . .* (Stuttgart, 1950), p. 306; *Trial of the Major War Criminals,* 37:550.

3. *Trial of the Major War Criminals,* 26:342–343.

4. Gisevius, *Bis zum bittern Ende,* 2:138, 140.

5. *Goerdelers politisches Testament,* ed. Krause, pp. 59–61.

6. Ulrich von Hassell, "Das Ringen um den Staat der Zukunft," *Schweizer Monatshefte,* 44 (1964–65), 320–321, 323, 326–327.

7. Ger van Roon, *Neuordnung im Widerstand: Der Kreisauer Kreis innerhalb der deutschen Widerstandsbewegung* (Munich, 1967), p. 83.

8. Thomas, "Gedanken und Ereignisse," pp. 542–543.

9. Rudolf Pechel, *Deutscher Widerstand* (Erlenbach and Zurich, 1947), p. 153.

10. Schacht, *Abrechnung mit Hitler,* p. 26.

11. Gisevius, *Bis zum bittern Ende,* 2:118–120; Foerster, *Beck,* p. 149.

12. Carl Goerdeler, "Reisebericht: Algerien," April 17, 1939, p. 18, Bundesarchiv (Koblenz), NL Goerdeler, 15; idem, "Heads of Agreement between Great Britain and Germany," December 1938, Public Record Office (Kew), FO371/21659, C15084, pp. 208–10; idem, undated memorandum, spring 1939, pp. 1–3, Bundesarchiv (Koblenz), NL Goerdeler, 16.

13. A. P. Young, *The 'X' Documents,* ed. Sidney Aster (London, 1974), pp. 234–235.

14. *Akten zur deutschen auswärtigen Politik,* series D, 6:565–566, 569–570.

15. Gisevius, *Bis zum bittern Ende,* 2:142–143.

16. Groscurth, *Tagebücher,* p. 173.

17. Galen, *Akten, Briefe und Predigten,* 2:747.

18. Bentley, *Niemöller*, pp. 147, 160.
19. Bonhoeffer, *Gesammelte Schriften*, 1:320.

16. German Successes or Nazi Triumphs?

1. *Times* (London), September 5, 1939.
2. *Hitler: Reden und Proklamationen*, ed. Domarus, 2:1386–87.
3. Ibid., p. 1396.
4. Great Britain, *Parliamentary Debates: House of Commons, 1938–39*, 5th ser., 352:564–566.
5. *Trial of the Major War Criminals*, 37:467–468.
6. Peter Hoffmann, *Widerstand, Staatsstreich, Attentat: Der Kampf der Opposition gegen Hitler* (Munich, 1969), p. 147; Pechel, *Deutscher Widerstand*, p. 153.
7. Groscurth, *Tagebücher*, p. 238.
8. Thomas, "Gedanken und Ereignisse," p. 543; Hoffmann, *Widerstand, Staatsstreich, Attentat*, p. 185.
9. Groscurth, *Tagebücher*, pp. 487–488. 490, 497.
10. Kordt, *Nicht aus den Akten*, p. 369.
11. Hoffmann, *Widerstand, Staatsstreich, Attentat*, pp. 192–193.
12. Reynolds, *Treason Was No Crime*, pp. 177, 208–209.
13. Hassell, *Vom andern Deutschland*, pp. 89–90.
14. Ibid., pp. 129–133.
15. Roon, *Neuordnung im Widerstand*, pp. 479–480.
16. *Die Mittwochs-Gesellschaft*, ed. Scholder, pp. 262–263.
17. *Beck und Goerdeler*, ed. Schramm, pp. 95–96; Ritter, *Goerdeler*, p. 569.
18. Hassell, *Vom andern Deutschland*, p. 158; Ulrich v. Hassell, "Die Knochen des pommerschen Musketiers," *Auswärtige Politik*, 9 (1942), 762–763; Christian Augustin [Ulrich von Hassell], "*Dominium maris baltici*," *Auswärtige Politik*, 9 (1942), 211–212.
19. Kommando der Panzergruppe 4, Abt. 1a Nr. 20/41, LVI. A.K., 17956/7a, Anlage 2 and Anlage 14, May 5, 1941, Bundesarchiv-Militärarchiv, (Freiburg).
20. Stieff, *Briefe*, p. 124.
21. Heinemann, *Ein konservativer Rebell*, pp. 78, 224.
22. Galen, *Akten, Briefe und Predigten*, 2:902.

17. The Moral Dilemmas of Hegemony

1. Müller, *Stauffenberg*, pp. 215–216.
2. Hassell, *Vom andern Deutschland*, pp. 91, 154, 158, 166.
3. *Beck und Goerdeler*, ed. Schramm, pp. 147–148.
4. *Landesbischof D. Wurm*, ed. Schäfer, p. 122.
5. Galen, *Akten, Briefe und Predigten*, 2:848–849.
6. Groscurth, *Tagebücher*, p. 487; Hassell, *Vom andern Deutschland*, p. 127.
7. Groscurth, *Tagebücher*, p. 216.
8. Stieff, *Briefe*, pp. 107–108.
9. Rudolph-Christoph v. Gersdorff, *Soldat im Untergang* (Frankfurt am Main, Berlin, and Vienna, 1977), p. 87.

10. Stieff, *Briefe*, p. 127.
11. Helmuth James von Moltke, *Briefe an Freya, 1939–1945*, ed. Beate Ruhm von Oppen (Munich, 1988), p. 278.
12. Hassell, *Vom andern Deutschland*, pp. 92, 166.
13. *Beck und Goerdeler*, ed. Schramm, p. 105.
14. Hassell, *Vom andern Deutschland*, pp. 92, 127; Stieff, *Briefe*, p. 108.
15. Moltke, *Briefe an Freya*, p. 308.
16. *Beck und Goerdeler*, Schramm, pp. 105–107.
17. Höhne, *Canaris*, pp. 443–445, 466; Karl Bartz, *Die Tragödie der deutschen Abwehr* (Salzburg, 1955), pp. 96, 98–107.
18. Heinemann, *Ein konservativer Rebell*, pp. 78, 221, 279–280.
19. Kommando der Panzergruppe 4, Abt. 1a Nr. 20/41, LVI. A.K., 17956/7a, Anlage 2 and 14, May 5, 1941, Bundesarchiv-Militärarchiv, (Freiburg).
20. Büchler, *Stülpnagel*, p. 125, Helmut Krausnick and Hans-Heinrich Wilhelm, *Die Truppe des Weltanschauungskrieges: Die Einsatzgruppen der Sicherheitspolizei und des SD 1938–1942* (Stuttgart, 1981), pp. 218–220.

18. The Ebbing Tide of Conquest

1. *Landesbischof D. Wurm*, ed. Schäfer, p. 168.
2. Galen, *Akten, Briefe und Predigten*, 2:878, 984.
3. *Akten Kardinal Faulhabers*, ed. Volk, 2:824–825, 845, 856.
4. *Kölner Aktenstücke zur Lage der katholischen Kirche in Deutschland, 1933–1945*, ed. Wilhelm Corsten (Cologne, 1949), p. 269.
5. Ibid., pp. 301, 303.
6. *Landesbischof D. Wurm*, ed. Schäfer, p. 144.
7. Ibid., p. 159.
8. Ibid., pp. 160, 164–165.
9. Ibid., pp. 167, 373–374.
10. Ibid., pp. 155, 158, 161–162, 312.
11. *Kirchliches Jahrbuch für die Evangelische Kirche in Deutschland, 1933–1944*, ed. Joachim Beckmann (Gütersloh, 1948), p. 401.
12. *Kirche im Kampf*, ed. Hermelink, pp. 650–651.
13. *"Spiegelbild einer Verschwörung,"* ed. Jacobsen, p. 19.
14. Scheurig, *Tresckow*, p. 151; Gersdorff, *Soldat im Untergang*, p. 133.
15. *"Spiegelbild einer Verschwörung,"* ed. Jacobsen, pp. 98–99.
16. Ibid., p. 452.
17. Ibid., p. 448.
18. Gisevius, *Bis zum bittern Ende*, 2:314–315; *"Spiegelbild einer Verschwörung,"* ed. Jacobsen, p. 19; Detlef von Schwerin, *"Dann sind's die besten Köpfe, die man henkt": Die junge Generation im deutschen Widerstand* (Munich and Zürich, 1991), p. 227; Höhne, *Canaris*, p. 455.
19. *"Spiegelbild einer Verschwörung,"* ed. Jacobsen, pp. 34, 110, 168–169; Hassell, *Vom andern Deutschland*, p. 314.
20. Stieff, *Briefe*, ed. H. Mühleisen, p. 137; Hoffmann, *Stauffenberg und seine Brüder*, p. 337; Müller, *Stauffenberg*. p. 382; Hassell, *Vom andern Deutschland*, p. 314.

21. Axel von dem Bussche, "Eid und Schuld," *Göttinger Universitäts-Zeitung,* March 7, 1947, p. 2.

22. *"Spiegelbild einer Verschwörung,"* ed. Jacobsen, p. 474.

19. Searching for a Negotiated Peace

1. *"Spiegelbild einer Verschwörung,"* ed. Jacobsen, p. 34; Eberhard Zeller, *Geist der Freiheit: Der zwanzigste Juli,* 4th ed. (Munich, 1963), pp. 257–258.
2. *"Spiegelbild einer Verschwörung,"* ed. Jacobsen, pp. 19, 115–116.
3. Hoffmann, *Widerstand, Staatsstreich, Attentat,* pp. 387–388.
4. *"Spiegelbild einer Verschwörung,"* ed. Jacobsen, pp. 19–20, 34.
5. Ibid., pp. 19, 34, 116.
6. "Zwei aussenpolitische Memoranden der deutschen Opposition (Frühjahr 1942)," ed. Hans Rothfels, *Vierteljahrshefte für Zeitgeschichte,* 5 (1957), 393–394.
7. *"Spiegelbild einer Verschwörung,"* ed. Jacobsen, p. 210.
8. Hoffmann, *Widerstand, Staatsstreich, Attentat,* pp. 435–436; *"Spiegelbild einer Verschwörung,"* ed. Jacobsen, pp. 59–61, 210; Ritter, *Goerdeler,* pp. 601–603; Zeller, *Geist der Freiheit,* pp. 318–319.
9. *"Spiegelbild einer Verschwörung,"* ed. Jacobsen, p. 452.
10. Roon, *Neuordnung im Widerstand,* p. 554.
11. *"Spiegelbild einer Verschwörung,"* ed. Jacobsen, p. 452; Otto Kopp, "Theodor Bäuerle und der Bosch-Kreis: Die wiederentdeckte Goerdeler-Rede," in *Widerstand und Erneuerung: Neue Berichte und Dokumente vom inneren Kampf gegen das Hitler-Regime,* ed. Otto Kopp (Stuttgart, 1966), p. 174.
12. *"Spiegelbild einer Verschwörung,"* ed. Jacobsen, p. 149; Kopp, "Theodor Bäuerle," pp. 174, 179.
13. *"Spiegelbild einer Verschwörung,"* ed. Jacobsen, p. 473.
14. "Goerdeler und die Deportation der Leipziger Juden," ed. Helmut Krausnick, *Vierteljahrshefte für Zeitgeschichte,* 13 (1965), 338; Ritter, *Goerdeler,* p. 597.
15. "Zwei aussenpolitische Memoranden," ed. Rothfels, p. 394; Roon, *Neuordnung im Widerstand,* pp. 589–590.
16. *"Spiegelbild einer Verschwörung,"* ed. Jacobsen, p. 59.
17. Gisevius, *Bis zum bittern Ende,* 2:314–315; Heinemann, *Ein konservativer Rebell,* p. 168.
18. Roon, *Neuordnung im Widerstand,* p. 584.
19. *"Spiegelbild einer Verschwörung,"* ed. Jacobsen, p. 127.
20. Hassell, "Die Knochen des pommerschen Musketiers," pp. 759, 763; idem, *"Dominium maris baltici,"* pp. 210–211.
21. *"Spiegelbild einer Verschwörung,"* ed. Jacobsen, pp. 126–127, 411; Müller, *Stauffenberg,* p. 393.
22. *"Spiegelbild einer Verschwörung,"* ed. Jacobsen, p. 34.

20. On the Brink of Redemption

1. *Landesbischof D. Wurm,* ed. Schäfer, pp. 459–460.
2. *Kölner Aktenstücke,* ed. Corsten, p. 310.

3. *"Spiegelbild einer Verschwörung,"* ed. Jacobsen, pp. 437, 535; Ritter, *Goerdeler,* p. 516.
4. *"Spiegelbild einer Verschwörung,"* ed. Jacobsen, p. 438.
5. Friedrich Meinecke, *Die deutsche Katastrophe: Betrachtungen und Erinnerungen* (Wiesbaden, 1946), p. 149.
6. Schlabrendorff, *Offiziere gegen Hitler,* p. 129.
7. Peter Hoffmann, "Der militärische Widerstand in der zweiten Kriegshälfte, 1942–1944/45," in *Aufstand des Gewissens: Der militärische Widerstand gegen Hitler und das NS-Regime, 1933–1945* (Herford and Bonn, 1984), p. 132.
8. Hoffmann, *Stauffenberg und seine Brüder,* pp. 452–453; *"Spiegelbild einer Verschwörung,"* ed. Jacobsen, p. 127; Schlabrendorff, *Offiziere gegen Hitler,* p. 129; Zeller, *Geist der Freiheit,* p. 361.
9. Zeller, *Geist der Freiheit,* p. 514 n. 2.
10. Schwerin, *"Dann sind's die besten Köpfe,"* p. 425.
11. Ibid., pp. 390–391.
12. *"Spiegelbild einer Verschwörung,"* ed. Jacobsen, p. 34; Zeller, *Geist der Freiheit,* p. 361.
13. Schwerin, *"Dann sind's die besten Köpfe,"* pp. 425, 427.
14. *"Spiegelbild einer Verschwörung,"* ed. Jacobsen, p. 127.
15. Ibid., pp. 126–127; Müller, *Stauffenberg,* pp. 393, 582.
16. Meinecke, *Die deutsche Katastrophe,* p. 150; Schwerin, *"Dann sind's die besten Köpfe,"* p. 391.
17. Marie Vassiltchikov, *The Berlin Diaries, 1940–1945* (London, 1985), pp. 186–187.
18. Zeller, *Geist der Freiheit,* p. 361.
19. Schlabrendorff, *Offiziere gegen Hitler,* p. 129.
20. Meinecke, *Die deutsche Katastrophe,* p. 149; Foerster, *Beck,* p. 164.
21. *"Spiegelbild einer Verschwörung,"* ed. Jacobsen, pp. 155–156.

21. A Mortal Failure

1. *New York Times,* July 22, 1944.
2. Great Britain, *Parliamentary Debates: House of Commons, 1943–44,* 5th ser., 402:596–597; *Times* (London), July 26, 1944.
3. *New York Times,* July 24, 1944; *Krasnaia Zvezda* (Moscow), July 23, 1944.
4. *New York Times,* July 23, 1944.
5. Great Britain, *Parliamentary Debates: House of Commons, 1943–44,* 5th ser., 402:1487.
6. *Times* (London), July 22, 1944.
7. Ibid., July 24, 1944.
8. John W. Wheeler-Bennett, memorandum of July 25, 1944, Public Record Office (Kew), F0371/39062, C 9896, p. 1.
9. *New York Herald Tribune,* August 2, August 9, 1944.
10. *Nation,* July 29, 1944, p. 116.
11. Alfred Vagts, "The Putsch That Failed," *Nation,* August 5, 1944, pp. 153–154.
12. *New Republic,* July 31, 1944, pp. 118–119.
13. Karl O. Paetel, "The Crisis in Germany," *New Republic,* August 7, 1944, p. 155.

14. National Archives (Washington, D.C.), Department of State, MS 862.20200 Goerdeler, Karl (DR)/8-544, pp. 1–2.
15. *Hitler: Reden und Proklamationen,* ed. Domarus, 2:2128.
16. *"Spiegelbild einer Verschwörung,"* ed. Jacobsen, pp. 1–2.
17. *Meldungen aus dem Reich, 1938–1945: Die geheimen Lageberichte des Sicherheitsdienstes der SS,* ed. Heinz Boberach, 17 vols. (Herrsching, 1984), 17:6684–85.
18. *Landesbischof D. Wurm,* ed. Schäfer, pp. 357–358.
19. *"Spiegelbild einer Verschwörung,"* ed. Jacobsen, p. 304; *Akten Kardinal Faulhabers,* ed. Volk, 2:1026.
20. *Time,* June 18, 1945, p. 26; *Times* (London), June 6, 1945.
21. Friedrich Percyval Reck-Malleczewen, *Tagebuch eines Verzweifelten* (Schwäbisch-Gmünd, 1946), pp. 219–221.
22. Ritter, *Goerdeler,* p. 306; Theodor Steltzer, *Von deutscher Politik: Dokumente, Aufsätze und Vorträge,* ed. Friedrich Minssen (Frankfurt am Main, 1949), p. 86; Moltke, *Briefe an Freya,* p. 609; Alison Owings, *Frauen: German Women Recall the Third Reich* (New Brunswick, 1994), p. 255.
23. Hoffmann, *Widerstand, Staatsstreich, Attentat,* pp. 602–603.
24. Zeller, *Geist der Freiheit,* p. 514 n. 2.
25. Hoffmann, *Widerstand, Staatsstreich, Attentat,* p. 603.
26. Schlabrendorff, *Offiziere gegen Hitler,* p. 153.

22. The Passion of the German Resistance

1. Hoffmann, *Widerstand, Staatsstreich, Attentat,* pp. 630–631; idem, *The History of the German Resistance, 1933–1945* (Cambridge, Mass., 1977), p. 712 n. 21.
2. Hoffmann, *Widerstand, Staatsstreich, Attentat,* pp. 626–627.
3. Helmuth J. von Moltke, *Letzte Briefe aus dem Gefängnis Tegel* (Berlin, 1951), p. 9.
4. Moltke, *Briefe an Freya,* pp. 602–603, 608.
5. Stieff, *Briefe,* pp. 178–179.
6. *"Spiegelbild einer Verschwörung,"* ed. Jacobsen, p. 795.
7. Ibid., pp. 796–797.
8. Ibid., pp. 799–800.
9. Hoffmann, *Widerstand, Staatsstreich, Attentat,* pp. 626–627, 869.
10. *"Spiegelbild einer Verschwörung,"* ed. Jacobsen, pp. 447–448.
11. Ibid., p. 448.
12. Carl Goerdeler, "Unsere Idee," November 1944, pp. 5–6, Bundesarchiv (Koblenz), NL Goerdeler, 26; *"Spiegelbild einer Verschwörung,"* ed. Jacobsen, pp. 353, 448; Carl Goerdeler, "Gedanken eines zum Tode Verurteilten über die deutsche Zukunft," September 1944, p. 38, Bundesarchiv (Koblenz), NL Goerdeler, 26.
13. *"Spiegelbild einer Verschwörung,"* ed. Jacobsen, pp. 168, 448.
14. Ibid., pp. 168, 452.
15. Ibid., pp. 168–169, 353, 450.
16. Ibid., pp. 110, 449–450, 474.
17. Carl Goerdeler, "Gedanken eines zum Tode Verurteilten über die deutsche Zukunft," September 1944, p. 37, Bundesarchiv (Koblenz), NL Goerdeler, 26.

18. Carl Goerdeler, "Die Aufgaben der deutschen Zukunft: Anlage," August 1944, p. 26, Bundesarchiv (Koblenz), NL Goerdeler, 26.

19. Hoffmann, *Widerstand, Staatsstreich, Attentat,* p. 603; Höhne, *Canaris,* p. 567; Schwerin, *"Dann sind's die besten Köpfe,"* p. 425.

20. Albrecht Haushofer, *Moabit Sonnets,* trans. M. D. Herter Norton (London and New York, 1978), p. 79.

21. *Verfolgung und Widerstand, 1933–1945; Christliche Demokraten gegen Hitler,* ed. Günter Buchstab, Brigitte Kaff, and Hans-Otto Kleinmann (Düsseldorf, 1986), p. 217.

22. *"Spiegelbild einer Verschwörung,"* ed. Jacobsen, p. 792.

23. Through Martyrdom to Beatitude

1. Galen, *Akten, Briefe und Predigten,* 2:1102.

2. Reinhold Sautter, *Theophil Wurm: Sein Leben un sein Kampf* (Stuttgart, 1960), pp. 80–81.

3. Galen, *Akten, Briefe und Predigten,* 2:1106.

4. *Akten Kardinal Faulhabers,* ed. Volk, 2:1061, 1072.

5. *Time,* June 18, 1945, p. 27.

6. Theophil Wurm, *Erinnerungen aus meinem Leben* (Stuttgart, 1953), p. 176.

7. Anton Gill, *An Honourable Defeat: A History of German Resistance to Hitler, 1933–1945* (New York, 1994), p. 1.

8. *Jahrbuch der öffentlichen Meinung, 1947–1955,* ed. Elisabeth Noelle and Erich Peter Neumann (Allensbach, 1956), p. 138.

9. Ibid.

10. Rothfels, *German Opposition,* pp. 165–166.

11. *Times* (London), October 4, 1951.

12. John W. Wheeler-Bennett, memorandum of July 25, 1944, Public Record Office (Kew), F0371/39062, C 9896, p. 1; idem, *Nemesis of Power,* pp. 689–690.

13. Zeller, *Geist der Freiheit,* pp. 294–295.

14. Annedore Leber, *Das Gewissen steht auf: 64 Lebensbilder aus dem deutschen Widerstand, 1933–1945* (Berlin and Frankfurt am Main, 1954), pp. 5–6.

15. Stauffenberg, "Die deutsche Widerstandsbewegung," p. 161.

16. Theodor Heuss, *Würdigungen: Reden, Aufsätze und Briefe aus den Jahren, 1949–1955,* ed. Hans Bott (Tübingen, 1955), p. 424.

17. Albert Norden, "Die Bedeutung des 20. Juli," *Die Weltbühne,* 2 (1947), 556.

18. Werner Plesse, "Zum antifaschistischen Widerstandskampf in Mitteldeutschland (1939–1945)," *Zeitschrift für Geschichtswissenschaft,* 2 (1954), 835–836.

19. Kurt Finker, "Widerstand und Geschichte des Widerstandes in der Forschung der DDR," in *Widerstand: Ein Problem zwischen Theorie und Geschichte,* ed. Peter Steinbach (Cologne, 1987), p. 105.

20. Norden, "Bedeutung des 20. Juli," pp. 558–559.

21. Karl-Eduard v. Schnitzler, "Der Mythos des 20. Juli," *Horizont,* 12, no. 29 (1979), p. 4.

22. *Neues Deutschland,* December 16, 1983.

23. Finker, "Widerstand und Geschichte des Widerstandes," p. 106.

24. *Frankfurter Allgemeine Zeitung,* July 21, 1994.

References

The following listing of historical documents and writings pertaining to the German resistance is intended primarily as a guide to the notes. It does not purport to be a comprehensive bibliography of the anti-Nazi movement under the Third Reich. Indeed, an attempt to prepare such a bibliography would have been not only a daunting or foolhardy task; it would have been a near impossibility. The bibliography in Peter Hoffmann's *Widerstand, Staatsstreich, Attentat,* published in 1969, contains close to eight hundred titles. The English translation of that work, which appeared in 1977 as *The History of the German Resistance, 1933–1945,* presents a list of approximately a thousand items. Regine Büchel in her study of 1975 entitled *Der deutsche Widerstand im Spiegel von Fachliteratur und Publizistik seit 1945* cites some two thousand books and articles. And that was two decades ago. Since then the scholarly literature on the subject has at least doubled. Hence the chief purpose of the following enumeration of historical materials is to enable readers to identify the sources on which this book rests. If thereby they should also acquire greater familiarity with at least a part of the scholarly literature on the German resistance, so much the better.

Primary Sources

ARCHIVAL MATERIALS

Leo Baeck Institute (New York). Julie Braun-Vogelstein Collection, part IV, box 28, folder 5 [Diana Hubback (Hopkinson)], unpublished manuscript on Adam von Trott zu Solz [1946].

Busser, Ralph C. Letter of August 5, 1944. National Archives (Washington, D.C.), Department of State, MS 862.20200 Goerdeler, Karl (DR)/8-544.

[Canaris, Wilhelm]. "Die nationalpolitsche Stellung des Offiziers in der Deutschen Wehrmacht: Vortrag Vizeadmiral Canaris, Oberkommando der Wehrmacht, am 22. April 1938 in Wien." Institut für Zeitgeschichte (Munich), F6.

"Die nach Amerika gerichtete Rundfunkrede des Herrn Generalsuperintendenten Dibelius vom 4. April 1933." Evangelische Arbeitsgemeinschaft für kirchliche Zeitgeschichte (Munich).

Evangelisches Zentralarchiv in Berlin, NL Dibelius, 50/R19.

Falkenhausen, Alexander von. Autobiographical report, November 15, 1946. National Archives (Washington, D.C.), Foreign Military Studies, MS B-289.

Goerdeler, Carl. Economic memorandum of 1930–31. Bundesarchiv (Koblenz), NL Goerdeler, 21.

————. Memorandum of August 1934. Bundesarchiv (Koblenz), NL Goerdeler, 12.

————. Memorandum of July 9, 1937. Bundesarchiv (Koblenz), NL Goerdeler, 12.

————. Report on the United States, January 2, 1938. Bundesarchiv (Koblenz), NL Goerdeler, 22.

————. Report on England and France, April 30, 1938. Bundesarchiv (Koblenz), NL Goerdeler, 14.

————. Undated memorandum, spring 1939. Bundesarchiv (Koblenz), NL Goerdeler, 16.

————. "Reisebericht: Algerien," April 17, 1939. Bundesarchiv (Koblenz), NL Goerdeler, 15.

————. "Reisebericht: Palästina," July 1939. Bundesarchiv (Koblenz), NL Goerdeler, 15.

————. "Die Aufgaben der deutschen Zukunft," August 1944. Bundesarchiv (Koblenz), NL Goerdeler, 26.

————. "Gedanken eines zum Tode Verurteilten über die deutsche Zukunft," September 1944. Bundesarchiv (Koblenz), NL Goerdeler, 26.

————. "Unsere Idee," November 1944. Bundesarchiv (Koblenz), NL Goerdeler, 26.

————. "Heads of Agreement between Great Britain and Germany," December 1938. Public Record Office (Kew), FO 371/21659, C 15084.

Habermann, Max. "Der Deutschnationale Handlungsgehilfen-Verband im Kampf um das Reich, 1918–1933: Ein Zeugnis seines Wollens und Wirkens." Deutscher Handels- und Industrieangestellten-Verband (Hamburg).

Kommando der Panzergruppe 4. Abt. 1a Nr. 20/41, LVI. A.K., 17956/7a, Anlage 2 and Anlage 14, May 5, 1941. Bundesarchiv-Militärarchiv (Freiburg).

"Niederschrift des Vortrags Konteradmiral Canaris bei der Ic-Besprechung im O.K.W. am 3.3. 1938." National Archives (Washington, D.C.), T-77/roll 808/frames 5540874–5540885.

Ott, Eugen. "Bemerkungen zu den Akten des Instituts für Zeitgeschichte." Institut für Zeitgeschichte (Munich), Zs 279.

Schulenburg, Fritz-Dietlof von der. "Preussisches Beamtentum," March and June 1931. Bundesarchiv (Koblenz), NL Schulenburg, 1.

————. "Neuaufbau des höheren Beamtentums," April 1933. Bundesarchiv (Koblenz), NL Schulenburg, 1.

————. "Reichsreform," spring 1934. Bundesarchiv (Koblenz), NL Schulenburg, 1.

Walz, Hans. "Meine Mitarbeit an der Aktion Goerdeler," November 1945. Bundesarchiv (Koblenz), NL Gerhard Ritter, 131.

PUBLISHED DOCUMENTS AND WRITINGS (ORIGINAL)

Bussche, Axel von dem. "Eid und Schuld." *Göttinger Universitäts-Zeitung,* March 7, 1947.

Canaris, Wilhelm. "Politik und Wehrmacht." In *Wehrmacht und Partei,* ed. Richard Donnevert. Leipzig, 1938.

Dibelius, Otto. *Ein Christ ist immer im Dienst: Erlebnisse und Erfahrungen in einer Zeitenwende.* Stuttgart, 1961.

Faulhaber, Michael von. *Judentum, Christentum, Germanentum: Adventspredigten gehalten in St. Michael zu München 1933.* Munich, 1934.

Fritsche, Hans Karl. *Ein Leben im Schatten des Verrates: Erinnerungen eines Überleben-den an den 20. Juli 1944.* Freiburg, Basel, and Vienna, 1984.

Gersdorff, Rudolph-Christoph v. *Soldat im Untergang.* Frankfurt am Main, Berlin, and Vienna, 1977.

Gisevius, Hans Bernd. *Bis zum bittern Ende,* 2d ed., 2 vols. Zurich, 1946.

Great Britain. *Parliamentary Debates: House of Commons, 1943–44,* 5th ser.

Hassell, Ulrich von. "Bismarck als Meister der Diplomatie." *Die neue Rundschau,* 50, no. 1 (1939).

———. *Deutschlands und Italiens europäische Sendung.* Cologne, 1937.

——— (Christian Augustin). "Dominium maris baltici." *Auswärtige Politik,* 9 (1942).

———. "Die Knochen des pommerschen Musketiers." *Auswärtige Politik,* 9 (1942).

"Die katholische Kirche und die Judenfrage." *Eine heilige Kirche,* 16 (1934).

Kleist-Schmenzin, Ewald von. "Eine Absage." *Mitteilungen des Hauptvereins der Kon-servativen* (Berlin), March 1933.

Kordt, Erich. *Nicht aus den Akten. . . .* Stuttgart, 1950.

Manstein, Erich v. *Aus einem Soldatenleben, 1889–1939.* Bonn, 1958.

Meinecke, Friedrich. *Die deutsche Katastrophe: Betrachtungen und Erinnerungen.* Wiesbaden, 1946.

Niemöller, Martin. *Alles und in allen Christus! Fünfzehn Dahlemer Predigten.* Berlin, 1935.

———. *. . . dass wir am Ihm bleiben: Sechzehn Dahlemer Predigten.* Berlin, 1935.

———. "Sätze zur Arierfrage in der Kirche." *Junge Kirche: Halbmonatschrift für reformatorisches Christentum,* 1 (1933).

———. *Vom U-Boot zur Kanzel.* Berlin, 1935.

Norden, Albert. "Die Bedeutung des 20. Juli." *Die Weltbühne,* 2 (1947).

Paetel, Karl O. "The Crisis in Germany." *New Republic,* August 7, 1944.

Pechel, Rudolf. *Deutscher Widerstand.* Erlenbach and Zurich, 1947.

Plesse, Werner. "Zum antifaschistischen Widerstandskampf in Mitteldeutschland (1939–45)." *Zeitschrift für Geschichtswissenschaft,* 2 (1954).

Popitz, Johannes. "Eugen Schiffer zur Kritik unserer Zeit." *Juristische Wochenschrift,* February 27, 1932.

———. "Finanzausgleich." In *Handwörterbuch der Staatswissenschaften,* 4th ed., 9 vols. Jena, 1923–1929.

———. *Der Finanzausgleich und seine Bedeutung für die Finanzlage des Reichs, der Länder und Gemeinden.* Berlin, 1930.

Die Reden gehalten in den öffentlichen und geschlossenen Versammlungen der 62. Gene-ral-Versammlung der Katholiken Deutschlands zu München 27. bis 30. August 1922. Würzburg, 1923.

Schacht, Hjalmar. *Abrechnung mit Hitler.* Hamburg and Stuttgart, 1948.

Schnitzler, Karl-Eduard v. "Der Mythos des 20. Juli." *Horizont,* 12, no. 29 (1979).

Schulenburg, Fritz-Dietlof von der. "Das Erbe des Preussischen Staates." *Württem-bergische Verwaltungs-Zeitschrift,* 33 (1937).

———. "Partei und Beamtentum." *Deutschlands Erneuerung: Monatsschrift für das deutsche Volk,* 6 (1932).

Speidel, Hans. *Invasion 1944: Ein Beitrag zu Rommels und des Reiches Schicksal.* Tübingen and Stuttgart, 1949.

Stauffenberg, Alexander von. "Die deutsche Widerstandsbewegung und ihre geistige Bedeutung in der Gengenwart." In *Bekenntnis und Verpflichtung: Reden und Aufsätze zur zehnjährigen Wiederkehr des 20. Juli 1944.* Stuttgart, 1955.

Stein, Leo. *I Was in Hell with Niemöller.* New York, London, and Edinburgh, 1942.

Thomas, Georg. "Gedanken und Ereignisse." *Schweizer Monatshefte,* 25 (1945–46).

Trial of the Major War Criminals before the International Military Tribunal, 42 vols. Nuremberg, 1947–1949.

Vagts, Alfred. "The Putsch That Failed." *Nation,* August 5, 1944.

"Die Wahlen zum Reichstag am 4. Mai 1924 und am 7. Dezember 1924." *Statistik des Deutschen Reichs,* 315, nos. 2–3 (1925).

"Die Wahlen zum Reichstag am 20. Mai 1928." *Statistik des Deutschen Reichs,* 372, no. 2 (1930).

"Die Wahlen zum Reichstag am 14. September 1930." *Statistik des Deutschen Reichs,* 382, no. 1 (1932).

"Die Wahlen zum Reichstag am 31. Juli und 6. November 1932 und am 5. März 1933." *Statistik des Deutschen Reichs,* 434 (1935).

Watzdorf, Bernhard. "Die getarnte Ausbildung von Generalstabsoffizieren der Reichswehr von 1932 bis 1935." *Zeitschrift für Militärgeschichte,* 2 (1963).

Wurm, Theophil. *Erinnerungen aus meinem Leben.* Stuttgart, 1953.

———. *"Habt die Brüder lieb, fürchtet Gott, ehret den König!": Predigt am Sonntag Jubilate, 22. April 1934 über 1. Petri 2, 11–17 im Münster zu Ulm.* Stuttgart, 1934.

PUBLISHED DOCUMENTS AND WRITINGS (EDITED)

Akten zur deutschen auswärtigen Politik, 1918–1945, series C, 6 vols. Göttingen, 1971–1981.

Akten zur deutschen auswärtigen Politik, 1918–1945, series D, 13 vols. Baden-Baden, Frankfurt am Main, Bonn, and Göttingen, 1950–1970.

Akten zur deutschen auswärtigen Politik, 1918–1945, series E, 8 vols. Göttingen, 1969–1979.

Beck und Goerdeler: Gemeinschaftsdokumente für den Frieden, 1941–1944, ed. Wilhelm von Schramm. Munich, 1965.

Bonhoeffer, Dietrich. *Gesammelte Schriften,* ed. Eberhard Bethge, 6 vols. Munich, 1958–74.

Ciano, Galeazzo. *1937–1938 Diario.* Bologna, 1948.

Deutsche Parteiprogramme, ed. Wolfgang Treue, 2d ed. Berlin and Frankfurt, 1956.

Deutschland-Berichte der Sozialdemokratischen Partei Deutschlands (Sopade), 1934–1940, 7 vols. Frankfurt am Main, 1980.

Documents on British Foreign Policy, 1919–1939, 3d series, 10 vols. London, 1949–1961.

Die Evangelische Landeskirche in Württemberg und der Nationalsozialismus: Eine Dokumentation zum Kirchenkampf, ed. Gerhard Schäfer, 6 vols. Stuttgart, 1971–1986.

Akten Kardinal Michael von Faulhabers, 1917–1945, ed. Ludwig Volk, 2 vols. Mainz, 1975–1978.

Galen, Clemens August von. *Akten, Briefe und Predigten, 1933–1946,* ed. Peter Löffler, 2 vols. Mainz, 1988.

"Goerdeler und die Deportation der Leipziger Juden," ed. Helmut Krausnick. *Vierteljahrshefte für Zeitgeschichte,* 13 (1965).

Goerdelers Politisches Testament: Dokumente des anderen Deutschland, ed. Friedrich Krause. New York, 1945.

Groscurth, Helmuth. *Tagebücher eines Abwehroffiziers, 1938–40,* ed. Helmut Krausnick, Harold C. Deutsch, and Hildegard von Kotze. Stuttgart, 1970.

Hassell, Ulrich von. "Das Ringen um den Staat der Zukunft." *Schweizer Monatshefte,* 44 (1964–65).

———. *Vom andern Deutschland: Aus den nachgelassenen Tagebüchern, 1938–1945.* Zürich, 1946.

Haushofer, Albrecht. *Moabit Sonnets,* trans. M. D. Herter Norton. London and New York, 1978.

Heuss, Theodor. *Würdigungen: Reden, Aufsätze und Briefe aus den Jahren, 1949–1955,* ed. Hans Bott. Tübingen, 1955.

Hitler: Reden und Proklamationen, 1932–1945, ed. Max Domarus, 2 vols. Munich, 1965.

Katholische Kirche und Nationalsozialismus: Dokumente, 1930–1935, ed. Hans Müller. Munich, 1963.

Kirche im Kampf: Dokumente des Widerstands und des Aufbaus in der Evangelischen Kirche Deutschlands von 1933 bis 1945, ed. Heinrich Hermelink. Tübingen and Stuttgart, 1950.

Kirchliches Jahrbuch für die Evangelische Kirche in Deutschland, 1933–1944, ed. Joachim Beckmann. Gütersloh, 1948.

Kölner Aktenstüke zur Lage der katholischen Kirche in Deutschland, 1933–1945, ed. Wilhelm Corsten. Cologne, 1949.

Kopp, Otto. "Theodor Bäuerle und der Bosch-Kreis: Die wiederentdeckte Goerdeler-Rede." In *Widerstand und Erneuerung: Neue Berichte und Dokumente vom inneren Kampf gegen das Hitler-Regime,* ed. Otto Kopp. Stuttgart, 1966.

Leber, Julius. *Schriften, Reden, Briefe,* ed. Dorothea Beck and Wilfried F. Schoeller. Munich, 1976.

Meldungen aus dem Reich, 1938–1945: Die geheimen Lageberichte des Sicherheitsdienstes der SS, ed. Heinz Boberach, 17 vols. Herrsching, 1984.

Die Mittwochs-Gesellschaft: Protokolle aus dem geistigen Deutschland 1932 bis 1944, ed. Klaus Scholder. Berlin, 1982.

Moltke, Helmuth James von. *Briefe an Freya, 1939–1945,* ed. Beate Ruhm von Oppen. Munich, 1988.

———. *Letzte Briefe aus dem Gefängnis Tegel.* Berlin, 1951.

A Noble Combat: The Letters of Shiela Grant Duff and Adam von Trott zu Solz, 1932–1939, ed. Klemens von Klemperer. Oxford, 1988.

"Ein NS-Funktionär zum Niemöller-Prozess." *Vierteljahrshefte für Zeitgeschichte,* 4 (1956).

Reck-Malleczewen, Friedrich Percyval. *Tagebuch eines Verzweifelten.* Schwäbisch-Gmünd, 1946.

Schlabrendorff, Fabian v. *Offiziere gegen Hitler,* ed. Gero v. S. Gaevernitz. Zurich, 1946.

"Spiegelbild einer Verschwörung": Die Opposition gegen Hitler und der Staatsstreich vom 20. Juli 1944 in der SD-Berichterstattung, ed. Hans-Adolf Jacobsen. Stuttgart, 1984.

Steltzer, Theodor. *Von deutscher Politik: Dokumente, Aufsätze und Vorträge,* ed. Friedrich Minssen. Frankfurt am Main, 1949.

Stieff, Hellmuth. *Briefe*, ed Horst Mühleisen. Berlin, 1991.

Die Synode zu Steglitz: Die dritte Bekenntnissynode der Evangelischen Kirche der Altpreussischen Union, ed. Wilhelm Niemöller. Göttingen, 1970.

Vassiltchikov, Marie. *The Berlin Diaries, 1940–1945*. London, 1985.

Verfolgung und Widerstand, 1933–1945: Christliche Demokraten gegen Hitler, ed. Günter Buchstab, Brigitte Kaff, and Hans-Otto Kleinmann. Düsseldorf, 1986.

Landesbischof D. Wurm und der nationalsozialistische Staat, 1940–1945, ed. Gerhard Schäfer. Stuttgart, 1968.

Young, A. P. *The 'X' Documents*, ed. Sidney Aster. London, 1974.

"Zwei aussenpolitische Memoranden der deutschen Opposition (Frühjahr 1942)," ed. Hans Rothfels. *Vierteljahrshefte für Zeitgeschichte*, 5 (1957).

Zwischen Widerspruch und Widerstand: Texte zur Denkschrift der Bekennenden Kirche an Hitler (1936), ed. Martin Greschat. Munich, 1987.

NEWSPAPERS AND PERIODICALS

Allgemeine Evangelisch-Lutherische Kirchenzeitung (Leipzig)

Amtsblatt d. Erzdiözese München u. Freising

Augsburger Postzeitung

Berliner Evangelisches Sonntagsblatt

Berliner Evangelisches Wochenblatt

Berliner Tageblatt

Deutsches Volksblatt: Tageszeitung der Deutschen Jugoslawiens (Novi Sad)

Das Evangelische Deutschland: Kirchliche Rundschau für das Gesamtgebiet des Deutschen Evangelischen Kirchenbundes (Berlin)

Frankfurter Allgemeine Zeitung

Jahrbuch der öffentlichen Meinung, 1947–1955, ed. Elisabeth Noelle and Erich Peter Neumann (Allenbach, 1956)

Junge Kirche: Halbmonatschrift für reformatorisches Christentum

Kölnische Zeitung

Krasnaia Zvezda (Moscow)

Manchester Guardian

Nation

Neues Deutschland

New Republic

New Statesman and Nation

New York Herald Tribune

New York Times

Der Tag (Berlin)

Time

Times (London)

Secondary Works

BOOKS

Abshagen, Karl Heinz. *Canaris: Patriot und Weltbürger*. Stuttgart, 1950.

Bartz, Karl. *Die Tragödie der deutschen Abwehr*. Salzburg, 1955.

Bayern in der NS-Zeit, ed. Martin Broszat, Elke Fröhlich, Falk Wiesemann, Anton Grossmann, and Hartmut Mehringer, 6 vols. Munich and Vienna, 1977–1983.

Bentley, James. *Martin Niemöller, 1892–1984.* New York, 1984.

Bethge, Eberhard. *Dietrich Bonhoeffer: Theologe, Christ, Zeitgenosse.* Munich, 1967.

Buchheit, Gert. *Soldatentum und Rebellion: Die Tragödie der deutschen Wehrmacht.* Rastatt, 1961.

Büchler, Heinrich. *Carl-Heinrich Stülpnagel: Soldat, Philosoph, Verschwörer.* Berlin and Frankfurt am Main, 1989.

Castellan, Georges. *Le réarmament clandestin du Reich, 1930–1935: Vu par le 2e Bureau de l'état-major français.* Paris, 1954.

Conway, J. S. *The Nazi Persecution of the Churches, 1933–45.* London, 1968.

Conze, Werner, Erich Kosthorst, and Elfriede Nebgen. *Jakob Kaiser,* 4 vols. Stuttgart, Berlin, Cologne, and Mainz, 1967–1972.

Finker, Kurt. *Graf Moltke und der Kreisauer Kreis,* 2d ed. Berlin, 1980.

Foerster, Wolfgang. *Generaloberst Ludwig Beck: Sein Kampf gegen den Krieg.* Munich, 1953.

Foertsch, Hermann. *Schuld und Verhängnis: Die Fritsch-Krise im Frühjahr 1938 als Wendepunkt in der Geschichte der nationalsozialistischen Zeit.* Stuttgart, 1951.

Gill, Anton. *An Honourable Defeat: A History of German Resistance to Hitler, 1933–1945.* New York, 1994.

Heinemann, Ulrich. *Ein konservativer Rebell: Fritz-Dietlof Graf von der Schulenburg und der 20. Juli.* Berlin, 1990.

Hoffmann, Peter. *Claus Schenk Graf von Stauffenberg und seine Brüder.* Stuttgart, 1992.

———. *The History of the German Resistance, 1933–1945.* Cambridge, Mass., 1977.

———. *Widerstand, Staatsstreich, Attentat: Der Kampf der Opposition gegen Hitler.* Munich, 1969.

Höhne, Heinz. *Canaris: Patriot in Zwielicht.* Munich, 1976.

Kramarz, Joachim. *Claus Graf Stauffenberg, 15. November 1907–20. Juli 1944: Das Leben eines Offiziers.* Frankfurt am Main, 1965.

Krausnick, Helmut, and Hans-Heinrich Wilhelm. *Die Truppe des Weltanschauungskrieges: Die Einsatzgruppen der Sicherheitspolizei und des SD, 1938–1942.* Stuttgart, 1981.

Leber, Annedore. *Das Gewissen steht auf: 64 Lebensbilder aus dem deutschen Widerstand, 1933–1945.* Berlin and Frankfurt am Main, 1954.

Lewy, Guenter. *The Catholic Church and Nazi Germany.* New York, London, Sydney, and Toronto, 1964.

Mammach, Klaus. *Widerstand, 1933–1939: Geschichte der deutschen antifaschistischen Widerstandsbewegung im Inland und in der Emigration.* Berlin, 1984.

Müller, Christian. *Oberst i. G. Stauffenberg.* Düsseldorf, 1970.

Müller, Klaus-Jürgen. *General Ludwig Beck: Studien und Dokumente zur politisch-militärischen Vorstellungswelt und Tätigkeit des Generalstabschefs des deutschen Heeres, 1933–1938.* Boppard am Rhein, 1980.

———. *Das Heer und Hitler: Armee und nationalsozialistisches Regime, 1933–1940.* Stuttgart, 1969.

Neuhäusler, Johann. *Kreuz und Hakenkreuz: Der Kampf des Nationalsozialismus gegen die katholische Kirche und der kirchliche Widerstand,* 2d ed., 2 vols. Munich, 1946.

Owings, Allison. *Frauen: German Women Recall the Third Reich.* New Brunswick, 1994.

Reynolds, Nicholas. *Treason Was No Crime: Ludwig Beck, Chief of the German General Staff.* London, 1976.

Ritter, Gerhard. *Carl Goerdeler und die deutsche Widerstandsbewegung.* Stuttgart, 1954.

Roon, Ger van. *Neuordnung im Widerstand: Der Kreisauer Kreis innerhalb der deutschen Widerstandbewegung.* Munich, 1967.

———. *Widerstand im Dritten Reich,* 4th ed. Munich, 1987.

Rothfels, Hans. *The German Opposition to Hitler.* Hinsdale, Ill., 1948.

Sautter, Reinhold. *Theophil Wurm: Sein Leben und sein Kampf.* Stuttgart, 1960.

Scheurig, Bodo. *Henning von Tresckow,* 2d ed. Oldenburg and Hamburg, 1973.

Schöllgen, Gregor. *Ulrich von Hassell, 1881–1944: Ein Konservativer in der Opposition.* Munich, 1990.

Schwerin, Detlef von. *"Dann sind's die besten Köpfe, die man henkt": Die junge Generation im deutschen Widerstand.* Munich and Zurich, 1991.

Teske, Hermann. *Die silbernen Spiegel: Generalstabsdienst unter der Lupe.* Heidelberg, 1952.

Volk, Ludwig. *Der bayerische Episkopat und der Nationalsozialismus, 1930–1934.* Mainz, 1965.

Wheeler-Bennett, John W. *The Nemesis of Power: The German Army in Politics, 1918–1945.* London and New York, 1953.

Zeller, Eberhard. *Geist der Freiheit: Der zwanzigste Juli,* 4th ed. Munich, 1963.

Zipfel, Friedrich. *Kirchenkampf in Deutschland, 1933–1945: Religionsverfolgung und Selbstbehauptung der Kirchen in der nationalsozialistischen Zeit.* Berlin, 1965.

ARTICLES AND CHAPTERS

Bonkovsky, Frederick O. "The German State and Protestant Elites." In *The German Church Struggle and the Holocaust,* ed. Franklin H. Littell and Hubert G. Locke. Detroit, 1974.

Elias, Otto L. "Der evangelische Kirchenkampf und die Judenfrage." *Informationsblatt für die Gemeinden in den niederdeutschen lutherischen Landeskirchen,* 10 (1961).

Finker, Kurt. "Widerstand und Geschichte des Widerstandes in der Forschung der DDR." In *Widerstand: Ein Problem zwischen Theorie und Geschichte,* ed. Peter Steinbach. Cologne, 1987.

Graml, Hermann. "Hans Oster." In *Der zwanzigste Juli: Alternative zu Hitler?* ed. Hans Jürgen Schultz. Stuttgart and Berlin, 1974.

Hoffmann, Peter. "Der militärische Widerstand in der zweiten Kriegshälfte, 1942–1944/45." In *Aufstand des Gewissens: Der militärische Widerstand gegen Hitler und das NS-Regime, 1933–1945.* Herford and Bonn, 1984.

Krüger-Charlé, Michael. "Carl Goerdelers Versuche der Durchsetzung einer alternativen Politik 1933 bis 1937." In *Der Widerstand gegen den Nationalsozialismus: Die deutsche Gesellschaft und der Widerstand gegen Hitler,* ed. Jürgen Schmädeke and Peter Steinbach. Munich and Zurich, 1985.

Noakes, Jeremy. "German Conservatives and the Third Reich: An Ambiguous Relationship." In *Fascists and Conservatives: The Radical Right and the Establishment in Twentieth-Century Europe,* ed. Martin Blinkhorn. London, 1990.

Ringshausen, Gerhard. "Evangelische Kirche und Widerstand." In *Deutscher Widerstand—Demokratie heute: Kirche, Kreisauer Kreis, Ethik, Militär und Gewerkschaften,* ed. Huberta Engel. Bonn and Berlin, 1992.

Index

APR 1997

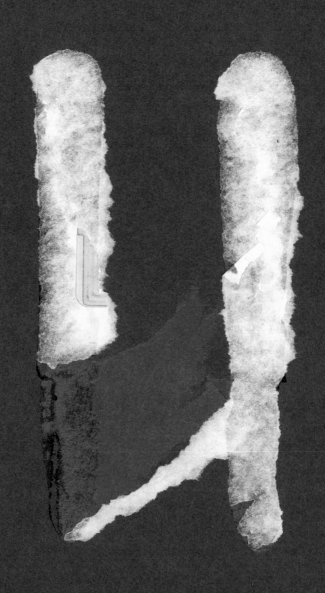